**Exemplaire de démonstration**

BLANK FORMS EDITIONS 2019

# 2 OTHER MATTERS

## BY CATHERINE CHRISTER HENNIX

EDITED BY LAWRENCE KUMPF

| | |
|---|---|
| 7 | **Introduction,** by Lawrence Kumpf |
| 11 | **ABSTRACTS FOR INFINITARY COMPOSITIONS** |
| 17 | $\Box_\kappa$ **(EXCERPT FROM NOTES ON THE COMPOSITE SINE-WAVE DRONE OVER WHICH THE ELECTRIC HARPSICHORD IS PERFORMED)** |
| 35 | **BROUWER'S LATTICE** |
| 39 | Notes on Intuitionistic Modal Music, by Catherine Christer Hennix |
| 41 | Excerpt from the Score for Cha-gaku, by Catherine Christer Hennix |
| 44 | The Basic Acts of Intuitionism, by L.E.J. Brouwer |
| 46 | Life, Art, and Mysticism, by L.E.J. Brouwer |
| 51 | A Brief Presentation of *Brouwer's Lattice* and the *Deontic Miracle*, by Rita Knox, edited by Catherine Christer Hennix |
| 55 | The Artists, by Keith Knox |
| 57 | The Deontic Miracle: Program |
| 61 | **NOTES ON TOPOSES & ADJOINTS** |
| 68 | Notes for the (Non-Alien) Reader |
| 73 | Spectra of Modalities and the Theory of the Creative Subject, Th($\Sigma$) |
| 90 | Semiotics I |
| 102 | Semiotics II |
| 108 | Toposes, Sheaves, and Adjoints |
| 115 | Appendix 1: Th($\Sigma$) and the Structure of Mind |
| 119 | Appendix 2: Cardinals in 1-Modal Spectra |
| 128 | Appendix 3: The Environment Toposes and Adjoints, Moderna Museet, Stockholm |
| 135 | **MODALITIES AND LANGUAGES FOR ALGORITHMS,** edited by Henry Flynt |
| 161 | **THE ELECTRIC HARPSICHORD,** by Henry Flynt |
| 169 | **PHILOSOPHY OF CONCEPT ART: A CONVERSATION WITH HENRY FLYNT** |
| 195 | **MYSTERIUM FASCINANS: THE EPISTEMIC ART OF CATHERINE CHRISTER HENNIX,** by Ulf Linde with Catherine Christer Hennix |
| 203 | **LA SÉMINAIRE** |
| 225 | **WSTNOKWGO** |
| 227 | Henry Flynt: WSTNOKWGO |
| 229 | Henry Flynt: version of WSTNOKWGO |
| 231 | **LANGUAGE AND LIGHT IN MARIAN ZAZEELA'S ART** |
| 239 | **THE BERLIN MAHNMAL** |
| 241 | Project for a (Non?-) Berlin Metamahnmal |
| 250 | Eisenman I, Eisenman II, Eisenman III |
| 257 | **REVISITING *BROUWER'S LATTICE* THIRTY YEARS LATER** |
| 263 | ***HALLUCINOGENIC/ECSTATIC SOUND ENVIRONMENT* PROGRAM NOTES,** by Henry Flynt |
| 267 | ***THE ILLUMINATORY SOUND ENVIRONMENT* PROGRAM NOTES,** by Henry Flynt |
| 271 | **RAG INFINITY/RAG COSMOSIS (MYOBU NO OMOTO IN MEMORIAM)** |
| 277 | **HILBERT SPACE SHRUTI BOX (OF THE (QUANTUM) HARMONIC OSCILLATOR)** |
| 295 | **THE YELLOW BOOK** |

# Introduction
Lawrence Kumpf

*The following is an abridged introduction to* Poësy Matters and Other Matters *by Catherine Christer Hennix; the full introduction, which includes a more comprehensive look at Hennix's life and work, is included in volume one of this two-volume set,* Poësy Matters.

This book represents the first major text survey of writing and thought by Swedish musician, visual artist, and mathematician Catherine Christer Hennix. The writings contained in these two volumes were written from the early 1970s through 2016 — in some cases, with revisions in 2017 and 2018 — and draw on a wide range of references, including formal logic, intuitionist mathematics, modal music, topos theory, cybernetics, medieval Japanese theater, Islam, psychoanalysis, and the specifics of Hennix's own intermedia practice. These writings alternately — and sometimes simultaneously — take the form of poetry, drama, musical composition, and prose essays. While this collection is extensive, it is in no way comprehensive; rather, it is a first attempt to introduce Hennix's immense, diverse, and under-acknowledged body of written work to a larger public. This effort, which coincides with Hennix's similarly overlooked music and visual art, has been reaching wider audiences in recent years through numerous exhibitions and newly released recordings. We hope that this two-volume set — comprising *Poësy Matters*, which focuses on Hennix's poetry and drama, and *Other Matters*, which, in prose, focuses on her art as well as topics like psychoanalysis and mathematics — will give readers a glimpse into the complexity of Hennix's thought, which has staked a singular position throughout the past fifty-plus years. These two volumes will also allow readers to reimagine some of the artistic and historical narratives and lineages in which Hennix played an active part during this timeframe.

*Poësy Matters and Other Matters* is split into four total sections across the two volumes: in *Poësy Matters*, poetry and abstract Nō dramas (the latter section titled "Theater of the Eternal Mind"); and in *Other Matters*, program notes and essays appear in one section, and the other section hosts the self-contained work *The Yellow Book*. With the exceptions of *Poetry as Philosophy, Poetry as Notation* (1985), *The Yellow Book* (1989), *Mysterium Fascinans* (1992), $\square_K$ *(Excerpt from Notes on the Composite Sine-Wave Drone Over Which The Electric*

Harpsichord is Performed)* (2010) and *The Electric Harpsichord* (2010, written by Henry Flynt), the texts included within the volume have not been previously published for wider audiences, and most have never been published at all, though some — namely *Notes on Toposes & Adjoints* (1976), *Brouwer's Lattice* (1976), and selections from *Ṭarīqah Nūr-Samad* (2016) — were published in small editions as mimeographs or printouts to accompany exhibitions or performances. Even when published, many of Hennix's writings were only preliminary drafts, in need of further work, which has made her reluctant to reprint them.

The texts included here only represent a small selection of Hennix's written oeuvre. Many of her writings have been lost over time; others, meanwhile, have been purposefully excluded from this collection because Hennix has deemed them failures. Although she is a prolific writer, she considers the majority of her work unfinished and unsuitable for publication. Some of the texts collected in these volumes are reproduced as they first appeared in their own time (with minor edits for typographical and grammatical mistakes), while several other texts have been significantly revised by Hennix, sometimes with this collection's editorial team and with Hennix's longtime collaborator, Henry Flynt. All but two pieces have been typeset according to this collection's layout; the two exceptions — *Notes on Toposes & Adjoints* and *The Yellow Book* — are printed as facsimiles of their original publications, with minor corrections for content and quality. We have noted each text's history on its own title page.

The work included here represents some of Hennix's most significant contributions to the numerous discourses in which she has been involved over the last fifty years, with a special focus on her creative writing as it relates to her work as a musician and visual artist. While Hennix's work in mathematics has played an important role across disciplines, we have not included any of her purely mathematical writings. Hennix's writing creates a concatenation of complex abstract thought that is also reflected in her art installations, which utilize a variety of mediums and forms — both visual and auditory — which the viewer is expected to navigate seamlessly. Hennix does not necessarily consider her paintings or sculptures "art"; her work collapses these fields, often presenting mathematical concepts in the form of paintings or drawings — as is the case with *Algebraic Aesthetics* (1973–1975) and, later, *Algebras w/ Domains* (1973–1991) and *Triptyque Lacanien* (1975–1991) — or, through her use of Brouwer's principles of intuitionism, as a method for framing her musical compositions and work with her ensembles, such as The Deontic Miracle and, more recently, Chora(s)san Time-Court Mirage.[1] Similarly, in her writing, Hennix places fragments and formulations in juxtaposition, each piece acting as a supplement to its partner, often with the order of a certain text possessing a variable component.

One of the primary difficulties in approaching Hennix's work — both as a reader and as an editor — is the machination of her cross-disciplinary approach to thought. *The Yellow Book* — one of the few pieces collected here that has been published in (slightly) wider circulation, as part of a special issue of the journal *IO*, edited by the poet Charles Stein, titled *Being = Space × Action: Searches for Freedom of Mind through Mathematics, Art, and Mysticism* — is perhaps the clearest example of Hennix's working method in written form, given the variation in writerly approach and discursive material from page to page. But this method of variegation is reflected in all of her work, not just on a formal level but also, simply, through the interconnected nature of her diverse pursuits. Her background in different disciplines and her unique writerly voice manifest themselves in idiosyncratic forms of personal notation and crop up throughout Hennix's writings; the notes draw from topos theory, formal languages, psychoanalytic formulas, and predicate calculus as means of articulating internal subjective states. An example of this use of notation can be found in *Notes on Toposes & Adjoints* (1976) or, more specifically, her diagraming of Dutch mathematician L.E.J. Brouwer's concept of two-ity, which describes the Creative Subject's ability to unite the discrete events within a continuous flow of time. Originally created for an exhibition at the Moderna Museet, Stockholm, Hennix's diagram was not published until 1989 — as part of the *The Yellow Book* — and is a prime example of her working method. This volume, *Other Matters*, demonstrates the breadth of Hennix's ingenuity not only as a writer but also as an artist and thinker across disciplines, too, as her practice has developed from the late 1960s to today.

1   Hennix's dating of her work often follows the year when she conceived of the concept and recorded it in her notebook. In the case of the *Algebraic Aesthetics*, which Hennix considers to be a mathematical concept and not necessarily a work of "art," the black and white decidable word problem was originally conceived in 1973, and the four-color undecidable word problem was conceived in 1975. Both pieces were meant to be included to some capacity in Hennix's 1976 exhibition at the Moderna Museet but were not executed and shown until 1979, as works on paper. The images later appeared in a series of paintings made for the Museum Fodor, Amsterdam, in 1991 called *Algebras w/ Domains*, dated 1973–1991, and *C-Algebra w/ Undecidable Word Problem*, dated 1975–1991. Hennix and I continued with this dating model for the 2018 exhibition *Catherine Christer Hennix: Traversée du Fantasme* at the Stedelijk Museum, Amsterdam.

# ABSTRACTS FOR INFINITARY COMPOSITIONS

Written in Stockholm, 1973. Previously unpublished.

# FIXED POINTS
## February 1973

### Abstracts
### $\Sigma_o^w$ – Structures

Let w = {1,2,3, ...} denote a numeration of all fractions σ st $1 \leq \sigma \leq 2$, i.e., all fractions confined to the closed unite interval (1,2) — In a natural way these can be made to correspond to the corresponding rational intervals within the octave, e.g., 1 corresponds to the unison interval 1:1, 2 to the octave endpoint 2:1, etc.

Suppose an initial segment $\Sigma_o^i$ of w given. Then $\Sigma_o^w$ will denote the increasing reflexion of $\Sigma_o^i$ throughout w. This reflexion is obtained by certain continuous functions F with domain $\Sigma_o^i$ and range $\Sigma_o^w$ where $\Sigma_o^w$ is a subset of w i.e., $\Sigma_o^w \subseteq w$. The values of F are called fixed points (in w), and w will naturally enough be called the *continuum* of intervals within the perfect octave. Since the conditions given for functions F are expressed by $\Sigma_o$ sentences of first-order logic, there exists a trivial translation of these conditions to programming languages such as Fortran.

# FORCING
## February 1973

### Abstracts

Assume the course-of-values of a fixed point function in an open topological space T.

If $a_q$ is a fixed point in T, then there is a generic subspace G of T such that T[G] forces all intervals $a_p$, $p < q$, when they contain "less" information than $a_q$ i.e., all intervals that are part of the construction of $a_q$ in T will be those intervals that appear in G and such that $a_p \in T[G]$ implies $a_p$ constructable from G and fitting some part of the space T.

One could look at the generic sets as if they represented some "undecidable" intervals $a_q < a_r$ and which some elements of G force by means of the forcing conditions given below. At the same time, of course, T is a purported model of ZFC set theory (which is why we have notions such as generic applicable to elements of T).

Consider a space T with given points and relations (ratios) between the points. Let G be a subspace of T and let P denote the set of conditions of G of the form $q_{w_1} \in G$, $q_{w_2} \in G$, $q_{w_3} \in G$, ... . Let A be a statement that yields an element in T for its satisfaction id est there is an $a_{q_{w_i}}$ in T such that the statement is satisfied by it.

Then the relation P⊩A (P forces A) is defined by the following forcing conditions:

I   For all A, not P⊩A and P⊩¬A

II  For each generic P, there exists an extension P'⊇P st for all A P'⊩A or P'⊩¬A

These are the basic forcing conditions. Now we turn to the different forms that A can take:

(i) A is atomic. Then P⊩A iff A∈G

(ii) A=BvC. Then P⊩A iff B∈G or C∈G

(iii) A=∃xB(x). Then P⊩A iff for some $a_{q_{w_i}} \in T$, $B(a_{q_{w_i}})$ is in P id est iff P⊩B(a) for some point a

(iv) A=-B. Then P⊩-B iff no extention P' of P is such that P⊩B

The set of conditions, P, is very similar to a tree or, more specifically, to an Yessenin-Volpin tree, T. But it has more "power" than T since it is not dependent on time for its development but given simultaneously with the information on satisfaction by T[G].

$$\square_\kappa$$
March 1973

## Abstracts

$\square_\kappa$ is the following combinatorial structure.
There is a sequence $<C_\lambda : \lambda = \cup \lambda < \kappa^+>$ such that:

(i)   C is *closed* and *unbounded* in $\lambda$ for each fixed point $C_\kappa$
(ii)  $\text{cf}(\lambda) < \kappa \rightarrow |C_\lambda| < \kappa$
(iii) if $\delta$ is a limit interval point of $C_\delta$, then $C_\delta = \delta \cap C$

Now, it is assumed that $V=L \rightarrow (\forall_\kappa)(\square_\kappa)$

So if $\Omega$ is a Cohen extension in a structure where V=L holds, then the combinatorial principle $\square_\kappa$ is applicable to all generic elements of $\Omega$

A realization of $\square_\kappa$ is a closed and unbounded extension of a generic structure $\Omega$

Obviously, a Souslin Tree can be generated by means of $\square_\kappa$

(EXCERPT FROM NOTES ON THE COMPOSITE SINE-WAVE DRONE OVER WHICH THE ELECTRIC HARPSICHORD IS PERFORMED)

Written in Stockholm, 1976. Originally published in a limited edition as The Electric Harpsichord by Etymon Editions, 2003. Re-published in *The Electric Harpsichord* (Die Schachtel, 2010). See also: "The Electric Harpsichord" by Henry Flynt in this volume, and "Dedication for the Electric Harpsichord" in Hennix, *Poësy Matters* (Blank Forms Editions, 2019).

## Monistic Universes B.

Ib. Σ contemplates the existence of *non-empty universes*

□ □ □ ..... □ □ .....

and the embedding(s)

$$R: E^{\square} \rightarrow \acute{E}.$$

Again, the identity of a non-empty, monistic universe, □, shall be determined by an inverse limit or range $R^{-1}(\acute{E})$. And, again, it is possible that

$$R^{-1}(\acute{E}) \neq R(E^{\square})$$

(if the reality of the situation is lacking in symmetries. Cf. *Monistic Universes A*).

*Standard Examples* (Classical Set Theory):

Singleton Sets: { • }, { Λ }, { **e** }.

# É-Examples: **Soliton Compositions. (Solitones)**

*0. Agrapha Harmonia.*
*(Cognitio Matutina).*

0.1     [ॐ]     The Sound of Shiva—
                            OMSAHASRANAMA
                            [For Pandit Pran Nath]

0.11     $\square_\kappa$     —The κ-times Repeated Constant Event.
                            [Infinitary Composition. Locally Infinite Space.
                            Fixed Point Structure, $\kappa = \kappa + 1$.]

0.111     $\square^N$     The **N**-times Repeated Constant Event.
                            [The Five Times Repeated Music, etc.]

0.111a           **N** = 3. Short Infinitary Processes. *White* $\overline{MA}$.

                            $\square \ \square \ \square \Rightarrow . \ \square \ ...$

|  |  |
|---|---|
|  | [where '.' refers to the initial empty space left by the leftmost $\square$ merging with its successor while '...' refers to the (possibly inductive) transfinite term which covers the future(s) of the constantly present boundary or middle term $\square$. (Cf. the Black & White Algebra of the formal (binary ontology) $\wedge\square\blacksquare$).] |
| 0.1111 | *The **N**-Times Repeated Constant Event* [Version For Sound Waves]. |
| 0.1111a | **N=0. 0-D** <u>Topologies For A Vertical Sound</u>. The *Zero—Times Repeated Event*, $\square^0$, or *The Sound of* MA, is defined by the *Sound of an Indestructible Moment of Silence* contained by a space equipped with a vertical topology.<br><br>$\square^0$—The Empty Sound |

0.1111b.  □$_{<x,y,z>}$ *Crystal Oscillators* (Quartz). *Digital Wave Forms*. (Programs).

Transfinite Cases;

□$_\kappa$ —The κ-Infinite Sound,

□$_{<x,y,z>}$ — x, y, z transfinite real variables.

. . . . . . . . . . . . .

The complexity of *constant events* may be measured in various ways. A convenient complexity measure for a constant event **e** shall be a certain ordinal number, ord(**e**). The non-empty constant events

$\acute{E}^{\square v}$:   □ □ □ . . . . . □ □ . . . . □

are usually characterized by *limit ordinals v*. Ord (□) and ord (■)

are two distinct species of limit ordinals which define two families of initial segments of the continuum of ordinal numbers, $\Omega$, which (naturally) give rise to two (families of) *natural number series* denoted here by $\mathbf{N}_\square$ and $\mathbf{N}_\blacksquare$, respectively. The series of constant (canonical) empty events is usually denoted $\mathbf{N}_\Lambda$ [**MA**-ordinals].

. . . . . . . . . . . . .

(Summary): The constant events $\square$ are defined by the (point-wise) composition of the three distinct curves:

$\square_{<x>}$ : a × sin (x)

$\square_{<y>}$ : b × sin (y)

$\square_{<z>}$ : c × sin (z)

the continuous point-wise compositions of which are omnidirectionally distributed in the interior of **É** as a mixture of a triple of phase-locked sine waves at constant frequencies and amplitudes such that the objects

$\square^N$ or $\square_x$ obtain as the respective limit constructions of this continuous process of (sine wave) composition based on fixed (eternal) quartz crystal oscillations in pre-determined ratios. The constants a, b, c take any (suitable) rational number triple as values.

More specifically, each sine-wave compactum $\square_{<w>}$, describes an infinitely proceeding sequence of constant events $\square_{<w_i>}$ the fixed amplitudes of which are inversely proportional to the frequency of the constant events that build up this indefinitely, ongoing wave structure. The possible frequencies of these constant events are determined by a certain set of *odd* prime numbers. Thus, 2 certainly does *not* belong to this set, but, say, 5 *may* belong to it, or all prime numbers larger than any large but otherwise arbitrary prime number may belong to it with certainty. Hence, this set may certainly be infinite.

If the $k^{th}$ (odd) prime $P_k$ does not belong to this (possibly infinite) set and $P_k$ divides m/n—the ratio between two sine-wave components—then any ratio m:n:$P_k$ is a possible (but not necessary) determination of a sine-wave component in a (É-) realization of the composition $\square^N$ or its transfinite extension $\square_k$.

(The eternal presence being constantly controlled or determined by what is eternally absent. This latter condition derives from La Monte Young's theory of tuning as developed and documented in the long awaited work ***The Two Systems of Eleven Categories 1:07:40 AM 3 X 67—ca. 6:00 PM 7 VII 75*** from ***Vertical Hearing or Hearing in the Present Tense***.)

**Remark;** In La Monte Young's works the second odd prime, i.e., 5, is uniformly included in this set for which Young uses the somewhat abusive notation X = 5 (and for which X = { 5 } would be more accurate).

Also, I wish to stress that in the *finite case*, the sets of prime numbers here defined were discovered by La Monte Young in the mid-'60s. I consider these sets of prime numbers as the most important source for studying concurrent intervals in just intonation. [End of remark.]

Elements which belong to the composite wave form $⊞^N$ are called *chronons* or *time elements*. Here, the technique of *analytic continuation* is presupposed as well as the most efficient programs for the FFT (Fast Fourier Transform).

. . . . . . . . . . . . .

At the moment when the Creative Subject enters a frame for a topos, $\mathcal{E}$. as defined by the interior of $\acute{E}$, the time manifold $\square^N$ is supposed to already contain indefinitely many time elements which have not yet or never will be experienced by the Creative Subject (i.e., which belong to her remote or never accessed future).

The moment at which the Creative Subject's tactics of attention include attention to the time process, $\boxplus^N$ corresponds to a point in her life-world where a moment of life falls apart with one part retained as an image and stored by memory while the other part is retained as a continuum of new perceptions. (Cf. Brouwer's construction of the intuitionistic natural number series.)

This incisive moment marks the beginning phase of the Creative Subject's experience of the *fixed point composition*

$\square^N$, i.e.,

*The **N**-times Repeated Constant Event*

[begun in Stockholm during the winter months of 1970 and continued into the present].

In a later phase of the Creative Subject's experience of $\Box^N$, the obtaining continuum of perceptions becomes gradually attenuated by a *continuum of memories* of an **N**-times repeated constant event ⊞. Thus, the Creative Subject gradually comes to experience $\Box^N$ as a *transfinite object* order-isomorphic to the set of rational numbers **η**, i.e., a countably infinite ordering without a first or last element (in which each element may be identified as pairs of integers m,n, except for the rational number 0 (zero), which may be identified with the usual 0 in the set of natural numbers).

In particular, at this later stage of experiencing $\Box^N$, the Creative Subject is endowed with the (not necessarily unique) experiences carried by the (n-ary) conjunction of the continuum of perceptions and the continuum of memories forming a dense ordering *of (the falling apart of) her moments of life*, i.e., an ordering of life without first or last elements and of Cantorian order-type **η**.

Finally, the "transfinite stages" of experiencing $\Box^N$, the Creative Subject arrives at a stationary subset of the generated continuum of perceptions at which she retains complete facultative control of the continuum of time-elements which defines the transfinite time-object $⊞_\kappa$ [here κ denotes (an ordinal of) some "large cardinal" and not merely a "large number" as connoted by the symbol **N**].

. . . . . . . . . . . . .

(Summary, cont.)

There exists a *unique time-interval*, $\tau$, in the space $\acute{\mathbf{E}}$ defined by the length of the period of the resulting *composite sound wave form* $\square_{<x,y,z>}$. When the time-interval $\tau$ has repeated itself **N** times, the time-arc $\tau_N$ corresponds to the repetition, i.e., the recursive iteration of the constant event $\square^N$-times, also written $\square^N$, or, more accurately

Remark that the unicity of the infinitesimal time-arc element $\tau$ is here based squarely on *geometrical* considerations alone so that the constancy of the invisible events $\square^N$ may be defined in terms of a unique geometrical consequence between the areas of the curves (boundaries)

$$\square^0 = \square^1, \square^2, \square^3, \ldots \square^k, \square^{k+1}, \ldots, \square^N = \square^{N+1}$$

which, in turn, are defined by a *point-wise composition* of images under the analytic functions $\lambda\xi\ \sin(\xi)$.

The triad <x,y,z> defines a class of equations E(x,y,z) which, in turn, determines a certain set of algebraic theories, Th(**E**), among which *triples* <X,Y,Z> and *co-triples* <$X^{co}, Y^{co}, Z^{co}$> have played an important role in my early formulations of an ALGEBRAIC AESTHETICS.

For each Creative Subject Σ who attends the space É*, in which the composition $\square^N$ is freely developing, there exists a (subjective) time-interval, τ*, during which the Creative Subject experiences a *constant* event $\square^*_{<x,y,z>}$ as a subobject of the É-universal infinitely proceeding sequence of geometrically congruent composite wave forms $\square^\tau_{<x,y,z>}$.

In general, the constancy of the subjective event $\square^*_{<x,y,z>}$ can be experienced also as a "fluctuating" manifold (as a function of a "fluctuating tactic of attention") so that the subobject $\square^*_{<x,y,z>}$ of $\acute{E}^*$ (created by a Creative Subject's attendance) as a submanifold $\square^{N*}$ of $\acute{E}^*$ defines a *continuously or discretely variable set* (of (fluctuating) experiences of a temporal constancy of time).

Thus, $\square^*_{<x,y,z>}$ corresponds to $\Sigma$'s perception or image of $\square_{<x,y,z>}$ along the subjective time-arcs $\tau^*$ iterated $N^*$ times. Obviously, $N^* < N$. In consequence of the latter inequality, the $N^*$-times iterated time-element $\tau^*$ may be made to correspond to an "arrow of time" in $\acute{E}^*$ (point-wise speaking). Thus, $\acute{E}_{\square}$ is obtained as a subjective space-time manifold of indefinitely iterated, invisible constant events $\square_{<x,y,z>}$.

$$\acute{E}^{\square v}: \square_0 = 1, \square_1, \square_2, \square_3, ....$$

are considered the objects of this *category* and consequently

$1 \to \square, \square \to \square_2 ....$

are its morphisms.

More precisely, $\square^N$ has as *objects*

$1, \square_1, \square_2, \square_3, ....$

and for each n = 0, 1, 2, 3, ... , n *morphisms*

$\square^N \xrightarrow{\Pi^{(n_i)}} \square, i = 0, 1, ... , n-1,$

such that for any n morphisms (in $\square^N$)

$\square^N_n \xrightarrow{\theta_i} \square, i = 0, 1, ... , n-1,$

there exists exactly one morphism

$\square^N_n \xrightarrow{<\theta_0, \theta_1, \theta_2, ... , \theta_{n-1}>} \square^N_n$

so that, in $\square^N$,

$$<\theta_0, \theta_1, \theta_2, \ldots, \theta_{n-1}> \Pi_i^{(n)} = \theta_i, \; i = 0, 1, \ldots, n-1.$$

If the arbitrary morphisms

$$\square^{Nm} \xrightarrow{\Phi} \square$$

are regarded as n-ary operations of $\square^N$, then $\square^N$ can be regarded as the *category of constantly shifting events* (which is simultaneously an *algebraic theory*), intitiated by the event $1 \to \square$.

# BROUWER'S LATTICE

Written in Stockholm, 1976. First published as a program note on the occasion of Hennix's presentation of *Brouwer's Lattice* at Spring Music Festival. Hennix's ensemble performed her compositions alongside works by La Monte Young, Terry Jennings, and others, at Moderna Museet, Stockholm, March 20–30, 1976. The following spread includes a facsimile of the original publication's cover, replacing uses of the letters a and b to black and white squares.

# Christer Hennix
# Brouwer's Lattice

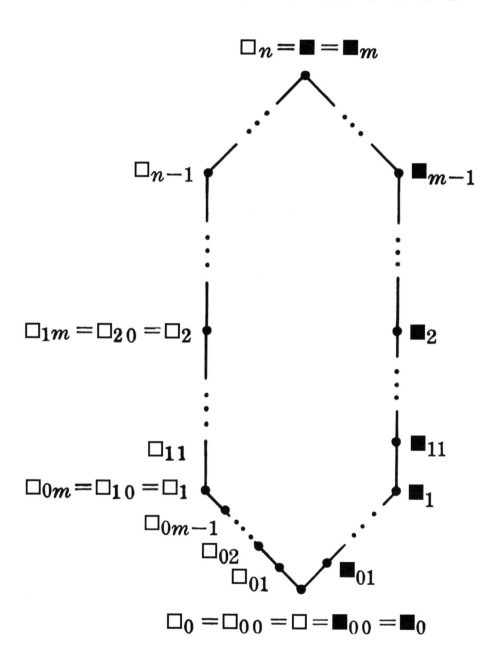

**Moderna Museet 20/3-76 – 30/3-76**

CONTENTS

| | |
|---|---|
| Catherine Christer Hennix: | Notes On Intuitionistic Modal Music |
| Catherine Christer Hennix: | Excerpt from the Score for Cha-gaku |
| L.E.J. Brouwer: | The Basic Acts of Intuitionism |
| L.E.J. Brouwer: | Life, Art, and Mysticism |
| Rita Knox: | A Brief Presentation of *Brouwer's Lattice* and *The Deontic Miracle* (Ed. Catherine Christer Hennix) |
| Keith Knox: | The Artists |
| The Deontic Miracle: | Program |

# Notes On Intuitionistic Modal Music

Catherine Christer Hennix

ASPECTS OF INTUITIONISTIC MODAL MUSIC

The *meaning* of Modal Music has a two-fold mark. This mark in its turn refers to the *Mode* of the scale and to the *Modalities* for which the scale remains valid.

The latter aspect of the mark is far more basic and important than the former, despite the fact that it is seldom considered at all in western-oriented music, except perhaps on an unconscious level.

Maybe the most vivid of the Modalities of Modal Music is the *Modality of Infinity*. The idea of the infinite refers to an unending process, i.e., a process without any conceivable end, reaching out towards the Future, while constantly leaving the Past pulsing behind. Here one can find the basic substance of the intuition of Time as it reveals itself in its most undisturbed form. But although Time might be the most requisite part of music, there are nonetheless equally vivid and important *vertical* tactics of attention, each requiring its specific spectra of Modalities, all of which unfold with the directed spreads of Time. It is the liberation of the latter Modalities that the creative subject constructs when one is subject to an activity involving the *2 Basic Acts of Intuitionism* (see Brouwer's text below). Here the Mind is cleaned from its excess garbage by controlled acts of intuitions, and the vertical Modalities crystallize out to abstract configurations of intensions and arrow diagrams.

.............................

Among the vertical Modalities, the *Modality of Tea* is perhaps the most convivial expression for the relation between addresser and one's addressees. The concept of Tea originated in Japan and developed to an integrated style of life based on simplicity and harmony of action. Its formal expression, the Tea Ceremony, became a practice with the purpose of bringing to consciousness the application of the law of sufficient reason (for actions and intensions) and is well known as it is exemplified within the general spirit of Zen. Hence the Tea Ceremony is perhaps the first participatory attempt to install a continuous tradition for refining the ecology of the human Mind, while at the same time denying any value to activities that retard its growth.

.............................

Although our western-oriented cultures have developed an *increasing* insensibility towards the finer points of the ecology of Mind, despite the efforts of such people as Bateson, Brown, Fuller, and Illich (among others), all the same there has been a kind of thinking manifesting a unique attitude towards the process of refining the mechanism of our thinking capacities. This trend has been recognized as *the research in the foundations of mathematics*, and it has attracted the most eminent mathematicians of our century, as for example, the names of Hilbert, Brouwer, and Gödel bear witness to.

--------------------

One of the main interests in the foundations of mathematics focuses on the *Modality of Infinity*. In particular, Brouwer's Intuitionistic School aimed, from its very beginning, at providing *constructions* (finitely presented) for infinite processes of all dimensions. Brouwer connected the constructions of infinities with the stages of consciousness that the Creating Subject rises through when immersed in the unlimited iterations of the basic acts of intuitionism.

--------------------

It turns out, upon comparison, that the conceptual basis for musical structures involving infinite domains is almost totally *affine* with Brouwer's account of the infinite above, and, in particular, with his notion of an ever denumerable continuum (of points of time). If this basis is *totally affine*, the end result is called *Intuitionistic Modal Music*, which now also satisfies the *Brouwerian Deontic Doctrine* (*Brouwer's Doctrine* for short).

--------------------

In Cha-gaku, the part books are written out in formulas involving the Creating Subjects as parameters immersed in constructions based on the acts of intuitionism. Each section of Cha-gaku is an exposition over freely generated *Modules of Modalities*, each one carrying its characteristic spectral lines of *Modal Operators*. Their successful deliverance is, by definition, their successful liberation.

In order to indicate the presence of a Modality, one simply introduces the corresponding sign in an operational position on the part book formula being operated upon and then read off the operational value of the formula so obtained.

RE: Brouwer's Lattice. Recalling our first installment, Hilbert's Hotel, we are pleased to announce the *reversal* of arrows for the morphisms that trace our continuous development. Our slogan has now become "Syntax poor, Semantics rich," or what amounts to the same "Let the Diagrams Commute." Our program is now restricted to develop only in accordance with the *Doctrines* and *Clubs* spelled out by the fundamentalistic ideals of Brouwer's 1905 manifesto, "Life, Art, and Mysticism." As is apparent from the manifesto, Brouwer's thinking is involved with the same modal spectral lines that the Mind of Tea has formed an Art from. Consequently, we have allowed ourselves to formalize the Tea Ceremony and the ancient tradition of Cha-gaku in Brouwer's Intuitionistic Logic.

# Excerpt from the Score for Cha-gaku

Catherine Christer Hennix

I connect Tea with the Soul of a Proof, i.e., its Establishment of Convincingness.

The air of Tea contains simplicity & purposefulness.

The concept of Tea (or Nō) is a Topos.

A Topos is like footprints of emptiness, its arrows reducing to the empty event.

--------------------

A domain I of basic objects $a_i$, I ∈ N, is *given* ......

On the intended interpretation, the basic objects $a_i$ correspond to *basic intensions* connected with the expanded eleutheric activities defined by *Relevance Theory*.

There are two main construction principles for obtaining composite complexes of intensions of basic intensions, viz:

1. The first principle, connected with the singular *bracketing operation*, yielding expressions of the form [..............], where the dots stand for any term with value in I

2. The second principle, connected with the operation of collecting together iterated applications of the singular bracketing operations yielding expressions of the form U (...., ...., ......, ....), where the dotted places mark the argument places for terms only with value in I

A formula or design is any expression Φ Ψ & c in a language λ(I) appropriate for I such that, for any free variables in Φ Ψ & c, I ($x_1$......$x_n$) is a sign which value at the coordinates $x_1$......$x_n$ is defined, if, and only if, the value of each term substituted at the places for the free variables in Φ takes at least *one value* in I if the values remain undefined or are appropriate only for other domains than I. Φ is said to be a mere *sign* (i.e., a formula without design).

For any activity α, if I is the field of α then all acts subsumed under α may be described by an appropriate λ(I). Subsets of λ(I) are called *Texts* for α. The rules for interpreting a Text determine the *meaning* of the formulas of the Text.

--------------------

Syntactically, meaning is constructed out of intensions that competent-wise determine the range of the semantics involved (i.e., subsets of the semantic domain).

We start with two objects, $E\!E$ and $T\!T$, that contain, respectively, *possible objects* and *atomic intensions*. The meaning of any formula $\Psi$ is then decided by the functional evaluation of the composite of elements in $T\!T$ over the elements in $E\!E$ (the arguments for the elements of $T\!T$).

According to Montague, $E\!E$ and $T\!T$ are conceived of as *basic categories*, while their combinatorial range is considered the domain of *derived categories*. For example, any modifier that is syntactically distinguishable in a formula belongs to a derived category.

Given the basic categories $E\!E$ and $T\!T$, we can inquire about their combinatorial modes. Consider, for instance, the complex formula $\Psi(x)$, which can be seen as a syntactial object of category $T\!T/E\!E$ :

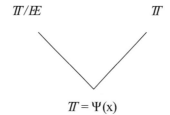

$$T\!T = \Psi(x)$$

Other derived categories are, for example:
$(T\!T/E\!E)/(T\!T/E\!E), (T\!T/E\!E)/(T\!T/E\!E)/E\!E)$ etc.

By these formal conventions, our logical constants receive the following syntactical definitions:

$\neg \quad \equiv_{def} \quad /\,T\!T$

$\& \quad \equiv_{def} \quad /\,T\!T\;T\!T\;T\!T$

$\vee \quad \equiv_{def} \quad /\,T\!T\;T\!T\;T\!T$

$\Rightarrow \quad \equiv_{def} \quad /\,T\!T\;T\!T\,/\,T\!T\;T\!T\;T\!T$

$\forall \quad \equiv_{def} \quad /\,T\!T\;T\!T\;T\!T,\;\ldots\ldots\ldots\ldots,\,/\,T\!T\;T\!T\;T\!T$

$\exists \quad \equiv_{def} \quad /\,T\!T\;T\!T\;T\!T,\;\ldots\ldots\ldots\ldots,\,/\,T\!T\;T\!T\;T\!T$

It is an easy but elaborate exercise to construct further definitions wherever they are required.

The *W–Doctrine* is that there is a *Morphism* between *Logical Space* and the values of formulas of basic or derived categories without free variables.

................

# The Basic Acts of Intuitionism
L.E.J. Brouwer

...... *The intervention of intuitionism* by two acts of which the first seems necessarily to lead to destructive and sterilizing consequences, whereas the second yields ample possibilities for recovery and new developments ......

*The first act of intuitionism completely separates mathematics from mathematical language*, in particular from the phenomena of language which are described by theoretical logic. It recognizes that mathematics is a languageless activity of the mind having its origin in the basic phenomenon of the perception of a *move of time*, which is the falling apart of a life moment into two distinct things, one of which gives way to the other but is retained by memory. If the two-ity thus born is divested of all quality, there remains the common substratum of all two-ities, the mental creation of the *empty two-ity*. This empty two-ity and the two unities of which it is composed, constitute the *basic mathematical systems*. And the basic operation of mathematical construction is the *mental creation of the two-ity of two mathematical systems previously acquired* and the consideration of this two-ity as a new mathematical system.

It is introspectively realized how this basic operation, continually displaying *unaltered* retention by memory, successively generates each natural number the infinitely proceeding sequence of the natural numbers, arbitrary finite sequences and infinitely proceeding sequences of mathematical systems previously acquired, finally a continually extending stock of mathematical systems corresponding to "separable" systems of classical mathematics.

SECOND ACT OF INTUITIONISM

which recognizes the possibility of generating new mathematical entities:

firstly, in the form of *infinitely proceeding sequences* $P_1 P_2 ....$, whose terms are *chosen more or less freely from mathematical entities previously acquired*; in such a way that the freedom of choice existing perhaps for the first element $p_1$ may be subjected to a lasting restriction at some following $p_v$, and again and again to sharper lasting restrictions, while all these restriction interventions, as well as the choices of the $p_v$'s themselves, at any stage may be made to depend on possible future mathematical experiences of the creating subject;

secondly, in the form of mathematical *species, i.e., properties supposable for mathematical entities previously acquired,* and satisfying the condition that, if they hold a certain mathematical entity, they also hold for all mathematical entities which have been defined to be equal to it, relations of equality having to be symmetric, reflexive, and transitive; mathematical entities previously acquired for which the property holds are called *elements* of the species.

With regard to this definition of species we have to remark firstly that, during the development of intuitionist mathematics, some species will have to be considered as being re-defined time and again in the same way, secondly that a species can very well be an element of another species but never an element of itself.

Two mathematical entities are called *different* if their equality has been proved to be absurd.

Two infinitely proceeding sequences of mathematical entities $a_1, a_2, ....$ and $b_1, b_2 ....$ are called *equal* or *identical* if $a_v = b_v$ for each $v$ and *distinct* if a natural number $s$ can be indicated that $a_s$ and $b_s$ are different.

From L.E.J. Brouwer, *Collected Works I*, ed. Arend Heyting,
North-Holland Publishing Company, 1975.

# Life, Art, and Mysticism (Excerpts)
L.E.J. Brouwer

Originally man lived in isolation; with the support of nature, every individual tried to maintain his equilibrium between sinful temptations. This filled the whole of his life, there was no room for interest in others nor for worry about the future; as a result, labour did not exist, nor did sorrow, hate, fear, or lust. But man was not content, he began to search for power over others and for certainty about the future. In this way the balance was broken, labour became more and more painful to those oppressed and the conspiracy of those in power gradually more diabolical. In the end everyone wielded power and suffered suppression at the same time. The old instinct of separation and isolation has survived only in the form of pale envy and jealousy.

TURNING INTO THE SELF

Having contemplated the sadness of this world look into yourself. In you there is a consciousness, a consciousness which continually changes its content. Are you master of these changes? You say no, for you find yourself placed in a world which you have not created yourself, you are bewildered by its continuous state of flux.

The content of your consciousness, however, is to a great extent determined by your moods, and these are within your power. Is the motto "Control your passions" only an empty phrase to you? Sometimes you must have experienced that religious feeling of escape from your passions, from fear and desire, from time and space, from the whole world of perception. Finally, you do know that very meaningful phrase "turn into yourself." There seems to be a kind of attention which centers round yourself and which to some extent is within your power. What this Self is we cannot further say; we cannot even reason about it, since—as we know—all speaking and reasoning is an attention at a great distance from the Self; we cannot even get near it by reasoning or by words, but only by "turning into the Self" as it is given to us.

This "turning into oneself" is accompanied by a feeling of effort, it seems as if some inertia has to be surmounted, that your attention is strongly inclined to linger where it is, and that the resistance felt in the move towards the inner Self is much greater than in the move away from it. If, however, you succeed in overcoming all inertia, passions will be silenced, you will feel dead to the old world of perception, to time and space and to all other forms of plurality. Your eyes, no longer blindfolded, will open to a joyful quiescence.

. . . . . . . . . . . . . . . .

Now you will recognize your Free Will, insofar as it is free to withdraw from the world of causality and then to remain free, only then obtaining a definite Direction which it will follow freely, reversibly. The phenomena succeed each other in time, bound by causality because your coloured view wants this regularity, but right through the walls of causality "miracles" glide and flow continually, visible only to the free, the enlightened.

## MAN'S FALL CAUSED BY THE INTELLECT

Without pain, the free man sees mankind cast down by fear and desire, by avarice and lust for power, by time and space, aimlessly wandering without wings, incapable of lifting itself in self-reflection, chained to the spawn of time and space, the Intellect, which has become fossilized in the form of the human head, the symbol of man's fall.

. . . . . . . . . . . . . . . .

This highly esteemed Intellect has enabled and has forced man to go on living in Desire and Fear, rather than—from a salutary sense of bewilderment—take refuge in self-reflection. Intellect has made him forfeit the staggering independence and directness of each of his rambling images by connecting them with eachother rather than with the Self. In this way, the Intellect made him persevere in a state of apparent security, in a "reality" which man, in his arrogance had made himself, which he had tied to causality, but in which, eventually, he must feel totally powerless.

In this life of lust and desire, the Intellect renders man the diabolical service of connecting the two images of the imagination as means and end. Once in the grip of desire for one thing, he is made by the Intellect to strive after another as a means to obtain the former.

. . . . . . . . . . . . . . . .

The act aimed at the means always overshoots the mark to some extent; the means has a direction of its own, at an angle, however small, from the end. It acts not only in the direction of the end, but also in other dimensions. Man's blinkered view prevents him from recognizing the sometimes very detrimental effects of such action, but, worse, the end is gradually lost sight of and only the means remains.

In this sad world, where a clear view of all human activity is impossible, a world dominated by Drill and Imitation, the other offspring of Fear and Desire, many recognize as an end what was originally only a means. They seek what we might call an end of second order and in so doing may discover a means again out of line with the corresponding end. If this deceptive jump from ends to means is repeated several times, it may happen that a direction is pursued which not only deviates into other dimensions but even opposes the direction of the original end and therefore counteracts it.

Industry originally supplied its products in order to create the most favourable conditions for human life. But one ignored the fact that in manufacturing these products from the resources of nature one interfered with and disturbed the balance of nature and of human conditions, thereby causing damage greater than the advantages of these products could ever justify.

. . . . . . . . . . . . . . . . .

But worse: manufacturing these industrial goods has become an end in itself, new industries were called into existence merely to supply instruments to facilitate production. Another blow was dealt to the balance of nature. Raw materials were recklessly seized from far away lands, commercial and naval enterprises were created with all their physical and moral misery, all leading to oppression of one people by another.

Now that the Self had been abandoned, the Self that knows all about the past and the future, man grew anxious about the future and craved for the power to predict. Science originates in this desire to predict, in its early stages it is completely subservient to industry. Science asserts generalizing propositions in and about the world of perception; these will come true as long as it pleases God, sometimes they are contradicted by the facts. The scientists then exclaim: "Yes indeed, but we had made this or that tacit assumption." In their incompetence they then set about complicating the proposition further and making so called improvements.

Science does not remain confined to serving industry, again the means becomes an end in itself and science is practised for its own sake. A further aberration has been the concentration of all bodily awareness in the human head thereby excluding and ignoring the rest of the body. At the same time, man became convinced of his own existence as an individual and that of a separate and independent world of perception. At that stage, the full extent of the deviation of human scientific thinking became clear, for scientific thinking is nothing but a fixation of the will within the confines of the human head, a scientific truth no more than an infatuation of desire restricted to the human mind. Every branch of science as it proceeds will therefore always run into deeper trouble; when it climbs too high it becomes blindfolded in even more restricted isolation, the remembered results of that; science take on an independent existence. The "foundations" of this branch of science are then investigated and this soon becomes a new branch of science. Then one begins to search for the foundations of science in general and knocks up a "theory of knowledge." As they climb higher and higher trouble increases and in the end everyone is thoroughly confused. Some in the end quietly give up. Having thought for a long time about the elusive link between the intuiting consciousness—which itself develops from the world of phenomena—and this world of phenomena (which again itself exists only through and in the form of the intuiting consciousness)—a confusion which originated in a sinful foundation of the world of intuition—they then plug the hole with the concept of the Ego which was self-created with and at the same time as the phenomenal world. And then they say, "Yes, of course, something must remain incomprehensible and that something is the Ego that comprehends." But there are others who do not know when to stop, who keep on and on until they go mad; they grow bald, shortsighted and fat, their stomachs stop working properly, and moaning with asthma and gastric trouble, they fancy that in this way equilibrium is within reach and almost reached. So much for science, the last flower and ossification of culture.

...Even if Conscience penetrates into the enclaved categories, man's attention is diverted away from it by the strongly felt stimulation and satisfaction of other needs, or it is assimilated, i.e., it is recognized as a need within the closed system and capable of satisfaction in the system. The main function of art and poetry, but also of religion, is to silence the human conscience by recognizing this need and by apparent but not real satisfaction. Art and religion in this world are only morphine industries, the yearning for a better life is only lulled into sleep or into a state of torpidity...


RECONCILIATION

This corrupt world, as you now recognize, only exists because of its very corruption, its deviation from the paths of rectitude. A world of righteousness seems to you as contradictory as your own mortality...

In language transcendent truth—even less than immanent truth—cannot be revealed without causing an outrage. A clear and true statement, Seriously and emphatically pronounced, is no more acceptable than the manifest performance of miracles.

. . . . . . . . . . . . . . . . .

In language transcendent truth seems to be the prerogative of imitators who have vaguely understood the words of the prophet and recognized them as truth, but only after watering it down to suit themselves.

. . . . . . . . . . . . . . . . .

They will liberate the world of all sorts of vices, stupidity and injustice, and be hailed as the benefactors of mankind but leave mankind as miserable as it was.

. . . . . . . . . . . . . . . . .

The advice to get rid of the intellect, "this gift of the devil," is qualified by some added remark in defence of the viewpoint of the repudiated intellect, such as for example: "The structure of nature is so infinitely subtle and complex that your intellect will never fully grasp it and so you will never find there the stability you aim for." For those who relinquish the intellect, however, the world is anything but subtle or complex—it is immediately clear: it appears subtle only to the intellect that struggles laboriously and sees no end to its struggle.

. . . . . . . . . . . . . . . . .

Look at this world, full of wretched people, who imagine that they have possessions, afraid they might lose them, always hopefully toiling in an effort to acquire more; look at people who strive after luxury and wealth, at those whose riches is secured, whose stocks and shares are safely deposited, but who nurture an insatiable appetite for knowledge, power, health, glory, and pleasure.

Only he who recognizes that he has nothing, that he cannot possess anything, that absolute certainty is unattainable, who completely resigns himself and sacrifices all, who does not know anything, does not want anything and does not want to know anything, who abandons and neglects everything—he will receive all; to him the world of freedom opens, the world of painless contemplation and of—nothing.

From L.E.J. Brouwer, *Collected Works I*, ed. Arend Heyting, North-Holland Publishing Company, 1975.

# A Brief Presentation of *Brouwer's Lattice* and *The Deontic Miracle*

Rita Knox (Ed. Catherine Christer Hennix)

The following text is based on an interview with Catherine Christer Hennix on March 7th, 1976. The interview took place at Christer's studio where also Keith Knox and Hans Isgren contributed to the discussions following my questions. Christer contributed extensively to the editing of this nearly four-hour interview which appears here in a rather condensed form.

By way of introduction, it should be stressed that Catherine Christer Hennix conceives of Music as a particular Language Form, or more accurately, as an extension of our ordinary language faculties. Her conception implies that music, paralleling ordinary language, defines "styles of life" or "life forms" as Wittgenstein used to call it, and that, in turn, implies that the languages of music define states of knowledge or awareness connected with our perceptions of the real world and the way the corresponding mental images become interpreted.

Christer always stresses that listening to music involves activating certain aspects of our collective awareness, which she describes in terms of Wittgenstein's "Modules of Modalities." What she means is that listening to music activates a kind of "private" language similar in form and flow to the "private" inner dialogs that accompany our awakened states of consciousness. As soon as we try to put this inner dialog into words its flow becomes disrupted and its form cracks into disconnected fragments. But in music there is a more immediate connection between our private thoughts and the musical expressions which, in a way, form "closed figures" of private language patterns.

This is the way music extends language, in particular, it extends our *freedom* of interpreting semantic-intended events. This should be understood in the sense that acts of interpretation serve as *means* for some higher order aims, in this case, in particular, the aim of extending our *tactics of attention* connected with the growth of knowledge of our continuously developing environment ...

    Rita Knox
... What is the difference between conventional music and your music, with its long performances and these modal infinity qualities?

Catherine Christer Hennix

The difference is that I believe very strongly in the psychological impact of modal intervals. As I see it music should be considered as a source of knowledge and not just entertainment: the specific feelings you are brought to under exposure to music is a specific form of knowledge or awareness. And, further, it is also a vital nourishment for your fantasy and concept formation processes. Actually, the whole inner self can be mapped onto modal structures, as is well known from the classical Indian and Japanese musical traditions, and even European music before the Renaissance. What you get aware of by exposure to our music is awareness of general patterns, it's a purely abstract and private imprint, not a factual thing.

...

And that is why I insist on claiming that music should open up new tactics of attention, in which terms the audience can redevelop their ambiguously acquired modalities. That is the aim ...

This strong belief is connected with the fact that we really need music that has this function in order to neutralize the rapid intensification of horrible conditions that degrade the quality of life. Music with this function serves the aim of cleaning up people's awareness of their own mental capabilities and intuitions and their whole strategy of searching tor knowledge, albeit not being the only means for that aim.

RK

What is the basis for the ensemble's music? And why does it reach such high-power levels of amplification? It seems to me that you depend a great deal on amplifiers to bring out the relevant combination notes and their relevant amplitudes.

CCH

It is a very unusual aspect of modal music we perform ... The movement of one note to another is grounded in the law of sufficient reason. This is what we call *Brouwer's Doctrine* ... Nobody has been able to bring out these aspects before the availability of electronic equipment and Brouwer's logic. We owe the inauguration of this tradition to La Monte Young and his fabulous New York City group in the 1960s ... Another aspect is that we aim at *evolving* frames of musical structures, rather than trying to obtain completeness. In this context completeness is misconceived.

Instead, the thing is to be extensive. That is why repetition is so important in this context, primarily emphasized by the drone ... The drone can be considered as a wave package that makes a copy of itself for each period of its waveform as it moves forward in time. The new copy is exactly the same as the preceeding ones and it is copied anew and anew with the same exactness each time. In congruence with this exactness, all our musical parameters are set, and that is how we can achieve extensiveness with very simple means. That is, we don't introduce any more complications into the music than is warranted by the law of sufficient reason ... The high power levels of amplification are simply a means for achieving this aim.

RK

Isn't your computer music done at EMS an idealized version of this, where the creative subjects have become precise algorithms?

CCH

Yes, the computer adds to the technical precision. You are never limited by physical exhaustion and there are no obstacles or proceeding with infinitely long spreads of musical events, locked together by some appropriate algorithm that recursively generates each new step on the basis of the proceeding ones. This technique permits nearly ideal conditions for a composer concerned with long measures of a musical performance ...

RK

But the ensemble is not fulfilling these conditions ideally?

CCH

No, but it should be noted that length is restricted by the standards of ethics in our society—a cardinal example of a conventionalistic restriction of a useful modality ...

Length has to do with space in society, how much space can be taken up by musical performance? ... Our long performance styles are very good pedagogic examples of *overcoming* the obstacles existing tor Freedom$_1$ and Freedom$_2$ in our society (§). This is how musical performance connects with ethics. There are obstructions for these long style performances and our music documents the overcoming of those obstructions ...

RK

... And this overcoming is the miracle achieved by exclusively deontic means?

CCH

Yes, here we relate to the modalities developed in the arts of Gagaku and Nō with their long style performances. The idea is, of course, that living music should be allowed performance space that allows it to be in progress for at least half a day or more. The musician should be able to perform as long as he is capable and inspired to do that. It is a characteristic feature of our society that it never allows a musician to perfect his art, which, of course, is true of all the other fine arts as well ...

In my music, the end of a performance does not indicate the end of the composition, but is merely an indication of a temporary stop caused by external factors. The compositions should be considered to evolve for durations of weeks and months, rather than limited to what the present standard of ethics permits.

RK

Would the ideas of Brouwer's bring any change with respect to these obstacles if they were generally accepted and known?

**CCH**

Well, as you know, Brouwer and the Significes movement derived the sources for the decadent trends in our society from the misconceptions caused by language and the sloppiness of the treatment of consciousness in the context of political decisions... So they wanted to refine people's thinking and to claim this as a political demand. We in our group think it is high time to reinforce this demand, it having gestated sufficiently long.... There is no doubt that the general recognition of Brouwer's thinking would have a healthy effect, not just on the standards of music in performance, but on the whole development of our society...

As I have already pointed out in my notes on Intuitionistic Modal Music, it seems to us that Brouwer's thinking is the closest analog in the Western Hemisphere of the Mind of Tea and, in particular, his conception of the roles of the creative subjects has a corresponding analog in the logical grammar of the Gagaku part books... since, as a matter of fact, the musicians in the Gagaku orchestra constitute, historically, the first example of creative subjects where each member has his Independent-part book handed down by the tradition, which, furthermore, is inaccessible to members not addressed by the text of the part book in question.

(§) See Catherine Christer Hennix: *Toposes & Adjoints*

# The Artists
Keith Knox

Catherine Christer Hennix was attracted early to Japanese music and to the modal music of John Coltrane. Hennix met Terry Riley and La Monte Young in 1969 in New York and became seriously interested in modalities and composing in relation to a drone. She became acquainted also at this time with the music of Terry Jennings. The influence of the saxophone techniques developed by Young and Jennings is heard in Christer's performances on electric renaissance oboe, which at times also comes close to John Coltrane's modal techniques.

In 1970 Christer met the remarkable singer Pandit Pran Nath, and this caused her music to change, as she began studying classical North Indian vocal music of the Kirana tradition. Christer became a disciple to Pandit Pran Nath, in company with Riley and Young, and the three have travelled and played together a great deal since then.

The fine structure of the overtone series became more and more important for Christer after her meeting with Pandit Pran Nath, which can be seen expressed by her move towards the Brouwerian Lattice and computer compositions involving infinitely many intervals. The original ideas of Japanese and Indian modal music were a means of liberating the blocked channels of mind caused by uncautious exposure to non-modal contexts.

In one of her main compositions for ensemble, "Chagaku," Christer is concerned with liberating these modalities in the general spirit of fundamentalism, while at the same time asserting the depth of the potentials of modal music.

Fundamentalism in a still stricter sense is exposed by Christer in her computer music of infinitely long musical events developed at EMS, Stockholm, in part together with La Monte Young. At present Hennix is designing her own computer systems in order to be able to work uninterruptedly with her infinitely proceeding sequences of musical events at his studio in Stockholm.

§ § § §

Hans Isgren began his career as a film maker with Ture Sjolander and others. He started to play drone music with Catherine Christer Hennix in 1970 on the latter's return from New York. The band known as Hilbert's Hotel was formed together with Peter Hennix, to develop the performance of live electronic music using built-in drones in the tradition of La Monte Young.

Hans Isgren's main instrument is sarangi. In 1971, he became a disciple to Pandit Ram Narayan, the famous North Indian sarangi artist. He has played and recorded with the American jazz trumpeter Don Cherry. He also studied with Jan Bark and Karlheinz Stockhausen.

Isgren has developed a special technique of using amplified sarangi to be congenial with the moods and possibilities of the group. At present, he is playing electric, she with a technique worked out in cooperation with Catherine Christer Hennix, to achieve the particular performance attributes required by the environment. He has recently experimented in the same way with amplified koto.

§ § § §

Peter Hennix introduced Catherine Christer Hennix to music, mainly that of Miles Davis and Charlie Parker, and they played jazz together through the 1950s and '60s. Peter Hennix studied trumpet very extensively with Idries Suliemann during the 1960s. He has played and recorded with Gunnar Lindqvist's UNIT.

He has worked for a decade with Swedish Radio/TV and recently recorded Ingmar Bergman's production of *The Magic Flute*. Lately, he recorded sitarist Nikki Banerjee during Banerjee's Swedish tour.

Peter Hennix has studied sitar, rudra vina, and Surbahar since 1971. The oboe technique he is presently using was developed for performance of the Christer Hennix scores.

# The Deontic Miracle: Program

Brouwer's Lattice with Dream Music Festival
Present "The Deontic Miracle"
March 20–30, 1976

Days 11–21                           Brouwer's Lattice


Evenings 20–30 III 76                Cha-gaku (Music for Tea) Catherine
(except 25, 26) at 7–9               Christer Hennix, Choshi, Netori, Music of
                                     Auspicious Clouds, Waves of the Blue Sea,
                                     Five Times Repeated Music,
                                     Central Palace Music...

                                     Well Tuned Organ/
                                     Well Tuned Piano     of Catherine
                                                          Christer Hennix
                                     Church Street Blues,
                                     Venice Boulevard Blues

Afternoons at 15–17

Saturday 20 III 76 and
Sunday 21 III 76                     Well Tuned Organ/Well Tuned Piano

                                     Swedish performances of
Monday 22 III 76                     Composition 1960 no. 7 by La Monte Young
Tuesday 23 III 76                    Dream Chord by La Monte Young
Wednesday 24 III 76                  Piano Piece 1960 by Terry Jennings
Thursday 25 III 76                   String Quartet 1960 by Terry Jennings
                                     (transcribed for organ)

Friday 26 III 76                     Dream Chord by La Monte Young
Saturday 27 III 76 and               Well Tuned Organ/Well Tuned Piano
Sunday 28 III 76
Monday 29 III 76                     Blank Page Music by Charles Ives
Tuesday 30 III 76                    Concert for two pianists and tape-
                                     recorders by Terry Riley

| | |
|---|---|
| Catherine Christer Hennix | Electric renaissance oboe, well-tuned keyboard, electric shō, sine-wave generator |
| Peter Hennix | Electric renaissance oboe |
| Hans Isgren | Electric shō<br>Electric sarangi |
| Environment design | Catherine Christer Hennix |
| Silkscreen | Alison Knowles |
| Photography | Lennart Halling<br>Rita Knox |
| Sound System | Lab |
| Laser Technology | Stocktronics |
| Tuning Assistant | Andre Studencki |

- - - - - - - - - - - - - - - - - - - - - - -

The Deontic Miracle play Fender pianos and Yamaha organs. Catherine Christer Hennix sits on Ackerman Komfort.

This event has been made possible through contributions from Rikskonserter and the Stockholm Cultural Council.

# NOTES ON TOPOSES & ADJOINTS

Written in Stockholm, 1976. First published on the occasion of Hennix's solo installation *Toposes & Adjoints* at Moderna Museet, Stockholm, September 4 – October 17, 1976. Included in this volume is a facsimile of the original publication. Hennix views this text as intentionally unfinished — a conscious bridge between a preliminary draft and the finished project.

# CHRISTER HENNIX

*Notes on*

# TOPOSES & ADJOINTS

*Moderna Museet*

*Sept 4 – Oct 17, 1976*

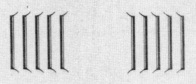

CHRISTER HENNIX

## NOTES ON
## TOPOSES AND ADJOINTS

COPYRIGHT
CHRISTER HENNIX
1976

NOTHING IS MORE FANTASTIC, ULTIMATELY,
THAN PRECISION.

      ALAIN ROBBE-GRILLET


IN PHILOSOPHY WE ARE ALWAYS IN DANGER
OF GIVING A MYTHOLOGY OF THE SYMBOLISM,
OR OF PSYCHOLOGY: INSTEAD OF SIMPLY
SAYING WHAT EVERYONE KNOWS AND MUST
ADMIT.

      LUDWIG WITTGENSTEIN

## CONTENTS

0. NOTES FOR THE (NON-ALIEN) READER .............. I - IV
1. SPECTRA OF MODALITIES AND THE
   THEORY OF THE CREATIVE SUBJECT, $T_H(\Sigma)$ ....... 1 - 15
2. SEMIOTICS I ................................... 16 - 27
3. SEMIOTICS II .................................. 28 - 33
4. TOPOSES, SHEAVES AND ADJOINTS ................. 34 - 40
5. APPENDIX 1: $T_H(\Sigma)$ AND THE STRUCTURE OF MIND  41 - 42
6. APPENDIX 2: CARDINALS IN 1-MODAL SPECTRA ..... 43 - 50
7. APPENDIX 3: THE ENVIRONMENT TOPOSES AND
   ADJOINTS, MODERNA MUSEET, STOCKHOLM ........ 51 - 53

# NOTES FOR THE (NON-ALIEN) READER

## NOTES FOR THE (NON-ALIEN) READER

1. ARROWS, I.E. LOGICAL CONNECTIONS, ARE INVISIBLE CONSTRUCTIONS MADE IN THE PRESENCE OF A LOGICAL SPACE OR L-SPACE.

THERE ARE INFINITELY MANY L-SPACES AVAILABLE, CORRESPONDING TO THE FORMS OF AWARENESS OR REALITIES THAT THE INTELLIGENCE MAY COMPREHEND.

THE INDICATION OF AN L-SPACE MUST NOT BE CONFUSED WITH ITS CORRESPONDING CONSTRUCTION. AN INDICATION IS JUST A SEMIOTICAL EVENT WHOSE SURFACE STRUCTURE REFLECTS SOME OR ALL OF THE ABSTRACTIONS UNDERLYING THE L-SPACE. THESE CONSTRUCTIONS OR SO-CALLED DEEP STRUCTURES OF A SEMIOTICAL EVENT ARE THE ACTUAL CONSCIOUSNESS BEING AWARE OF THE PRESENCE OF AN L-SPACE. IT IS ASSUMED THAT EACH SUCH PRESENCE IS REAL IF AND ONLY IF ITS MODAL SPECTRA HAVE ARRIVED FOR THE SITUATION IN QUESTION. MODALITIES, LIKE AWARENESS, COME IN DEGREES, THE DEGREE BEING SUFFICIENT OR NOT DEPENDING ON OPTATIVE CONTINGENCIES. MODALITIES CORRESPOND TO INTEGRATED FORMS OF CONSCIOUSNESS AND FORM THE SUBSTANCE OF THE AWARENESS OF THE UNIVERSE OF ALL LOGICALLY POSSIBLE WORLDS. WE THINK OF THIS UNIVERSE AS "STANDARD", I.E. AS A UNIVERSAL IN THE SENSE OF CATEGORY THEORY (FOLLOWING LAWVERE ET AL.).

2. THE PRESENT FORMAT OF OUR STYLE OF THINKING IS INSPIRED BY THE GREAT BREAKTHROUGHS IN THE STUDIES OF THE FOUNDATIONS OF MATHEMATICS. WE EMPHASIZE OUR AWARENESS OF THIS INTELLECTUAL TRADITION BY BRINGING FORTH TWO OF THE MOST CONTROVERSIAL CONTEMPORARY STARS IN THE FIELD TOGETHER WITH SOME OF THEIR MOST FAR-OUT CONCEPTUAL INNOVATIONS, MEANING OF COURSE ALEXANDER S.

YESENIN-VOLPIN'S ULTRAINTUITIONISTIC PROGRAM AND WILLIAM LAWVERE'S STUDIES OF MODELS OF TOPOI CONSTRUCTIONS.

3. THIS DEPENDENCY IS, HOWEVER, SUBORDINATED THE GENERAL PATTERN OF EPISTEMOLOGICAL ANARCHISM WHICH OUR COSMOLOGICAL CRITIQUE ENVELOPS. BESIDES SPOTTING EPISTEMOLOGICAL ILLUSIONS OUR CONCERN IS RELATED TO THE CREATION OF AN ATMOSPHERE OF ATTENTION IN EVERY (NON-ALIEN) SITUATION WHERE THE CONTRARY MAY OBTAIN. THAT IS, ONLY SUSTAINED FEELINGS OF AWARENESS ARE REAL OBJECTS IN OUR ONTOLOGY OF INTENSIONS. IT FOLLOWS THAT ANY SITUATION $S$ WHICH IS NOT PARAMETERIZED BY $\Sigma$ IS ALIEN FOR OUR PRESENT AIMS.

4. SPACES IN WHICH SUSTAINED FEELINGS OF AWARENESS OCCUR FORM A <u>PARTIAL ORDER</u> $<$ OF THEIR APPEARANCES. IN ABSENCE OF AN ATMOSPHERE OF ATTENTION THE <u>CONTINUITY PROPERTY</u> OF THIS ORDER IS VIOLATED. THE RESTORATION OF THE INJURED ORDER IS MARKED BY BARRING THIS ABSENCE (APPLICATION BAR - INDUCTION (BROUWER)).

5. THE ALIENNESS OF THE TACTICS OF ATTENTION BY WHICH THE ABOVE MODAL CONSIDERATIONS ARE SUSTAINED IS A FUNCTION OF THE <u>TOLERANCE OF ERROR</u> WHICH IS PERMITTED BY THE CORRESPONDING <u>OBJECTS OF ALIENATION</u>. IT IS SUGGESTED THAT EVERY SUCH CHARACTER IS EXPOSED FOR <u>DENIAL OF CONFIDENCE</u> SINCE EVERY OBJECT OF ALIENATION BY DEFINITION HAS ITS SPHERE OF CONFIDENCE REDUCED TO AN INFINITESIMAL. THIS BEING SAID, WE REMARK THAT THE CHOICE OF <u>BASIC CONSTRUCTION PRINCIPLES</u> IN <u>TOPOSES</u> AND <u>ADJOINTS</u> IS MADE WITH A PREFERENCE FOR THE LEAST PRESUMPTIOUS, ONLY TAKING

III

$\in$            (CANTORIAN MEMBERSHIP)

AND

$\sqcup$            (DIRECTED SUM)

AS UNDEFINED.

BY THESE PRIMITIVES, WE MAY RECOVER THE $\longrightarrow$ - OPERATION, VIZ. $\alpha \in \beta$ IF AND ONLY IF $\beta \longrightarrow \alpha$ AND $\sqcup \alpha \in \beta$ IF AND ONLY IF $\beta \longrightarrow \alpha_1$, OR $\beta \longrightarrow \alpha_2$ OR ........ OR $\beta \longrightarrow \alpha_n$, FOR $\alpha_1, \ldots\ldots\ldots, \alpha_n \in \alpha$.

FOR EVERY PROCESS $\alpha_1 \longrightarrow \alpha_2 \longrightarrow \ldots\ldots\ldots \longrightarrow \alpha_k \longrightarrow \alpha_{k+1} \longrightarrow \ldots\ldots\ldots$ THE FOLLOWING <u>DIALECTICAL TRIANGLE</u> IS <u>BASIC</u>, VIZ.

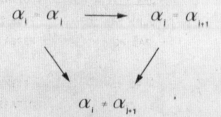

$$\alpha_i = \alpha_i \longrightarrow \alpha_i = \alpha_{i+1}$$
$$\alpha_i \neq \alpha_{i+1}$$

UNDERLYING THE INFINITELY PROCEEDING INVISIBLE PROCESSES PRESENTED IN TOPOSES AND ADJOINTS. (ALTHOUGH INFINITELY MANY IDENTIFICATIONS AND DISTINCTIONS ARE SUGGESTED BY THE <u>TIME CATEGORIES</u>, INITIAL SEGMENTS COVERED BY <u>GALOIS CONNECTIONS</u> SUFFICE FOR THE DESCRIPTION OF THESE <u>COHERENCE SINGULARITIES</u>).

6. IT GOES WITHOUT SAYING THAT THE PRESENT PRESENTATION ONLY REFLECTS THE FIELD FROM A RATHER SMALL (LIMIT) ORDINAL. ON THE OTHER HAND, BY FURTHER RARIFYING THE ATMOSPHERE OF ATTENTION FROM

IV.

A REFLECTION AT A HIGHER LIMIT ORDINAL, THE POSSIBILITY OPENS UP FOR A SUSTAINED FEELING OF AWARENESS EMBEDDED BY A <u>CONTINUOUS REFLEXION PRINCIPLE</u> (ALONG THE LINES OF BROUWER'S IDEAS OF THE CREATIVE SUBJECT, I.E. CONTINUOUS AT LIMITS). BUT THE USE OF THE REFLEXION PRINCIPLE AT LIMITS MUST BE GOVERNED BY SOME <u>PRINCIPLE OF CAUTION</u>, SINCE EMBARRASSING CONSEQUENCES MAY FOLLOW STEPS BEYOND PROJECTED LIMITS IF THE BASIC PRINCIPLES LACK THE PROPERTY OF BEING <u>WELL-FOUNDED</u>. THEREFORE, IN ALL EXTENSIONS OF THE <u>NOTES ON TOPOSES AND ADJOINTS</u> (I.E. SEMIOTICAL OBJECTS LISTED IN APPENDIX 3) THE PRESENCE OF <u>COLLAPSING TECHNIQUES</u> HAVE TAKEN PRECEDENCE. TOGETHER WITH AN <u>ULTRA-INTIMATE PEDAGOGY</u> GOVERNING THE INSTALLATION OF THE ENTIRE ENVIRONMENT <u>TOPOSES</u> AND <u>ADJOINTS</u>, THE GIVEN <u>BASIC PRINCIPLES</u> ARE INTENDED TO GROUND THE POSSIBILITY OF FOLLOWING A CONTINUOUS REFLEXION PRINCIPLE (LIKE FOLLOWING A CLEAR LANGUAGE $\mathcal{L}$ ).

7. TO THE ABOVE CLARIFYING TEXT WE WISH TO ADD SOME OF THE SOURCES OF OUR CONCEPTUAL FRAMEWORK.

L.E.J. BROUWER: COLLECTED WORKS I, ED. HEYTING, 1975
L.E.J. BROUWER: COLLECTED WORKS II ED. TROELSTRA, 1976
A.S. YESENIN-VOLPIN: INTUITIONISM AND PROOF THEORY, ED. KINO, MYHILL, VESLEY, 1970.
W. LAWVERE: SPRINGER LECTURE NOTES IN MATHEMATICS NO. 445, 1975.

SOME READERS MAY ALSO ENJOY

C. HENNIX: BROUWER'S LATTICE (MODERNA MUSEET, 1976).

FINALLY, WE MUST EMPHASIZE THAT THE FOLLOWING TEXT ONLY CONTAINS RATHER CONDENSED EXCERPTS FROM NOTEBOOKS THAT WE HAVE WRITTEN DURING THE LAST FIVE YEARS OR SO.

# SPECTRA OF MODALITIES AND THE THEORY OF THE CREATIVE SUBJECT Th$(\Sigma)$

## SPECTRA OF MODALITIES
## AND
## THE THEORY OF THE CREATIVE SUBJECT, $T_H(\Sigma)$

I.  It is a well-known fact that activities ending in art may not always carry a well-determined meaning or sense. On the contrary, the lack of meaning(-fulness) is compensated for by (purported) aim(s) expressed by the purpose(s) governing the installment of the generating activities for which end some particular object is taken as a witness. This somewhat confused reality shows the indisputable importance of the interpretation of the <u>optative modalities</u> underlying any goal-oriented activity $\mathcal{A}$.

II.  In order to fix the purposefulness of an activity $\mathcal{A}$, several ratios are to be measured, such as

$$1) \quad \frac{\text{Interest of results}}{\text{Efforts involved}}$$

and

$$2) \quad \frac{\text{Long-term satisfaction}}{\text{Efforts required}}$$

Given some satisfactory measures of these ratios for an activity $\mathcal{A}$ there is a further requirement on the <u>means</u> available by which the result(s) of $\mathcal{A}$ are achieved. Viz. it is generally required that any aim achieved through $\mathcal{A}$ is acquired only as far as <u>fair</u> means have been provided.

Any violation of this <u>fairness principle</u> is to be considered harmful for the continuation of the situations $S$ generated by $\mathcal{A}$, on account of the <u>displacement of modalities</u>, caused, in particular, by the displacement of goals relative the installment of $\mathcal{A}$.

III. Clearly, the condition of fairness for purposeful activities $\mathcal{A}$ imposes an obvious restriction as to the availability of means for realizing $\mathcal{A}$. This restriction must be evaluated relative the higher-order aims under which $\mathcal{A}$ is subsumed. As far as clarity and certainty is sought, the fairness principle is but a higher-order means for our epistemic development, and its violation poses obstacles as far as (foundational) communication is aimed at (to wit, its deepest threat).

IV. For the purpose of <u>restricting</u> the above-mentioned restriction, two <u>spectra of modalities</u> are defined for the sake of optimal freedom in activities $\mathcal{A}$ restricted by fair means, viz.

(1) The first spectrum which will be designated $Freedom_1$ or $F_1$ and is defined as that <u>regime</u> $P$ governing activities $\mathcal{A}$ in the <u>absence of any obstructions</u>. Id est, $F_1$ assigns the following interpretation to the fulfilment of the optative modalities connected with $\mathcal{A}$: If $T$ is an aim in $\mathcal{A}$ and $\mathcal{A}$ provides ($\alpha$) sufficient means and ($\beta$) all necessary means for realizing $T$ in $\mathcal{A}$, then $T$ is fulfill<u>able</u> in $\mathcal{A}$. $F_1$ clearly corresponds to the <u>purposefulness</u> of $\mathcal{A}$ and would be violated in any situation where ($\alpha$) ($\beta$) hold but $T$ has been (or will be) obstructed.

(2) The second spectrum which will be designated Freedom$_2$ or F$_2$ and which is defined as that REGIME $P$ governing activities $\mathcal{A}$ such that NO ACT IN $\mathcal{A}$ IS FORCED BY COERCION, FRAUD OR ANY OTHER VIOLATION OF THE FAIRNESS OF MEANS PROVIDED FOR THE COURSE OF $\mathcal{A}$. Id est, $\mathcal{A}$ is said to possess property F$_2$ whenever every act in $\mathcal{A}$ is free from compulsion, id est exercised in accordance with the creative subject's free will. Clearly, the satisfiability of F$_2$ captures exactly what is intended by JUSTFULNESS of $\mathcal{A}$ and the SPECTRUM OF F$_2$-MODALITIES is precisely all instances of installments of given activities $\mathcal{A}$ for which fair means have been provided.

V. The spectra of modalities for $\mathcal{A}$ thus split into two basic components, F$_1$ and F$_2$. By passing to the DIRECT LIMIT of the projections of F$_1$ and F$_2$ on any $\mathcal{A}$, the composite F$_1$ F$_2$ obtains. It corresponds to that REGIME $P$ for which Freedom$_1$ and Freedom$_2$ hold SIMULTANEOUSLY and if $\mathcal{A}$ possesses property F$_1$ F$_2$ we shall say that $P$ is ELEUTHERIC FOR $\mathcal{A}$ or that the activities comprised by the situations generated by $\mathcal{A}$ are ELEUTHERIC ACTIVITIES in the regime $P$. - The basic tenet of Yesenin-Volpin's ELEUTHERIC ETHICS or our ULTRA ETHICS is that all modalities connected with just and purposeful activities $\mathcal{A}$, including their spectra, are REDUCIBLE to the modalities of the direct limit F$_1$ F$_2$.

VI. A rough indication of the growth of $\mathcal{A}$ may be given by describing the TREE STRUCTURE associated with $\mathcal{A}$, designated by $\mathcal{T}_{\mathcal{A}}$. At its root, $<\quad>_{\mathcal{S}}, \mathcal{T}_{\mathcal{A}}$ indicates the initial act in $\mathcal{A}$, while at every branch $<\ldots\ldots>_{\mathcal{S}}$ above $<\quad>_{\mathcal{S}}, \mathcal{T}_{\mathcal{A}}$ indicates for each node of a branch, the CATEGORY of the decision invited at the node in addition

TO THE <u>INTENSION</u> FOR THAT CATEGORY AT THE GIVEN LOCI.

TREES OF THE KIND $\mathcal{T}_\mathcal{A}$ DEPICT THE <u>SEARCH</u> IN WHICH THE CREATIVE SUBJECT DEVELOPS ACTIVITIES FOR THE PURPOSE OF ATTAINING SOME DESIRED RESULT(S) INVOLVING $\mathcal{A}$.

TO DESCRIBE THE INNER MAP PRESUPPOSED BY WAY OF $\mathcal{T}_\mathcal{A}$, IT IS NOT SUFFICIENT TO LOOK ONLY AT THE INDICES AT THE NODES OF $\mathcal{T}_\mathcal{A}$ BUT, IN ADDITION, IT IS NECESSARY TO MAP $\mathcal{T}_\mathcal{A}$ INTO AN EXTENDED TREE, $\mathcal{T}_\Sigma$, IN WHICH THE SEARCH IN $\mathcal{A}$, FUNCTOR-WISE, GOES OVER INTO THE <u>DOMAIN OF THE THEORETICAL ACTIVITY</u> CONNECTED WITH THE FULFILMENT OF THE SEARCH IN $\mathcal{A}$. THIS FUNCTOR IS CALLED THE $\Sigma_\mathcal{T}$-<u>PROJECTUM</u> OF TREES OF KIND $\mathcal{T}_\mathcal{A}$ (CF. DIALOGUE AND IMPASSE DIAGRAMS).

VII. WHEN UNDERSTOOD AS AN <u>EPISTEMIC OPERATOR</u>, THE <u>CREATIVE SUBJECT</u>, $\Sigma$, MAY BE CONCEIVED OF AS GROUNDED BY THE FOLLOWING AXIOMS. THE CLOSURE OF THESE AXIOMS UNDER THE CONSEQUENCE RELATION IS DENOTED $\text{TH}(\Sigma)$, I.E. THE THEORY OF $\Sigma$.

<u>AXIOMS FOR $\Sigma$</u>:

I: $\Sigma \vdash_n \mathcal{A} \vee \Sigma \vdash_n \neg \mathcal{A}$

II: $\Sigma \vdash_n \mathcal{A} \rightarrow \mathcal{A}$

III: $\Sigma \vdash_n \mathcal{A} \,\&\, n > m \rightarrow \Sigma \vdash_m \mathcal{A}$

IV: $\neg \exists(x) \Sigma \vdash_x \mathcal{A} \rightarrow \neg \mathcal{A}$

V: $\dfrac{\Sigma \vdash_n \mathcal{A}, \; \mathcal{A} \rightarrow \mathcal{C}}{\Sigma \vdash_n \mathcal{C}}$

$$\text{VI:}\ \frac{\Sigma \vdash_n \exists(x)\,\mathcal{A}(x)}{\exists(x)\,\Sigma \vdash_n \mathcal{A}(x)}$$

### INFERENCE SCHEMA FOR $T_H(\Sigma)$

$$\text{VII:}\ \frac{\Sigma \vdash_n \mathcal{F},\quad \Sigma \vdash_m \mathcal{F} \rightarrow \mathcal{G}}{\Sigma \vdash_{n,m} \mathcal{G}}$$

The general idea is now as follows. The basic relation $\vdash$ in the context $\Sigma \vdash_n \mathcal{A}$ is interpreted as "$\Sigma$ has <u>decided</u> or <u>solved</u> $\mathcal{A}$ at the n<sup>th</sup> stage of his investigation or research in $\mathcal{A}$", where $\mathcal{A}$ designates an <u>intension</u> or <u>problem</u> connected with $A$. The logical operators $\neg$, $\&$, $\vee$ and $\rightarrow$ are given the following interpretations.

$\neg[\mathcal{A}]$ signifies the task of obtaining the absurdity of the solution of $\mathcal{A}$

$\&[\mathcal{A},\mathcal{B}]$   "   "   "   " solving <u>both</u> $\mathcal{A}$ and $\mathcal{B}$

$\vee[\mathcal{A},\mathcal{B}]$   "   "   "   "   " <u>either</u> $\mathcal{A}$ or $\mathcal{B}$

$\rightarrow[\mathcal{A},\mathcal{B}]$   "   "   "   "   " the problem $\mathcal{B}$ given any solution of $\mathcal{A}$

IN ADDITION:

$\exists(x)[\mathscr{A}(x)]$ SIGNIFIES THE TASK OF SOLVING THE VALUE OF $x$ SUCH THAT $\mathscr{A}(x)$,

WHERE $\exists(x)$ IS THE OPERATOR DESIGNATING THE <u>EXISTENTIAL CONSTRUCTION PRINCIPLE</u>.

AMONG SOLVABLE PROBLEMS IN $\text{Th}(\Sigma)$ WE MENTION THE FOLLOWING TASKS (EXERCISE!):

$$\mathscr{A} \to \mathscr{B} \,\&\, \mathscr{B} \to \mathscr{C} \to \mathscr{A} \to \mathscr{C} \quad (1)$$

$$\mathscr{A} \to \mathscr{C} \,\&\, \mathscr{B} \to \mathscr{C} \to \mathscr{A} \vee \mathscr{B} \to \mathscr{C} \quad (2)$$

$$\neg \mathscr{A} \to \mathscr{A} \to \mathscr{B} \quad (3)$$

$$\mathscr{A} \to \mathscr{B} \to \neg \mathscr{B} \to \neg \mathscr{A} \quad (4)$$

$$\mathscr{A} \to \neg \mathscr{B} \to \mathscr{B} \to \neg \mathscr{A} \quad (5)$$

$$\neg(\mathscr{A} \vee \mathscr{C}) \to \neg \mathscr{A} \,\&\, \neg \mathscr{C} \quad (6)$$

$$\neg(\mathscr{C} \,\&\, \mathscr{E}) \,\&\, \mathscr{C} \vee \neg \mathscr{C} \to \neg \mathscr{C} \vee \neg \mathscr{E} \quad (7)$$

$$\neg(\mathscr{A} \,\&\, \neg \mathscr{A}) \quad (8)$$

<u>REMARK</u>: BY (8), <u>CONSISTENCY</u> OF $\text{Th}(\Sigma)$ IS ESTABLISHED, I.E. $\text{Th}(\Sigma)$ IS A <u>NON-TRIVIAL</u> THEORY (I.E. EPISTEMICALLY PALATABLE).

<u>(HISTORICAL) REMARK</u>: <u>L.E.J. BROUWER</u> WAS THE FIRST LOGICIAN TO FORMULATE PRINCIPLES SIMILAR TO THE ONES GIVEN ABOVE.

## THE HIERARCHY OF DEGREES OF MODALITIES

**(n°)** — Increasingly Stricter and Stricter Condensations of Acts of Confidence (by Arrows)

**(5°)** $\mathcal{A} \longrightarrow \Sigma^{\Sigma}$  Eleutheria (in Arrows)

**(4°)** $\longrightarrow\!\!\!\!\!/\longrightarrow$  Metamathematics (Consistency of Arrows (Hilbert's 2ⁿᵈ problem))

**(3°)** $\underset{\approx}{\Sigma}$  Actions and Processes (with Arrows)

**(2°)** $\Sigma$  Awareness (of Arrows)

**(1°)** $|\ \ |$  Arrows (at points of Condensation)

**(0°)** $\square$  Plasma (per Arrows)

VIII: Let us now briefly pause over the formalism so far introduced for the purpose of achieving a broader view of our subject.

It is a general fact that any activity $\mathcal{A}$ proceeds on the background of other activities $\mathcal{A}_j$ for which the relation

$$(\star) \quad \mathcal{A} \subset \mathcal{A}_j$$

holds for every $j$ (where $\mathcal{A} \subset \mathcal{A}_j$ reads $\mathcal{A}$ is included in $\mathcal{A}_j$ or $\mathcal{A}_j$ extends $\mathcal{A}$).

The exteriorized elements of $\mathcal{A}$, i.e. those belonging to some $\mathcal{A}_j$ but not in $\mathcal{A}$, can often be encountered as objects mentioned in any relevant part of $\mathcal{A}$. But, significantly, they may not participate constructively in any creative situation in which $\mathcal{A}$ is realized (as opposed to the given interior elements of $\mathcal{A}$). The processes of exteriorizing parts of an activity that is given, proceed on the unfolding of the modal components of the activity, which, essentially, determine the scope or ranges of the conceptual frameworks that go into the interior of the activity.

When we say that a modal component acts on an activity, we are referring to a hierarchy of (degrees of) modalities, that, when fully developed, constitutes the spectra of modalities in $\mathcal{A}$ (cf. the diagram of the hierarchy of degrees of modalities).

By a rank 2 or 2nd degree modal operator is to be understood those modalities which participate in shorter (i.e. fragmentary) lines of reasonings or other more general activities involving the use of interpreted signs (like the bracketing operation). Rank 1 is assigned to those modalities whose carrier activities consist in the use of (at most) <u>uninterpreted signs</u> or no signs at all (like the singular awareness of the presence of a <u>PLASMA</u>). There is no upper bound on the assignment of ranks to modalities in this hierarchy, as should be expected if $\mathcal{A}$ has the property $F_1 F_2$. The rank of a modality reflects the complexity of its dependence on modalities of lower rank as well as of the <u>degree of confidence</u> vindicated by the situations generated by $\mathcal{A}$. Any $\mathcal{A}$ for which the participating modalities are assigned rank $\geqslant 3$ is called a <u>theoretical activity</u>. On the other hand, ranks below 3, i.e. $< 3$, are connected with <u>dream activities</u>. (There exist some borderline cases of 3rd degree modalities, notably Intuitionistic Modal Music, which, although grounded in the law of sufficient reason, nevertheless may be said to be a dream activity, due to the presence of a <u>deontic miracle</u> in the activity).

As to be expected, the theoretical activity of $\Sigma$, as determined by the $\Sigma\sigma$-projectum, makes essential use of modalities of rank $> 3$. In particular, for any prospective interpretation of an element in the class of objects referred to as <u>TOPOSES</u>, it is essential to note the rank of modalities participating in the object. By way of example (and intimate pedagogy!), in <u>TOPOSES</u> rank is increased by introducing stronger concepts of <u>infinity</u> at points where an end could have been prescribed. The un-ending of a process, i.e. its points of infinity, is connected with the <u>future</u> of its unfolding, which may be <u>near</u> or <u>remote</u>. By reasonings about the <u>scales</u> between these points, we can imagine different lengths of ramifying infinitary processes including their "Zeonian" embeddings which distinguish themselves by the degree of infinity to which they converge. The diagram $\mathcal{E}$ may be understood as a

"UNIVERSAL" (LAWVERE) FOR SUCH SITUATIONS.

IX: As will soon become apparent, <u>CLASSIFICATIONS OF ARROWS</u> may be considered the <u>MAIN PROBLEM</u> of CONSTRUCTIVE CONCEPT-<u>UALISM</u> in <u>CARTESIAN CLOSED CATEGORIES</u>, where $C$ is <u>CONCEPT</u> or <u>CATEGORY</u>. That is, we will look at morphisms of the (developmental) kind $C \leftarrow CC \leftarrow CCC \leftarrow \ldots\ldots\ldots$ (Vide intimate pedagogy, exercises in the arts of <u>BELLES LETTRES</u>!).

Generally, what is intended is that <u>ARROWS</u> go proxy for the <u>MEANING RELATION</u> obtaining between the terms situated on both sides of the arrow-<u>SIGN</u>. There are, generally, no restrictions on the kind of objects that are permitted to appear as (the) fixed values of the terms. The collection of <u>ALL OBJECTS</u> which may be substituted for the values of the terms of the arrow-signs, is called the <u>UNIVERSE</u>, $U$, which the meaning relation will be said to <u>REFER TO</u>, whenever interpreted.

The means for designating terms in their occurrences in some collection of arrow-signs require access to some vocabulary, $V$, by which these designations become expressed. By $L_V$ we designate the language generated over $V$, i.e. all finite sequences of symbols of $V$. $G_L$ shall designate the <u>GRAMMAR</u> generating $L_V$. (For further details, see the theory of semiotics).

X: When we are considering the abstract mechanisms of our language or of collections of signs in general, their underlying reality or "DEEP STRUCTURE" is what essentially contributes to the sense or meaning of these mechanisms. For each fragment of a language or collection of signs, we have to consider what kind of <u>WORLD</u> or <u>FORM OF LIFE</u> is depicted by this fragment (its MODEL(s)). Depending on the context, the meaning that a sign receives may be called the <u>WORLD-LOCATION</u> or <u>LOCI</u> of that sign. If the sign is a <u>LOGICAL</u> sign, we may also speak of the <u>LOGICAL COORDINATES</u> as the meaning(s) that the sign receives.

These locations or coordinates make up the core of the underlying reality of our signs. Reality being a result of authority, to wit, the result imposed by its author(s), the life of this "reality" is restricted by the standards of ethics which the author legislates by his demarcation between admissible and inadmissible symbols and signs. The mental vacuum of our conventionalistically sustained culture is but a second-order consequence of society's fallaciously developed modalities. In order to correct our first impressions of this state of affairs it is advisable to look at some of the deeper modalities of our existence, as exemplified by the <u>DEONTIC</u> and <u>OPTATIVE</u> ones.

Consequently, we may note that connected with the underlying reality of the use of signs is what may be termed <u>RELEVANCE THEORY</u>, id est the study of <u>AIMS</u> and <u>MEANS</u> associated with any reality. Some signs may lack a meaning simply because they were intended as an <u>ACT</u> or <u>GESTURE</u>, which, of course, may lack meaning (in a well-defined sense) but must be associated with an <u>AIM</u>. An aim is any desire to accomplish a construction by some <u>GIVEN</u> means. If the latter are lacking (or insufficient) we shall speak about <u>IDEALS</u> and instead of a construction we shall speak of a <u>TENDENCY</u> (towards the ideal).

One of the basic tenets of <u>OUR</u> (Eleutheric) Relevance Theory is its commitment to <u>JUST AND PURPOSEFUL ACTS OF COMMUNICATION</u>, id est acts freed from obstacles, fraud and coercion. Obviously, this principle is clearly related to ideas in ethics as well as epistemology (of certainty) and it constitutes a cornerstone of our GENERAL THEORY OF MODALITIES, which will be developed in a subsequent paper.

PURPOSEFULNESS means, above all, that the means associated with the aims are SUFFICIENT for achieving the aims. That is to say, an aim which is not remaining an ideal is by definition without purpose if it lacks the necessary and sufficient means associated with its fulfillability. Of course, if an aim is found purposeless, it can still be retained, if desired, as an IDEAL. But then the ideal is properly called IDLE unless it becomes (or already is) associated with a SEARCH for means that suffice for sustaining the tendency on which the ideal depends.

The JUSTNESS of an act is simply its admissibility in the context of its appearance. For instance, it is required that a new act is compatible with previously committed purposeful acts in the sense that it does not obstruct already achieved acts of communication. If an obstruction would follow from some specific act in $\mathcal{A}$, then this fact would be an indication of the faultiness of the logic behind the activity, which, accordingly, one is obliged to revise or simply abandon in order to secure the eleutheric continuation of $\mathcal{A}$.

XI. Activities decompose into individual sequences of acts which ultimately exhaust the activity. Among the "atomic" acts yielded under any such decomposition it is desirable (in order to avoid confusion) to distinguish between ORGANIC ACTS, i.e. those connected with interference with the physical world, and EPISTEMIC ACTS, which involve interference with our abstraction capabilities, i.e. those acts which may be described as PURELY MENTAL. As is plain, Constructive Conceptualism focuses mainly on activities where the latter acts dominate. Usually,

𝒜s of this kind are referred to as THOUGHT PROCESSES and coded in their extensiveness by the universal ℰ-diagram.

An appearance of a sign has at least two epistemic structures associated with it, viz. its SURFACE STRUCTURE and its DEEP STRUCTURE, respectively. Only in a logically perfected language (a SATURATED language) do these two structures coincide. In other languages the coincidence may vary, and it belongs to the TACTICS OF ATTENTION of those languages to determine the exact projection of surface form onto its companion deep structure form.

The projection rules of the sign determine its world location and thus give us the coordinates of the sign's underlying reality. This is part of the criterion for the meaningfulness of the sign's appearance and it is also part of the criterion for every INTRODUCTORY OCCURRENCE of a sign, in which the rules of projections are laid down.

The acquisition and use of a sign is a highly intricate network of mental processes conducted under various spectra of modalities which operate on all actions that require participation under the rules of use of signs. It is rather a tragedy that people have overlooked the deep contribution of these modalities to the functional and creative aspects of the use of signs, which, incidentally, partially accounts for the deteriorating standards not only of colloquial and political language but also of such highly stylized forms of conduct as are prescribed by the codes of jurisprudence and international law.

DIGRESSION: Present standards are truly a poor monument to the intellectual achievements of this century and there is even an urgency to call for some (fundamentalistic) regimentation on the part of our semantics so that these achievements may not

DETERIORATE INTO OBLIVION. A PLEA FOR A <u>CONVIVIAL SEMANTICS</u>
ON A PAR WITH ILLICH'S PROGRAM FOR A CONVIVIAL RETOOLING OF
OUR SOCIETY IS CERTAINLY CALLED FOR, IF THE LATTER AIM SHALL
NOT REMAIN AN (IDLE) IDEAL. IN PARTICULAR, THE FACT THAT <u>OUR</u>
LANGUAGE (IN DISTINCTION TO <u>THEIRS</u>) IS ALSO ONE OF OUR MOST
PRECIOUS TOOLS (FOR ANY AIM) CANNOT BE EMPHASIZED SUFFICIENTLY
IN THIS CONTEXT. (<u>WARNING</u>: DON'T CONFUSE THIS PLEA WITH ANY
CONVENTIONALISTIC REVISION OF OUR SPEECH HABITS!)

XII. TO SUM UP. ONE OF OUR BASIC AIMS IS TO IMPLEMENT A
FAMILY OF LANGUAGES $\mathcal{L}$ WHICH MAY REFLECT BY ITS VERY DESIGN
THE CONDITIONS FOR PURPOSEFUL ACTS OF COMMUNICATION. SUCH AN
AIM OF IMPLEMENTING OUR SEMIOTICAL CAPABILITIES INVOLVES A
CERTAIN AMOUNT OF "DEBUGGING" OF SOME (AND ULTIMATELY, ALL)
OF THE IDLE SEMANTICAL OR HABITUAL CIRCUITS THAT PREVENT THE
MIND FROM A CLEARED ACCESS TO ITS FUNDAMENTAL(ISTIC)
CREATIVE POTENTIALS.

WITHIN SOME MODALITIES THE VERY DEBUGGING ACTIVITY ITSELF
RESULTS IN A REFINEMENT OF OUR LANGUAGE TO THE DEGREE THAT ITS
DESIRED IMPLEMENTATION HAS BECOME FULFILLED WHEN SUCCESSFULLY
KILLING OFF THE BUGS.

OTHER MODALITIES, HOWEVER, REQUIRE THAT MORE CONSTRUCTIVE
PROCESSES (MEDIATED BY INTIMATE PEDAGOGY) TAKE THE PLACE OF
THOSE "FREE" PLACES ALONG THE DEBUGGED CIRCUITS. GENERALLY,
THESE PROCESSES WILL NOT REMAIN FIXED AT THEIR CORRESPONDING
SUBSTITUTED PLACES, BUT WILL PARTICIPATE IN THE INTEGRATION OF
OTHER STREAMS OF CONSCIOUSNESS. (OBVIOUSLY, THE "FLOATING"
CHARACTER OF THIS ACTIVITY DEMANDS ELEUTHERIA FOR THE SAKE OF
ITS STABILITY AND (NON-PARALYZED) DEVELOPMENT). THIS PARTICI-
PATORY FUNCTION WILL BE REGARDED AS THE <u>MAIN SOURCE</u> FOR THE
ARISING OF <u>NEW</u> MODALITIES AND WITH THE LATTER NEW MOODS OF

CONSCIOUSNESS AND THEIR ASSOCIATED TACTICS OF ATTENTION.

DIGRESSION: As people seem to have failed to notice, one of the main obstacles for the realization of this aim is the otherwise well-known circumstance that in art (and elsewhere), we are usually involved with interpretations that yield to multiple forms of understanding, i.e. moods of understanding that lack UNIQUENESS (one of the causes being, of course, the "free fall" into associative thinking). Consequently, when we try to fix, in some way, this understanding, we fail to provide for even the most elementary aspects of $Freedom_1$ and $Freedom_2$, thereby depriving us of the possibility of providing for just and purposeful acts of communication in a field that purports to defend these very values. Thus, no fixed meaning can seriously be claimed for works of art or any other symbolic activity (including jurisprudence and codifications of human rights) that society has provided for up till now. Of course, there is SOMETIMES (but not always) a certain economical gain involved when a multiple set of meanings can be compressed into a single sign. But if the clarity of the sign suffers too much during the course of this conceptual compression, its purposefulness becomes doubtful, and hence, ceases to fulfill its presumed role (as far as that role involves any exact purpose).

REMARK: When an author shows the addressee a sign, an ACT OF CONFIDENCE towards the author takes place when the addressee interprets the sign. This confidence is expressed by TACTICS FOR IDENTIFICATIONS AND DISTINCTIONS that the addressee brings forth during the act of interpretation. In addition the TACTICS OF ATTENTION, which the allowance or admissibility of the sign in part defines, further restricts the possible moods of understanding of the sign. On the other hand, TACTICS OF NEGLECT are determined by the SPHERE OF CONFIDENCE that emanates from the author when addressing the addressee. That is to say, what is not explicitly expressed but presupposed by context or other relevant clues, can only be retraced by following the tactics of neglect authorized by the situation in which the act of communication takes place. Any neglect not authorized by this tactic will be considered a violation of the condition of fairness for just and purposeful acts of communication and consequently inadmissible for the context in question. It is important to note, however, that any neglect based on <u>alien</u> circumstances plays no relevant role when declaring a neglect inadmissible. The alienness of circumstances is prescribed by Relevance Theory and the Ethical Doctrine associated with it.

# SEMIOTICS 1

# SEMIOTICS - I

The idea of an <u>abstract language</u> originated with the discovery of some simple <u>algebraic properties</u> pertaining to the combinatorial or syntactical rules governing the productions of strings of symbols. One of the most elementary algebraic structures involving these properties is the <u>semi group with</u> $1$, generally designated $a = \langle \mathcal{A}, \circ \rangle$, where the first coordinate designates the <u>domain</u> of the semi group (also called the carrier of the semi group) and the second coordinate designates an <u>associative operation</u> (concatenation) closed with respect to the domain of the semi group.

Operations performed on a carrier $\mathcal{A}$ are termed <u>productions</u> of the structure $a$ and they correspond to sentence forms and other grammatically significant units on the syntactic level.

Chains of productions over $\mathcal{A}$ are given structural descriptions in terms of <u>trees</u>, $\mathcal{T}_A$, where the "root" designates the initial production (or "start symbol") and the branchings designate the successive applications of operations on previously obtained "<u>words</u>". By the closure of $\mathcal{A}$ we mean all trees $\mathcal{T}_A$ such that $\mathcal{T}_A$ obtains in $a$. This closure corresponds to the <u>language</u> generated by $a$, designated $\mathcal{L}(\mathcal{A})$.

By generalizing the concept of a semi group with $1$ we may obtain a global presentation of $\mathcal{L}(\mathcal{A})$. This generalization brings us to the concepts of <u>category theory</u>, one of the highlights of exact thinking after the creation of Cantor's "Paradise". By a <u>category</u> $\mathbf{C}$ we shall understand a collection of <u>objects</u>, corresponding to the words on $\mathcal{A}$ above, together with a collection of <u>morphisms</u>, corresponding to the productions generating $\mathcal{L}(\mathcal{A})$.

Objects will be denoted $А, В, Г, Д, \ldots$ and morphisms $Я, Ю, Э, \ldots$. For each pair of objects $А, В$, there is a set $C(А, В)$ of morphisms $Я$ carrying $А$ to $В$, and, in addition, for each $А$ in $C$, an <u>identity morphism</u> $\epsilon_А (А, А)$, also written $\mathcal{I}_А$.

Now, if there are three morphisms $Я, Ю, Э$ such that

$$Я: А \Rightarrow В, \quad Ю: В \Rightarrow Г, \quad Э: Г \Rightarrow Д$$

then the <u>composition</u> of them satisfies

$$(ЯЮ)Э = Я(ЮЭ)$$

Also, if $Я: А \Rightarrow В$, then $\mathcal{I}_А Я = Я = Я \mathcal{I}_В$

To complete our definition we remark that a Category $C$ is always <u>closed</u> under arbitrary <u>compositions</u> of morphisms, i.e. if

$$Я \in C(А, В) \text{ and } Ю \in C(В, Г), \text{ then always}$$

$$ЯЮ \in C(А, Г)$$

The <u>syntax</u> of $\mathcal{L}(А)$ can now be specified as a category $\mathcal{F}$ where the Objects are strings of letters drawn from some fixed alphabet and the Morphisms are derivations (trees) of one string from another.

By a derivation $\mathcal{D}$ we shall now understand the following ordered triple

$$\mathcal{D} = \Big\langle (А_0, \ldots, А_n), (Я_0, \ldots, Я_{n-1}), (\lambda_0 - \zeta_0, \ldots, \lambda_{n-1} - \zeta_{n-1}) \Big\rangle$$

WHERE

$(A_0, \ldots, A_n)$ DESIGNATES THE <u>WORD COORDINATE</u>,

$(Я_0, \ldots, Я_{n-1})$ IS THE <u>DERIVATION COORDINATE</u>, AND

$(\lambda_0 - \zeta_0, \ldots, \lambda_{n-1} - \zeta_{n-1})$ IS THE <u>NEIGHBOURHOOD COORDINATE</u>,

THE LATTER GIVEN A <u>TOPOLOGICAL</u> INTERPRETATION (SEE BELOW).

THE <u>LENGTH ZERO</u> DERIVATION $\langle (A), (\ ), (\ ) \rangle$ IS REGARDED AS THE $A$-<u>IDENTITY DERIVATION</u>, WHILE THE <u>LENGTH ONE</u> DERIVATION $\langle (A, B), (Я : A \Rightarrow B), (\lambda - \zeta) \rangle$ WILL BE "ABBREVIATED" $Я : A \Rightarrow B$ AND PURPOSELY CONFUSED WITH THE "REAL" PRODUCTION $A \Rightarrow B$ IN $\mathcal{L}(A)$. CLEARLY $\mathcal{D}$ MAY BE TURNED INTO AN INDEPENDENT CATEGORY, ID EST INDEPENDENT OF $\mathcal{L}(A)$.

THE IMPORTANCE OF THE ABOVE CONCEPTS COMES FROM THE FACT THAT MORPHISMS ARE EXAMPLES OF A GENERAL CLASS OF <u>ARROWS</u>. ANOTHER EXAMPLE IS THE CLASS OF <u>FUNCTORS</u> THAT EXISTS BETWEEN CATEGORIES THEMSELVES.

A FUNCTOR $\Upsilon$ FROM A CATEGORY $C_0$ TO A CATEGORY $C_1$ IS SIMPLY TWO CLASSES OF ARROWS, ONE SENDING OBJECTS IN $C_0$ TO OBJECTS IN $C_1$ AND THE OTHER SENDING MORPHISMS IN $C_0$ TO MORPHISMS IN $C_1$. FORMALLY, THE FOLLOWING SITUATION OBTAINS: IF $\Upsilon$ IS A FUNCTOR BETWEEN $C_0$ AND $C_1$, ID EST

$$\Upsilon : C_0 \longrightarrow C_1$$

, THEN FOR EVERY $A \in C_0$, $\Upsilon$ ASSIGNS AN OBJECT $\Upsilon(A)$ IN $C_1$ AND FOR EACH $Я \in C_0$ $\Upsilon$ ASSIGNS THE MORPHISM $\Upsilon(Я)$ IN $C_1$.

## 20

Now, by the SEMANTICS of $\mathcal{L}(\mathcal{A})$ we mean a CO-FUNCTOR

$$\mathcal{G} : \mathcal{F} \rightrightarrows \mathcal{U}.$$

where $\mathcal{U}$, of course, denotes the SEMANTIC CATEGORY associated with $\mathcal{L}(\mathcal{A})$ when generated by the Syntax Category $\mathcal{F}$.

More specifically, the Co-Functor $\mathcal{G}$ specifies an INTERPRETATION of $\mathcal{F}$ by taking Objects to CARTESIAN PRODUCTS in $\mathcal{U}$ and derivations to functions in $\mathcal{U}$. In other words, the Semantic Category $\mathcal{U}$ consists of a Category of SETS and FUNCTIONS and the image of the interpretation $\mathcal{G}$ is called the SEMANTICS of the interpretation. For example, the interpretation of an Object $\mathbf{A}_\mathcal{F}$ of the Syntax Category consists of those Functions Ш that are Contravariant in $\mathcal{U}$. (They correspond to retracts in a Topos).

If Я is a Morphism in $\mathcal{U}$ (i.e. Я is a Function), then the neighbourhood of Я is defined as those Morphisms $Я_1, \ldots, Я_n$ that act as Identities on the extended neighbourhood domain of Я. That is, $Я_1, \ldots, Я_n$ are neighbourhoods of Я if the following diagrams commute:

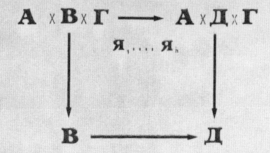

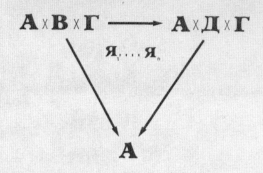

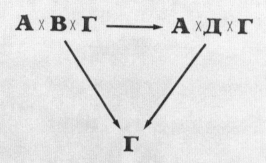

WHERE Я IS THE MORPHISM Я:В ⇒ Д AND × INDICATES CARTESIAN PRODUCT.

FURTHER EXAMPLES OF GENERAL CLASSES OF ARROWS TO BE MET WITH IN CATEGORY THEORY - BESIDES MORPHISMS AND FUNCTORS - ARE <u>MONO-MORPHISMS</u> AND <u>EPI-MORPHISMS</u>, AS IN THE FOLLOWING

<u>DEFINITION</u>. Ш IS A <u>MONO-MORPHISM</u> IN A CATEGORY C, IF FOR ALL Ю, Э ∈ C

$$Ю:Г ⇒ А, Э:Г ⇒ А$$

IMPLIES Ю = Э    IF ЮШ = ЭШ

## 22

<u>DEFINITION</u>. Ш IS AN EPI-MORPHISM IN A CATEGORY **C**, IF FOR ALL Ю, Э ∈ **C**

$$Ю:B \Rightarrow Г, Э:B \Rightarrow Г$$

IMPLIES    Ю = Э    IF    ШЮ = ШЭ

Ш AND Ш WILL BE OF IMPORTANCE FOR THE MAPPINGS OF THE INNER STRUCTURES OF TOPOSES.

TOPOSES GIVE RISE TO YET OTHER GENERAL CLASSES OF ARROWS LIKE <u>PULL-BACKS</u> AND <u>PUSH-OUTS</u>. FOR THE MOMENT WE WILL STOP THE PRESENT CLASSIFICATION OF ARROWS, ONLY MENTIONING ONE FURTHER CLASS, AND LEAVING THE OTHERS FOR ANOTHER OCCASION. THIS CLASS IS CALLED THE <u>CLUB OPERATORS</u>, $\Omega$, WHICH ASSIGNS TO EACH OBJECT **A** A MORPHISM

$$Ч_A : \varUpsilon A \longrightarrow \varPhi A$$

WHERE $\varUpsilon$ AND $\varPhi$ ARE **2**-FUNCTORS.

FURTHER, TO EACH MORPHISM Ч OF THE UNDERLYING **2**-CATEGORY **Г** OF **Д**, A **2**-CELL MORPHISM Ч$_A$ IN THE CO-DOMAIN **2**-CATEGORY **Д** IS ASSIGNED SUCH THAT THE FOLLOWING "SQUARE" OBTAINS:

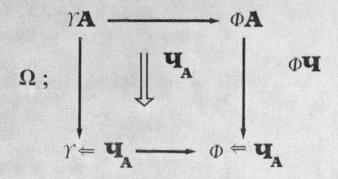

INTUITIVELY, $\Omega$ IS A <u>NATURAL TRANSFORMATION</u> BETWEEN CATEGORIES. SPECIFIC NATURAL TRANSFORMATIONS WILL BE PICTURED:

$$Ц_{\underline{\Omega}} : \Upsilon \rightsquigarrow X$$

THE CLUB OPERATOR PLAYS A PROMINENT ROLE FOR THE <u>PASSAGE</u> BETWEEN CATEGORIES, AS WHEN WE WISH TO GO FROM ONE SEMANTIC CATEGORY $\mathcal{U}_1$ TO ANOTHER SEMANTIC CATEGORY $\mathcal{U}_2$, WITH COMMON UNDERLYING SYNTACTIC CATEGORY $\mathcal{F}_0$. THE DEONTIC AXIOMS DETERMINING THE ADMISSIBLE PASSAGES FOR SOME $\Omega$ ARE CALLED THE <u>DOCTRINE OF THE CLUB OF CATEGORIES</u> (OR JUST <u>DOCTRINES FOR SCHOOLS</u>), WHERE THE "CLUB" NOTION NOW REFERS TO THE CATEGORIES IN THE DOMAIN AND CODOMAIN OF $\Omega$. FOR EXAMPLE, A SITUATION THAT IS TYPICAL FOR ANY DOCTRINE FOR SCHOOLS IS THE OPERATION OF <u>PASTING</u> OBJECTS (HERE, CATEGORIES) IN A CLUB. SO ONE THING PERMITTED IS TO PASS FROM THE SITUATION

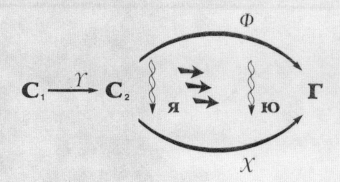

TO THE SITUATION

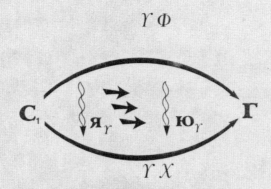

WHERE ⇉ DENOTES THE PASTING OPERATION AND $\Gamma$ IS AN ELEMENT OF THE CLUB.

DIAGRAMS OF CONCEPT FORMATION PROCESSES UNDERLYING FORESTS OF CORRECT REASONINGS MAKE HEAVY USE OF ⇉ , ESPECIALLY WHEN THE CLUB HAS MANY-SORTED DOCTRINES FOR SCHOOLS.

+ + + + +

SOME ELEMENTARY CATEGORIES (ARROW AND TIME CATEGORIES).

(1) LET $\mathcal{V}$ BE A (SMALL) UNIVERSE OF <u>SETS</u>. THE <u>ARROW CATEGORY</u>

$$\mathcal{V}^{\Rightarrow}$$

WILL CONSIST OF THOSE OBJECTS $\lambda : \mathbf{X}_0 \Rightarrow \mathbf{X}_1$ FOR WHICH $\mathbf{X}_0$ IS A DOMAIN FOR $\lambda$ AND $\mathbf{X}_1$ ITS

CO-DOMAIN AND WHERE THE MORPHISMS, I.E. ARROWS

$$\Lambda : \lambda : \mathbf{X}_0 \Rightarrow \mathbf{X}_1 \Rightarrow \lambda' : \mathbf{Y}_0 \Rightarrow \mathbf{Y}_1,$$ ARE

THE PAIRS OF FUNCTIONS $\lambda_0$, $\lambda_1$ SUCH THAT THE FOLLOWING DIAGRAM COMMUTES, I.E. $\lambda \Lambda^\circ = \Lambda' \lambda$

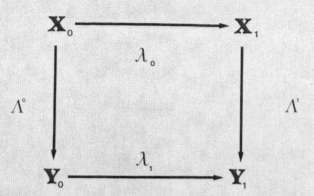

(2) IF $\mathcal{P}$ IS A (DISCRETE) <u>PROCESS</u>, THEN $\mathcal{V}^\mathcal{P}$ IS THE CATEGORY OF TIMES (RELATIVE $\mathcal{P}$ ). IF INSTEAD OF $\mathcal{V}$ AND/OR $\mathcal{P}$ WE PUT THE CATEGORY ON THE FORMS

$$\mathcal{V}^\mathcal{E} \quad \text{OR} \quad \mathcal{E}^\mathcal{E},$$

WE GET THE (UNIVERSAL) CATEGORIES OF LOCAL AND GLOBAL TIME, RESPECTIVELY.

FOR THE CATEGORY $\mathcal{V}^\mathcal{P}$ WE SHALL HAVE AS OBJECTS INFINITELY PROCEEDING SEQUENCES OR STRINGS

$$\mathbf{X}_0 \Rightarrow \mathbf{X}_1 \Rightarrow \mathbf{X}_2 \Rightarrow \cdots \Rightarrow \mathbf{X}_m \Rightarrow \cdots$$

OF ARROWS BETWEEN SETS $\mathbf{X}_j \in \mathcal{V}$ AND AS MORPHISMS SEQUENCES OF $\Lambda$-ARROWS, LIKE THE FOLLOWING:

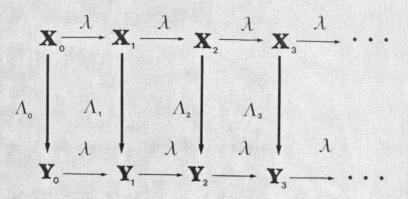

In terms of Arrows, $\mathcal{V}^{\Rightarrow}$ and $\mathcal{V}^{P}$ differ in the following way

$$\mathcal{V}^{\Rightarrow} : \cdot \Rightarrow \cdot$$
$$\mathcal{V}^{P} : \cdot \Rightarrow \cdot \Rightarrow \cdot \Rightarrow \cdots$$

## THE DEFINITIVE CATEGORY OF ALL CATEGORIES.

For Toposes as well as elsewhere, the DOCTRINAL CATEGORY $\mathcal{E}$ is the FORGETFUL CO-DOMAIN CATEGORY of the UNIVERSAL FORGETFUL FUNCTOR

$$\mathcal{E} \xrightarrow{\#}$$

Its Objects are many-sorted – Brackets, $|\;|$, and Cups, $\sqcup$ – and the Morphisms are obtained through iterations in the Cumulative Hierarchy $\mathcal{V}$ of Arrow Operations $\longrightarrow$ for denotational connections between Objects in $\mathcal{E}$.

Any diagram for a Concept Formation Process (guided by Correct Reasonings) has an ADJOINTED FORGETFUL CO-FUNCTOR mapping elements in the Process to Cartesian Products of Objects in $\mathcal{E}$ and Morphisms to Functions (Arrows) in $\mathcal{E}$. Evidently, Cartesian Closed Categories (CCC's) will be the most prominent tool for constructing Toposes. By this last step we attempt a move from Lawvere's <u>OBJECTIVE DIALECTICS</u> to <u>NATURAL DIALECTICS</u> where Club Operations and other Natural Transformations (⌁▶) dominate over the specifications of Category Objects. Clearly, $\mathcal{E}$ considered as a Category will be our alternative to the Category of all Categories as a foundation of mathematics and Generalized Constructive Conceptualism.

Of course, $\mathcal{E}$ and its Sub-Objects will still serve as our favorite example of Inaccessible Cardinals, Toposes, Cosmois and what not that will be encountered in the pursuit of the delights of Exact Thinking.

# SEMIOTICS 2

# SEMIOTICS-II

In order to understand our idea of a Topos it is necessary to introduce some notions from TOPOLOGY, i.e. the theory of INVISIBLE SPACES. In particular, Toposes are intended as exact formalizations of TACTICS OF PARTIALLY ORDERED SPACES, abbreviated as TOPOS.

Corresponding to the CONTINUOUS vs. DISCRETE modes of thinking we introduce CONTINUOUS and DISCRETE SPACES. Continuous spaces are termed MEASURABLE CANTOR SPACES generated on the core of a Continuous Product Topology (C-Spaces). Discrete spaces are of a Boolean kind and are represented by, for example, the Measurable 2-Space. Clearly, from a semiotical point of view, the interpretation differentiating between a Space Sign $\square$ of the kind C- or 2-, respectively, is determined by the TACTIC OF ATTENTION on the ORDER of $\square$.

Beyond the above (Black and White) dichotomy of Spaces and their Topologies, we wish to recognize some additional "chromatic" characteristics. Thus we shall distinguish between point-spaces with properties such as COMPACTNESS, CONNECTEDNESS, SEPARABILITY and their negative counterparts INCOMPACTNESS, UNCONNECTEDNESS and INSEPARABILITY, respectively. It turns out that all spaces $T_\square$ may effectively be determined by such properties alone and that the combinations of them determine the CHROMATICS induced by degrees of attention directed towards Spaces $T_\square$ of exact Thinking. We prefer to call such Spaces $T_\square$ CHROMATIC TOPOLOGIES when, and only when, the fixing of Arrows for their points and basis are given in terms of the above properties.

## DIGRESSION: CHROMATIC THREADS

SPACES WITH POINT-BASES ARE EXAMPLES OF <u>CHAINS OF CORRECT REASONINGS</u> WHERE THE CHAINS COME OUT AS <u>CHROMATIC THREADS</u>.

LET $\theta_1, \ldots, \theta_s$ BE A CHAIN OF CORRECT REASONING. EACH $\theta_i$, $i \in s$, IS A COLLECTION OF $\vdash$ -SENTENCES (IN THE STYLE OF FREGE), EACH ONE BEING OF THE FORM $\Gamma \vdash \Delta$, WHERE $\Gamma, \Delta$ ARE COLLECTIONS OF SENTENCES (I.E. OBJECTS IN A STRUCTURE $\mathfrak{a}$). $\Gamma \vdash \Delta$ IS READ $\mathcal{R}_\Delta \Gamma$, I.E. THERE IS A (NOT NECESSARILY UNIQUE) CORRECT REASONING $\mathcal{R}$ FOR OBTAINING $\Delta$ FROM $\Gamma$.

THE CORRECTNESS OF $\mathcal{R}$ DEPENDS MAINLY ON THE POSSIBILITY OF ASSIGNING <u>ARGUMENTAL SUPPORTS</u> TO THE OCCURRENCES OF $\vdash$ -SYMBOLS BELONGING TO $\theta_i$, FOR ALL $i \in s$. THE A.S. OF A $\vdash$ -SENTENCE IS A <u>JUSTIFICATION</u> FOR THE <u>ACCEPTANCE</u> OF THE REASONING $\mathcal{R}$ REFERRED TO BY THE OCCURRENCE OF $\vdash$ IN THE CONTEXT OF A $\vdash$ - SENTENCE. THE TOTALITY OF A.S.'S ASSIGNED TO A CHAIN OF CORRECT REASONING $\theta$ IS CALLED THE <u>ENVELOPE</u> OF $\theta$. THE ENVELOPE IS <u>CHROMATIC</u> IF ITS THREADS ARE.

$\theta$:

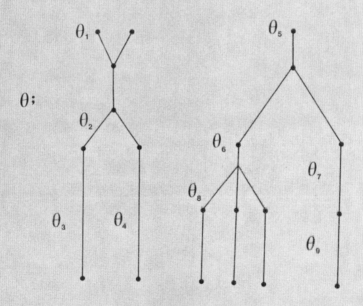

(END OF DIGRESSION)

Besides the Topological notions considered above, Semiotics may be considered as providing for those <u>construction procedures</u> $\mathcal{M}$ required to obtain a fixed <u>text</u> $\mathcal{T}$.

By a construction procedure $\mathcal{M}$ for $\mathcal{T}$ we shall understand a collection of <u>rules</u>, $\mathcal{R}$, and <u>methods</u>, $\mathcal{M}$, such that any part $\mathcal{T}'$ of $\mathcal{T}$ is obtained by some following of $\mathcal{R}$, $\mathcal{M}$. Intuitively, $\mathcal{R}$ is the <u>logic</u> for the means $\mathcal{M}$ when aimed at $\mathcal{T}$, i.e. the Envelope for $\mathcal{M}$.

If a language $\mathcal{L}$ is understood as a method for introducing and eliminating signs, each appearance of a sign $\sigma$ will be connected with a method $\mathcal{L}\{\sigma\}$ in effect of which the appearance of $\sigma$ is obtained.

<u>The following of a language</u> $\mathcal{L}$ is indicated by certain constructions of parts of the objects we have designated $\mathcal{T}$. Generally, an object $\mathcal{T}$ may be obtained through the following of a set $\mathcal{L}_1, \ldots, \mathcal{L}_m$ of languages. For each $\mathcal{L}_i$, $1 \leq i \leq m$, there shall correspond a unique set of parts $\mathcal{T}_{i_1}, \ldots, \mathcal{T}_{i_k} \in \mathcal{T}$ such that for each $\mathcal{T}_{i_j}$, if $\mathcal{L}_i|\mathcal{T}_{i_j}|$ <u>constructs</u> the part $\mathcal{T}_{i_j}'$, then $\mathcal{L}_j|\mathcal{T}_i|$ <u>constructs</u> $\mathcal{T}$ (the partial image of $\mathcal{L}_i$).

$\mathcal{L}$ may be considered as the collection of all $\mathcal{L}\{\sigma\}$ for which $\mathcal{L}$ constructs $\sigma$.

If $\mathcal{L}\{\sigma\}$ and a following of $\mathcal{L}\{\sigma\}$ is indicated, $\Diamond |\mathcal{T}_{i_j}(\sigma)|$, then $\mathcal{T}_{i_j}$ is said to be <u>clear in the sign</u> $\sigma$. The same applies to $\mathcal{T}_{i_j}(\bar{\sigma})$, $\mathcal{T}_i(\bar{\sigma})$ and $\mathcal{T}(\bar{\sigma})$. Consequently, if $\bar{\sigma} = \sigma_1, \ldots, \sigma_n$ exhausts the signs

APPEARING THROUGH $\mathcal{T}_i(\sigma_1, \ldots, \sigma_n)$ AND $\mathcal{T}$ IS CLEAR IN EACH $\sigma_j$ FOR ALL APPEARANCES THROUGH $\mathcal{T}_i$, THEN $\mathcal{T}$ IS SAID TO BE CLEAR IN ALL OF ITS SIGNS.

BY A <u>SEMIOTICS</u> OF A (PRE-)THEORY FOR A TEXT $\mathcal{T}$, $\text{Th}(\mathcal{T})$, WE SHALL UNDERSTAND A METHOD $\mathcal{m}$ OF A CLASS OF CONSTRUCTION PROCEDURES $\mathcal{M}$ SUCH THAT

(1) $\mathcal{R} \subset \mathcal{M}$

(2) ANY APPLICATION OF AN ELEMENT $r \in \mathcal{R}$ ON ANY PREVIOUSLY CONSTRUCTED OBJECTS $\mathcal{T}_1, \ldots, \mathcal{T}_k$ IS <u>SECURED</u> (I.E. PERMITTED) IF THE RESULT OF APPLYING $r$ TO $\mathcal{T}_1, \ldots, \mathcal{T}_k$ ONLY DEPENDS ON $m_1, \ldots, m_i \in \mathcal{M}$ AND PARTS $\mathcal{T}_1, \ldots, \mathcal{T}_{k'}$ SUCH THAT $m_1(\mathcal{T}_1) = \mathcal{T}_1, \ldots, m_i(\mathcal{T}_k) = \mathcal{T}_k$

(3) IF $\mathcal{T}'$ IS ANY PART OF $\mathcal{T}$, THEN THERE ARE $m_1, \ldots, m_k \in \mathcal{M}$ SUCH THAT FOR ALL PARTS $\mathcal{T}''$ PRECEDING $\mathcal{T}'$, $m_1, \ldots, m_k(\mathcal{T}'') = \mathcal{T}'$.

LET $\mathcal{T}$ BE A FIXED TEXT. IF $\mathcal{T}$ IS <u>CLEAR</u>, THEN $\mathcal{T}$ MIGHT BE UNDERSTOOD AS A <u>DISCRETE PROCESS</u> $\Pi\mathcal{T}$. IN PARTICULAR, THE FOLLOWING OF $\mathcal{L}(\mathcal{T})$ FOR CLEAR $\mathcal{T}$ MIGHT BE UNDERSTOOD AS THE FOLLOWING OF A <u>CLEAR LANGUAGE</u>.

AS EXPECTED, THERE IS NO DECISION PROCEDURE FOR RECOGNIZING CLEAR $\mathcal{T}$'S. SO TO SHOW THAT $\mathcal{T}$ IS CLEAR, IT IS NECESSARY TO CONSTRUCT A METHOD $\mathcal{L}$ SUCH THAT $\mathcal{L}(\mathcal{T})$ <u>DISCRETELY</u> CONSTRUCTS $\mathcal{T}$. GIVEN $\mathcal{T}$, THE <u>MEANING PROBLEM</u> FOR $\mathcal{T}$ IS THE PROBLEM OF RECOVERING A SUITABLE $\mathcal{L}$ SUCH THAT $\mathcal{L}(\mathcal{T})$ CONSTRUCTS $\mathcal{T}$ DISCRETELY.

THE FOLLOWING SCHEME IS FOLLOWED IN EVERY SITUATION ESTABLISH-

ING DENOTATIONAL CONNECTIONS BETWEEN SIGN-EVENTS OF DISCRETE CHARACTER.

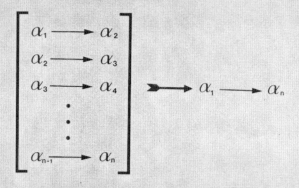

THE ABOVE SCHEMA GENERATES THE ADMISSIBLE FIBRATIONS STEMMING FROM ITERATIVE DENOTATIONAL INDICATIONS. AT ITS ORIGIN THE SCHEMA INDICATES THE CONNECTION BETWEEN THE SIGN $\alpha_1$ AND ALL VALUES $\alpha_2$ OF $\alpha_1$. THE VALUES $\alpha_2$ ARE THE <u>POINTS</u> OR <u>MEANINGS</u> OF $\alpha_1$. IN ORDER FOR $\alpha_i$ TO BE <u>DEFINITE</u>, THE CONNECTION $\alpha_i \longrightarrow \alpha_j$ MUST BE CLEAR, ID EST THE POINTING OF $\alpha_i$ TO $\alpha_j$ MUST BE CONSTRUCTED AS $\mathcal{M}(\alpha_i \longrightarrow \alpha_j)$ AND, IN ADDITION, $\alpha_j$ MUST BE A SINGLETON OR A TERMINAL OBJECT. EVERY SIGN FOR TOPOSES IS DEFINITE BY DEFINITION OF AN EXACT LANGUAGE AND, CONSEQUENTLY, COLLAPSES ON THE INITIAL NOEAMA $\Pi^o$ WHEN THE CORRECT LOGICAL ANALYSIS IS PROVIDED FOR.

<u>WARNING</u>: OUR USE OF THE NOTION $\text{Th}(\mathcal{T})$ OR OF THE TERM "SEMIOTICS" IS TOTALLY INDEPENDENT OF THE PRESENT FRENCH FASHION OF THE "LITERARY" STUDY OF "THEORIES" OF SIGNS (VIDE BARTH ET AL.)

# TOPOSES SHEAVES & ADJOINTS

# TOPOSES,
## SHEAVES AND ADJOINTS

An initial point of the <u>support</u> of an abstract concept formation process $\Pi$ is called the <u>noema</u> of $\Pi$ and is denoted $\Pi^o$ (in terms of CCC's, $\Pi^o$ is a <u>terminal object</u> of the associated category).

The chain(s) of arrows originating at a noema $\Pi^o$ and ascending in the diagram of $\Sigma$, i.e. $\Delta(\Sigma)$, is the <u>fibration</u> $\Phi$ associated with $\Pi^o$.

A fiber bundle $\Phi$ is a network or <u>lattice</u> of fibrations $\Phi_1, \ldots, \Phi_n, \ldots$, originating on different noemas and acting on the formation of a <u>pre-topos</u>, where a pre-topos is a non-empty collection of <u>sites</u> in a topos (the <u>external category</u> relative the pre-topos formation). Generally, sites are identified by the image of the continuous fixed-point functions on the fiber bundles underlying a correct reasoning in CCC contexts.

For each pair of objects $|a_i|^k$, $|a_j|^m$ participating in a fibration $\Phi$, the <u>sub-object fiber</u> or <u>arrow</u> connecting them is called a <u>pre-morphism</u>. A <u>complete morphism</u> is a family of pre-morphisms belonging to a fiber bundle $\Phi$ of an abstract concept formation process $\Pi$.

A <u>topos</u>, finally, consists of a collection of objects, the <u>sites</u>, together with the pre-morphisms on the <u>stacks</u> of sites and the complete morphisms of the fiber bundles $\Phi_\omega$ underlying the topos.

REMARK: Clearly, and as expected, a Topos turns out to be a particular instance of Objects $\Pi$ and we note with satisfaction the Cartesian Closedness of Objects $\Pi$ when viewed as Toposes. If $\Pi$ is a Topos, we will write $\Pi \underset{\text{Def.}}{=} \Pi^E$

(Note the Adjointed Forgetful Functor $\mathcal{Q}_E : \Pi^E \Rightarrow \mathcal{E}$ !)

Now we turn to the technical details of the properties of Toposes.

A <u>RETRACING FUNCTION</u> (RF) is an Object which acts on a fiber such that the (Terminal) Objects $\mathbf{a}_i$, i.e. the noemas, are <u>FIXED POINTS</u> of the function. Formally, if $r$ designates the RF we have

$$r(|\mathbf{a}_i|^{k+1}) \leq r(|\mathbf{a}_i|^k)$$

$$r(\mathbf{a}_i) = \emptyset$$

The set of Retracing Functions of a Fiber Bundle $\Phi$ is called the <u>RETRACT</u> of the Stack generated by the collection of Sites for which Fibrations are defined.

Next, a <u>PULL-BACK</u> ($pb$) is the "Stack" of Retracts of a Topos such that the Fixed Points of the Retracts (generated by the Retracing Functions) <u>COLLAPSE</u> on the <u>INITIAL NOEMA</u> $\mathbf{a}_o$, which then is a <u>UNIVERSAL TERMINAL OBJECT</u> $\Pi^o$. The Pull-Back function can be described as that function which takes a Topos $\Pi^E$ as argument (its domain) and yields as value the Initial Noema, $\mathbf{a}_o$. - Characteristically, a Pull-Back reverses all Arrows in a Topos $\Pi^E$, i.e. it is locally contravariant.

The dual concept of a Pull-Back function $pb$ is the notion of a

PUSH-OUT function $p_0$ with interchanged domain and co-domain. Characteristically, then, the PUSH-OUT takes as argument the Object $a_0$ and yields as value the Topos $\Pi^E$. Intuitionistically, this will mean that the Push-Out provides us with a (derivational) METHOD for generating $\Pi^E$ given any presentation of $a_0$. (A $p_0$ determines a Spread).

REMARK: A somewhat paradoxical situation arises from the fact that the dual nature of Push-Outs requires that THEIR Fixed Points must also collapse. But the Fixed Point of a Push-Out is a non-empty set of Toposes (!), or, what amounts to the same, it collapses the class of all Toposes $\Pi^E_j$ on the singular Topos $\Pi^E$. Unfortunately, $\Pi^E$ is not unique upon this definition. But that may not necessarily be a problem, since every Topos $\Pi^E$ has a Pull-Back associated with it, and the PULL-BACK yields a unique image for each Topos, viz. the Universal Terminal Object $a_0 = \Pi^o$. Thus the paradox disappears if the Doctrine of Clubs over the Clan of Toposes restricts proliferations of Fibrations that lead out of the Doctrine proper, i.e. the Doctrine advocates the AXIOMS of IRREPROACHABILITY and INCONTESTABILITY at every application of the LAW OF SUFFICIENT REASON.

By a SHEAF we mean a Lattice of Toposes. Simplified, but not misleadingly, a Sheaf can be described as a "higher-order" Topos concept where quantification now is permitted over the entire class of Toposes. Thus, Sheaves might be regarded as many-sorted ramified type-structures over the universe of Toposes. As such, we should expect them to REFLECT certain lower-order properties, i.e. properties associated with Toposes (such as CCC).

38

Consider any RANK FUNCTION appropriate for a Sheaf. Then the Sheaf is said to be NORMAL if its Rank exceeds the Rank of the Toposes belonging to it. Formally, we mean that a Sheaf forms, in a certain sense, the SUPREMUM of the Ranks of its Toposes. On the other hand, if the Rank of the Sheaf forms the INFIMUM of the Ranks of its Toposes, it will be said to be REGRESSIVE. We can express this situation by noting that each Topos $Л^E$ in a REGRESSIVE Sheaf $Л^{E,Л}$ has Rank $> 1$, and for most cases the Rank of a regressive Sheaf will be equal to $1$.

It is desirable to adhere to Doctrines that avoid regressive Sheaves as they tend to be too similar to conventional(istic) art objects and their fallacious Modalities. Clubs that are unable to miss out on regressive structures are delegated to those entertaining impeachable logics.

The notion of Rank for a (normal) Sheaf Reflects down to its associated Toposes, as we noted above. The Reflexion is effected by a Natural Transformation (actually, a GALOIS CONNECTION) ∿∿⟶ preserving global properties of the Sheaf at its local regions occupied by Toposes and taking as image a prefabricated CCC Object $Л^E$.

Recall that the Objects of the Doctrinal Category $\mathcal{E}$, i.e. the denotational connections between signs of type $|a_i|^k$ or $\sqcup (|a_{i_1}|^{k_1}, \ldots, |a_{i_n}|^{k_m})$ consist of the points of indications connected with the local Arrow or Pre-Morphism appear-

ING IN SOME FIBER FOR A SITE BELONGING TO THE TOPOS $\mathcal{E}$.
THE RANK OR DEPTH OF ANY SUCH SIGN IS GIVEN BY ITS ASSOCIATED
INDEX, I.E. $i+k$ OR $i+k+\frac{n+m}{2}$, AS THE CASE MAY BE. IN OTHER WORDS,
THE DEPTH OF A SIGN $[a_i]^k$ OR $\bigsqcup([a_{i_1}]^{k_1}, \ldots, [a_{i_n}]^{k_m})$ EQUALS
THE NUMBER OF ARROWS OR PRE-MORPHISMS OF THE UNDERLYING BUNDLE
OR SINGLE FIBER THAT DEFINES THE CORRESPONDING INDICATIONS.

THE DEPTH OF AN INDICATION, IN TURN, IS GENERALLY EQUAL TO
THE INVERSE OF THE RANK OF THE SITE OR STACK THAT ENVELOPES THE
INDICATION. ANALOGOUSLY, THE DEPTH OF A TOPOS IS IN GENERAL
EQUAL TO THE INVERSE OF THE RANK OF ITS SHEAF AND SO ON FOR THE
REMAINING STRUCTURES (FIBER BUNDLES, $pb$'s, $po$'s, SHEAVES, ETC.).

IN THE OTHER DIRECTION WE MAY REFLECT UPWARDS OVER THE ENTIRE
UNIVERSE OF SHEAVES. AS A FIRST STAGE OF THIS REFLEXION, WE
ARRIVE AT A PRE-COSMOI, WHILE AT A LATER STAGE THE APPEARANCE
OF A COSMOI OF COLLECTIONS OF SETS OF SHEAVES BECOMES POSSIBLE.

FOR COSMOIS, WE MAY DEFINE LEFT AND RIGHT ADJOINTS AS A
UNIVERSAL PROPERTY OF EVERY COSMOI. THAT MEANS IN PARTICULAR
THAT EVERY COSMOI IS SYMMETRICALLY SELF-REFLEXIVE WITH RESPECT
TO ADJOINTNESS.

ADJOINTS ASSOCIATED WITH SHEAVES AND TOPOSES ARE NOT NECESS-
ARILY SYMMETRIC, BUT NEVERTHELESS DEFINED IN LEFT OR RIGHT FORM
FOR EVERY SHEAF AND TOPOS. IF BOTH FORMS ARE PERMITTED BY THE
DOCTRINE ON A SHEAF OR TOPOS, THE UNIVERSAL PROPERTY IS RE-
COVERED. SUCH SITUATIONS ARE REFERRED TO AS DOCTRINAL CLUB
CONSPIRATIONS - DCC'S - AND THEIR OBJECTS ARE THE ADJOINTED
SHEAVES AND TOPOSES.

In this way we can continue to Reflect upwards beyond the Cosmois towards more and more comprehensive Units and there seems to be no conceivable end to the iterative applications of the <u>Reflexion Principle</u>. On the other hand, due to the normality of our Sheaves, there is no corresponding infinite regress or descent downwards, since all structures below the Sheaves collapse ultimately on the void indication $\mathbf{a}_o$, i.e. the Universal Terminal Object $\underset{\sim}{\Pi}^o$. This property will henceforth be referred to as the well-foundedness of the structure in question. On the contrary, regressive Sheaves or Toposes can never be well-founded and the same holds for their (inadmissible) Doctrines.

However, recalling Brouwer's insight concerning wasteful proliferations of Units, we shall stop at the Cosmois, for the time being, and leave to the interested reader to work out the details of the next stage, for which we on Doctrinal grounds have withdrawn every preassigned name. It occurs to us that this next stage is likely to behave more like a Black Hole, rather than, say, Continuous Plasmas, while the Pull-Back diagrams of Cosmois would be much more rewarding objects of study.

# APPENDIX 1

## TH($\Sigma$) AND THE STRUCTURE OF MIND

By a creative subject $\Sigma$ we shall now mean an idealized collection of <u>STREAMS OF CONSCIOUSNESS</u>, $\zeta_1$, $\zeta_2$, ........., $\zeta_k$, ......... .

By <u>CONSCIOUSNESS</u> we mean any non-empty set $\Xi$ of streams $\zeta_{k_i}$.

The <u>BASIS</u> of a Consciousness $\Xi$ is a set $\Lambda$ of <u>POTENTIALS</u> $\lambda_1$, $\lambda_2$, ......., $\lambda_m$, ......, determining the range of the corresponding Streams $\zeta_k \in \Xi$. Typically, a Potential $\lambda_{m_j}$ initiates and supports the development of a stream $\zeta_{k_i}$. The properties of $\lambda_m$ are described in terms of the <u>CURRENTS</u> $\zeta_{n_j}$ that $\lambda_m$ may give rise to along $\zeta_{k_i}$ and whose totality will be designated $Z$.

Clearly $\Theta\{\Xi \sqcup \Lambda \sqcup Z\}$ describes the generating field of the <u>TACTICS OF ATTENTION</u> conducting activities of $\Sigma$ at different stages of his consciousness development.

By <u>AWARENESS</u> we shall mean the Consciousness of <u>ARROWS</u> $\alpha_i \longrightarrow \alpha_{i+1}$ occurring along the streams $\zeta_{k_j}$. By $\alpha_i \longrightarrow \alpha_{i+1}$ we establish, as usual, the denotational connections between all values of $\alpha_{i+1}$ that are values of $\alpha_i$.

Arrows participate in concept formation processes. The knowledge of Arrows is subsumed under those <u>ARROW POTENTIALS</u> $\psi_\omega$ which <u>FORCE</u> $\zeta_k$. This forcing relation brings into attention the denotational connections which spring from the fibration of the underlying concept formation process. When $\zeta_k$ belongs to some $\Sigma$, the stream $\zeta_k$ designates any <u>SUSTAINED FEELING</u>

OF AWARENESS DIRECTED TOWARDS THE <u>FIXED POINTS</u> OF SOME MENTAL PHENOMENON WITHIN THE REALM OF $\Sigma$'S CONSCIOUSNESS. THE CORRESPONDING ARROW POTENTIALS $\psi_\kappa$ ARE REFERRED TO AS THE <u>NOEMAS</u> $\Pi^j$ OF $\xi_k$. FINALLY, THE <u>MIND</u> OF $\Sigma$ IS DESIGNATED

$$\Xi \cup \Lambda \cup Z \cup \Psi$$

THE CONSTRUCTION OF THE (INFINITE) CLASS $\Xi \cup \Lambda \cup Z \cup \Psi$ IS BASED ON TWO <u>CONSTRUCTION PRINCIPLES</u> AS FOLLOWS:

GIVEN A NOEMATIC BASIS $\Psi$ FOR OBJECTS $a_{00}$, $a_{01}$, ......., $a_{mn}$, ......, (WHICH ACT AS OUR DESIGNATED ELEMENTS), A <u>SIMPLEX</u> $\sigma$ OBTAINS IFF ONE OF THE FOLLOWING HOLDS:

1) $\sigma = |a_{mn}|\cdot$, OR THE <u>BRACKETING OPERATION</u>

OR

2) $\sigma = \cup(\ |a_{ii}|^{'}\ ,\ |a_{nj}|^{''}\ \cdots\cdots\cdots\cdots\ |a_{mn}|^{ij}\ \cdots\cdots\ )$
     OR THE <u>UNION OPERATION</u>.

THE <u>CLOSURE</u> OF 1) AND 2) OVER $\Psi \subset \Xi \cup \Lambda \cup Z \cup \Psi$ DESIGNATES THE <u>UNIVERSAL MIND</u> OF $\Sigma$ RELATIVE THE BASIS $\Psi$. WE USE $\Sigma^\Sigma$ TO SIGNIFY THE CORRESPONDING OBJECT.

THE DIAGRAM $\Delta$ OF $\Sigma$, $\Delta(\Sigma)$, INDICATES THE BASIS AND THE STATE OF GROWTH OF THE STREAMS OF CONSCIOUSNESS $\xi_k$ EMANATING FROM THE DESIGNATED ELEMENTS $a_{00}$, $a_{01}$, ......., $a_{mn}$, ........

THE DIAGRAM FOR $\Sigma$ OVER $\Psi$ IS DISPLAYED ON THE FOLLOWING PAGE.

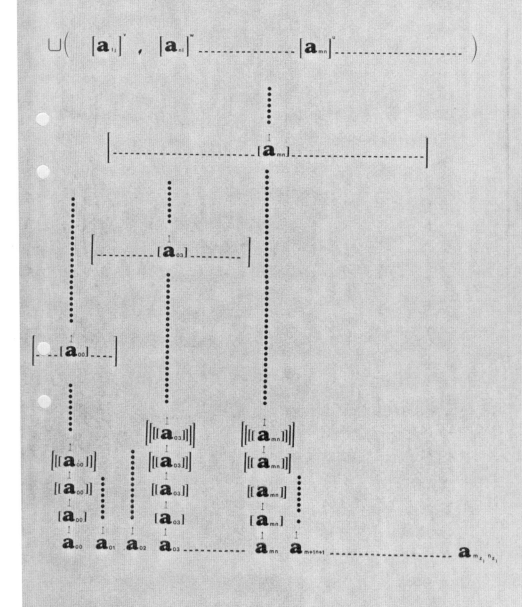

# APPENDIX 2

# 1— CARDINALS IN MODAL SPECTRA

# CARDINALS IN 1-MODAL SPECTRA

By the <u>CARDINAL</u> of an Object K, Card(K), we mean the <u>measure</u> of the size of K. There is a <u>smallest</u> Cardinal, viz. Card(∅), where (∅) points to an <u>empty</u> Object.

<u>OPEN PROBLEM</u>: Is there an Object K such that for every Object K′ different from K, Card(K) > Card(K′), where > designates the binary predicate "greater than"?

Let $\mathbf{K}$ be a <u>class</u> of Cardinals. If there is a Cardinal $K \in \mathbf{K}$ such that for all Cardinals $K' \in \mathbf{K}$ Card(K) > Card(K′), then $\mathbf{K}$ is <u>bounded above</u>. If there is no such Cardinal, then $\mathbf{K}$ is <u>unbounded</u> and <u>closed</u> in its <u>cofinality</u>. The <u>cofinality</u> of $\mathbf{K}$ is the class of Cardinals belonging to the <u>ultrafilter</u> in the <u>upper semi-lattice</u> of $\mathbf{K}$ and which is closed under all regular Cardinal Operations Card$\left| \Rightarrow \right|$.

The invention of <u>new</u> Cardinals became one of the more fashionable pastimes during the 60's. Thus we have become acquainted with Sachs Cardinals, Silver Cardinals, Solovay Cardinals, Ramsey Cardinals, Rowbottom Cardinals, just to mention a few. The invention of these Cardinals was often connected with the <u>new models for set theory</u>, as they became known in connection with Paul Cohen's famous <u>forcing constructions</u>.[1]

This fashion has been well documented in the recent literature and its Objects constitute solid pieces of the Art of Conceptual Thinking, and certainly a specimen of A-Art. Independently of these contributions, we now wish to introduce the notion of a <u>SPREAD CARDINAL</u> Card($\underset{\sim}{\Sigma}$), where $\underset{\sim}{\Sigma} = <\Sigma, \Sigma^c>$ is a <u>SPREAD</u> with $\Sigma$ its <u>SPREAD LAW</u> of functions from sequences $n_0 \ldots \ldots n_j \ldots \ldots$ into the <u>TRUTH SPACE</u> $[0,1]$ and $\Sigma^c$ its <u>COMPLEMENTARY LAW</u> defined on the field of $\Sigma$ and taking values among <u>PREVIOUSLY CONSTRUCTED MATHEMATICAL ENTITIES</u>.

Card($\underset{\sim}{\Sigma}$) exists <u>SOLELY</u> in <u>1-MODAL SPECTRA FOR INTUITIONISTIC REASONINGS</u>. By the prefix 1- we express as usual <u>MAXIMAL MODAL DEPTH</u>, so that the notion Card($\underset{\sim}{\Sigma}$) will depend on the following basic operation:

$$\Theta$$

the <u>CLOSURE OPERATOR</u> over the <u>SPACE OF INTENSIONS</u> $\mathcal{E}$.

For example, by

$$\Theta[\pi_j]$$

we mean the <u>CLOSURE OF INTENSION</u> $\pi_j \in \mathcal{E}$, or, in other words, the <u>INTUITIONISTIC INTERIOR IMAGE</u> of the <u>NOEMA</u> $\pi_j$ in the modality $\Theta$, as indicated above. The III yielded by an application of $\Theta$, as above, is such that Card(III) = Card($\underset{\sim}{\Sigma}$) for the Spread $\underset{\sim}{\Sigma}$ <u>ASSOCIATED</u> with this application.

Preparing for the theorems below, we introduce the distinction between <u>SMALL CARDINALS</u> and <u>LARGE CARDINALS</u>. By <u>SMALL CARDINALS</u> we mean Objects K such that Card(K) and K is <u>CONSTRUCTIBLE</u> within <u>GÖDEL'S CONSTRUCTIBLE UNIVERSE</u> L or in its <u>JENSEN</u> refinement J. We think of the "real" (Cantorian) world V as containing, at least, the hierarchies L or J.

If we restrict our attention just to the <u>constructible levels</u> in $V$, we shall write $V = L$ or $V = J$. (The former expression is also known as the <u>Axiom of Constructibility</u>, first formulated by Gödel, 1938).

If $K$ is an Object and Card($K$) and $K$ is not constructible in $L$ or $J$, then Card($K$) is a <u>large cardinal</u>. In our language, the most obvious Large Cardinal is, of course, Card($\mathcal{E}$).

By what was said about the relation $\Theta[\pi_j] = III$ above, we may now state

<u>THEOREM 1</u>: <u>Every Spread Cardinal Card($\Sigma$) is contained in the Large Cardinal $\mathcal{E}$</u>

<u>Re</u>: <u>The Open Problem above</u>. One might think $\mathcal{E}$ is such that for all $K$ in our universe, Card($\mathcal{E}$) > Card($K$). Trivially, this holds in every <u>0-modal spectrum</u> due to the complete cofinal character of every $K$ in 0-Modal Spectra. For which other prefixes it may hold still remains an open problem!

Although the notion Card measures a <u>size</u> of $K$, which was expressed by Card($K$) above, it might not always be the case that <u>every</u> $K$ is <u>measurable</u> although we have Card($K$). Hence we may introduce another notion about Cardinals, <u>viz</u>. the <u>measurable cardinals</u>. For a complete distinction, we shall also introduce <u>non-measurable cardinals</u>.

By a <u>measure</u> $\mu$ on $K$, we shall understand the <u>map</u> $\mu : 2^K \to [0, 1]$, where $2^K$ is the total partition of the parts and subparts of $K$ collected together (i.e., $2^K$

IS THE <u>POWER SET</u> OF K) AND WHICH SATISFIES:

$$\left| \begin{array}{l} \mu(K) = 1 \\ \mu(K') = \overline{\angle} \mu(K_i') \end{array} \right.$$

WHERE $K' \in 2^K$, $K' = K_1' \cup K_2' \cup \ldots \cup K_j'$ AND $K_1' \cap K_2' \cap \ldots \cap K_j' = 0$ (N.B.: WE USE $\angle$ AS AN <u>ADDITIVE SIGN</u>, WHILE $\cup$, $\cap$ ARE USED AS REGULAR UNIONS AND INTERSECTIONS RESPECTIVELY).

<u>THEOREM 2</u>: IF A SPREAD CARDINAL CARD($\Sigma$) IS A LARGE CARDINAL THEN IT HAS A NON-TRIVIAL TOTAL MEASURE $\mu = 1$

THE FOLLOWING THEOREM IS, THEN, RATHER OBVIOUS:

<u>THEOREM 3</u>: A SPREAD CARDINAL IS A MEASURABLE CARDINAL IFF[1] IT IS LARGE

[1] IF, AND ONLY IF

WE NOW STATE TWO THEOREMS FOR THE ADJOINTS ☐ AND ▬

<u>THEOREM 4</u>: ☐₁ IS NON-MEASURABLE

<u>PROOF</u>: BY EXPERIENCE (AND CONSEQUENTLY, ALREADY BY DEFINITION)

THEOREM 5: ███████████ H A S   M E A S U R E   1 :

$$\mu(\blacksquare\blacksquare\blacksquare) = |\pi^\circ|$$

PROOF: By definition, every 1-Modal Spectrum has $1 \stackrel{\nabla}{=} |\pi^\circ|$ ($\nabla$ is, of course, our past tense operator)

Of interest is also:

THEOREM 6: F O R   A N Y ███████████, ███████████ I S
E L E M E N T A R I L Y   E Q U I V A L E N T
W I T H $\mathcal{E}$ :

$$\blacksquare\blacksquare\blacksquare \equiv \mathcal{E}$$

Not surprisingly, then:

COROLLARY: Card(███████████) I S   A   L A R G E
C A R D I N A L

As was to be expected, ███████████ is consequently not in L or J. So,

COROLLARY: ███████████ I S   N O T   C O N S T R U C T -
I B L E   I N   L.

where we recall that L stands for GÖDEL'S CONSTRUCTIBLE UNIVERSE.

FOR THE EXPERT, WE MAY ALSO MENTION:

COROLLARY: BY CONSTRUCTING ▮ IN J, WE OBTAIN A MIRACLE

FOR ADJOINTS $\square\ \square$ WE HAVE THE FOLLOWING:

THEOREM 7: $\square\ \square$ IS ONLY MEASURABLE BELOW $|\pi^\circ|$ IMPLIES CARD( $\square\ \square$ ) = CARD($\Sigma$)

AND FURTHER, FOR NO $j > 0$ IS $[\pi_j]$ MEASURABLE

THUS, WE HAVE THE RATHER SENSATIONAL

THEOREM 8: IF CARD( $\square\ \square$ ) = CARD($\Sigma$), THEN CARD( $\square\ \square$ ) IS THE LEAST MEASURABLE CARDINAL

PROOF: EITHER BY FINE SENSES OR, ALTERNATIVELY, BY THE FOLLOWING CONSIDERATIONS.

PUT $\mu(|\square|) = \mu(|\square|) = 0$,

THEN WE MAY PUT

$$\mu(\text{CARD}(\square\ \square)) = 1 = |\pi^\circ|$$

Ad (1). In THEOREM 4 above, we stated the Non-Measurability of $\square_1$. By arrows, it follows that ■ also is Non-Measurable and in fact each ■$_j$ is Non-Measurable. This is one of the basic facts underlying the FINE SENSES LEMMA given in another part of this work.

---

[1] (cf. A.R.D. Mathias: The Surrealistic Landscape of Set Theory after Cohen. Dept of mathematics, UCLA, Underground, 1967)

# APPENDIX 3

# TOPOSES & ADJOINTS

| 4 | 11 |
| 1x | am |
| — | — |
| 17 | 9 |
| x | pm |
| 76 | |

# TOPOSES AND ADJOINTS

by Christer Hennix

A survey of the formation of abstract concepts
from Cantor to Lawvere

Moderna Museet, Stockholm

4.9.1976 - 17.10.1976

I. <u>Invisible Process Pieces</u>

    0. <u>Composite Continuous Infinitary Wave-Form</u> ((Electronic sine waves) - (Quoted word object from LINCOS for La Monte Young, 1969 -    ))

    $0^1$. <u>Aromatic Chains #4</u> ((Susanna's) Super Sensualism, collaboration piece with Susanna Kae, 1973 -   ) -------
    ------------------------- (Organic molecules in air)

II. <u>Set & Spread Pieces</u> (Topologies)

    1. <u>Short Infinitary Process</u> ................ (Acrylic, 1973)
    (Using the Restricted Tactic of Attention)

    2. <u>Model for Set Theory</u>, $\varepsilon$ ................ (Acrylic, 1973)
    (Object in the Category of all Categories)

3. <u>Open Point Set of Measure 0</u> ............ (Letraset, 1971)
   (Continuously Variable Lawverian Set)

4. <u>Straight Lines</u> ........................ (Acrylic, 1971)

5*. <u>Brouwer's Bar</u> ..................... (Stainless steel, 1975)
   (Answering a question of Walter De Maria by use of Brouwer's Bar Theorem)

6*. <u>The Least Non-Measurable Cardinal</u> ..................... (Stainless steel, 1973- )

7*. <u>The Least Measurable Cardinal</u> ..(Stainless steel, 1973- )

8*. <u>Brackets</u> ....................... (Stainless steel, 1970)

(*= Made 1976 by special agreement with Nord Verkstad AB, Molkom (Uddeholm))

III. <u>Exercise Pieces</u> ...................................... (1976- )

  9. <u>Exercise #1</u> .................................. (Letraset)

  10. <u>Exercise #2</u> ................................. (Letraset)

  11. <u>Exercise #3</u> .................... (Soot on aluminum)
     (**2** - and **C** -Spaces of Abstract Topologies)

IV. <u>Toposes</u>   Computer Monitor Displays     (Dia projections
   12. Topos #1                                        1974- )

   13. Topos #2

14. Topos #3         20. Topos #9
15. Topos #4         21. Topos #10
16. Topos #5         22. Topos #11
17. Topos #6         23. Topos #12
18. Topos #7         24. Topos #13
19. Topos #8         25. Topos #14

V. LANGUAGE PIECES

26. (Fragments from) LINCOS (For          (Illuminated dias)
    Intergalactic Communications) - (Infinitary Drawing, 1969)

VI. ABSTRACT NONSENSE PIECES          (Typewriter & letraset)

27. Excerpts from Notes on Toposes and Adjoints (1969-76)

VII: HISTORICAL DEPARTMENT

28. Kleene's Slash ........................... (Letraset)

29. First Commutative Diagrams ... (Reproduction technique)
    (After Eilenberg - MacLane, 1942)

VIII: APPENDIX

30. Gödel's L .................... (Reproduction technique)

31. Jensen's J .................. (     "            "    )

# MODALITIES AND LANGUAGES FOR ALGORITHMS

© Henry A. Flynt, Jr.

Edited version, by Henry Flynt, of *Notes on Toposes & Adjoints* by Catherine Christer Hennix. Flynt's introductory notes are included. In the body of the text we have excluded the sections "Semiotics I," "Semiotics II," "Toposes, Sheaves, and Adjoints," and "Cardinals in 1-Modal Spectra"; readers can refer to the original sections in *Notes on Toposes & Adjoints* in this volume. Second edition edited in 1983. Previously unpublished.

Contents

Ch. I    Modalities and the Theory of the Creative Subject
Ch. II   Semiotics I
Ch. III  Semiotics II
Ch. IV   Toposes, Sheaves, and Adjoints
Ch. V    Cardinals in 1-Modal Spectra


Motto

Nothing is more fantastic, ultimately, than precision.
—Alain Robbe-Grillet

*Prelude*

In Richard Dedekind's *Essays on the Theory of Numbers* (Chicago: Open Court, 1909), page 64, the following passage appears:

66. Theorem. There exist infinite systems.
Proof. My own realm of thoughts, i.e., the totality S of all things which can be objects of my thought, is infinite. For if s signifies an element of S, then the thought s' that "s can be an object of my thought" is itself an element of S. If we regard this as transform ø (s) of the element s, then the transformation ø of S, thus determined, has the property that the transform S' is part of S; and S' is certainly a proper part of S, because there are elements in S (e.g. my own ego) which are different from such thought s' and therefore not contained in S'. Finally, it is clear that if a, b are different elements of S, their transforms a', b' are also different. Therefore the transformation ø is a distinct (similar) transformation. Hence S is infinite, which was to be proved.[1] [I have somewhat modernized the Open Court text. —Editor]

The fact that such a passage as this appears in a modern classic of mathematics —together with the examples of Wittgenstein's *Tractatus* and Montague's *Formal Philosophy*—give a precedent for some of the ideas in the work which follows.

*Prefatory*

The technical prerequisites for what follows can be found in the following books. Books will be cited in the text by author or editor.

L.E.J. Brouwer, *Collected Works I*, ed. Arend Heyting (1975).
L.E.J. Brouwer, *Collected Works II*, ed. Troelstra (1976).
C.C. Chang and H. J. Keisler, *Model Theory*, North-Holland, Amsterdam, first edition 1973; second edition 1977.
Frank R. Drake, *Set Theory: An Introduction To Large Cardinals*, North-Holland, Amsterdam, 1974..
Kurt Gödel, *The Consistency of the Continuum Hypothesis* (Princeton, 1940).
Peter Hilton, ed., *Category Theory, Homology Theory and their Applications II*, Springer Lecture Notes in Mathematics No. 92 (1969).
R.B. Jensen, "The Fine Structure of the Constructible Hierarchy," in *Annals of Mathematical Logic* 4 (1972), pp. 229–308.
G.M. Kelly, ed., *Category Seminar*, Springer Lecture Notes in Mathematics No. 420 (1974).
Lawvere(1):
F.W. Lawvere, ed., *Toposes, Algebraic Geometry and Logic*, Springer Lecture Notes in Mathematics No. 274 (1972).
Lawvere(2):
F.W. Lawvere et al., eds., *Model Theory and Topoi*, Springer Lecture Notes in Mathematics No. 445 (1975).
Saunders MacLane, *Coherence in Categories*, Springer Lecture Notes in Mathematics No. 281 (1972).
M. Nakkal and G. E. Reyes, *First-Order Categorical Logic*, Springer Lecture Notes in Mathematics No. 611 (1977).
A.R.D. Mathias, *The Surrealistic Landscape of Set Theory After Cohen*, UCLA Department of Mathematics, Los Angeles, 1967..
Richard Montague, *Formal Philosophy*, Yale University Press, New Haven, 1974.
Jean van Heijenoort, ed., *From Frege to Gödel* (1967).
Volpin(1):
A.S. Yessenin-Volpin, "Le programme ultra-intuitioniste des fondements des mathématiques," in *Infinistic Methods*, Pergamon, New York, 1961, pp. 201–223.
Volpin(2):
A.S. Yessenin-Volpin, "The Ultra-Intuitionistic Criticism and the Antitraditional Program for Foundations of Mathematics," in *Intuitionism and Proof Theory*, ed. A. Kino, J. Myhill, and R. E. Vesley, North-Holland, Amsterdam, 1970, pp. 3–45.
Volpin(3):
A.S. Yessenin-Volpin, "About Infinity, Finiteness, and Finitization." in *Constructive Mathematics*, ed. Fred Richman, Springer Lecture Notes in Mathematics No. 873 (1981).


In many cases, the theories proposed in this work call for syntheses whose details are not worked out. I think of this working through as rather straightforward and tedious. To others it may not be straightforward.

*Chapter I: Modalities and the Theory of the Creative Subject*

*Activities* decompose into individual sequences of acts which ultimately exhaust the activities.

Among the "atomic" acts yielded under any such decomposition, it is desirable (in order to avoid confusion) to distinguish the following:

1. *Organic* acts, i.e., *those connected with interference with the physical world.*
2. *Epistemic* acts, which involve interference with our abstraction capabilities, i.e., *those acts which may be described as purely mental.*

As is plain, *constructive conceptualism focuses mainly on activities where the latter acts dominate. Usually, activities of this kind are referred to as thought-processes.* They are coded in their extensiveness by the diagram for the Category $e$, which Category corresponds to the mapping of all meanings onto constructions. ("Category" is meant in the sense of Category Theory. $e$ is defined strictly in Chapter II, on page 100 in this volume. The $e$-diagram is much like the diagram for the Creative Subject, to be explained on pages 151–155 below and displayed on page 154.) As for the *"epistemic"* modality, to explain it further, it refers to the aspiration to certainty or incontestability.

Obviously, a linear presentation of these technical details is not possible. The exposition has to zigzag and to be fragmentary, mentioning ideas which are subsequently explained more fully. A considerable number of cross-references will be supplied with the hope that they will moderate the difficulty.

An appearance of a sign has at least two epistemic structures associated with it, its surface structure and its deep structure. Only in a logically perfected language (a saturated language) do these two structures coincide. In other languages, the coincidence may vary, and it belongs to the tactics of attention of those languages to determine the exact projection of surface form onto its companion deep-structure form. (There will be more about *tactics of attention* throughout; the idea goes back to Volpin(2).)

The projection rules of the sign determine its *world location* (cf. pages 141–142); and thus give us the coordinates of the sign's underlying reality. This is part of the criterion for the meaningfulness of the sign's appearance; and it is also part of the criterion for every introductory occurrence of a sign, in which the rules of projections are laid down.

\*\*\*

MODALITIES, DEGREES, SPECTRA. The modalities associated with an activity give it its import—narrowly, in regard to whether the objective is to be *actualized*, vs. whether its *preconditions* are to be satisfied *without its actualization*—etc. Awareness of modalities reinforces your understanding of your consciousness. In other words, your awareness of a logical reality is real only if it is a self-conscious awareness, only if you understand what makes the logical reality possible and real. The hope that you could stumble on a highly articulated consciousness-state by accident, without an algorithm, is not taken seriously.[2] We are given colloquial thought without effort, but to rise above it, we must progressively destroy it by analyzing it and replacing it with formalizations or explicit linguistic rules.

The ideas here go back to Volpin(2), pp. 14–15.

a. *The deontic modality* is the logic of rules, including permissions and prohibitions.
b. *The optative modality* is the logic of goal-directed activity.
c. *The epistemic modality*, again, concerns the aspiration to certainty or incontestability.

Again, the import is that mastery of consciousness is self-consciousness of procedures and conditions through which consciousness is transformed. *Degrees* refer to the idea that one starts with colloquial thinking and then achieves illumination by progressively analyzing and formalizing it. *There is a major departure here, also going back to Volpin(2): the axiomatic method is rejected.* It is replaced by a "helical" method in which colloquial thinking is progressively replaced by analysis and formalization. Each degree is a level of formalization. Roughly speaking, the lowest degree is colloquial discourse without explicit syntax or semantics. It is the profane conceptual medium which society thrusts you into. It is a morass which demands no effort. At the next degree, you begin to formulate rules for the language you think you are using, e.g., fixing the meanings of words. The achievement of the higher degree takes effort.

The spectrum of a degree pertains to the idea that a given degree may split up into sub-levels, i.e., that some activities may be borderline between degrees. Example: having a rational basis, yet not algorithmic.

It is a general fact that any activity proceeds on the background of other activities, so that the background activities extend the given activity, or the given activity is included in its background activities. The exteriorized elements of an activity, those belonging to the background but not to the given activity itself, can often be encountered as objects mentioned in pertinent parts of the given activity $A$. But, significantly, they may not participate constructively in any creative situation in which $A$ is realized (as opposed to the given interior elements of $A$). The processes of exteriorizing parts of a given activity proceed on the unfolding of the *modal* components of the activity, which components basically determine the scope or ranges of the conceptual frameworks that go into the interior of the activity.

***

Returning to signs, the acquisition and use of a sign is a highly intricate network of mental processes conducted under various spectra of modalities which operate on all actions that require participation under the rules of use of signs. It is unfortunate that people have overlooked the deep contribution of these modalities to the functional and creative aspects of the use of signs.

***

When we are considering the abstract mechanisms of our language or of collections of signs in general, their underlying reality or "deep structure" is what essentially contributes to the sense or meaning of these mechanisms.

*For each fragment of a language or collection of signs, we have to consider what kind of world or form of life is depicted by this fragment (its model(s)).* Depending on the context, the meaning that a sign receives may be called the world-location or locus of that sign. (A notion already invoked on page 140.) If the sign is a logical sign, we may also speak of the logical coordinates as the meaning(s) that the sign receives.

These locations or coordinates make up the core of the underlying reality of our signs. *Reality is a result of authority—the result imposed by its author(s)*. Thus, the life of this "reality" is restricted by the standards of ethics which the author legislates by his demarcation between admissible and inadmissible symbols and signs. The mental vacuum of our conventionalistically sustained culture is but a second-order consequence of society's fallaciously developed modalities (meaning, again, the realm of gradations of fulfillment of requirements of or in purposive human activity, preferably, as explicitly understood and formalized). In order to correct our first impressions of this state of affairs, it is advisable to look at some of the deeper modalities of our existence, as exemplified by the deontic and optative modalities (again, logic of rules, logic of goal-directed activity).

Consequently, we may note that connected with the underlying reality of the use of signs is what may be termed *Relevance Theory*, i.e., the study of aims and means associated with any reality. Some signs may lack a meaning simply because they were intended as an act or gesture, which, of course, may lack meaning (in a well-defined sense) but must be associated with an aim. An aim is any desire to accomplish a construction by some given means. If the latter are lacking (or insufficient), we shall speak about ideals and instead of a construction we shall speak of a tendency (towards the ideal).

One of the basic tenets or our Relevance Theory is its commitment to just and purposeful acts of communication, i.e., acts freed from obstacles, fraud and coercion. Obviously, this principle is clearly related to ideas in ethics as well as epistemology (the science of how we achieve certainty); and it constitutes a cornerstone of our general theory of modalities.

Purposefulness means, above all, that the means associated with the aims are sufficient for achieving the aims. That is to say, an aim which is not just meant as an ideal is by definition without purpose if it lacks the necessary and sufficient means associated with its fulfillability. Of course, it [sic] an aim is discovered to be purposeless, it can still be retained, if desired, as an idea. But then the ideal is properly called futile unless it becomes (or already is) associated with a search for means that suffice for sustaining the tendency on which the ideal depends.

The justness of an act is simply its admissibility in the context of its appearance. For instance, it is required that a new act is compatible with previously committed purposeful acts in the sense that it does not obstruct some specific act in the given activity $A$, then this fact would be an indication of the faultiness of the logic behind the activity, which logic the doer is thus obliged to revise or simply abandon in order to secure the continuation of $A$ free from obstacles, fraud, or coercion. (Hereafter freedom from obstacles, fraud and coercion will be designated by "Freedom" or "Free.")

* * *

One of our basic aims is to implement a family of languages which may reflect by its very design the conditions for purposeful acts of communication. Such an aim of implementing our semiotic (linguistic and self-understood) capabilities involves a certain amount of unblocking (and rectifying) of some (and ultimately all) of the futile semantic or habitual circuits that restrain the mind from an unobstructed access to its fundamental(istic) creative potentials.

Within some modalities, the very unblocking activity itself results in a refinement of our language to the degree that its desired implementation has become fulfilled when successfully removing the blocks.

Other modalities, however, require that more constructive processes, to be taught by vivid manifestations, take the place of those unblocked places along the unblocked circuits. Generally, these processes will not remain fixed at their corresponding substituted places, but will participate in the integration of other streams of consciousness. (Obviously, the "floating" character of this activity demands Freedom from obstacles, fraud and coercion for the sake of its stability and (non-paralyzed) development.) This participatory function will be regarded as the main source for the arising of new modalities, and, with the latter, new moods[3] of consciousness and their associated tactics of attention.

People seem to have failed to notice that one of the main obstacles for the realization of this aim is the otherwise well-known circumstance that we are usually involved with interpretations that yield to multiple forms of understanding, i.e., moods of understanding that lack uniqueness (one of the causes being, of course, the "free fall" into associative thinking). Consequently, when we try to fix, in some way, this understanding, we fail to provide for even the most elementary aspects of Freedom from obstacles, fraud and coercion, thereby depriving us of the possibility of providing for just and purposeful acts of communication in a field that purports to defend these very values. *Thus, no fixed meaning can seriously be claimed for any symbolic activity (including jurisprudence and codifications of human rights) that society has provided for up till now.* Of course, there is sometimes (but not always) a certain economical gain involved when a multiple set of meanings can be compressed into a single sign. But if the clarity of the sign suffers too much during the course of this conceptual compression, its purposefulness becomes doubtful, and hence, ceases to fulfill its presumed role (as far as that role involves any exact purpose).

When an author shows the addressee a sign, an act of trust towards the author takes place when the addressee interprets the sign. This trust is expressed by *tactics for identifications and distinctions* that the addressee brings forth during the act of interpretation. In addition, the tactics of attention, which the allowance or admissibility of the sign in part defines, further restrict the possible moods of understanding the sign. On the other hand, tactics of neglect are determined by the sphere of trustworthiness or certainty that emanates from the author when addressing the addressee. That is to say, what is not explicitly expressed but presupposed by context or other relevant clues can only be retraced by following the tactics of neglect authorized by the situation in which the act of communication takes place. Any neglect not authorized by this tactic will be considered a violation of the condition of fairness for just and purposeful acts of communication and consequently inadmissible for the context in question. It is important to note, however, that any neglect based on non-contributing (irrelevant or obstructionist) circumstances plays no relevant role when declaring a neglect inadmissible. The irrelevance of circumstances is prescribed by Relevance Theory and the ethical doctrine associated with it (again cf. Volpin(2)).

***

By a *Creative Subject* we mean an idealized collection of streams of consciousness. When an abbreviation is needed, we will use "Subject" or $\Sigma$.

By consciousness we mean any non-empty set of streams of consciousness.

The basis of a consciousness is a set of *potentials*, determining the range of the corresponding streams of consciousness. Typically, a potential initiates and supports the development of a stream of consciousness. The properties of the potentials are described in terms of the currents that the potentials may give rise to along the streams of consciousness.

***

SEMIOTICS. The term goes back to C.S. Peirce and Charles W. Morris and means the theory of language: syntax, semantics, pragmatics (contextual determination). Caution: Our use of the term "semiotics" or the notion "theory of a text" is totally independent of the French fashion of the "literary" study of "theories" of signs (Barthes, et al.). The notion of Semiotics is made formal in Chapter III.

***

INTENSION. A map from the Creative Subject onto the "real world" or a world. Roughly, a meaning, or an interpretation, or a thrust from subject to world.[4]

***

ARROW. Roughly, an arrow is a denotation or a map.

More rigorously, an arrow is a proxy for the meaning-relation obtaining between the terms situated on both sides of the arrow-sign. There are, generally, no restrictions on the kinds of objects that are permitted to appear as (the) fixed values of the terms. The collection of all objects which may be substituted for the values of the terms of the arrow-signs is called the universe, which the meaning relation will be said to refer to, whenever interpreted.

The means for designating terms in their occurrences in some collection of arrow-signs require access to some vocabulary V, by which these designations become expressed. By $L_V$ we designate the language generated over V, i.e., all finite sequences of symbols of V. $G_L$ shall designate the grammar generating $L_V$.

The choice of basic construction principles in this work is made with a preference for the most frugal, taking only

and
$\in$ (Cantorian membership)
$\cup$ (directed sum)

as undefined.

Having done so, arrows may be defined in terms of these primitives. $b \to a$ (i.e., a is a meaning of b, b points to a) if and only if $a \in b$. Also, given $a_1, ..., a_n \in a$, $b \to a_1$ or ... or $b \to a_n$ if and only if $\cup a \in b$.

Resuming our continuing discussion of the logic of given activity $A$, a rough indication of the growth of activity $A$ may be given describing the tree structure associated with $A$, designated by $T(A)$ or just $T$. At its root, notated $(\;)_T$, $T$ indicates the initial act in $A$. At every branch $(...)_T$ above the root $(\;)_T$, $T$ indicates, for each node of a branch,

a) the type or label of the decision invited at the node
b) the intension for that type at the given locus.

Trees depict the search in which the Creative Subject develops activities for the purpose of attaining some desired result(s) involving given activity $A$.

To describe the inner map presupposed by way of the tree $T(A)$, it is not sufficient to look only at the indices at the nodes of $T$. It is in addition necessary to map $T$ into an extended tree, in which the search in the activity, functor-wise, goes over into the domain of the theoretical activity connected with the fulfillment of the search in the activity. The functor in question is called the Subject$_T$-projectum of trees of kind $T$. (Cf. dialogue and impasse diagrams.)

***

Let us refer to the relation of given activity $A$ to its modal components, introduced also at the bottom of page 4. When we say that a modal component acts on an activity, we are referring to a hierarchy of (degrees of) modalities, that, when fully developed, constitutes the spectra of modalities in given activity $A$. The diagram of the hierarchy of degrees of modalities is displayed on the next page, page 10. Its elucidation will be a continuing task throughout this work.

Degree 1 is assigned to those modalities whose underlying activities consist in the use of (at most) uninterpreted signs or no signs at all (like the singular awareness of the presence of a plasma—the morass of colloquial thought).

Nodal operators of degree 2 are those modalities which participate in shorter (i.e., fragmentary) lines of reasonings or other more general activities involving the use of interpreted signs. An example of the latter is the singular bracketing operation as converted by arrows, which yields sets. This operation is notated $[\;]$.

## THE HIERARCHY OF DEGREES OF MODALITIES

(n°) ┊ | INCREASINGLY STRICTER AND STRICTER CONDENSATIONS OF ACTS OF TRUST CERTAINTY (BY ARROWS)

(5°)      $A \to \Sigma^{\underline{\Sigma}}$      *FREEDOM* (IN ARROWS)

(4°)      $\nrightarrow$      *METAMATHEMATICS* (CONSISTENCY OF ARROWS (HILBERT'S 2ND PROBLEM))

(3°)      $\underset{\approx}{\Sigma}$      *ACTIONS AND PROCESSES* (WITH ARROWS)

(2°)      $\Sigma$      *AWARENESS* (OF ARROWS)

(1°)      [ ]      *ARROWS* (AT POINTS OF CONDENSATION)

(0°)      □      *PLASMA* (PER ARROWS)

There is no upper bound on the assignment of degrees to modalities in this hierarchy—as should be expected, if the activity is Free. The degree of a modality reflects the complexity of its dependence on modalities of lower degree, as well as of the degree of trustworthiness/certainty vindicated by the situations generated by the activity. Any activity for which the participating modalities are assigned degree $\geq$ three is called a theoretical activity. [Or an algorithm.—Editor] On the other hand, degrees below three are connected with dream activities.

A thesis to which I have repeatedly recurred is that in order to reach a highly articulated result, you have to have an algorithm. (The choice of noemas is the exception.) If a highly articulated result could happen spontaneously without guarantees that its prerequisites had been met, I would call that a miracle. Or an outcome that happened in violation of prerequisites that had been met would be a miracle.

My personality is not especially consistent. For example, I claim that my intuitionistic modal music, exemplified by "Electric Harpsicord No. 1," is one of these "miracles" by the norms of rule-logic (deontic logic). This music is a borderline case between a theoretical activity and a dream activity because it is grounded in the law of sufficient reason (in this case, the requirement to be rational and not arbitrary); yet a miracle relative to rule-logic is present in it (a highly articulated result comes without an algorithm). This borderline case at degree three of modalities shows that *degrees can split into finer gradations. That is the basis for speaking of spectra of degrees of modalities.*

As is to be expected, the theoretical activity of the Creative Subject, as determined by Subject$_T$-projectum, makes essential use of modalities of degree greater than three. In particular, for any prospective interpretation of an element in the class of objects referred to as Toposes, it is essential to note the degree of modalities participating in the object.

\*\*\*

TOPOSES are formally defined for the purposes of this work in Chapter IV (page 109).

\*\*\*

*Zenonian situations* were introduced and discussed extensively in Volpin(2). They arise because of Volpin's claim that there can be different-length natural number series. A Zenonian situation arises when an infinite series is embedded in a finite part of another series. The label is taken from Zeno's paradoxes. Cf. Volpin(2), p. 8, especially.

\*\*\*

To continue in regard to the theoretical activity of the creative subject, degrees of modalities, and Toposes, let us consider the following. *In Toposes, the degree of a modality is increased by introducing stronger concepts of infinity at points where an end could have been mandated. The un-ending of a process, i.e., its points of infinity, is connected with temporality and tense in respect to the future of its unfolding, which may be a near future or a remote future. By reasoning about the scales between these points, we can imagine different lengths of ramifying infinitary processes, including their Zenonian embeddings, which distinguish themselves by the degree of infinity to which they converge.* The *e*-diagram first mentioned on page 140 may be understood as a Universal (per Lawvere) for such situations.

\*\*\*

Let me now recapitulate with some remarks which are of an introductory character, but which can only be appreciated after the foregoing definitions and explanations have been assimilated. (Indeed, without the foregoing material, the following would definitely lend itself to misunderstanding.)

Arrows, i.e., logical connections, are invisible constructions made in the presence of a logical space.

There are infinitely many logical spaces available, corresponding to the forms of awareness or realities that the intelligence may comprehend.

The indication of a logical space must not be confused with its corresponding construction. An indication is just a semiotic event whose surface structure reflects some or all of the abstractions underlying the logical space. These constructions, or so-called deep structures of a semiotic event, are the actual consciousness being aware of the presence of a logical space. It is assumed that each such presence is real if and only if that awareness is self-conscious, comprehending what makes the particular logical space possible and real. (A highly articulated result requires an algorithm supported by an unflawed and self-understood language.) Or, in my vocabulary, the presence of a logical space is real if and only if the modal spectra of that presence have arrived for the situation in question. Modalities, like awareness, come in degrees of self-understanding or formalization. A given degree of formalization is sufficient or not depending on the contingencies of the purpose or purposefulness in question. Modalities—which again are the realm of gradations of fulfillment of requirements of or in purposive human activity, preferably, as explicitly understood and formalized—correspond to integrated forms of consciousness. They form the substance of the awareness of the universe of all logically possible worlds. We think of this universe as "standard," i.e., as a Universal in the sense of Category Theory (following Lawvere, et al.).

While this work depends on the ideas of Volpin and Lawvere, that dependency is overruled by our general vision and its cosmological critique. Besides discerning epistemological illusions, our concern is related to the creation of an atmosphere of attention in every relevant and contributing situation where the atmosphere of attention may be absent. To come to the point, the only real objects in our ontology of INTENSIONS are SUSTAINED STATES OF ILLUMINATION. In other words, this general theory of algorithms only wants algorithms for SUSTAINABLE VISIONARY OR ILLUMINATORY STATES OF CONSCIOUSNESS. That should make it plain enough what is unique about my sort of "mathematics." It follows[5] that any situation which is not parameterized by the CREATIVE SUBJECT is non-contributing to the aims of this work.

Spaces in which sustainable states of illumination occur form a partial order, notated < , of their appearances. In the absence of an atmosphere of attention, the continuity property of this order is violated. (In other words, gaps appear in your memory of illuminatory intensions.) The restoration of the continuity of the order is designated formally by barring the absence of an atmosphere of attention. The mathematical formalism for this is Brouwer's inductive principle for proving that a given property propagates backwards along a series, all the way to the earliest term (*bar induction*).

This work subscribes to the principle of cognitive parsimony, that the less you assume, the less your chance of error. So, basic construction principles are chosen as frugally as possible. I state the case for cognitive parsimony in a negative way, expressing the relevant correlation as a correlation between what we *don't* want. Irrelevance of tactics of attention by which the modal considerations are sustained *is a function of* tolerance of error which is permitted by corresponding objects of irrelevance or obstruction. Every such character is liable to denial of trust or certainty, since every object of irrelevance by definition its sphere of trust or certainty reduced to an infinitesimal. Thus it is that we opt for meager construction principles.

When we defined "b points to a" in terms of $\in$ and $\cup$ on page 145, we noted that we can have $a_1,\ldots, a_n \in a$. Continuing, for every process

$a1 \to a2 \to \ldots \to ak \to ak+1 \to \ldots$, the following dialectical triangle is basic

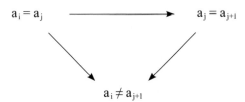

as underlying the infinitely proceeding invisible processes presented in this work. This triangle also corresponds to the progressive present tense orientation of Buddhist epistemology. In other words, if you enforce this regime on mundane consciousness, it means that identification of $x_{past}$ with $x_{present}$ and identification of $x_{present}$ with $x_{future}$ does not entitle you to conclude that $x_{past}$ is the same as $x_{future}$. (And Volpin(2), page 7, mentions Heraclitus on the notion of identity.) Without the temporal transitivity of identity, things become split up into many unanalyzed objects. Continuing with the technical details, infinitely many identifications and distinctions are suggested by the time Categories. (Local, global time, etc. Defined in Chapter II, page 27.)

However, for the description of coherence singularities such as displayed by the dialectical triangle, initial segments covered by Galois connections[6] are sufficient.

***

*A limit ordinal* is an ordinal which cannot be reached by any ordinal operation (such as iterated exponentiation, Ackermann's function, general recursive functions).

***

*Reflection; Reflection Principle.* "Reflection" is sometimes used in the colloquial sense of ponder or analyze. The Reflection Principle is a set-theoretic notion which was investigated by R. Montague and A. Lévy. Adding the Reflection Principle to Zermelo-Fraenkel set theory assures its consistency: to say that a property can be "reflected" throughout set theory means that the set theory is uniform; properties are preserved and there are no surprises (e.g., very large numbers behaving differently from numbers of familiar size).

***

The present presentation only reflects the field from a rather small (limit) ordinal. On the other hand, by further rarifying the atmosphere of attention from a reflection at a higher limit ordinal, the possibility opens up for a sustainable state of illumination embedded by a continuous Reflection Principle (along the lines of Brouwer's ideas of the Creative Subject, i.e., continuous at limits). But the use of the Reflection Principle at limits must be governed by some principle of caution, since embarrassing consequences may follow steps beyond projected limits if the basic principles lack the property of being well-founded. Therefore, in all extensions of this work (i.e., semiotic objects), *the presence of collapsing techniques has taken precedence*. Together with our ultra-intimate pedagogy, the given basic construction principles are intended to ground the possibility of following a continuous Reflection Principle. (Like following a "clear language" L. This very formal concept is defined in Chapter III.)

***

Let us continue the explanations regarding the Creative Subject begun on page 8. The closure of

Consciousness ∪ Potentials ∪ Currents

describes the generating field of the tactics of attention conducting activities of the Creative Subject at different stages of his development of consciousness.

By awareness we shall mean the consciousness of arrows $a_i \rightarrow a_{i+1}$ occurring along the streams of consciousness. By these arrows we establish, as usual, the denotational connections between all values of $a_{i+1}$ that are values of $a_i$.

Arrows participate in concept-formation processes. The knowledge of arrows is subsumed under those arrow-potentials (very roughly, objects-in-the-world for consciousness; note that the term "potential" was already used) which force one or another stream of consciousness. This forcing relation brings into attention the denotational connections which spring from the fibration[7] of the underlying concept-formation process. When a stream of consciousness belongs to some Subject, the stream designates any sustainable state of illumination directed towards the fixed points[8] of some mental phenomenon within the realm of the Subject's consciousness. The arrow-potentials for a state of illumination are referred to as the *noemas* of the stream of consciousness.

***

NOEMA. Roughly, noemas are the objects-in-the-world or possibilities-in-the-world for consciousness. In our terminology they are also arrow-potentials; and in Category-theoretic terms they are terminal objects. In other words, they are the possibilities-in-the-world-for-consciousness (shifting from context to context), prior to any definite reflection or self-analysis. Although they are among the most important elements of my ontology, I do not theorize about them because they are not chosen by algorithm. One's choice of one's *collection of arrow-potentials or noemas*—one's choice of one's Noematic Basis—is very personal, like artistic expression. Noemas are formally defined in Chapter IV.

***

The mind of the Subject is designated as

Consciousness ∪ Potentials ∪ Currents ∪ Noematic Basis

The construction of this mind which is an (infinite) class is based on two construction principles as follows. Given a Noematic Basis for objects $a_{00}, a_{01}, \ldots, a_{mn}, \ldots$ (which act as our designated elements), a simplex σ obtains if and only if (i) or (ii) stated below holds.
Remarks: The notation σ is chosen to indicate that simplexes are like elements of Σ. The superscripts on right brackets in (ii) below indicate the number of times bracketing is *iterated*.

i) $\sigma = [a_{mn}]$, the bracketing operation of fixing and sustaining the designated element $a_{mn}$
ii) $\sigma = \cup ( [a_{lj}]^v, [a_{nl}]^w$ _____ $[a_{mn}]^u$ _____ ), the union operation of stringing together and collecting bracketed elements

The closure of (i) and (ii) over Noematic Basis ⊂ Consciousness ∪ Potentials ∪ Currents ∪ Noematic Basis designates the mind-Universal ("Universal" as in Category Theory) of Σ relative to the Noematic Basis.
Remark: ⊂ has not been defined but is an inclusion.
We use $\Sigma^\Sigma$ to signify the corresponding object.
Remark: The 5th degree of modalities, page 10, is now explained. $\Sigma^\Sigma$ is isomorphic to the Category *e*.
The diagram of the Creative Subject, $\Delta(\Sigma)$, indicates the basis and the state of growth of the streams of consciousness emanating from the designated elements $a_{00}, a_{01}, \ldots, a_{mn}, \ldots$ . These elements are the Noematic Basis and appear on the diagram as the bottom row. The diagram is displayed on the next page, page 154.

***

The Creative Subject $\Sigma$, relative to the quest for certainty, solves problems and makes inferences; and the system of problem-solving and inferences is the *Theory of the Creative Subject*. In detail, A is an intension or problem connected with activity A. It is also possible to use A in the expression A(x) when the intension or problem depends on a parameter x. The basic relation $\vdash$, in the expression $\Sigma \vdash_n A$, is interpreted as "Creative Subject $\Sigma$ has decided or solved A at the nth stage of his investigation or research in *A*."

Four logical operators are interpreted as follows.

| | |
|---|---|
| $\neg A$ | signifies the task of obtaining the absurdity of the solution of A |
| A & B | signifies the task of solving both A and B |
| A ∨ B | signifies the task of solving either A or B together with a determination of which has been solved |
| A → B | signifies the task of solving the problem B given any solution of A |

$\exists x [A(x)]$ signifies the task of finding the value of x such that A(x) where $\exists x$ is the operator designating the existential construction principle.

The Creative Subject as an epistemic operator may be conceived of as grounded by the following axioms:

*Axioms for $\Sigma$*

1. $\Sigma \vdash_n A \vee \Sigma \vdash_n \neg A$
2. $\Sigma \vdash_n A \rightarrow A$
3. $\Sigma \vdash_n A \,\&\, m > n \rightarrow \Sigma \vdash_m A$
4. $\neg \exists x [\Sigma \vdash_n A] \rightarrow \neg A$

5. $\dfrac{\Sigma \vdash_n A,\ A \rightarrow C}{\Sigma \vdash_n C}$

6. $\dfrac{\Sigma \vdash_n \exists x [A(x)]}{\exists x [\Sigma \vdash_n A(x)]}$

*Inference Schema for Theory of $\Sigma$ (Axiom of Frictionless Epistemology)*

7. $\dfrac{\Sigma \vdash_n F,\ \Sigma \vdash_n F \rightarrow G}{\Sigma \vdash_{n+m} G}$

The closure of the foregoing Axioms under the consequence relation is the Theory of the Creative Subject, Th($\Sigma$).

Historical remark: L.E.J. Brouwer was the first logician to formulate principles similar to the ones given above.

On the basis of these principles, the following tasks are solvable problems in Th($\Sigma$). Note: These are not mere propositional tautologies, because A etc. are intensions or problems which may depend on parameters, and because these tasks have to be accomplished from axioms for $\Sigma$.

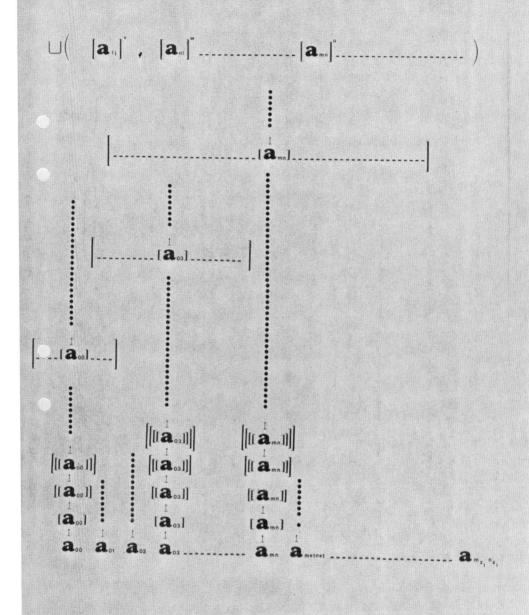

i) $A \rightarrow B \,\&\, B \rightarrow C \rightarrow A \rightarrow C$
ii) $A \rightarrow C \,\&\, B \rightarrow C \rightarrow A \vee B \rightarrow C$
iii) $\neg A \rightarrow A \rightarrow B$
iv) $A \rightarrow B \rightarrow \neg B \rightarrow \neg A$
v) $A \rightarrow \neg B \rightarrow B \rightarrow \neg A$
vi) $\neg(A \vee C) \rightarrow \neg A \,\&\, \neg C$
vii) $\neg(C \,\&\, E) \,\&\, C \vee \neg C \rightarrow \neg C \vee \neg E$
viii) $\neg(A \,\&\, \neg A)$

Remark: By (viii), consistency of Th($\Sigma$) is established. What consistency of a theory means to me is that the theory is epistemically worthy and non-negligible.

\*\*\*

[In *Notes on Toposes & Adjoints*, Hennix devoted several pages to given activity $A$, defining Freedom for $A$ and giving mechanical measures of $A$'s effectiveness. While this passage is rather redundant, it is retained because it provides a little more information on how Hennix uses the terminology of modalities. —Editor]

It is a well-known fact that activities with some resulting product or output (and arising from the choice of a Noematic Basis) may not always carry a well-determined meaning or sense. On the contrary, the lack of meaning(-fulness) is compensated for by (purported) aim(s) expressed by the purpose(s) governing the installment of the generating activities for which end some particular object is taken as a manifestation. This somewhat confused reality shows the indisputable importance of the interpretation of the optative modalities underlying any goal-directed activity $A$.

In order to fix the purposefulness of an activity $A$, several ratios are to be measured, such as

(1) $\dfrac{\text{interest of results}}{\text{efforts involved}}$

and

(2) $\dfrac{\text{long-term satisfaction}}{\text{efforts required}}$

Given some satisfactory measures of these ratios for an activity $A$, there is a further requirement on the means available by which the result(s) of $A$ are achieved. That is, it is generally required that any aim achieved through $A$ is acquired only as far as fair means have been provided. Any violation of this fairness principle is to be considered harmful for the continuation of the situations S generated by $A$ on account of the displacement of modalities, caused, in particular, by the displacement of goals relative to the installment of $A$.

Clearly, the condition of fairness for purposeful activities $A$ imposes an obvious restriction as to the availability of means for realizing $A$. This restriction must be evaluated relative to the higher-order aims under which $A$ is subsumed.

As far as clarity and certainty are sought, the fairness principle is but a higher-order means for our epistemic development; and its violation poses obstacles insofar as (foundational) communication is aimed at—indeed, the deepest threat to such communication.

For the purpose of restricting the above-mentioned restriction, two spectra of modalities are defined for the sake of optimal freedom in activities $A$ restricted by fair means.

(1) The first spectrum is defined as that regime $P$ governing activities $A$ in the absence of any obstructions; it is designated freedom, or F1. In other words, F1 assigns the following interpretation to the fulfillment of the optative modalities connected with $A$: if T is an aim in $A$ and $A$ provides (i) sufficient means and (ii) all necessary means for realizing T in $A$, then T is fulfillable in $A$. F1 clearly corresponds to the purposefulness of $A$ and would be violated in any situation where (i)–(ii) hold but T has been (or will be) obstructed.

(2) The second spectrum is defined as that regime $P$ governing activities $A$ such that no act in $A$ is forced by coercion, fraud, or any other violation of the fairness of means provided for the course of $A$; it is designated freedom$_2$, or F2. In other words, $A$ is said to possess property F2 whenever every act in $A$ is free from compulsion, i.e., is exercised in accordance with the Creative Subject's free will. Clearly, the satisfiability of F2 captures exactly what is intended by justfulness of $A$, and the spectrum of F2 modalities is precisely all instances of installments of given activities of $A$ for which fair means have been provided.

The spectra of modalities for A thus split into two basic components: F1 and F2. By passing to the direct limit of the projections of F1 and F2 on any $A$, the composite F1F2 obtains. It corresponds to that regime $P$ for which freedom$_1$ and freedom$_2$ hold simultaneously, and if $A$ possesses property F1F2, we shall say that $P$ is "Free" for $A$ or that the activities comprised by the situations generated by $A$ are "Free" activities in the regime $P$. The basic tenet of Yessenin-Volpin's Free ethics, or our ultra-ethics, is that all modalities connected with just and purposeful activities $A$, including their spectra, are reducible to the modalities of the direct limit F1F2.

* * *

As will become apparent in the following chapters, classifications of arrows may be considered the main problem of constructive conceptualism in Cartesian Closed Categories.

*Cartesian Closed Categories* are defined in MacLane, *Categories*, pages 95–6[9]. Although the present work is more than just a technical monograph in algebra, Toposes and Cartesian Closed Categories are sophisticated objects, and it would be misleadingly facile to tell the non-expert reader that e.g., a Category is a semigroup with unit.

To continue, in the following chapters, we will look at morphisms of the developmental kind

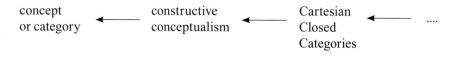

concept or category ← constructive conceptualism ← Cartesian Closed Categories ← ....

\*\*\*

An overall purpose of this work is to extend the realm of the tautologous. Methods are provided for analyzing the grammar of partially intuitive, partially human-constituted systems so that their outputs can be duplicated by computations employing the most meager choice of elements. The systems are thus considered to have been incorporated in the realm of the "trivial." Thus, for example, the system of "trivialities" expounded in this book (including what is developed in the following chapters) can be used to model the whole of mathematics. Cf. the work of Lawvere or Yessenin-Volpin.

On the other hand, one's relation to noemas never becomes an algorithm.

*Chapter I, Appendix: Further Explanations*

There are a few basic "images" underlying the "mental atomism" propounded in this work. You have formulas, which express thoughts when they are interpreted. These formulas can be generated and collected; then they stand for some particular segment of knowledge. They arise from reflection over perceptions: giving names to perceptions, distinguishing them, operating on them, etc.

On the one hand, we want to look at the foundation, the unreflected moments where something is giving rise to a thought process (the thought process is starting). Some kind of impingement on your consciousness is happening.

On the other hand, you can remember this process. You can focus in on it repeatedly, and it becomes more and more detailed. Now you are viewing it in retrospect and analyzing it. That retrospection by itself is complicated.

What is happening continuously is the dialectic of, on the one hand, building up certain abstract thought patterns; and on the other hand, looking at them (and using the fact that you reflect on this particular way of building thoughts) as you proceed anew. But the noemas (shown as the bottom row of the diagram of the Creative Subject, page 154) stream forth all the time. So you have ongoing reflections, and then more noemas appear, and you proceed anew; but now your previous mentation is stored in memory. If, at some point, you look back at your previous activity of consciousness (upper left of the diagram of the Creative Subject) it is dense to the point of being obscure. In order to make this genesis or history transparent, you must have procedures which cut through the detail, which can retrospectively analyze with little effort—which can re-view frictionlessly.

The dialectical process just described is what goes on in theory-building of this kind. To give a further example: Recall another procedure, the so-called "dialectical triangle." The "dialectical triangle" means that you refuse to identify a previous experience with a present or future experience. You regard an experience as pristine in building on it. In this way you dissociate yourself from everything— you encapsulate your present. But nevertheless, you still have your mental history in your unconsciousness.

*&#42;&#42;&#42;*

An intension is a "sense" supplied to an apparition by the Subject. Or, it is an interpretation of a semantics-intended event. One's state of mind forces the "meaning" of a perception. An intension is structured by collations, which include acts of discernment, identification, and distinction. (An intension thereby involves maps from the Subject to the "real world.") Collations are made unwittingly and are unrecoverable without further analysis. They have the import of assumptions.

*&#42;&#42;&#42;*

Referring to the diagram of the Creative Subject, the bottom row consists of the noemas as they are continuously given (left to right is temporal order). Noemas are languageless, unformalized, epistemically non-classifiable perception-objects. To be aware of a noema is a refined form of consciousness. A perception which is not a noema is said to be "without support" and is considered unworthy.

Set-theoretically, noemas are treated equivocally as distinct empty sets (atoms), or as singletons. (There is some precedent for this in Quine's set theory, in which individuals are equated with their singleton sets, more about this below.)

The entire diagram of the Creative Subject can be interpreted as Volpin's model for intuitionistic Zermelo-Fraenkel set theory without inaccessible cardinals. (Cf. Volpin(2), pages 42–43 for this model.) The columns of the diagram are finite. The bottom row is the proxy for a Dedekind-infinite set in the model. Reading from the left, the elements of the bottom row, the atoms, are indexed by a natural number series outside the model. This indexing series is exhausted by the series of atoms, and there are atoms beyond the indexing series. In one context, the atoms may be thought of as containing the extrinsic indices, which are necessary to reason about them. In another context, the indices are disregarded and the atoms are empty and "unordered." It is not decidable whether an arbitrary perception contains a noema; or whether an arbitrary noema is a genuine empty set.

This work relies on my Postulate of Refined Intuition. A precedent for this postulate was Volpin's Axiom of Irreproachability, stated in Volpin(1), page 221. The Axiom of Irreproachability said that if each step of a construction had a justification in Volpin's prototheory, then the entire construction was correct. This claim was not stronger than Church's Thesis.

My *Postulate of Refined Intuition* requires a Free activity of the Creative Subject. If this is satisfied, then the ambiguity of the noemas as empty sets or singletons can be apprehended.

1 A similar consideration is found in §13 of Bernard Bolzano, *Paradoxes of the Infinite*.
2 The choice of *noemas* is the exception (see page 152).
3 Attitudes toward the modalities of situations.
4 The category $e$ mentioned on page 140 can also be characterized as the space of intensions.
5 A situation S is defined as a class of (meanings of) sentences; see Volpin(2), page 15.
6 Galois connections have to do with the Reflection Principle described here. They are transformations ensuring uniform behavior as between familiar and large objects.
7 "Fibration" is treated mostly in Chapter IV; also Chapter III. The notion has to do with columns in the diagram $\Delta(\Sigma)$ on page 154, and also with transitivity of arrows.
8 Fixed points are defined in Chapter IB in connection with retracts.
9 *Categories for the Working Mathematician* (Springer, 1971).

# THE ELECTRIC HARPSICHORD

© Henry A. Flynt, Jr.

Written in New York, 1998. First published in
*The Electric Harpsichord* (Die Schachtel, 2010).

Catherine Christer Hennix performed *The Electric Harpsichord* (hereafter *EH*) on March 23, 1976, as part of her program *Brouwer's Lattice* at the Moderna Museet in Stockholm. At the time, all I knew about the event was the program notes she sent me, which seemed to return to the fifties practice of justifying music by scientific references. That summer, she was in New York and temporarily stored a satchel of documentations in my apartment. For some reason, out of curiosity, I took *EH* out and played it. It took me completely by surprise. It came from a place I didn't know existed; and I wouldn't have expected it to be technically realizable. One felt as if one had tuned to a broadcast originating somewhere other than planet Earth. Not that it was oddly clanky or screechy or incomprehensibly boring—"modern" composers had been writing that for decades. There was a luminous intelligence embodied in a tonal and justly tuned program. The frequency spectrum was dense, saturated, with twinkling attacks, humming bass, diffraction, and pulsing—without any thematic organization. The tonality and timbre were delectable (with an edge of anxiety)—that's why you could draw near it. Twinkling frequencies swept through the spectrum in waves, boiling through each other—shifting the phase. One apprehended a new kind of logic/*ratio* in the event. I wanted to call it a hallucinatory sound environment.

To me, the most wonderful moments were the beginning and end of the tape, which were created by the way the sound check was produced. The long fade-up of the hum, which resolves into high twinkling attacks. And the end, when the hum drops away to uncover a sine tone, which is abruptly faded, leaving an extraordinary charged silence.

Later I learned more about how Christer had come to the integration of methods. Christer's father was an amateur Arabic scholar. Christer's mother, Margit Sundin-Hennix, was a woman of independent means and a jazz composer. Christer played drums in her brother's jazz band, starting as a child, and as a teenager met prominent New York jazz musicians on their visits to Stockholm.

Christer joined the Electronic Music Studio of the Swedish Broadcasting Corporation in the late sixties. "International Style" composers such as Xenakis were her models. She had two compositions of note published—including *Text/Sound Composition 5*, one of the first published records of computer music.

In 1969, at age 21, Christer met La Monte young; and hearing Young's constantly maintained sine-wave drone transformed her conception of music. Young played a tape of "The Well-Tuned Piano" for Christer. She soon began to assist Young, realizing one of Young's "Drift Studies" for him in 1970.

In July 1970, Young insistently invited Christer to come to St. Paul de Vence to hear Pandit Pran Nath, who was touring with Young and Terry Riley. Hearing Guruji's tamburas transformed Christer's conception of music once again. She went to Berkeley in 1971 and 1973 to study mathematical logic and pursue music. In May 1971, she became a disciple of Guruji's in a ceremony in Terry Riley's loft in San Francisco.

Meanwhile, she continued to work in algorithmic music theory, announcing "infinitary compositions" as a genre inspired by Young. In 1973, she was a teaching assistant to Guruji at Mills College and toured in California with Guruji and Terry. That same summer, she wrote a proposal for a course in algorithmic music theory (for computer realization), a course which never took place.

In *Brouwer's Lattice*, Christer speaks of computer synthesis as the ideal means of realizing the music, and she says it again in an interview in 1982 (when she was teaching mathematics and computer science at New Paltz). Christer's work with computer music ended in the early Seventies because the funding was cut. All the same, Christer told me in a conversation in 1978 that she had concluded that the commercially manufactured synthesizers were inadequate. Their designers knew nothing about the musical goals (aesthetics, sensibility). Nothing worthwhile could be done with them. So it was that Christer came to perform on musical instruments fed into electronic processors, supported by custom-made precision audio generators.

It is hard to say whether one enjoys the recording more if one does not know how it was made or if one knows how it was made. Playback should be without excessive bass. The effects change with the listener's spatial position. You hear dense, twinkling frequencies, and bass tones—with the density of a hum; and waves sweep through the spectrum. (One less appreciative listener called it the smoke-alarm philharmonic.) In fact, Christer used a tunable Yamaha keyboard with the harpsichord stop. The scale is an interpretation of the scale of raga Multani. (Christer had been given Daniélou's *Tableau comparatif des intervalles musicaux* by La Monte and Marian, and consulted it when composing the scale.) Christer devotes the left hand to a broken open chord, and the right hand to melismas. The input is layered with a long delay using the two tape recorder method. Periodically, Christer drops out, and the tape system plays by delay. So there comes to be a saturation of harpsichord attacks, and waves of frequencies boiling through the spectrum, turning the pulsation.

The first live performance of *EH* was the last. I assume it would have been extraordinary to witness, to experience this mass of unearthly sound being driven by a keyboard player. In the late Seventies, when we were exchanging proposals for a new science, a number of ideas suggested themselves. One was of a science neither psychology nor physics, which sought the (verifiable-by-inspection) law of what consciousness discerned or recognized in an involuted external process. Another was the idea of a process largely set in motion mechanically, wherein improvisational control was necessary to drive the process. (A mechanical process with nonautomatable control.) Another was to ingest a psychotropic drug, and use the induced consciousness as a lens onto the drug's physical structure.

These projects had a common feature, which traces back to the culture of tuning championed by La Monte Young. The thrust of modern technology was to transfer the human act to the machine, to eliminate the human in favor of the machine, to study phenomena contrived to be independent of how humans perceived them. In contrast, the culture of tuning, which Young transmitted by example to his acolytes, let conscious discernment of an external process define the phenomenon. The next step is to seek the laws of conscious discernment, or recognition, of the process. And the next step is to invent a system driven by improvisation monitored by conscious apperception of the process.

If I had known what *EH* was, and if I had known that the first live performance would be the last, I would have gone to Stockholm to hear it. Later that year, Christer mailed me the catalogue for her second installation at Moderna Museet,

*Toposes & Adjoints.* Looking at this document after hearing *EH*, I began to wonder if the algebraic epistemology therein was the *ratio* which had informed *EH*.

I had the tape played on WBAI-FM in New York on October 17, 1977. Arriving in New York on December 11, 1977, Christer seemed a person who took Establishment rank for granted, who was poised for increasing success. But it didn't exactly play out that way. Christer became a mathematics professor at New Paltz. But her art did not really acquire a public, and the public never became involved in *EH* as I did. All the same, she played the tape at Experimental Intermedia in April 1978 (a stressful time for her personally because of her opening at Redbird Gallery the preceding New Year's).

To me, *EH* was something other than music. Christer and I had extensive exchanges assessing the genre as part of our proposals for a new science. It was a new genre, or chapter, in "psychology."[1] Called a hallucinatory sound environment or illuminatory sound environment, it is a taped synthesis of musical sounds, typically using modal scales and sensuously appealing timbres. Source programs come from musical instruments, but envelopes may be disguised. The source programs are semi-regular, but detail is improvised. The input is layered electronically, producing accidental concurrences and diffraction effects or phasing. The resulting aural events are elusive and saturate the spectrum. The listener's attention is monopolized; the physical vibration is physically felt; the uniformity of texture produces a sense that time is suspended. This aural texture works, without any themes to recognize, to stimulate hallucination or logically anomalous perceptions. They call, in turn, for new logico-mathematical *ratios*.

As an homage to Christer's discovery, I produced two tape compositions in the genre. We presented our tapes at a concert at The Kitchen in New York in 1979. There was a catalogue in which I had a six-page essay on *EH*, and Christer supplied the text "17 Points on Intensional Logics for Intransitive Experiences." As the one-page "Program Notes" that I prepared makes clear, I was intensely aware that we were defending a vision *from* the inimical, crushing weight of the prevailing sensibility.

Somehow I insisted on retyping and editing Christer's essay for the catalog. That led to a separate dispute—because the first sentence seemed to me to have a category error. It said that the music gave you gratifying feelings of dignity.[2] I objected that the phrasing disregarded the meaning of dignity as intrinsic worth; Christer wanted something outside to give you a gratifying impression of intrinsic worth. I changed the sentence; but Christer and a friend complained that an urgent meaning had been lost. When we edited the text again in the nineties, we brought the sentence back close to the original.

I mentioned *EH* in the prospectus for a new science in "The Crisis in Physics and the Question of a New Science" in 1978.

I had *EH* in mind when I talked in personhood theory about inspiration beyond anything you ever want to encounter. Encounter with something that solves a problem for you, that you would not have scripted; it has the advantage of you.

I had *EH* in mind when I stated the problem of the new medium (a non-discursive medium) of the transmission of cultural values.

Let me suggest the flavor of Christer's explanations of the work. In a conversation this year, Christer equated the feeling of dignity with the feeling of enjoying the world's respect; and went on to say that the sound was meant to create a "charged space" for the mind so the mind is *charged* in a conducive manner—the mind becomes open-ended in both temporal directions, so that consciousness glides without friction, and ideas link up effortlessly. In an unused draft from 1979, Christer wrote:

> *Music is here considered as an extension of the language of inner representations in situations in which both spoken and written languages are impossible. ... The term "music" is here reserved for what I have called realizations of subjectively—real environments in sound and light. ... It would be an understatement to say that music is just an extension of the language of inner representations because the music I have in mind also serves as an amplification of that language. For example, I consider the sound waves of this music to induce states of awareness which have a modulatory effect on perceptions and states of inner illuminations, to a degree that gives the concept "reality" an extrapolated meaning in the presence of these sound waves. This extension of meaning can be accounted for by the concept of intensionality, a concept which functions as a selector for interpretations of semantics-intended events, and which receives a particularly critical excitation in the presence of my music. So does also the concept of intransitivity of the relationship between the self and the world.*

We have the notices which the 1979 Kitchen concert received from critics, and they were hardly encouraging.[3] I knew Tom Johnson, the key reviewer in New York, personally; he had recently moved around the corner from me and from The Kitchen.[4] His mention of our concert came in a review of another event; he said that our music did not have its intended effect on him.

In Stockholm, in March 1976, the audience had been enthusiastic about the concerts, but the curators discouraged Christer. Christer had wanted to follow Young's precedent, maintaining the setup over a long stretch of time, performing periodically so that the realization was sampled by the audience. In the interview in *Brouwer's Lattice*, Christer emphasized the battle for sponsorship of long performances. But it ended abruptly. After the 1976 installations, Christer was blackballed in Sweden by the curators. The tape was never broadcast on Swedish radio.

So, the donated support, which is the precondition for any cultural submission becoming publicly visible or being publicly sustained, didn't reach the necessary threshold for Christer (or for our joint efforts in this area). *EH* remained invisible. As a resource that accomplished, and intimated, unearthly imaginative modalities and technologies, *EH* drove me to an explosive reexamination—but the excitement remained my private affair.

Today, unfortunately, Christer no longer has the tuning standards and scale computations. Only an approximate setup diagram can be reconstructed. The master tape was crushed in storage. This landmark of imagination and consciousness just barely survives.

I should say something about Christer's relation to the European scene. I have often expressed a dim view of the path European civilization took—from the beginning. As I have to keep repeating to defensive readers, I do not mean to compare Europe invidiously to the U.S.A. By "European," I include the settler colonies and those parts of Asia which have embraced capitalism and modernism. *EH* escapes the European tradition's course. As we see from the many references in *Brouwer's Lattice* and *Toposes & Adjoints*, Christer wanted to join the cultural elite—but the cultural elite wasn't having any part of it.

I don't classify *EH* as music. That label limits it far too much, since *EH* is like a model for an environment, without a beginning or end—since it concerns tuned texture rather than thematic articulation. Up through 1976, Christer had used the phrase "infinitary composition." The nearest term for the point I want to make, in the culture we are trapped in, is "psychology." *EH* certainly has a *ratio*—that aspect was a profound one in informing the piece—but it is not the *ratio* of European music (especially serious modern music). Somehow Christer absorbed modern audio techniques but managed to find a purpose for the devices totally disconnected from the precedents. The International Style's authority was swept away by Young's drone and Guruji's tamburas. Christer is one of a tiny number of European artists who escaped the tradition's course and did something unclassifiable and out of this world.

1. That we only have this one word for everything from quality and structure of perception, to personality and identity, to life with others governed by value-hierarchies is more evidence of the culture's loathing of humanness.
2. I had spoken of dignity in "Geniuses' Liberation Project" in 1975; Christer's writing of the late Seventies foregrounded the notion. Later I worked at creatively explicating the word.
3. *New York Times* reviewer Ken Emerson was more generous to me than to Christer. He assumed, overall, that our purpose was to entertain by producing mental vacancy.
4. A review Johnson wrote of my band in 1975 had been killed by Robert Christgau.

*References*
Catherine Christer Hennix, *Identitäten II* (Kerberos, Stockholm, 1968).
Catherine Christer Hennix, *Text/Sound Composition 5* (Fylkingen, Stockholm, 1969).
Catherine Christer Hennix, *Brouwer's Lattice* (Moderna Museet, Stockholm, March 1976).
Catherine Christer Hennix, *Notes on Toposes & Adjoints* (Moderna Museet, Stockholm, October 1976).
Catherine Christer Hennix, *17 Points on Intensional Logics for Intransitive Experiences, 1969–1979*, 1979, manuscript.
Henry Flynt and Christer Hennix, "HESE Logic & Intensional Logics," booklet, 1979.
Press Release (one page), The Kitchen, New York, February 7, 1979.
Program Notes (one page), The Kitchen, New York, February 7, 1979.
Ken Emerson in *The New York Times*, February 9, 1979, p. C27.
Tom Johnson in *The Village Voice*, March 19, 1979; also *The Voice of New Music* (1989), p. 378.

# PHILOSOPHY OF CONCEPT ART: A CONVERSATION WITH HENRY FLYNT

Conversation took place in New York City, December 6, 1987. First published in *Io #41: Being = Space × Action*, ed. Charles Stein (North Atlantic Books, 1989). Reprinted and revised on the occasion of the joint exhibitions, *7 Homotopies (How One Becomes the Other) Homotopies Between Sounds and Lights* by Catherine Christer Hennix and *Concept Art 50 Years Anniversary* by Henry Flynt, at Grimm Museum, Berlin, July 15 — August 14, 2011.

Henry Flynt

I'm going to give a summary of how I originated Concept Art in order to bring it up to the point where it's understandable why I speak of you [Catherine Christer Hennix] as my only successor in the genre. Summarizing briefly, I see two things coming together. One of them was my involvement with the modern music community of the time—Stockhausen, Cage, La Monte Young—and the other aspect was that I had been a mathematics major at Harvard and already knew that I thought of myself primarily as a philosopher; that my intention had been when I was very young, when I didn't understand the situation that I was in, to become a philosopher with nevertheless a specialization in mathematics. Of course, many people actually did that.

So, having said that, one of the things that I began to notice about the modern music of that time was this extremely strong pseudo-intellectual dimension in Stockhausen—Stockhausen's theoretical journal *die Reihe*—the impression that they were actually doing science. For example, Stockhausen had a long essay on how the duration of the notes had to correspond to the twelve pitches of the chromatic scale...

Catherine Christer Hennix

"...how time passes..." [*die Reihe* 3].

HF

Yes, and what is more, the other rhythms had to correspond to the overtone structure above those frequencies as fundamentals.

CCH

Yes, I'm quite familiar with that.

HF

Yes, I would expect you would be. I remember Bo Nilsson—you will like this—in 1958 at the same time I saw Stockhausen's score. [Nilsson] went even one step further than Stockhausen because he used fractional amplitude specifications—so this is even more than Stockhausen, and so forth and so on.

Cage took a considerable step further in the sense that, in Cage, this kind of play with structure is carried to the point where there is an extreme dissociation between what the composer sees and what the performer sees in terms of the structure of the piece and what the audience knows. They are completely divorced from one another. Cage would compose a piece on a graph in which the time that a note begins is on one axis and the length of the note is on another axis. What he would do was to superimpose that on some picture, like from a star catalog—

CCH

*Atlas Eclipticalis.*

HF

Yeah, well, that's the particular piece. I'm making up a composite of his compositional techniques, but the result is that when you break up a sequential event in that way, it's not like a pitch-time graph where there's an intuitive recognition of the way the process unfolds. He would have one structure for beginnings and another structure for durations. Well, at any rate, already in Cage's music there was a kind of ritual aspect to performing classical music. I mean in Cage's piece, which is actually all silence—the only thing the pianist does is open and close the lid of the piano or something like that.

Then La Monte Young comes along. His word pieces were the first that I ever saw, composed in mid-1960. I saw them in December 1960. It was a very different kind of structural game. It was no longer like twelve-tone organization and so forth, but, rather, it was like playing with paradoxes—it was nearer to making a paradox than making some kind of complicated network.

And I felt that matters had reached the point where there was some kind of inauthenticity here, because the point of the work of art had become some kind of structural or conceptual play, and yet it was being realized under the guise of music so that the audience had no chance of really seeing what was supposed to be the point of the piece. The audience was actually prevented from seeing. Certainly Cage's methods had exactly that effect. The audience receives an experience which simply sounds like chaos, but, in fact, what they are hearing is not chaos but a hidden structure which is so hidden that it cannot be reconstructed from the performed sound. It's so hidden that it can't be reconstructed, but nevertheless Cage knows what it is. So I felt that the confusion between whether they were doing music or whether they were doing something else had reached a point where I found that disturbing or unacceptable.

At the same time, at that period, there was a great fascination in sort of taking the Stockhausen attitude and looking back at the history of music from that point of view. Stockhausen's analysis in *die Reihe* 2 of Webern's String Quartet [*Opus 28*] tried to show that Webern was composing total serial music and not just twelve-tone music. That was the attitude: they were rewriting the history of music, trying to show that all previous important figures were essentially preoccupied with structure, that they had been complete structuralists.

CCH

Really? I thought it was only Webern that was given that treatment.

HF

Well, they were digging up all these composers from the Middle Ages, the isorhythmic motet and everything like that. They were sort of dredging that up because that was the previous period—the medieval scores in the form of a circle and the use of insertion syncopation.[1] It appears with the red notes in a medieval score, and then it reappears in Stockhausen's *Klavierstück XI*. They were just jumping—they were dismissing what we would call the baroque, classical, and romantic periods as completely worthless. In other words, the last music before Stockhausen was in the fourteenth century—this is the way the history of music was being rewritten. And La Monte was getting into Leonin and Perotin and all that kind of stuff. Well, anyway, that's quite an excursion. At any rate, there is in music, there is this preoccupation with—it may be a kind of quasi-Pythagoreanism, I don't know.... .

CCH

The way I looked at it was, what they saw in Webern—first of all, the harmony was going away. And they saw in Webern a way of determining the note more and, more precisely, in terms of all of its parameters—pitch, duration, timbre, and all that. What was left was that timbre was not serialized yet. And that, as far as I see it, was what the Darmstadt School did. They added—

HF
Stockhausen's *Kontra-Punkte*—

CCH
Yeah. And they all considered Webern the god of the new music—

HF
Yes—

CCH
—and also a little bit Messiaen—

HF
Yes.

CCH
It was Webern and Messiaen that determined the entire Fifties in Darmstadt. In other words, they were saying that Cage was no good. He was just looking in *I Ching*—it was a random thing. And you cannot recover the structure—it's hidden, as you said. The problem was that Stockhausen, when he played his *Klavierstück XI*, you couldn't recover the structure either. It was so complex now. So the complexity of the serialist music became exactly the complexity of Cage. Cage looked his numbers up in random number tables; the others were sitting calculating rows of numbers. But in addition to that, they also had to fake it. Because— you find that yourself when you do serial music—the music moves too slowly. So you change the numbers to get the music up a little bit.

HF
Yes. We're taking longer on this than I meant to...

CCH
But I wanted to say this. The completely deterministic composition technique and the completely random aleatoric technique gave exactly the same results. And that was the complete breakdown of the Darmstadt School. That's when they started to improvise in Darmstadt. Not before that was there improvisation in Darmstadt.

HF
When they first tried to serialize duration, they tried to pick a fundamental unit and use multiples of it; in other words, that's not the way you serialize pitch. You don't take one cycle per second, and then use two cycles per second, up to twelve. That's not what you do. But that's what they did with duration. And that's what produced the Boulez pieces that move so slowly. In other words, if you treat rhythm as multiples of, like, a whole note then it was moving too slowly for them.

But Cage was for them what was wrong with America or something. I mean, the center of what Stockhausen was doing was the concept of scientificity. In other words, at the time I fantasized the composer appearing as performer, on the stage in a lab coat carrying a slide rule—there were no electronic calculators at that time, it would have to have been a slide rule—but that seemed completely appropriate. In other words, a composition was a laboratory experiment. I mean, they viewed Cage as a typical American—coming in a vacuum—American superficiality—a vacuum with no scientificity. But Cage was actually not using a random number table, he was flipping coins, he was using the *I Ching*. Yet it was not even that—what Cage was doing was much more whimsical than using a random number book. He would just copy a leaf—in the *Concert for Piano and Orchestra*, he just put the staff over a leaf, and then the main points defining a shape of the leaf, he just copied them on and he ended up with a circle—or not a circle, but a group of notes in cyclic shape—and so the pianist was supposed to play around the circle. The was completely whimsical actually and yes, I remember very well these debates that they had, the one and the other[2]—I didn't have any idea that I was going to spend this much time competing with the music critic of the *New York Times* about who remembers the 1950s the best.

At any rate… There is, of course, a larger tradition in art which has a kind of quasi-scientific involvement in structure that does go very much to the Renaissance, for example. Although I was not so conscious of that—I looked that up much later. But it was certainly there.

So, on the one hand, concept art came from the idea of lifting structure off and making a separate art form out of it. The structure or conceptual aspect, and making a separate art form out of it. The other thing that was coming—the development of my philosophical thinking—I have to explain first that the version of mathematics that I received at Harvard in the 1950s, in which W.V. Quine was the head of the department and editor of the *Journal of Symbolic Logic* and so forth, and the hottest thing in philosophy was considered to be Quine's debate with Carnap. And I was a schoolmate of Saul Kripke, Robert M. Solovay, Nelson Goodman, etc., etc., etc. I'm just mentioning that to locate the period of time. Actually my conversations with them were insignificant as far as the philosophy of mathematics was concerned, there was no discussion between me and them on any of that, but it will locate the time frame that I'm talking about.[3]

But observing what was going on at that time, I picked up the idea that the most plausible explanation of what mathematics is, is that it is an activity analogous to chess, or in other words, that chess captures the characteristic features of mathematics, even though, as I have told you privately many times, everybody knew who Brouwer was and what the intuitionist school was, but nobody studied it, and, from my point of view, looking at it and knowing what it was, I felt no inclination to pursue it further.

The reason why this chess game explanation of mathematics seemed so plausible—you know, at the end of the nineteenth century they found themselves with three geometries—this is not Henry Flynt saying this, this is the canard, the story in the text books—there were three geometries; one of them fit the real world. They thought it was Euclidean, but it might not be. It might be one of the others, like elliptic, for example; nevertheless, all three were consistent. Now, what was the epistemological status of the two out of the three geometries that were true without having any correspondence to the real world, while one of them did have a correspondence to the real world and was also true? But what of the other two—the ones that were called true even though they had nothing to with the world? You know presumably Hilbert wrote *Foundations of Geometry* as the original answer to that question.

Although—I can't pursue this here, it is much too technical—this is now an open question for me. It has never been an open question in the past. I just accepted what I was told—that Hilbert solved this by seeing that a system of mathematics that has no relation to the real world—in what does its truth consist? Its consistency as an uninterpreted calculus as they would say—axioms, proofs, formation rules, transformation rules. Certainly it was clear in the early twentieth century that the concept of an abstract space was established. This was what geometry was about. Geometry did not attempt—in Kant's time it was assumed that when you were talking about geometry you were talking about the geometry of the real world—that's the only geometry that there was—the idea that there was a different agenda for geometry other than the real world—how Kant could have moved geometry into the constitutive subject and said that it was congenital to the mind—Euclidean geometry. In hindsight that seems to be one of the biggest mistakes he made, tremendously embarrassing, because by the mid-twentieth century, it was completely taken for granted that the job of the mathematician was to study structures which do not have any reality. And that from time to time you will give an interpretation to one or the other of these structures, like a physical interpretation, and then it may be found to be true or false in reality or not. Meanwhile, you have another sense of the word "interpretation" which has to do with relative consistency proofs by something having a model.

This is now a completely open question for me, what they thought they were doing. In other words, what Hilbert thought that he was doing…he interpreted one or another non-Euclidean geometry—what was the interpretation that he used? It was a denumerable domain of algebraic numbers [*Foundations of Geometry*, page 27–30].

CCH

I think his ideas go back to Klein's models—which are Euclidean in the center of the circle and then at the periphery they have turned non-Euclidean (in the complex plane).

HF

You had to have an explanation of how mathematics could be true in any sense whatsoever even though any claim of a connection with the real world had been completely severed, and it was being pursued in some kind of vacuum. What does mathematics mean in that case? And the answer that Hilbert gave was that it does not have to mean anything.

That's the answer. So it's a chess game. And the only difference between mathematics and a chess game is that there are additional complications created in mathematics by the fact that it deals with infinitary games. By the way, I completely overlooked that aspect at that time. You know, I can only see it now, kind of like two superimposed pictures, because I see what I know now and compare it with what I knew then.

CCH

Yeah, the same for myself. I didn't know that this idea of Hilbert's was forced by Frege until later. Frege was the one who said that either the parallel axiom is true, or it's not. Which way do you want it? And so he caused the big stir in the foundations of geometry in the end of the nineteenth century, and that's why he became enemies with Hilbert. They were life enemies.

HF

The reason I see it like two superimposed transparencies—

CCH

But even today this debate with Frege—you have to go to a single volume in Frege's posthumous writings—it is not mentioned in any single textbook, no lecture mentions it, and, so far, nobody has explained it properly.[4]

HF

Yes, yes, yes. You're talking about an obscure origin of something, and what I'm talking about is a kind of consensus that had grown up, since everybody agreed that mathematics should study unreal structures.

CCH

But that consensus was *forced* on us, that *that* was what we were supposed to do.

HF

The problem then—I thought mathematics was like chess. What I understand now is that even a good formalist would not agree with that. A good formalist would say that when you have a finite game like chess, the problems of validity and soundness become transparent or intuitively ascertainable; therefore, a finite game is too trivial to be a proxy for mathematics. At that time I did not understand that distinction. I've read in many books since then that mathematics is the science of infinity—that is the way mathematics is defined now in half of the books that I look at. But at that point I did not understand. I thought the finite game was already—I mistakenly thought—a complex enough problem to stand for mathematics. Or that the reliability of a finite game was sufficiently complicated to stand for mathematics, so I basically focused just on a finite game.

CCH

By the way, this was exactly the late Wittgenstein's view of the philosophy of mathematics—it's not a complete misunderstanding. That is to say, other people thought of it that way too.

HF

The question then arose of even the soundness, the reliability, the consistency of a finite game—this then is the problem, for example, whether it is possible to follow a very simple rule correctly or not. The other thing that was feeding into everything that was going on was that Wittgenstein's *Remarks on The Foundations of Mathematics* was in the Harvard Bookstore when I walked in as a freshman my very first day there—so, in other words, I was looking at Wittgenstein's *Remarks on the Foundations of Mathematics* from 1956—

**CCH**
Ten years before me—

**HF**
—but very cursorily. Because I had a philosophical agenda—I passed over this material in a very cursory way because I had a philosophical agenda. I was not involved in that.

**CCH**
You thought there was no such distinction?

**HF**
Well, no, I thought that—it didn't seem that there was very much point in worrying about that when there were much more extreme problems to be worried about. But Wittgenstein wrote a lot about the possibility of following very simple rules. And I assumed if there were epistemological questions for mathematics that this game interpretation—this chess interpretation—had displaced the question of the soundness and reliability of the mathematics to the possibility of understanding a very simple rule like writing the series "plus 2."

And having gathered that this was the way that I should picture mathematics—I mean we understood very well that there were other pictures of mathematics, but we thought they were philosophically obsolete. In other words, the person who believed that mathematics was a description of a real supra-terrestrial structure, and certainly there were people like that—

**CCH**
Still today.

**HF**
—we thought that this was a philosophy that had been exposed as superstitious by Positivism and possibly even by Ockham several centuries earlier. So it was not that we didn't know about that. I drew a personal conclusion that that position could not be defended by any arguments that are acceptable by modern standards. What I really meant was by Carnap's standards. That's what modern standards meant to me.

In my philosophy I was not concerned with the specifics of mathematics; I was concerned with the problem of how I know a world beyond my immediate sensations. That was actually the question that I began with—the question of propositions of material fact, like "it is raining" or "the Empire State Building is at Fifth Avenue and 34th Street."

I had read a very simplified exposition—it was actually some lectures that Carnap gave in England in the 1930s on what Positivism was.[5] They were very simple lectures and very different from his actual published books with all these supposed apparatuses and symbols and so forth. A very simple exposition of what it is for a proposition to be meaningful—that it must be empirically testable and so forth and so on, and the solution of questions of metaphysics that make assertions that are not testable are therefore meaningless. That seemed to me, at the time, to be a stunning contribution. Because I come out of a background—I was in high school reading Kant and so forth and so on—and Carnap's solution was much more attractive to me than trying to participate with Kant, to experience his question and try to take one side or the other when he already said it's not really answerable. I solve it by simply having faith or something like that, which is what he said about the famous god, freedom, and immortality—I found it immensely attractive when Carnap came along and said that there is no way of answering questions; therefore, words are being used nonsensically.

I went through a process of thinking about that without ever having seen Carnap's *The Logical Structure of the World*. When I was in Israel Scheffler's philosophy of science class, I tried to write a text which in effect gave my own empiricist constructions of what it means to say that A causes B and so forth, to give empiricist constructive definitions of those—which is, I suppose, in the spirit of Carnap's program, even though I hadn't actually seen what he had written, and if I had it would have confused me—no, I wouldn't say "confused," I would say it would have discredited him completely. I wouldn't say "confused" because that's too modest.

CCH

No, I wouldn't think "confused." I would think it would have upset you.... .

HF

No, I wouldn't say "confused." I would say he had been discredited. I very quickly passed to the position that the propositions of *natural science* were meaningless metaphysics.

CCH

On what basis? Can you pin that down? A little bit, only.

HF

This is something I want to compress—it says a little bit about this in *Blueprint for a Higher Civilization*[6]—like the proposition, "this key is made of iron," or something like that. I comment on that in the essay "Philosophical Aspects of Walking Through Walls."

CCH

I didn't recall the example actually.

HF (reading)

*The natural sciences must certainly be dismantled. In this connection, it is appropriate to make a criticism about the logic of science as Carnap rationalized it. Carnap considered a proposition meaningful if it had any empirically verifiable proposition as an implication. But consider an appropriate ensemble of scientific propositions in good standing, and conceive of it as a conjunction of an infinite number of propositions about single events (what Carnap called "protocol-sentences"). Only a very small number of the latter propositions are indeed subject to verification. If we sever them from the entire conjunction, what remains is as effectively blocked from verification as the propositions which Carnap rejected as meaningless. This criticism of science is not a mere technical exercise. A scientific proposition is a fabrication which amalgamates a few trivially-testable meanings with an infinite number of untestable meanings and inveigles us to accept the* whole conglomeration at once. It is apparent at the very beginning of *Philosophy and Logical Syntax* that Carnap recognized this quite clearly; but it did not occur to him to do anything about it.

    The only point that I'm trying to make here is that I began to move very quickly when I was still very young towards a position of extreme disillusionment and cognitive extremism. I moved very quickly. This was not a slow process. I just immediately took Carnap's critique of metaphysics, decided that it applied directly to natural science—you dismiss natural science as meaningless. The problem: is there an object that is beyond my experience, is there a glass which is beyond what they would call the "scopic" glass, the "tactile" glass [gestures toward the glass from which he has been drinking]—is there a glass other than those glasses? When you first think about it, that question seems to have exactly the status of the propositions about god, freedom, and immortality that Kant said are unanswerable and that Carnap said are meaningless. However, there is one additional step for people who are interested in the history of philosophy. Kant, in the second edition of *Critique of Pure Reason*, added this notorious refutation of idealism to prove the existence of the real world independent of my sense impressions. You may not know about this—this was the basis of Husserl's phenomenology—Husserl's phenomenology was invented in the passage, and it also tremendously preoccupied Heidegger. It was one of the sources which causes Heidegger to say that the essence of Being is Time. Kant said that essentially it is the passage of time which proves that there must be an external world. This is notorious in the history of philosophy. Because, on the one hand, it is so deeply influential for later thinkers; and on the other hand, for example, Schopenhauer said it was a complete disgrace—it was such an obvious sophistry that it was just disgusting, that it had the effect of ruining the *Critique of Pure Reason*.

    Actually this refutation of idealism is distributed throughout the *Critique of Pure Reason*, it's not in any one place—a footnote here, a preface there, another passage somewhere else. In one of the footnotes, Kant makes the same point. In order to ask the question whether there is a glass beyond my sense impression of it—I cannot ask that question... .

CCH

Oh, you mean the *Ding an sich* question.

HF

Well, that's what Kant would have been talking about, but I don't want to fit that narrowly into Kant's controlling the terms of the discussion. I'm trying to ask it as someone who has embraced Logical Positivism and is now turning around to question Logical Positivism—you see the point that I was just making there—when you say that this key is made of iron, which is Carnap's favorite example —and then a protocol sentence, for example, "If I hold a magnet near this key, the key will be attracted to the magnet"—it is not clear where Carnap stands on the question whether only my sense impressions are real—just talking about this situation only my sense impressions are real—or is there supposed to be a *substantial* key?

    By the way, I don't know Carnap's work that well. I passed over these people in a very offhand way, so much so that many times I've talked to people and they've concluded in their own mind that I don't really know philosophy because

I seem to have just glanced at these people—picked up one or two points—the reason for that is that I was moving so quickly to my own terminus, I only needed to see the slightest symptom from these people to know that they were spending all their time worrying about something that it was a waste of time to worry about since it could only be a secondary issue. Here is Carnap with this key made of iron—while I'm trying to ask, is there a key other than the scopic key, the tactile key *now*?—since the past and the future are beyond immediate experience. I mean, they cannot be cited as evidence—or, whether they are evidence or not is the same problem. Should I believe in the glass, even though what I presumably have is a scopic glass—at this very moment, a visual glass apparition, from that, should I conclude a glass?

The first reaction to that question for somebody who is coming from Kant and Carnap and who does not mind how extreme his answer is—that's the key thing. In other words, if I came to a conclusion that was completely untenable as far as social circumstances—that didn't bother me at all. At first, the question whether there is a real glass beyond the apparition would seem to be an unanswerable question—one of Kant's metaphysical questions—but then you think—that if you know what the question means then there must be a realm beyond experience because otherwise it is unclear how the question could be understandable.

From my point of view—if you want to make an issue out of semantics—this is the profound issue. What the mathematical philosophers and philosophers of mathematics were doing, talking about semantics, interpreting geometry as an algebra and algebra as a geometry—really for the purposes of relative consistency proofs or because they found they could solve problems by using a machinery developed in another branch of mathematics by seeing these structural similarities—but to confuse that with what I thought the bona fide semantic question is: How would I understand the question whether there is a substantial glass other than the scopic glass? You know the conclusion—I can't tell you the exact breakdown—but I am talking now about the 1961 manuscript, *Philosophy Proper*.[7] I may have already come to the conclusion at that time—that the question itself forces a yes answer. This does not mean that a proof of the existence of the external world has been given. It meant that the proposition of the existence of the external world would verify itself even if it were false!

CCH

I find this extremely interesting and rewarding what you are saying now because I never heard you say it this way before. I just want to ask you one question before you go on: namely, I see something for the first time which I hadn't seen before—the simple existential statement, "There is a glass on the table." You include that also in what will be doubtable here. In other words, not just "There is a glass on the table," but "There exists a glass"—the existential statement. I guess I wasn't very clear now.

HF

No, the thing is, the approach that I'm taking doesn't break it down the way that you're talking about. Let me tell you, you may not be *sympatico* with empiricism. When you are trying to deal with philosophy at all—you have to make some allowance for the fact—you have to understand that the philosopher may be carving up problems in a way that is temperamentally alien to you.

**CCH**
Yeah…

**HF**
You have to understand that. This is why somebody like Carnap would read Hegel and say it's not saying anything. Actually Hegel is saying something. In fact, you might go so far as to make a case that Hegel is actually rebutting Carnap, because if you understand what Hegel is doing, you realize even more than one would realize anyway that Carnap has an untenable position—that he's sort of—that he wants what he cannot have. He has made a set of rules that does not allow him to have the thing that he demands to have. Hegel would have seen that immediately. Carnap thinks that the problem of a logic of consistency is an easy problem and a solved problem. In effect, Hegel was saying there something very misleading in thinking that that is a solved problem. I'm trying to give you a sense of misunderstandings between philosophers that are the results of temperamental incompatibilities.

**CCH**
What you are giving me is a two-step way to skepticism. You ask a certain question—is there something beyond this perception of the glass? And you say the answer "yes" is forced on me, but then you realize this was a meaningless question.

**HF**
No, it's the other way around.

**CCH**
Oh, okay. But here's where you have to explain in detail, because here's where I miss you.

**HF**
Let me go through the steps again. The series of steps was…. . I'll have to do it all at the same time. You have to understand—I don't think that you even understand what an empiricist is. It's a peculiar attitude. And one of the reasons why you have very little training in this attitude is because people who claim to be empiricists—it's always a fraud. All people who appear in public and say they are empiricists, they are all lying all of the time. The reason that they're lying is that they have this doctrine of the construction of the world from sense impressions. That is their doctrine. But they do not stay with that doctrine. And the reason why they do not stay with that doctrine is because in addition to having the doctrine of the construction of the world from sense impressions, they also want to have things like science—

**CCH**
Ethics…

**HF**
No, not ethics—one of the characteristics of the twentieth-century philosopher was the appearance of the tough-guy philosopher who rejects all of ethics as

meaningless, which Carnap certainly did and people who are close to him like A.J. Ayer—no, they did not want ethics. But they wanted science. And the problem with wanting the construction of the world from sense impressions on the one hand and wanting science on the other is that the two finally have nothing to do with each other at all—and when they said that the two were the same thing, as Carnap did—he was lying. I made a hero out of Carnap—I derived some kind of positive impulse from him or something like that without—I never actually read—my serious reading of Carnap was like three or four pages of excerpts in a paperback popularization. I owned, I had in my library Carnap's so-called real books, like *Logical Foundations of Probability* and *Meaning and Necessity*, and all the rest of them and I never read them.[8] And in hindsight that was good, because I took his slogan seriously and assumed that he meant what he said and drew the necessary consequences of it. If I had actually read his books I would have been thrust into this massive hypocrisy, and I must say, stupidity, because the man did not realize that his answers were not adequate, did not realize how preposterous his constructions of the world were—

CCH
I would say vulgar.

HF
Yes, yes, and…what is even worse about empiricism is, in the case of somebody like Mach, not only does he want to have his sense impressions and does he want to have his science, but he wants to have science explain sense impressions! And, nevertheless, it was supposed to be the sense impressions that were primary, not the science. Mach is seriously telling you, I will tell you why you see a blue book—because the frequency of blue light is—and then he gives some uncountable number, I mean some number that is pragmatically infinite, or something like that. And how do you know that blue light is exactly 3.2794835 times ten to the fifteenth, and not one more or less? Well, certainly not by just looking—I'll guarantee you that! You have to go into a laboratory with a few million dollars' worth of equipment or something. But that's what it is to see that the book is blue.

I'm trying to give you the sense of what it would be to be an authentic empiricist. You ask, *does a glass exist?* An authentic empiricist would have to say that he already has a problem with that—that he has to regard that as an undefined question or statement. It's undefined, because, if you are asking me if at this moment I quote unquote *have*—interesting word there, "have"—that is what our ordinary language gives us as the idiom for this.

CCH
Or "suffer"!

HF
Yes, "have" or "suffer," that's right. *I have* or *I suffer* a scopic glass or visual glass apparition—then that is identically true. That is identically true. If you express any surprise at that, we have a problem here. *I have a scopic glass.* If I say I have an apparitional glass, would that be okay? I mean, from this point of view the sense impression is not open to dispute. It's meaningless to dispute it. It's an impression, an apparition—the sense impression is that for which seeming and being are

identical. For the empiricist, the phase of the world or range of the world for which seeming and being are identical is the sense impression. If that seems strange to you then maybe I can make it less strange by pointing out to you to make this as clear as possible—for the empiricist to say that I have an apparitional glass is to say nothing about Reality with a capital "R" at all! This is the so-called subjective psychological moment—although an empiricist would never say that. The reason an empiricist would never say that is that even to call it subjective is already much too strong because that implies that you can guarantee an objectivity to compare it to. And a bona fide empiricist would not agree that my sense impression is subjective—subjective in comparison to *what*?

CCH

So, an empiricist would be a person who would not doubt whether he had a toothache or not. In other words, if he had a toothache...

HF

I'm not sure about the word "toothache"—if you mean that he would not doubt whether he had a toothache sensation. Whether there is an organic—in the language of medicine—whether there is an organic substrate for the toothache impression—this, in a medical sense, is a question of what is called "hysteria" or something like that.

CCH

Suppose I have a toothache. But now I'm an empiricist, so I say I'm doubting this impression. I probably don't have a toothache.

HF

No, no...

CCH

I have to accept the toothache?

HF

No, you don't have—

CCH

The glass you said was—I couldn't doubt the perception of the glass. You said that was beyond doubt, in some sense, for the empiricist.

HF

It would be some kind of logical mistake to think that there was anything there to be doubted.

CCH

Okay. And the same with the toothache.

HF

Yes, yes. I mean the point is not so much that we have come into an area in which the empiricist is prepared to have faith—that would be completely missing the point. No faith is required—that's the point. The point is that it would be some kind of logical error. Once you understand what a sense impression is, the terminology of doubt does not apply to that level.

**CCH**

I see. Just, that was my question.

**HF**

The terminology of doubt does not apply to apparitions. It doesn't make sense to doubt subjective apparitions. The empiricist is already nervous when you ask, *does a glass exist?* If you are asking whether I have a "scopic" glass, it's identically true. Wait, wait. There are already problems there. I'll come back to them. But when you say—it sounds like what you're asking me is whether the fact that I see a glass is sufficient to prove an objective glass—that sounds like...

**CCH**

No, no, that's not what—

**HF**

Well, okay. Most people, when they say, "Do you concede that there is a glass on the table—I'm sitting here looking at it," what they mean is, "Do you concede that from your visual glass apparition you should conclude an objective glass, a substantial glass?" I'm taking it for granted that you know enough about philosophy to have a sense of the full weight those two words—"substantial" and "objective"—have in philosophy.

**CCH**

Yes.

**HF**

That, at great length, is my reaction to your question about doubting "there is a glass on the table" versus doubting "there exists a glass." A bona fide empiricist would say, "Why are you asking me this? The scopic glass is simply here for me." As far as concluding that an objective glass exists from the existence of that apparition—the traditional problem of concluding whether the apparition is symptom of some transcendent world—I think the word "transcendent" is sometimes used in that sense in philosophy—the world beyond any sense impression—

**CCH**

This is why I used the example of pain—because it would be senseless for me to claim that *I* can have *your* toothache!

**HF**

Now just a minute. An empiricist—what you're really getting at—what you're sort of squeezing out of me here—I'm glad to have it squeezed out of me, I have no embarrassment about this—is that with empiricism either you must be prepared immediately to depart absolutely from the conventional world view, or else you will just plunge yourself into a quicksand of hypocrisy. When you're asking me, *can I have your toothache...* A good empiricist would say, "I have not established so-called other people except the other-people apparitions that occur for me from time to time in waking life *as they do in my dreams!* And are you now going to ask me can I have the toothache of a person who appears to me in a dream?" Then the spotlight would be turned on *you*—what kind of an issue are you trying to make there? What do you believe is the reality status of the furniture in my dreams? For the empiricist, nothing remotely like that question has arisen yet because I haven't got outside of my own quote unquote head yet.

Maybe you're just squeezing more and more. Either the empiricist must be a "madman" or else he must be insincere. I took the alternative of the madman. This is important not for me but for the general public to be told—something which the general public has never been told—and I know why they have never been told—maybe it is necessary to complete this point. The point is that empiricism was contrived to paper over a kind of—I mean, there was sort of this epistemological—science epistemologically was resting on some sort of very shaky foundation. They saw that. They brought in this empiricism in the hope that it would solve a problem, that it would substantiate science while at the same time it would cut away the common-sense notion of causality as being unnecessary to science. Empiricism was going to give you a more sophisticated science that did not need the traditional metaphysical or common-sense notion of causality. It told you how to get along without that, but, at the same time, it validated everything that the scientist needed. And, at the same time, empiricism was supposed to be—in the case of Neurath—he wanted to make some kind of unification of empiricism with Marxism and make it like a complete de-mythified view of society.

CCH

There was even an attempt to bring ethics into it.

HF

Well, in Neurath's case, yes.

CCH

Schlick too, I think—Schlick, I recall, did something in ethics.[9]

HF

I was talking about why empiricism is not portrayed honestly in the general picture that exists of philosophy—the public picture of philosophy. It was brought in to solve the problem of what is a base for science—namely, sense impressions are going to be taken as elemental. Science is going to arise from sense impressions by construction. Nevertheless, it is required that both scientific knowledge and the common-sense social world be produced by this approach—

CCH

Neurath, you mean.

HF

No, no. Well, Carnap did not deny the existence of other people. All of the positivists…

CCH

Rather, he had nothing to say about it.

HF

I didn't say ethics—I said the common-sense social world. I wasn't talking about anything ethical…

CCH

The existence of tables and cars and—

HF

Well, what I'm saying is that the existence of other people is on the same level as the existence of tables and automobiles. And what is even worse than that is that the ones who were scientists in fact wanted to see the perception itself as the product of the abstract and quantified sequence that the biophysicist or the psychophysicist sees—the light, the lens, the retina, the optic nerve, the visual cortex, and so forth and so on. They wanted to have that as prior to the sense impression, but at the same time they wanted to have all that constructed up from the sense impressions. Why would this remain in place? Because it was more palatable—it's just like, why would formalism remain in place? Everybody learns that formalism dies with Gödel's incompleteness theorems—it certainly didn't die for me; it isn't even clear what the incompleteness theorems are supposed to have done or not to have done—the fact remains that if you don't explain mathematics as an uninterrupted calculus, then for us there was nothing left but superstition. Those are the choices that you are given. If you don't explain that science is constructed up from a ground of sense impressions, then how do you want it to be constructed? Down from God? You see, we don't take that seriously anymore.

As a matter of fact, Hume wrote two philosophical works, and in the first work[10] there is the notorious passage in which he himself understands what it means to be a genuine empiricist.[11] He says, "I feel that I am an outcast from the human race," and so forth, in this famous passage. He says, "I do not know if the glass continues to exist after I've looked away from it." That line in Hume should have told you whatever you wanted to know about the existence of the glass. You should be able to ascertain the appropriate answer to your question. Hume says, "I do not know if the glass exists when I look away from it."

Hume's second book,[12] when he was trying to vindicate himself, when he had dropped the whole business of being a madman—it was much nearer to what empiricism means today: An attempt to construct science from a more meager inventory of elements, namely sense impressions. And that is where Hume presents his doctrine that science does not need and should not invoke metaphysical causation; that it should replace the old-fashioned causation with some sort of construction, which is more flat or more network-like.

Well, at any rate, I'm going into this long thing. This is why it's never dealt with in public in a sincere way—the only time it was, was by the guy who invented it, Hume, in the book that he wrote when he was twenty-three years old. That's the only honest version of it, and everything after that is a fraud.

The way it goes is this: I ask the question whether there is a substantial glass, an objective glass, a material glass, something that is over and above the visual glass of the moment. When first considered, this seems to be a question which I have no method of answering. That would seem to place it like a Kantian metaphysical question, which doesn't have a provable solution, though, interestingly enough, Kant thought that the existence of the external world in general could be proved but only in the second edition. And, in that second edition, in those little passages, Kant did really get into the existence of this individual thing, like a unicorn and how that would or would not fit into the general proof of the existence of the world and, also, the question of how dreams would affect the validity of the proof. He touches on all of those in a way which is just awful. It's a disgraceful performance. But he had the issue there, actually.

Well, your first reaction is, "I have no way of answering this." Your second reaction is that if I understand the question, then there must be an external world. So it would seem that I have actually proved the external world—that's what Kant actually said. Or he came very near to saying something like that. The third step is the realization that the statement would validate itself not only if it's true—but if it's false it validates itself equally well!

CCH

Given this method of understanding the question and the method remained unspecified so far—as far as I know, nobody has been able to do very well at specifying it.

HF

What? Do you mean if somebody asks whether there is an external world—my last remark is a comment about semantics—the genuine semantic issue, as I said, and it's very different from the sort of thing that Tarski is going on about, which I think is just ridiculous.

Maybe I'd better stop and tell you why I think it's ridiculous. It's because I'm now talking about things which are exactly the fundamental issues. If Tarski thinks that he can talk about the theory of chess before the question of whether the universe exists or not has been answered—they are deliberately creating specialized problems which in their minds do have answers and then they are proceeding to answer them. The larger question of whether the work has any meaning at all—it's like somebody spending his whole life working on the King's Indian Defense in chess, or something like that, and thinking that somehow makes it necessary to answer such questions as does the chess board exist or is it only apparitional? If it's only apparitional then there is no guarantee of the continuity of the position of the pieces in the *absence of moves*. What happens is that people treat those basic questions as if they are so basic that it's sort of preposterous to make an issue of them. Kripke said very clearly in his book on Wittgenstein that once the question "Does language exist?" has been asked, not to give an affirmative answer is "insane and intolerable."[13] It's the same reaction as there is to solipsism—that solipsism is the philosophy of the man in the lunatic asylum.

The thing that may come before all the discussion so far is the question of *what is my position on being classified as insane?* This is the beginning of philosophy for me.

CCH

Well, this is the classical beginning of philosophy.

HF

Because if you're not willing to face up to being classified as insane—if you want to avoid that confrontation—you can't be a philosopher. That confrontation is at the center of bona fide philosophy.

CCH

Or was… .

HF

Yes. At any rate, I had reached this point in something like 1961. I had not yet done the "Is there language?" trap. But I had reached the point of saying that to claim the existence of a world beyond experience is untenable. However, I understood very well that it begins to create problems for me to say, "I have a visual glass apparition," because there is a lot of structure in that sentence. And it's not clear what is supporting that structure after the world has been cut away. Even the use of idioms like "have" and "suffer." The use of the word "I"—after the objective world has been cut away, it's unclear what is the basis for all of that. And this is the point I had reached in 1961, and this is the point when I did Concept Art.

On the one hand, you have an art which is about structure and conceptual things. On the other hand, this art is not going to *affirm* traditional doctrines of structuredness and conceptualization. It is deliberately in every case going to violate them. It is going to express the fact that there has been a philosophical discovery made. I would have said chess is not a sound game. It's not well founded. It can't be. The whole problem of Wittgenstein's famous question, *what is the meaning of a rule?* My answer would be it doesn't have one. When you look at it from the standpoint of Hume—when he says, "I have become a monster, I am outside the human race"—the standpoint of the person who chooses insanity as opposed to intellectual dishonesty!

The person who chooses being a madman—even chess doesn't work. [There is] the whole question of its consistency. The point of Concept Art is, on the one hand, to transmit the tradition from the isorhythmic motet and the five Platonic solids, in Leonardo—and, on the other, it's to blow it up because each work of Concept Art must be a counter-example to that tradition. And at the same time to say that it is art means—when I passed to Concept Art, I left behind many things that traditionally would have been considered crucial features of art, like sentiment, for example. Let me just leave it at that.

When the Renaissance people did study geometry and art, they developed perspective to paint people, not to paint abstractions. And, you know, I have to admit quite bluntly, my Concept Art was already the product of the acceptance of an abstract art. And now, many years later, I can see that that was an historical juncture, to consider it tolerable that art should break with sentiment and with the representation of people. It's like moving toward an Islamic view of art. And then saying now, however, in the future, instead of Mosque decoration we will do a piece that has the visual, sensuous delectation, but it's completely abstract. But, whereas Islamic art was trying to express the *truth* of a certain theorem in group theory, Concept Art must express that you can't have that—that that theorem fails. Now I'm formulating an unsolved problem—I never did a concept piece the purpose of which was to rebut the symmetry involved in a visual pattern, with that as the opponent to be hit. I mean, I very well could and perhaps should.

All of my pieces except one were uninterpreted calculi, because I accepted that that was the only way of explaining what mathematics is: That it consists of a body of truth about a world that does not exist, and explicitly so. And that all of the traditional explanations of mathematical content are now seen to be anachronistic superstitions. They are just indefensible in the modern world. Put those two things together, and mathematics becomes a chess game, an uninterpreted calculus.

All of my Concept pieces are using the terminology of Carnap's *Logical Syntax of Language*—the formation rule, the transformation rule—but in each case, they wish to express the violation, the failure of some traditional organizing principle of these uninterpreted calculi. For instance, there is one where, among other things, the very notation itself has an undisplaced active interaction with the subjectivity of the quote-unquote reader.[14] And that determines the structure of the derivation, the proof. It was pointed out to me many years later that it's not just that you don't get this in schoolbook mathematics—this is what they are *most concerned to exclude*.

I had another one in which there was no general transformation rule.[15] There were only completely nominalistic transformation rules. In other words, for each step you are told, for that step only and for this moment only, what the transformation rule is. And by the time you are ready to take the next step, that rule is forgotten and inoperative.

CCH
This is the *Energy Cube Organism*?

HF
No, no. The *Energy Cube Organism* was not Concept Art at all. No, no. It was a different genre. That one was the piece called *Transformations*. The *Energy Cube Organism* and the *Perception-Dissociator*, in my own classification, are not Concept Art. Only the pieces labeled "Concept Art" are Concept Art. And I only did five of them until 1987. Three of them are in *An Anthology*, and the fourth was published in *dimension* 14 (1963). The *Energy Cube Organism* and the *Perception-Dissociator* were in other genres. I drew these distinctions of genre rather narrowly, actually.

This is the one [pointing to 6/19/61 in *An Anthology*] where there is, in an uninterpreted calculus, interaction between notation and the subjectivity of the quote unquote reader.

This is *Transformations*. You are just taking these objects, you are burning them, melting them, doing all sorts of things to them. The point of this is that each step in the proof—you have to think of it as a proof—you see it has the tree structure of a proof. These are my nominalistic transformation rules, because each rule is stipulated only at that step, and then it is thrown away. The point that I was trying to express if was that's what they do in all of it—even in chess, when you move the pawn to king's bishop three, you think that you are conforming to a general rule written in heaven. But, in fact, there isn't any general rule, and when you move the pawn to bishop three, you're just making up what you are doing right at that moment, and there isn't any general rule.

CCH
You would label this ad hoc?

**HF**

That's right. That would be perhaps a better word for it. All transformation rules and probably even all formation rules are ad hoc, yes, yes.

I said "nominalistic" because they are only there individually. They do not add up to any general—

**CCH**

System of rules?

**HF**

No, not that. They do not add up to any generality, to a general rule that covers all cases of a certain class.

What is inadequate about this—and I realized very quickly that it's inadequate—is that this does not actually give some profound reason in concrete practice for questioning chess. That's what the inadequacy of the original Concept Art pieces is. That they don't really give you some kind of operative situation where you can see that following the chess rules is failing. I don't provide that. I only provide something that's ritualistic. Saying, *this is how you would behave if you realized that following any rule is ad hoc.*

A conventional mathematician would say, *you have not proved that the world that this is designed for is the world that I have to live in. That's* the inadequacy. He would say that I am only ritualizing the world of impoverishment or disorganization. I'm not showing that that's the world that people in general have to live in because it's in force. That's the difference between then and now. The reason that I want meta-technology would be to give a situation where somebody can actually see that you *can't* play a game of chess—or, that you want to play one, and that I, by putting it in the appropriate context, make it clear that the general rules on which playing it depends are not in fact available.

But to show that in a serious way, from the prevailing point of view, I would be talking about contriving a miracle. In other words, to actually substantiate any of these—what is interesting is not so much *Transformations*—but it would be some situation that would substantiate that the conventional view is actually unavailable. And to do that you have to violate what are considered today to be the soundest laws of science. I'd need a miracle to manifest that I'm right, so to speak. So, by the time I get to meta-technology, I'm in the job of constructing miracles—I mean, constructing situations that are absolutely physically impossible (or in some cases, logically impossible) by currently accepted scientific and commonsense views of what is the real world.

*Innperseqs* is the one that is visually sensuously the best. You are making a rainbow halo that you can get by breathing on your glasses and looking at a point light—you get a rainbow halo around the light. Eventually I will set it up so that you don't need glasses or anything, so that the whole business of seeing the rainbow halo is moved out and does not require any special preparation by the spectator. The rainbow halo is the sensuous delectation. The derivation, the proof, the specification of propositions, is something that you do as the halo is fading. You have to quickly specify—I never analyzed exactly what was going on there but it was as if—you have a notation which is externally changing, and therefore the quote unquote reading of a mathematical system has to be a process that is taking place in experienced time.

By acts of attention, you have to choose sentences, to choose implications—it's a display. You are given an external display which is changing out there, not in your head. And you have to place a structure on it by specified rules.

You know, another point that can be made is, that *Innperseqs* is philosophically inconsistent with *Transformations*—that these pieces are mocking each other.

At the time that I did this, I did not have the kind of maturity that I would have today to put it together in a strong way. These were gestures. And they are not even uniform on a question like whether a rule exists or not. Well, actually, frequently I'm too hard on myself. I think that in the essay "Concept Art" I do say something like objective language doesn't exist, but I'm still free to work with what you think the text says—I can use that in *art*—this is *art*!

There are three ways that the art part comes in. One is the visual display, the delectation. The second way the art part comes in is—well, if La Monte Young's Word Pieces are art, then this is art too. But the third thing is that this does not claim to have objective truth. It is a construction for the world-hallucination, or the world-apparition, or even a construction for the private world-apparition.

CCH

You are actually extending the world by new constructions.

HF

But it's the world-apparition. In a sense, if I believed that these rules were objectively established then it would almost indicate that I had not learned the lesson of the very piece which sits beside it on the page![16] And what am I doing talking about a page and a text? So the answer is that I have abandoned the provision of truth as the purpose of this activity and I have moved to the provision of experiences where the possibility of these experiences is a surprise.

CCH

And you don't have to be an empiricist to be surprised.

HF

Yes, yes. But the truth claim that you would have from a Kripke or a Goodman has been dropped. The meaning of the text is the meaning that the reader associates to it. And the thing is that in conventional intellectual work that's an unacceptable answer, because usually you are trying to get independent of the reader's distortion—that's the whole hope—that you can make something that is independent of the reader's distortion of it. This is a different game. This is not classical mathematics; it's not classical science. It's like giving a Rorschach blot. Then I don't mind if you have a unique subjective reaction. If my purpose is to make Rorschach blots, then I do not object, I have not failed if you have a unique personal reaction.

These pieces are designed for the individual reaction rather than in spite of it. The only other Concept Art piece—in *dimension* 14—one just has to guess whether this piece exists and, if it does, what its definition is. That was the piece. And that was a response to Cage's dissociation of what the composer sees, the performer sees, the audience sees. Starting from that, going through all the games that La Monte had played with the idea of performance, where we were performing pieces first and composing them second, maybe many months later. So, finally with the Concept Art piece, even whether the piece exists is completely indeterminate, but I meant for people to try to take that seriously. I was having a joke with the person who thinks that concepts form an objective world, which the individual who cognizes only discovers bit by bit. In effect, I am giving him this: Thank you for believing that there is a piece here—I'm leaving it to you to find it. I wash my hands of that problem—*you* find it!

Well, there's a natural pause that comes here because I think that I've summarized perhaps fairly thoroughly where I was when I did the work published in 1963. The entire subsequent career of the label Concept Art, its misapplication to Word Pieces, and all the rest of it, we have not begun with. After that, we can go on to the discussion of your visual pieces of the '70s and how they resume the genre of Concept Art.

(End of Part I)

1. My term for the rhythmic feature common to Magister Zacharias's *Simute Karissimi* and *Klavierstück XI*. See Willi Apel, *The Notation of Polyphonic Music* (4th ed.), p. 432, for *Sumite Karissimi*. [H.F., note added.]
2. Serial versus chance.
3. I'm being too diffident. I had quite significant discussions with Kripke and Goodman in 1961. [H.F., note added.]
4. Felix Meiner, *Nachgelassene Schriften und Wissenschaftlicher Briefwechsel*, vol. 2, Hamburg, 1976. (Gottlob Frege, *The Philosophical and Mathematical Correspondence*, University of Chicago Press, 1980.)
5. R. Carnap, *Philosophy and Logical Syntax*, 1935.
6. H. Flynt, *Blueprint for a Higher Civilization*, Milan, 1975.
7. Published in *Blueprint for a Higher Civilization*.
8. Again, I'm being too diffident. I thoroughly studied portions of the Carnap books I owned—beginning with *The Logical Syntax of Language*, which I bought while in high school. [H.F., note added.]
9. *Fragen de Ethik*, Vienna, 1930.
10. *A Treatise on Human Nature*.
11. Book 1, Part IV, VII "Conclusion."
12. *An Enquiry Concerning Human Understanding*.
13. S. Kripke, *Wittgenstein on Rules and Private Language*, p. 60.
14. Dated *6/19/61*—later titled *Illusions*.
15. *Transformations*, retitled *Implications* in the second edition.
16. *Innperseqs* versus *Transformations*, second edition.

# MYSTERIUM FASCINANS: THE EPISTEMIC ART OF CATHERINE CHRISTER HENNIX

Ulf Linde with remarks by Catherine Christer Hennix

Text by Ulf Linde written in Stockholm, 1991. Footnotes by Catherine Christer Hennix written in Amsterdam, 1991. First published on the occasion of *Parler Femme*, a group exhibition at Museum Fodor, Amsterdam, 1991.

MYSTERIUM FASCINANS
The Epistemic Art[1] of Catherine Christer Hennix
By Ulf Linde

1. To consider and properly judge the work of Catherine Christer Hennix on the level of her own philosophical inquiry certainly requires a working knowledge of highly technical logical methods—something which scarcely I have (and never will; advanced formal philosophy and logic requires an exacting discipline which is only available to a specialist).

    But, then, how can there be any point in writing about a work for which one can't summon the correct level of understanding?

2. The first time I visited her studio, I experienced something that ought to have turned me away. Whatever I was looking at in her studio—or environment-in-progress—concealed itself in its entirety; her own style of explaining the work stopped short of being just entirely useless. For in my own mind there now emerged a solid, sharply cut block of a radical lack of understanding; indeed, of my own thoughts there remained only emptiness surrounding this block. Now, certainly, it is most often the case that the border between knowing and not knowing runs in such a way that it lures the faculty of understanding to enter and occupy the area of knowledge's lack. However, this time it was distinctively not so: paradoxically, this solid block of absence or lack gradually induced an experience of rare comfort—an unforeseen modality of *jouissance*.

    The desire to know had ceased to be operative.[2]

3. Her semiotical objects appeared to emit or radiate some kind of negative aura which cancelled every attempted at a definition: a square was *not* a Malevich square, nor a Don Judd; it was *not* a specimen of some materiality, *not* a completed form of an integral whole, and *not* something participating in anything outside of its own space. The fact that the artist considered these intensions as entirely subordinated to the expressions of her logical doctrines did not concern me at all. But, instead, what concerned me was this aura: what I was looking at kept radiating a kind of light, in the interior of which all determinants faded, where all previous categories vanished. I certainly would not have had the same reaction had I merely come across these same formulae printed in a work of logic or the foundations of mathematics; rather, I would then leisurely have decided whether or not I should be deciphering them and find out further what they are about. By contrast, with Ms. Hennix's design and approach—size, material, color, etc.—their appearance in her studio was numinous: the negative aura was overwhelming.[3]

    Was this art? The question was superfluous, since its answer was entirely immaterial.

4.  When, later, she had moved her installation *Toposes & Adjoints* to Moderna Museet in Stockholm—that was in the autumn of 1976—the numinous radiation was increased beyond anything I could ever have anticipated. Suddenly, the aura was now taking possession of *everything* in its vicinity, art or not art—of the insignificant track lights and their unavoidable reflections on the surface of a continuously variable floor painting, of the doorknobs at the installations outer limits—everything suddenly became transformed, transported, everything took on the radiation of this strange light. Yet, at the same time, it was a *natural* light.

    When one looks at a lake and names it a lake, while, at the same time, thinking it is a lake in all appearance, one may suddenly fall prey to the complete indifference that the lake harbors in being called a "lake": the human *adscriptum* does not cause a single ripple on its surface: it exists in a beyond of what is human. Similarly, in *Toposes & Adjoints*, a stainless steel square, as soon as it was *called* a "stainless steel square," it became mentally unhinged and dislocated beyond all the normal human faculties: these conventional words turned into an echoing of veridical emptiness, while they didn't seem to retain anymore an ability of making connections with the world of appearance. This was cognition turned into a languageless activity. (It occurs to me that a bar of steel by Walter De Maria—as opposed to a steelbar of Ms. Hennix's—in no way resists being named "stellar": it is not natural in the same way.)

    But the most remarkable feature of Catherine Christer Hennix's work, is, for me, its incomprehensible serenity.

1) "Epistemic Art" was my response to the original formulation of "Concept Art" vide Henry Flynt. (Original version published in *An Anthology*, ed. La Monte Young [New York, 1963], reprinted in *Being = Space × Action*, *Io #41*, ed. Charles Stein [Berkeley, California, 1989]). While H.F. conceived Concept Art as syntax rich/semantics poor abstract constructions (à la Carnap), my inclination was to reverse the conceptual prerogatives in accordance with the slogan of semantics rich/syntax poor (known from F.W. Lawvere's arrow approach to the foundations of mathematics). Cf. C.C. Hennix, *Brouwer's Lattice* and *Notes on Toposes & Adjoints* (Moderna Museet Publications, Stockholm, 1976).

2) The mystery of fascination is a particular instance of the interplay between the fundamental processes of *semeiosis* and *homosemeiosis* (cf. *Io*, op. cit.), which, as a limit, transforms itself to a modality of ataraxia purely as a function of the signifier's grammatical structure. However, this grammar is not the ordinary one occupying the area of linguistic research, but, rather, the grammar of the unconscious, which includes the perception of one's own body in a symbolic register which is endowed with epistemic certainty. The alignment of the latter certainty with the epistemic certainty of one's own ongoing thought processes can never be directly influenced by the subject's own will power, but, rather, is an entirely unconscious process triggered or mediated by a specific semiotical event and its unfoldings. It is certainly a tribute to U.L.'s refined modalities of perception that he allowed himself to occupy this *topos* of his consciousness as a function of being confronted with my semiotical constructions. In fact, I know of no one (excepting myself) that has allowed herself to enter this space of the aesthetic experience during an exposure to my work. By the latter remark I wish to emphasize that this very space plays a central role in my work, and it takes precedence over any other epistemic aspect that it might offer. Superficially, this contradicts the reality principle, in terms of which the interpretation of a work of art's (on the level of its formal(-izable)) meaning has no common measure with the work's existence—which remains a logical enigma on the basis of the principle of sufficient reason. Yet, the cessation of meaning is the limit-case in which the signifiers become bound in an intransitive relation with the subject of cognition as a function of the ongoing process of *homosemeiosis*. And, passing beyond this limit, one may finally arrive at the initial structure in terms of which a sustained discourse of the *noemas* effectively takes place. It is *that* discourse in its singularity which the aesthetic experience of epistemic art aims at. And, by the way, it certainly gives a particularly striking credence to the medieval logical proverb: *grammatica tua sit tibi in perditionem!*

3) Continuing the topic of the previous footnote, I recall that the term "nūmen" is known as a n-epistemic term at least since the time of *Rg Veda*. In the occident the term goes back to Parmenides and Plato where it comprehends what is given for the thinking subject, i.e., the reality of thought in its independence from the *phenomena*. In more recent times the term plays a central role in Kant's epistemology, where it is maintained that thought in itself does not suffice for entering a state of real knowledge—in addition, Kant argues, intuitive considerations must be brought in as a negative limit-concept, towards which thought by itself leads by an inner necessity, a necessity which only affords a formalization within a stringent concept of ethics or morality. More recently, these ideas have been developed by the Dutch mathematician L.E.J. Brouwer on the basis of which he has conceived radical alternatives to classical mathematics. And most recently, the Russian-American logician and philosopher A.S. Yessenin-Volpin has begun isolating this formalizable intuition as a *logic of confidence* (see the relevant texts by Brouwer and the Yessenin-Volpin in *Io #41*, op. cit.).

While these aspects remain relevant to U.L.'s use of the concept of the *numinous*, I find it very interesting that U.L.'s use of this terminology is also consistent with the Latin root of "nūmin," especially when it is taken in the sense of "grace." In fact, my own use of this terminology is often ambiguous in the sense that both the Greek and Latin roots color its meaning simultaneously.

Returning to the topic of the second footnote, it is certainly not in general the case that the art of logic (*Ars Logica*) coincides with the logic of art. However, when the coincidence is obtained the result may deserve to be called "Epistemic Art." The rare occurrences of this coincidence make them often appear as moments of grace—as when the symbolic and imaginary dimensions of existence come to coincide with the real.

\*) Commenting on one's critics' writings always remains an uncompromising desire. I therefore want to thank Ulf Linde for inviting me to write the remarks that follow. C. H-x.

Amsterdam, 1991

# ~~LA~~ SÉMINAIRE

Written in Amsterdam, 1992, on the occasion of a June 2, 1992, talk at Museum Fodor, Amsterdam. This version is previously unpublished. Similar version published in *Beyond Logos*, ed. Zoran Gavric and Zana Gvozdenovic (Belgrade Museum of Modern Art, 1992).

..... [ Séminaire ] ....., Intervention Zéro;

[ Epistemic Art and Psychoanalysis ]

This text is *not* a final, critical edition of its original, but comprises about a third of it—and is here delivered in a preliminary "lecture notes" style. It was delivered the first time at Museum Fodor, Amsterdam, 2 VI 92 (as an apropos *Parler Femme*, a show at Fodor that I participated in earlier this year), where I also used five slide-projectors which showed, concurrently, the formulae diagrams, drawings, and other sem(e)iotical extensions of the delivered text, and which, for the most part, have been deleted from the present, preliminary text.

I wish to seize the occasion and thank Museum Fodor for so timely presenting the first installment La̶ *Séminaire*, and, in particular, Leontine Coelewij and Freud Wagemans for the pleasant experience everybody enjoyed at this intervention.

As the present context makes clear, this preliminary report has been given its present format as it serves to prepare the second installment of La̶ *Séminaire*, *Beyond Logos*, in Belgrade. While my main topics now are to be the homotopy theory and *Triptyque Lacanienne*; this intervention will depend on the availability of a complete, critical edition of the present text.

Grammatica tua sit tibi in perditionem.
–Nicholas of Autrecourt

Le fou est la victime de la rébellion des mots.
–Edmond Jabès

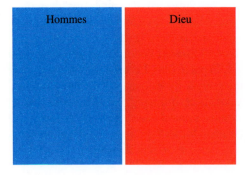

Tableaux du La portée du Signifiant

" ....."

In the ontological dimension, the aesthetics of $E_{ART}^*$ are in part occupied with that region of the inner event-horizon at which the *emergence* of the mental objects occurs. Its initial ontology is an interior ontology of *emerging objects*, which may be captured by (exterior) concepts, under which they can remain extracted or comprehended. As I have already alluded to above, this aesthetics makes certain connections with psychoanalysis to which I will now turn.

To begin with, I notice that while ontologies of emergence traditionally tend towards idealism on account of their evanescent objects, psychoanalysis offers an opportunity to radically depart from the received approaches and pose the question of the existence of "hidden ontologies" anew—that is to say, alternative ontologies which are outside the scope of any known scientific method and yet retain the power of advancing the presence of the Real (cf. *Le Séminaire, Livre VII, L'éthique de la psychanalyse*).

That the presence of the Real itself is accorded the status of an emerging object is only indicative of its non-trivial position in the psychoanalytic epistemic structure of a thinking subject. If the position occupied by the subject is not convergent with the emerging presence of the Real—if it [the subject] is positioned in a place determined by a modality of the *not*-Real—it is not necessarily in a unique place or determined by a unique force. To be propelled out of the presence of the Real is a multivalued function which may take the subject anywhere. Psychoanalysis, as a method, may be considered as the study of a certain *restriction* of this multivalued function, while its metatheory also includes certain of its *extensions*.

In psychoanalytic terms, disappearance—the aesthetics of absence—is preparatory for an aesthetics of emergence. Its initial object of contemplation, its *given episteme*, is the multibranching structure of the *signifying chain*, $S_2$. At each node $S_1, S'_1, S'_1{}', \ldots$, of the chain of signifiers, the subject, S, undergoes a *Vorstellung*, to which the signifier is connected by the *Vorstellungsrepräsentanz*. The latter connection is obtained by some specific *tactic of attention*, which, however, is unknown to the subject in the sense that it is a construction of its *unconscious*, a construction which is hidden from the operations of the ordinary episteme.

That a connection and a construction nevertheless can be obtained between *Vorstellung* and *Vorstellungsrepräsentanz* in the presence of the Real is one of the fundamental discoveries of psychoanalysis. While even the arbitrariness of a signifier doesn't prevent it from releasing a *Vorstellung*, if only fleetingly, in passing, there exist *designated signifiers* which occupy the subject constantly, even compulsively. The grammar of these latter signifiers is a most perplexing system of rules, of which most are non-recursive, and consist largely of a family of *substitution functions* specific for each subject and hence subjected to an *intensional* identity relation.

---

* The notion $E_{ART}$ was originally elaborated in *Brouwer's Lattice and Notes on Toposes & Adjoints*, Moderna Museet, Stockholm, 1976, parts of which have been reprinted in E[n], *Hors-texte*, 68-88, Berheleg, California, North Atlantic Books, 1989. For a compact presentation see my footnotes to Ulf Linde's *Mysticism Fascinans*, Museum Fodor, Amsterdam, 1991 (reprinted in this volume).

There can be no question concerning the epistemic modality which traditionally is accorded a subjective *Vorstellung*—the local conceptualization actualized in a subject since the time of Aristotle has been treated, in the sense of the term, φαντασία. And Freud undeniably connects with this venerable tradition when he places the ontology of the *Vorstellungsrepräsentanz* among the *primary processes*, thereby according the semantics of the designated signifiers, the master signifiers, the status of *hallucination*.

However, Freud proceeds from here by emphasizing that the irreducible hallucination which the subject suffers under the signifier (cf. Kristeva's *sujet-en-procès*)[1] also makes it non-transparent to itself, which, a priori, prevents philosophical idealism from claiming any coherence. Moreover, when the subject on trial is absent from the presence of the Real, it proceeds on the strength of alternative grammars by which it is condemned to enter the alternative orders of the *Symbolic* and the *Imaginary*, which, according to Lacan, is a necessary route for returning the presence of the Real. A specific "topology" is accorded these three orders by Lacan, which he designates with the *Borromean Knot* in order to emphasize their inseparableness in the constitution of the subject. To avoid the idealism by which Freud's *Entwurf* certainly was tainted, Lacan insists on the ontological absence of a psychogenesis of the subject without therefore according him emergence *ex nihilo*. The closest traditional epistemic term which covers the emergence of this subject is, perhaps, an *everywhere undefined recursive function*, the values of which may be considered *entirely arbitrary*.

(While the concepts of recursive function theory may be stretched to cover also the constitution of the subject it is not my intention to bring about such a development here.[2] Suffice it to mention, Lacan's position on the relevance of mathematics to meta-analytic studies by way of the following remark from *Encore*:

> *La mathématisation seule atteint à un réel—et c'est en quoi elle est compatible avec notre discours, le discours analytique—un réel qui n'a rien à faire avec ce que la connaissance traditionelle a supporté, et qui n'est pas ce qu'elle croit, réalité, mais bien fantasme.*
> *Le réel, dirai-je, c'est le mystère du corps parlant, c'est le mystère de l'inconscient.*
>
> *[Mathematization alone reaches a real—and it is in that respect that it is compatible with our discourse, analytic discourse—a real that has nothing to do with what traditional knowledge has served as a basis for, which is not what the latter believes it to be—namely, reality—but rather fantasy.*
> *The real, I will say, is the mystery of the speaking body, the mystery of the unconscious.]* [3]

Presently, I shall turn to Lacan's theory of the already emerged, constituted subject as modeled by a theory of continuous deformations, *Théorie Homotopique*, including the fundamental group of the Borromean Knot.)[4]

*Triptyque Lacanien* (1991) consists of presentations of the homotopic representations of the subject under the aspects of *Le Sinthome* (1991); *Schéma XX* (1991); and *La portée du Signifiant* (1991). The *Polyptyque Lacanien* (1991) is a modular addition to *Triptyque Lacanien* (1975–1991) and it defines the fundamental concepts of *La Séminaire* (1991). These works and the present text are a co-evolving whole of a work-in-progress, in a phase of multidirectionality and rapid expansions of views which allude to the completion of a theory.

Before I turn to technical mathematics such as algebraic topology and homotopy theory, I shall first develop a fragment of Lacan's theory of the *mathèmes* within a framework derived from the systems of notations in $E_{ART}$. In part III of the present report [in preparation], I will advance some of the topological machinery on which my studies of invariance of meta-psychological constructions depends (cf. *Théorie Des Schémas Analytique*).

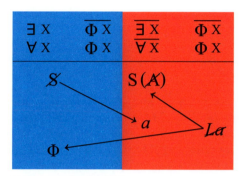

Tableaux du Schéma XX

To the objectives of psychoanalysis belong not only the observations of the obstacles to human love and sexuality, but also observations of the obstacles to truth—the *truth of the subject*.

That the subject surrounds itself with obstacles to its own realization as a loving and sexually fulfilled creature has been a cultural trait since the beginning of time—but so has the subject's own complicity in the "human condition."

The barriers against the knowledge of the truth of this complicity are a main objective of meta-analytic theory which studies the subject's resistance to and self-censorship of its own truth. The barriers against becoming conscious of the truth of one's own condition is a signature of an intricate elaboration, which ultimately expresses itself in the form of a *symptom*, a form which needs an equally intricate elaboration in order to be disentangled from its sources.[5]

*Le Sinthome* is the meta-analytic counterpart of the intuitionistic creating subject—together they form a structure of duality spanning the modalities between truth and absurdity over a double-negation topology. The elaboration of the theory of *Le Sinthome* is concordant with nothing less than the elaboration of the main obstacle to analysis itself. *Le Sinthome*, a notion that arose in the wake of Lacan's study of *Finnegans Wake*, is an episteme for a thinking subject whose thinking is outside of, or *out-of*, the episteme proper, a thinking which only signifies the contours of a body cut up by words and which speaks without the subject (being aware of) itself speaking (cf. *Le Séminaire, Livre XXIII, Le Sinthome*—unpublished). Diachronically, *Le Sinthome* defines the cumulative self-image of a subject in vain trying to protect itself from its own truth, the result of self-censorship and resistance which, originating in the unconscious, serves to protect the subject against revelations which would make life impossible to live. It is on this observation that Lacan rests when he says, "Who doubts that there is an order other than that along which the body thinks it is displaced?"[6]

*Le Sinthome*, regarded as an operator, is a function of some set of signifiers—the image of which writes the body as a signifier—that are led on and subtended by the hands of the Oedipal family, by the hands of the *Law-of-the-Father*. *Le Sinthome* is, in a way, a master signifier of the unconscious which presents a subject, *its subject*, for an another signifier—a signifier which at this juncture supplants, or stands for, a supposed subject of knowledge, the "*Homoinzune*" of the classical existential quantifier

$$\exists x\, Hx$$

which Lacan also denotes by the more familiar *mathème*

$$\exists x\, \Phi x$$

known from the schema of sexual division in Encore and to which I refer in this publication as *Schéma XX* (cf. *Le Séminaire, Livre XIX, ou pire*—unpublished, and *Le Séminaire, Livre XX, Encore*).

It is the negation, $\overline{\Phi x}$, of the open formula, $\Phi x$, of the Law which expresses ZXthe Dialectics of Desire, the subversion of the subject under an ineffable epistemic operator. It is this negation and its non-classical episteme which defines the speaking which comports with *objet petit a*, and the continuous deformations which comport the Cartesian subject with its sexless existential endpoints—the recurrent, incessant cover-ups of the truth of the subject.[7]

*Le Sinthome* may hence be taken to model the limit of this process of continuous deformations by which the truth which cannot be spoken—for which there is no audible speech—continuously makes itself heard in *symptoms*, such as our stunning cultural *Armod* and the mental anguish and twisted bodies attendant to it.

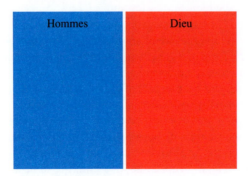

Tableaux du Sinthome

It is within the context of *Discours Analytique* that one may develop the techne (Τέχνη) and ontology (οντολογία) by which one nevertheless "hears" a meaning in these symptoms, which in their hieroglyphical configurations struggle to become speech, *logos* (λόγος). The rejection by the analytic discourse of the Aristotelian concept of logos is not only based on the latter's failure to model ontologies of emerging objects, but it also brings attention to the fact that Aristotle's logos is not universal, since it is not equipped to sustain a discourse on *perversion* about which it ostensibly wishes to know nothing in an equally perfectly pervert way—the perfectly pervert way by which it pretends to know nothing about sexuality. As Lacan has observed,

> *Pour Aristote en effet, s'agissant d'un certain type de désirs, il n'y a pas problème éthique. Or, ces désirs-là ne sont rien de moins que les termes promus au premier plan de notre expérience. Un très grand champ de ce qui pour nous constitue le corps des désirs sexuels est tout bonnement classé par Aristote dans la dimension des anomalies monstrueuses—c'est du terme de bestialité qu'il use à leur propos. Ce qui se passe à ce niveau ne ressortit pas d'une évaluation morale.*
>
> *[Where a certain category of desires is involved, there is, in effect, no ethical problem for Aristotle. Yet these very desires are nothing less than those notions that are situated in the foreground of our experience. A whole larger field of what constitutes for us the sphere of sexual desires is simply classed by Aristotle in the realm of monstrous anomalies - he uses the term "bestiality" with reference to them. What occurs at this level has nothing to do with moral evolution.]*[8]

Aristotle's ideal is "*horsexe*," or *transexuality*, but realized in the dimension of perversion where the sexual relation is always *empty*, is always *out-of-sex* (cf. *Encore*, p. 78).

The Aristotelian denial of perversion is already codified in the term to which "*Homoinzune*" evaluates and is a matter of another final symptom, fed by the processes *in absurdum* by which the masculine side of the sexual divide of the episteme maintains its identity as a foundation for a speaking subject. To which Lacan concurs:

> *[...] ce qui surgit sous l'épinglage dont le désigne Aristote, c'est trèés exactement ce qeu l'expérience analytique nous permet de repérer comme étant, d'au moins un côté de l'identification sexuelle, du côté mâle, l'objet—, l'objet qui se met à la place de ce qui, de l'Autre, ne saurait être aperçu. C'est pour autant que l'objet a joue quelque part—et d'un départ, d'un seul, du mâle—le rôle de ce qui vient á la place du partenaire manquant, que se constituter ce que nous avons l'usage de voir surgit aussi á la place du réel, à savoir le fantasme.*
>
> *[Hence, what emerges with the term by which Aristotle designates it is quite precisely what analytic experience allows us to situate as being the object—from at least one pole of sexual identification, the male pole—the object that puts itself in the place of what cannot be glimpsed of the Other. It is inasmuch as object a plays the role somewhere—from a point of departure, a single one, the male one—of that which takes the place of the missing partner, that what we are also used to seeing emerge in the place of the real, namely, fantasy, is constituted.]*[9]

While you may conclude from Lacan's theory that the "missing partner" (*partenaire manquant*) plays a central role in the masculine pursuit of epistemological and sexual perversions, a more radical and important conclusion is that (1) while there is no sexual relation in the dimension of the Real, (2) Aristotle's logic defines the same empty relation in the dimension of the Symbolic, which, (3) in the dimension of the Imaginary, is filled with any form except the empty form. That is, in the Imaginary dimension of the male side of the subject, there exists *at least one* sexual relation (*Homoinzune*), and further, there exists *no* empty sexual relation, i.e., all sexual relations are, by definition, *non-empty*. Such, then, is the *Law-of-the-Father*, a mere set-theoretical speculation by which empty sets are treated as the only *anomalous sets*.

While set-theoretically life (without empty sets) may appear simple and straightforward, it, nevertheless, crumbles under its own conceptualization, and on the male side of the episteme, the faltering foundation is already to be found in the interior of its unity, *l'Un*, which as a Zermelo ordinal receives the notation (cf. *Livre XIX, ou pire*).

or
$$\{\emptyset\}$$
$$\{\Lambda\}$$

depending on how you introduce the notation for the empty set, the classically anomalous ontological object, the existential import of which is logically equivalent to the destruction—the emptying-out—of the male epistemic position, i.e., the Aristotelian Categories.

The *crossed-out integral*, or the impossibility of the integration of the particular into the universal, may be seen to have been analyzed by Lacan as a case of *non-computability* which exceeds any formal degree of unsolvability. The prime non-computable term is isolated as *objet petit a*, the structure of which circumscribes the cause of the impossibility of the integration of a non-imaginary sexual (non-empty) relation with the Aristotelian episteme. As a graphic aid for this image, I offer the following (non-Lacanian) *mathème*, by which I designate the *crossed-out Integral*.[10]

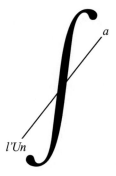

It is the lack of an other, the missing partner, in whom *objet petit a* can be inscribed, which is the condition under which a totalizing subject must operate and also where the subject meets its demise. This accounts for the non-computability of the crossed-out integrals' upper bound, *objet petit a*. The loss coded by *l'Un*'s empty interior, on which the impossibility of the male position in a discourse rests, plays a dual role for the non-computability of the integral's intractable lower bound. The founding act of this position is again that of the experience of lack, of a partner missing in force of whom the integral's lower bound becomes in the symbolic registrar its discourse's computable foundation, its *tertium non datur*, its *l'Un*.[11]

What is required in order to move beyond this position, this *phantasmagoria*, is, however, not a matter of switching logic alone but of assuming an entirely different epistemic position which does not block the entrance to any universe (of discourse). As Lacan has been the first to stress, this ulterior epistemic position cannot be offered by the female side of the divide of the episteme, by which *tout court*, "the woman does not exist." L̶a̶, in its dividing function, points to both the Law-of-the-father, Φ, and to S($\cancel{A}$), woman's "missing partner," both coordinates serving to obstruct access to an ulterior *l'Un*, to an ulterior discourse of the truth of the subject.[12]

Already, the *mathèmes* of Schéma XX allude to this dividing function, and Lacan seems to pose the problem of finding the *configuration of mathèmes*, the configuration of *contre-sense* by which this ulterior discourse may open up (cf. *Encore*, p. 85). Yet, we also seem to be in need of constant reminders of the request for this ulterior discourse, the coordinates of which appear as the always already missed, non-computable encounter, the forever avoided or undefined realization (thereby sharing the fate of *parler femme* as a future, conditional discourse).[13]

As another need for a constant reminder I find it necessary to stress the importance of observing the *non-classical* logics at work at the fundamental junctures outlined by psychoanalytic theory—even at the level covering elementary experiences. Thus, a reminder is needed to the effect that it seems the fate of analytic theory to concern itself with an ontology of *"emerging objects,"* of an evanescent presence of the Real which gives rise to notions which remain on the *threshold* of the knowable and which fail articulation by a speech act. As elementary examples you may think of the notions of the drive or of the aesthetic dimension of the signifier. Also, the knowledge specific to the unconscious and the episteme it spans (dream-structures, the structure of the phantasm, etc.) are "threshold phenomena," immune to the classical laws of logic. And, finally, the relation, the "*connexité*" between the epistemes of the unconscious and consciousness, respectively—two irremediably divided modes of the drive for knowledge, under which the subject is subtended—is a threshold for the emergence of *objet petit a* in the context of *Discours Analytique*, an emergence which defies the laws of classical logic in their entirety.

*Digression.* It is, of course, not without analytic interest that one observes Lacan's obsession with mapping out the irreconcilable discord between *objet petit a* and *l'Un* and how he, in perfect harmony with the obsessional neurotic's "epistemology of prohibition," prohibits the theoretical possibility of an *ulterior One*, a *l'Une*, with its implied existence of an Other beyond the Other, a *l'Autre de l'Autre*. But how could Lacan proceed otherwise than according to the law of castration, $\overline{\Phi x}$, which sustains the absence of the sexual relation outside the trajectory of the phantasm? The barrier against the truth of the subject is universal, and, consequently, it must also have the analyst himself as an object. But the impossibility of a bootstrap approach to this impasse is not discordant with a logical approach to its dissolution. Viz., it suffices to notice that the supposed existence of the supposed subject of knowledge—*Homoinzune*—is just that, a supposition, a hypothesis, and that this hypothesis *suffices* for a certain developing of meta-analytic schemes which aid in surpassing the obstacles offered by this theoretical (and existential) impasse. Some people appear to have the impression that Lacan's theory of *mathèmes* succeeds in pointing to the direction where such schemes will become available. However, a more general and abstract approach will eventually be needed: I will present it as the *Theory of Analytic Schemes* at a future seminar (*Théorie Des Schemas Analytique*). (End of digression.)

In terms of the crossed-out integral and its non-computable limits, *Le Sinthome* is the subject who offers increasingly greater resistance the closer it comes to a discourse which would be the ultimate one, the revelatory discourse the subject absolutely refuses. It is the problematic integral relation of the subject to itself which is the key to the meaning of the symptoms in that it is the subject's refusal of this meaning that poses an unsolvable problem for it. Resistance, even outside of analysis, is the inflection discourse adopts on approaching this nucleus (Lacan).

The fundamental epistemic relation for *Le Sinthome* is not that of acquiring knowledge still lacking, but of *resisting* knowledge already acquired. A well-known example, initially provided by Freud, is the use of *negation* smitten by the *sinthome*, whereby negating a proposition the subject prepares an order to assert its truth. But this subject is not only resisting truth but also *interrupting* its discourse no sooner than it approaches the vicinity of the Law, of which its understanding *this time* truly *is* lacking. This is the level of *censorship*. Here, the negation is realized by the subject's refusal of entering a relation of confidence with anybody else, including itself. Yet, according to Lacan's theory, censorship is on the same level as transference—there is a resistance of censorship just as there is a resistance of transference.

But the epistemic contorsions provided by the phantasm's logic of negation are far from exhausted, since in between resistance and censorship arises the modality of *hysterical disgust* and the particular knowledge which sustains it and that takes the form of a "passionate denial" or "passionate refusal" that issues from the symbolic body of *jouissance* in the presence of the Real, and from which the female's epistemic position situates itself in accordance with the division of Schéma XX.

By articulating in the exterior of the signifying chain an epistemology of disgust, the subject itself emerges as a *negation*, a passionate denial from which the symptom nevertheless elaborates itself through the field of *significance*—the sum total of the subject's tactics of attention and tactics of neglect—by a modality in which the subject's unconscious reveals itself. Besides, already the subject's body has the power of thought and its direction to the extent that it constructs itself through the signifying medium offered by its body of *jouissance*, the sensoriality of which is informed by the signifying elaboration of desire, or, even, of *jouissance*'s beyond. It is from this substance of the subject's own episteme's interiority the knowledge everyone resists, or else disrupts—that the field of *jouissance* is formed through an improbable organization of signifiers which is compulsively realized and rectified in a body where it converges on a message under censorship and resistance. Hence, the relation of hysteria to theory—perversion signified in the *interior* of the signifying chain—reduces to the *aesthetical problem* of the relation of a presentation of unspeakable desire to the representation of it by an epistemology, which, in its "nucleus," carries man's "forbidden knowledge"— or his "bestiality," to speak the language of Aristotle.

The fundamental epistemic relation for *Le Sinthome* is hence a bundle of trajectories through the phantasm sustained by the non-computable limits of the crossed-out integral. It is not clear to me to what extent the unsolvability of the integral's major terms is historically conditioned or not. I regard it as an open problem. Yet it does appear as if the semantics of the hystericized body are informed by its historicity, as is evidenced by the *vitae* of medieval female mystics. On the basis of this example, Ms. Bynum has advanced the conjecture that, indeed, the hysterical body, and consequently *parler femme*, does have a history all of its own. Inspection of available historical sources, beginning with the first known diagnosis of hysteria on an Egyptian medical papyrus scroll dated 1900 B.C., supports Bynum's case, but its detailed verification requires a separate study. The outcome of such a study will determine, however, the extent to which *objet petit a* and *l'Un* are diachronically dimensioned and therefore not *necessarily unsolvable* epistemic terms. In a digression below I will touch on an aesthetical phenomenon (Butō), by which a certain light may be shed on the question of the diachronic dimension of the "Freudian objects." Meanwhile, I return to the synchronic aspect of the phantasm and its relation with Schéma XX.

In this section, I shall continue the model theory of *contre-sense* with respect to the Freudian objects $a$ and *l'Un* in their modalities of emergence. In section V.a., I return to the "set theory" of *objet petit a* while section V.b. is concerned with the relation between *l'Un* and Schéma XX and its image in *La Portée de la Signifiant*. But first a reminder.

I recall, then, first of all, that the *language of the phantasm* is situated somewhere at the mid-point between the divergent epistemes of the unconscious and consciousness, respectively, where it acts as a certain go-between but *also* as a buffer making livable what is unlivable in ordinary language—*le-sujet-en-procès*—by modulating the *Vorstellungsrepräsentanz*'s logical possibilities. And it is by a semantics of *contre-sense*, the peculiar *sémantèmes* that inform the *mathèmes*, that Lacan approaches a new method by which a trapdoor to the language of the unconscious may be revealed. Underlying this method is a defiance of the classical laws of logic, of which ample reminders already have been given. There is no need, however, to stay within the limited development that Lacan succeeded in bringing about concerning the locality of this epistemic trapdoor, but as I have already intimated, bold generalizations are called for, such as the "theory" of *analytic schemes*. On the other hand, Lacan's discourse remains far from excavated, calling for prudence and attentive studies of *Le Séminaire, Livre I-XXVI*, the latter certainly a hopeless task for almost anyone. Thus, ~~La~~ *Séminaire* appears excused to proceed by its own pace and fashion. That being said, I return to my reconstruction of Lacan's theory of the phantasm.

V.a.
It is with *La Logique du Fantasme* (*Le Séminaire, Livre XIV*—unpublished) that Lacan introduces a new level of abstraction in the meta-theory of psychoanalysis. While Lacan still starts out from the premise that "there is something originally,

inaugurally profoundly wounded in the human relation to the world,"[14] the resulting defiance of the classical laws of logic is, in the end, a product of the intersection between the Real and the structure of the phantasm as a signifier all alone—but of which the classical laws yet form a remnant part, the part of the male side of the epistemic subject.

The logic which arrests this *locale*, this intersection, indicates how the phantasm and the Real stand in an immediate, reciprocal relationship where, concurrently but with variable forces, the Real undermines the phantasm, all while the phantasm protects them from the Real. Classical mathematics and transubstantiation in the modality of the eucharist are not the only cultural phenomena that come to mind as examples of this *locale*, but more prominently—and more pertinently—*the meta-discours over hysteria itself* in the historical dimension mapped-out by Monique David-Ménard, in her important work *L'Hystérique entre Freud et Lacan: Corps et langage en psychanalyse*, the most important independent theoretical contribution so far to Bynum's conjecture of the historicity of the hysterical body.

It is in terms of this last example we most clearly may see, from the female side of the epistemic subject, how the *locale* above comports the tension between desire and reality by delivering *objet petit a* as the result of an operation of its own internal logical structure (cf. *Livre XIV*). Set theoretically, Lacan places *objet petit a* in the image of the intersection between the subject and the Other (*l'Autre, A*).

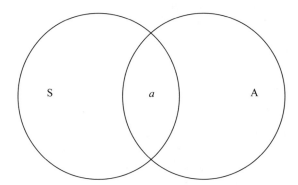

Put otherwise, or in terms of a (non-measurable) metric for Lacan's "primordial (topological) surface," when the subject, S, occupies the maximal distance to the other, A, the Other's image is reduced, contracted to *objet petit a*—whereas when the subject merges with the Other (minimal distance), *objet petit a* exhausts the substance of what they, ultimately, share as an effect by the subtended trajectories of the phantasm which Lacan indicates in the mathème

$$\mathcal{S} \lozenge a$$

While Lacan never ventured outside of ordinary (well-founded) universes of sets, the ephemeral emergences of *objet petit a* where its *ex-sis-tence* is sustained entirely on the strength of an operation of its own logical structure suggest a much more disorderly set universe such as offered by *extraordinary (non-well-founded)* sets. This is an obvious place, then, for introducing one of the called, for "bold generalizations." Thus, in terms of *extraordinary set theory* the following extraordinary set may serve to model the intractable existence of *objet petit a*

$$\{.....\{\{.....\{\{\{...\}\}\}\}.....\}\}.....\}$$

(When in the '70s I constructed this set, it was governed by axioms intended to model certain aspects of the "noemas." Some of these aspects carry over to *objet petit a* while, clearly, some additional "special axioms" are required to mark the "Freudian object" itself. I leave these specifications for another occasion.)

V.b.
According to Lacan, *contre-sense* is the instrument by which to cut the oedipal censorship which prevents a "*l'Une*" to replace the "*l'Un*" in the branches of the signifying chain. If this replacement was not always interrupted, censored, a new modality of discourse would arise which would stand in opposition to every other discourse—this is Lacan's *contre-discourse*, the discourses each instance of which would embody a transference relation. And as a *signum* for these discourses stands the *mathèmes* in their presentation as integral signifiers which in their alienness to the ordinary signifying chain—*significance commune*—undercut its Law, *Le-Nom-du-Pere*, thereby bypassing the sword of censorship. There is thus cause for surmising that in the semeiosis of the *mathèmes* a potential for a transference relation can progress. According to analytic theory, we have arrived at a critical *center of resistance*, which stands in need of a deep analysis of which Schéma XX and its fate can be taken as the starting point.

The general theorem which may verify the surmise above and on which Lacan's *contre-discours* depends states that, in its relation to the primary (hallucinatory) processes and within the regime of the phantasm's trajectory, the signifier carries a structure which, depending on the structure of the subject, is a potential site (*locale*) for *a transference relation*.

Each subject in search of its truth is directed by "algorithms of the unconscious" towards relations of transference which are grounded in the *locale* of certain signifiers (among which also the master signifiers circulate), which bear a specific, intrinsic relation with the organization of the subject's episteme and its internal processes of semeiosis. More generally, Lacan asserts that transference takes place as soon as a supposed subject of knowledge emerges among the others, i.e., *as soon as a qualified act of confidence takes place towards another*.

As has already been stressed, to this relation belongs, as one of its (logical) qualifications, a sense of *jouissance*, which conjoins the subject with the signifier at the level of the symbolic body and its *sinthome*. This is, of course, exactly the field of *jouissance* which is realized in a body but formed through an organization of certain signifiers—of the symbolic body, of love's body (Norman O. Brown). It is the relation between this modality of *jouissance* and language that informs the subject's sexual identity so that in the limit the Symbolic dimension *itself* can take on the function of *objet petit a*, cause of desire, and the splitting of the subject. Indeed, at the site of transference grammar undergoes a radical functional change—from having conducted the condemnation of the subject at its trials to becoming the living witness of a carrier of *jouissance*. Thus, the phantasm reveals itself in its trajectory as an algorithm for the interdiction by trauma to instruct the subject's actions towards a site of transference. It even appears as if psychoanalysis already exists *inside* the neurosis, as if the techniques of the self are themselves so many expressions of the symptom they aim to treat, so many expressions of our epistemic stigmas. It is quite ambivalent whether this "inside," this interiority, is of the Law or of what is *not*—not the Law but not the Law (in its exclusive positivity)—or, put differently, whether there can be a genuine *feminine technique* in the field of psychoanalysis, or are all analytic interdictions ultimately special cases of the Law, $\Phi$, *le Phallus*? According to Lacan, the case seems closed by necessity and therefore has no history—except the history of the subject, the fading or vanishing subject, who is the propagator and perpetrator of the Law-of-the-Father, the iron-law of the subject's strangulation at the threshold of emergence. On the other hand, Lacan insists on the possibility of the narrow escape offered by his notion of *contre-discours* and its *contre-senses*. Let me try to review Lacan's case.

By the quantification formulae of sexuation (Schéma XX), any author of the Law, identified by *Discours du Maître*, anyone posing as a possessor of the Phallus, is always a split, divided subject, $\not{S}$, which brings with each universal law, $\forall x\, \Phi x$, its recognized exceptions, $\exists x\, \overline{\Phi x}$, to which a sexual opposition is linked by the law of castration, $\overline{\Phi x}$, and which occludes the position of the Other, A, while entirely excluding the existence of the crossed-over Other, $\not{A}$, and its signifier, $S(\not{A})$, the signifier of a lack in the Other.

The negation of the Law is an apposition beyond the divided masculine subject, a position which presupposes the subject as a function of the crossed-over Other, $S(\not{A})$, i.e., the feminine subject defined by her beyond, i.e., by her capacity for *jouissance* in terms of which her "*pas tout*" takes on its signification. Lacan points out that the locale of the *jouissance* of this "*pas tout*" is not the entire body but is restricted to the "symbolic eye," the *gaze* by which "qu'il ex-siste un x de LA Femme que formule le 'Ne le gardez pas'" (cf. *Le Seminaire, Livre XXII, R.S.I.*—unpublished).

It is the content of her gaze from this beyond, this feminine vision, the limits which are revealed in ex-stasi, that which brings the Law to negate itself in spite of its universality and to position itself beyond yet another negation, the negation of its own negation, by which is underscored its submission to the beyond of the (still missing) feminine subject, $S(\not{A})$; *Dike, Justicia, Sophia, ...* , are all names of the childless, unnameable Virgin, the unmentionable Noblesse born under the sign of the immutable lack and therefore presiding over the unwritten laws of knowledge.

Hence, Lacan writes $\overline{\forall x}\, \Phi x, \overline{\exists x}\, \overline{\Phi x}$—asserting at most, by the last formula, the Law only under the (intuitionistic) law of the *double-negation* in the case of its feminine instance exceeded non-recursive behaviors, i.e., belongs to the undecidable formule of the Law as well as to the first-order monadic fragment of the predicate calculus. It is in this way "phenomena are saved," since it is not the case that the Law, when written, does not hold, i.e., it is absurd that the Law is absurd—*except* in the non-recursive beyond of the masculine subject.

Having reviewed Lacan's case this far, it seems safe to assert that that which is not-not the Law is yet the Law not surpassing itself, a Law without historicity. It is only when the (subverted) Law reaches the beyond of the feminine subject that it truly come to surpass itself—and only then can and may the (completely subverted) Law write—underwrite—a new cultural era based on the negation of its unsubverted form and, consequently, undivided by sexual difference.

# Epilogue

There is an exile from the forms of language as we have come to know them that awaits anyone at this beyond of the signification (in the *Names-of-the-Father*). A new church of language, a new passage into the body where the unwritten laws of the Real are confirmed at the moment of their revelation, is the type of non-recursive functions which need to be at hand—*Analog* computable functions rather than digital Turing machine solvability, that is to say. Hence, a logic of confidence (in the correctness of analog computations) becomes indispensable, and a new concept of freedom (of use of signs), therefore, is mandatory to take into attention.

Yet, however far we attempt to develop "new techniques," there are ample reasons for heeding Lacan's warning against "understanding too quickly," since such "egocentrism" might compromise and stand in violation of basic ethical principles on which the analytic discourse is founded.

The conclusion that Lacan's case is perpetually an enigma or inconclusive is therefore entirely in line with what one must expect from meta-analytic theory itself which serves, above all, the continuation of the interrogation the subject undergoes in its search for its own truth. Meanwhile, if no progress is in sight, one may always remind oneself of the singularity by which the *Discours Analytique* forms the speaking which comports *objet petit a* and which as a *"savoir l'absolument-non"* delivers a space for the Dialectics of Desire in which aesthetical judgements become unavoidable. (To be continued.)

Mathème of the phantasm of hysteria;

$$\frac{a}{-\Phi} \lozenge A$$

Mathème of the phantasm of obsession;

$$\cancel{A} \lozenge (a, a', a'', a''', \ldots)$$

*Digression* (on the aesthetical dimension of the signifier)
It is in the promiscuous dimensions of the arts that one may study, at one's leisure, the effect in the Symbolic of the ongoing displacements of the subject's uncertain sexual identifications, the subject's "four options" in the terminology of Schéma XX. Viz., along this trajectory you may find exposed the hidden philosophical problem concerning the degree to which consciousness is circumscribed by narcissistic drives, by unconscious desires and suppressed verbal myths which govern its relation to the field of knowledge, the episteme as we know it in its historicity, as artifact. When you add to this artifactual episteme—the "episteme of the unconscious"—and their "inmixing" in what Plato referred to as "ψυχή and λόγος" the soul's conversations with herself, the logic of the spirit, the logic of the inner voice—there emerge three epistemic options for the subject at which she may anchor her sexual identifications and which may be put into correspondence with the three *non-empty* sexual *options* left by Schéma XX. Yet, regardless of which epistemic option the subject chooses as the dimension of truth for its sexual identification, the subject is bound to approach this truth as representing the dimension of the unthinkable *for it* as it inhabits the *"trinité infernal"*—the Real,

the Symbolic, and the Imaginary in their interstitchings of the Borromean Knot (cf. *Livre XXII*, R.S.I.). The recoiling from the abreactions the subject ensues from its pursuit of the dimension of the unthinkable—the unthinkable *for it*—finds a strange place of rest in the aberrant movements of the aesthetical dimension of the signifier where the displacements of the subject's sexual identifications may be "unveiled by the bachelors, even."[15]

Here is undeniably a place, or, rather, a *delta*, where alternative ontologies of emergence and disappearance are opportune to arrive *en masse*, which are firmly belonging to the non-recursive beyond of the masculine subject (*l'homme*) and which represent a displacement, an epistemological migration, by which Aristotle will be contradicted on all his terms and by which the signifier and the *sex-ion* (wandering, unstable sex) form a dynamic union—sometimes referred to as "style" (Lacan), sometimes referred to as "aesthetics" (Freud). And it is with the latter references that one may precisely anchor this epistemological displacement in the locus of disgust designated as *objet petit a*.

According to psychoanalytic theory—and in sharp contrast with both Aristotle and Kant—aesthetic fascination has its origin in a perception of disgust, which the work of art offers the viewer the occasion to *turn attention away from*, and the mental displacement of this "turning away from" precisely constituting the aesthetic experience by embodying a *tactic of attention*, which is intrinsically subjected to the logic of the phantasm. Moreover, it was already Freud's contention that the mechanism of *Dichtung*, poetical creation, is the same as that of phantasies informed by the epistemology of hysteria (cf. letter to Fliess, May 31, 1897), which, if nothing else, again, only goes to affirm that all aesthetical satisfaction excites disgust, excites the power of horror surrounding the subject.

You know it all from Lacan's *Kant avec Sade*, of course. But you may also think of Bataille's *La Somme Athéologique*, Artaud's *Le Théâtre et son Double*, or the dimensions of darkness in the aesthetics of *Butō*.[16] In Bataille's case, the aesthetical dimension is captured by his obedience to the ancient Gnostic precept to challenge all limits by substituting for subordination superior principles, but only in order to confound the human spirit and the philosophy of idealism with something entirely base—in the moment corresponding to the subject's reflection of an unperceived totality of horror dispatched by the world's spirit's spur of the moment, by *chance*. According to Bataille, *l'expérience intérieure* attains its modalities of communication through fusion with *non-savoir*—the not knowing—as subject and the *inconnu*—the not known—as object, a process in the limit of which the subject-object dichotomy dissolves. But this mode of overcoming the fundamental Aristotelian dichotomy entails the subject's imminent disappearance in a perilous and accidental way—something which only confirms already existing analytic theory rather than positions a viable alternative. A different avenue is offered by Artaud and the aesthetics of Butō where the theme of "atheology" receives another twist through the *pure language of the body*, where the semanteme is exchanged for the "*pathéme*," an atomic configuration of the body of passion.[17]

Here is the arena for an immediate and unmediated confrontation with the subject's recoil from the discordant unconscious which circumscribes a knowledge (*savoir*) which originates out of an alien desire which confers on the human subject an object of separateness, estrangement, the topological dynamics of which is described by the primal losses surrounding us as they reappear in the movements of the body. Perhaps no aesthetics has captured this moment and its dynamics, this near-Freudian moment, more acutely than *Butō*, the *dance step of utter darkness*, which brings about an instantaneous illumination of the existential conditions of a culture where, impenetrable to others, each person is also a stranger to the entire universe. Long before I became interested in psychoanalysis, I was fascinated by the development of a "logic of the phantasm" in *Butō*, which led to a number of directions among which I especially mention *SAIDO-BUTŌ*, i.e., *Butō of the pulverizing moment* (cf. my Horstexte, 68–88).[18]

From the perspective of the history of hysteria, Butō formalizes, in terms of its *pathéme*, the former's atheological aspect with an edge that is only comparable to the pagan mystery cults of antiquity—such as seen on the fresco of the *Villa of Mysteries at Pompeii*. But Butō goes perhaps further than that by bringing forth the orders circulating the *"trinité infernal"* in its ineffable presentation—rather than representation—of *le Sinthome*. Among the contemporary exponents of Butō, no one has, perhaps, expressed this edge and its beyond more eloquently than Yoko Ashikawa. In her most recent piece of writing, "Searching For The Other Person In The Body,"[19] it is impossible not to recognize in it a "pilot study" for a *meta-analytic theory of movement* along the lines already suggested by Monique David-Ménard and alluded to above.

Yoko Ashikawa's text, like the *pathéme* of her dance, exposes in a perfectly clear language the radical ontological status of the symptom, conceived as *sinthome*, by presenting it, its aesthetical dimension, as our only substance, the only support of our Being by which the subject can endure existence's artificial separateness from Nothingness. This is the radical meaning of Freud's axiom *wo es war, soll ich werden*, the verification of which stands at the end of the analytic process where an identification with the symptoms brings the analysand and to recognize in the order of the Real that, without the symptoms, the subject would forever disappear.

But Ashikawa's text "Searching For The Other Person In The Body" also makes clear how movement implies a momentary extinction of discourse, logos, and a presentification of the impossible in the immediate presence of the Real, while simultaneously characterizing the hidden, reciprocal exclusion of language and *jouissance*, of *sense* and Being. As in the case of conversion hysteria, there is here a decisive, ontological moment where *jouissance* is no longer representation, a signifying relation, but is presented, embodied only as pure movement, unobstructed motility, *contre-sense*—which substitutes for an uninterrupted voice addressing a supposed subject of knowledge. It is in the nakedness of this movement, in this bare dance step of utter darkness, in which the residue of symbolization, *objet petit a*, resides, and which by a logic of its own permits us to sense the cause of our desire under the weight of an incomprehensible existence.

It is to the beauty (behind its shutters) that one must speak.
—Lacan

(End of digression.)

1. See Julia Kristeva in *Tel Quel*, nos. 52/53, 1973. Reprinted in *Polyogue*.
2. I have recently been informed that the "homotopy-approach" to Lacan's notions is not new. See for instance the work by Vappereau in *Ornicar?* [see bibliography].
3. Lacan, *Le Séminaire, livre XX, Encore*, Paris: Seuil, 1972–1973, p. 118, Lesson of May 15th.
4. cf. Lacan. "Tout ce qui est mental, en fin de compte, est ce que j'ecris du nom de sinthome, c'est-a'-dire signs" in *Le Séminaire, L'impossible a saisir, livre XXIV*, No. 17/18, 1979.
5. cf. Lacan's discussion concerning the "subversion on Sujet et dialectique du désire" in *D'un discours qui ne serait pas du semblant, Le Séminaire, livre XVII*.
6. See *Ornicar?* 3, 1975.
7. See Lacan, *Le Séminaire, livre XXII* and *livre XXIII*.
8. Lacan, *Le Séminaire, livre VII, L'éthique de la psychanalyse 1959-60*, Paris: Seuil, 1986, p. 13.
9. Lacan, *Le Séminaire, livre XX, Encore*, p. 58, Lesson of May 15th.
10. cf. Lacan's discussion concerning the "subvertion on sujet et dialectique du désir" in *D'un discours qui ne serait pas du semblant, Le Séminaire, livre XVIII*.
11. See Lacan, *Le Séminaire, livres XVIII, XX, XXIII*.
12. It would require a separate study to draw together all of Lacan's statements on this topic—a task I presently defer. I attempt a characterization of the problems involved.
13. This future, conditional discourse shares a number of structural features with the transference phenomena and, hence, poses as an alternative exit from the *analytic discourse* as the latter positions itself within the lattice of the four discourses in *L'envers de la psychoanalyse*.
14. See Lacan, *Le Séminaire, livre II*, p. 167.
15. Ulf Linde [private communication] has drawn my attention to the fact that the "Bride" corresponds to Duchamp's own silhouette as he once painted himself as playing chess with his brothers [the "bachelors"] *Portrait de jouer de schack*, 1911. Rose Sélavy thus stands for an equivalence, an imaginary identification, between the experience of transsexuality and aesthetics of the twentieth century's art myth [as, for example, *Mona Lisa* expressed a similar sentiment of Leonardo's time].
16. This topic deserves a new hearing which, in particular, relates it to the themes of pre-Christian and early Christian theology—a study I must defer.
17. See Lacan, *Le Séminaire, livre XXII* and *livre XXIII*.
18. See bibliography.
19. See bibliography.

# Bibliography

Ashikawa, Yoko. "*Searching for the Other Person in the Body*"; *Tsubushi* no. 1, Tokyo, 1989.
Bataille, George. *Oeuvres Complètes*, vols. V, VI. Paris: Gallimard, 1973.
Bynum, Caroline Walker. "The Female Body and Religious Practice in the Later Middle Ages" in *Fragments for a History of the Human Body, Part One*, ed. Michel Feher with Ramona Naddaff and Nadia Tazi. Cambridge: Zone Books, MIT Press, 1990.
—— *Holy Feast and Holy Fast, The Religious Significance of Food to Medieval Women.* Berkeley and Los Angeles: University of California Press, 1987.
David-Ménard, Monique. *L'Hysterique entre Freud et Lacan: Coprs et language en psychanalyse.* Paris: Editions Universitaires, 1983.
Doumit, Élie. "Les négations et les univers du discours," in *Lacan avec les philosophes*. Paris: Albin Michel, 1991.
e.l.p.. *Le Transfer Dans Tous Ses Errata.* Paris: E.P.E.L., 1991.
Hennix, Catherine Christer. *Notes on Toposes & Adjoints*, exhibition catalogue. Stockholm: Moderna Museet, 1976
—— *Brouwer's Lattice*, exhibition catalogue. Stockholm: Moderna Museet, 1976.
—— *Poetry as Philosophy, Poetry as Notation* in *Wch Way*. New York, 1985.
—— E[n] – Hors-texte, 68–88, in *Being = Space x Action, Io #41*, ed. Charles Stein. Berkeley: North Atlantic Books, 1989.
—— *Schéma XX and Intuitionistic Model Theory*. Stockholm, 1990, unpublished.
Irigaray, Luce. *Ce sexe qui n'en est pas un*. Paris: Editions de Minnit, 1977.
—— *L'éthique de la différence sexuelle*. Paris: Editions de Minnit, 1984.
—— *Parler n'est jamais nuetre*. Paris: Editions de Minnit, 1985.
—— *Sexe et parentés*. Paris: Editions de Minnit, 1987.
Kristeva, Julia. *Polylogue*, Paris: Seuil, 1977; *Tel Quel* nos. 52/53, 1973.
Lacan, Jacques. *Le Séminaire, livre VII, L'éthique de la psychanalyse*. Paris: Seuil, 1981.
—— *Le Séminaire, livre VIII, Le Transfer*. Paris: Seuil, 1991. Le Transfer dans sa disparité subjective, sa pretandue situation, ses excursions techniques—cf. e.l.p.: Le Transfer Dans Tous Ses Errata.
—— *Le Séminaire, livre XI, Les quatre concept fondamentaux de la psychoanalyse*. Paris: Seuil, 1973.
—— *Le Séminaire, livre XIV, Le logique du fantasme*. Paris, 1966–1967, unpublished.
—— *Le Séminaire, livre XVII, L'envers de la psychanalyse*. Paris: Seuil, 1991.
—— *Le Séminaire, livre XVIII, D'un discours qué ne serait pas du semblant*. Paris: 1970–1971, unpublished.
—— *Le Séminaire, livre XIX, ou pire*. Paris, 1971–1972, unpublished.
—— *Le Séminaire, livre XX, Encore*. Paris: Seuil, 1976.
—— *Le Séminaire, livre XXII, R.S.I.*. Paris, 1974, unpublished.
—— *Le Séminaire, livre XXIII, Le sinthome*. Paris, 1975, unpublished.
—— *Le Séminaire, livre XXIV, L'insu*. Paris, 1978, unpublished.
—— *Ornicar?* 3. Paris: Seuil, 1975.
—— *Ornicar?* 17/18. Paris: Seuil, 1979.
Linde, Ulf. "Mysterium Fascinans—The Epistemic Art of Catherine Christer Hennix [with footnotes by C.C. Hennix]," in *Parler Femme*, exhibition catalogue. Amsterdam: Museum Fodor, 1991.
Loparic, Andrea. "Les négations et les univers du discours," in *Lacan avec les philosophes*. Paris: Albin Michel, 1991.
Michel, Albin (ed.). *Lacan avec Les Philosophes*. Paris: Bibliothéque du College International De Philosophie, 1991.
Stein, Charles (ed.). *Being = Space × Action, Io #41*, Berkeley: North Atlantic Books, 1989
Vapperean, Jean-Michel. *D'un calcal dans les champ du noeud, Ornicar?* 28. Paris: Seuil, 1984.
Yessenin-Volpin, A.S. "On the Logic of the Moral Sciences" in *Being = Space × Action, Io #41*, ed. Charles Stein. Berkeley: North Atlantic Books, 1989. Originally published in *Social Problems* No. 12, 1972. [Samizdat–in Russian.]

# WSTNOKWGO

© Henry A. Flynt, Jr.

Piece by Flynt created in New York, July 1961. First circulated as a limited-edition hectograph print by Tony Conrad, September 1961. First performed at ONCE Festival, Ann Arbor, Michigan, February 1962. Published in *Dimension 14* (Ann Arbor) and *w*, ed. La Monte Young (self-published with Jackson Mac Low), both 1963. On the second page, the text in the first section constitutes the original work by Flynt. The second section reproduces an update by Flynt, sent via fax to Hennix in 1994; the third (bolded) section represents Hennix's new, original contribution to the work, created in Stockholm, June – September 1994.

Concept Art: Work Such That No One Knows
What's Going On (July 1961)

[One just has to guess whether this work exists and if it does what it is like.]

Version of Work Such That No One Knows
What's Going On (WSTNOKWGO)

Two works: composition, mathematical system
Mathematical system:

i) somebody stipulates, ordains axioms (formation, transformation rules)
ii) somebody concretely discovers specific theorems (discovers: theoremhood is not decidable)
iii) somebody takes the theorems on trust, like formulas for area and volume

it is dissociative logic (partitioned logic) if the experience of each of the three gives no clue to the other two phases:
no way to tell how axioms, rules were arrived at from seeing theorem, no way to tell how discovered or established

it is suspense logic if, for example, axioms are planned and there is concrete discovery of specific theorems *before the axioms are ordained*:
in general, the usual time sequence of i) ii) iii) is disrupted

Maybe call both of these *dissociations*.
WSTNOKWGO is supposed to be the closure of all possible dissociations.

A system of mathematics whose author is unknown has been sealed inside a box. Thus there is no author, no researcher, no lay reader—no addressee. There is only a subject in relation to a hidden system without an author. The axioms and theorems may be real, but they are permanently concealed.
No: does this system exist and what does it say?
You have to guess whether each phase (i, ii, iii) exists *yet* and what it says
…

---

"Presenting" WSTNOKWGO from Flynt's 1961 "anthology" (from letter to Young, 11/29/61). Way you "present" it is to print in program just what I have in anthol., title and bracketed note; and then after print a note giving your guess as to what it is. Then you act accordingly; for ex. if you guess it doesn't exist, you don't do anything, if that it does exist but is nothing then you don't do anything; if that it is such-and-such a piece when you perform it, if that it is Death Valley then you don't have to do anything, etc.

(Updated version H.F. – fax 06/22/1994 15:17.)

---

**My guess is that it would be absurd if this work does not exist & that it is of such a nature that one has to guess whether its non-existence is absurd and if it is, what it is like. (Hint: use intuitionistic logic.)**

C. H-x.
June–September 1994
Galleri Enkehuset, Stockholm

# LANGUAGE AND LIGHT IN MARIAN ZAZEELA'S ART

Written in Amsterdam, 1996. First published in *Sound and Light: La Monte Young and Marian Zazeela*, eds. William Duckworth and Richard Fleming (Associated University Press, 1996).

> So wie die Erkenntnis die Sprache ahndet,
> so erinnert sich die Sprache der Erkenntnis.
> —Hölderlin

While each installation of Marian Zazeela's major work *Light*[1] is an integral part of any *Dream House* installation—and inseparable from it—it must be recognized that *Light* carries an integral structure of its own that, like all of Zazeela's light works, defines a space-time event internal to itself and in complete independence from other programmed events concurrent with it. (The mobiles would keep turning even if the *Dream House* sound was absent or changed and, like La Monte Young's sound, would continue to turn even if no one was present.) There is no doubt, as emphasized by Henry Flynt, that the effects of Zazeela's works critically depends on the dimensions of the ambient space. However, since the artist's freedom to choose her own spatial dimensions is very limited, I shall, in what follows, abstract from any actual space dimensions in order to more fully elaborate on Marian Zazeela's originality as a light artist and calligrapher. Hence, my remarks will also apply to the general case of her light-mobile installations, including installations on high ceilings such as the Harrison Street installation of *The Magenta Lights*, which is discussed by Henry Flynt in "The Lightworks of Marian Zazeela" in [*Sound and Light: La Monte Young and Marian Zazeela*].

## From Light to Language

The mobiles obstructing the light turn on a precisely defined momentum that is intrinsic to their suspension in space. This angular momentum rests and is inscribed within the circumference of a circle (measuring $\pm 2\pi$ radians)—the unit circle of the letter—inside of which the mobile describes its continuous movements clockwise or counterclockwise. The continuity of this movement is nondeterministically broken up by the arrival of a "metastable" momentum at which the mobile assumes a continuously fixed position. The succession of these (continuous) configurations is that of a random pendulum, or an almost *perpetuum mobile*—a physically intractable state (analogous to the complexity of the integral movement of a calligrapher's hand).

Within the boundary conditions of this pendulum, each mobile describes and records, concurrently, a pair of shadow projections carrying fixed, complementary[2] colors (amber and blue in *Time Light Symmetry*, magenta and turquoise blue in many other installations), which are continuously changing or deforming[3] the concurrent projections as each mobile is continuously moving or metastable.

In *Light*, each pair of mobiles thus defines a continuous projection of four colored shadows that, in turn, define what may be conceived of as a *language of illuminated calligraphy* based on an alphabet of at least two characters (in complementary colors) together with their mirror forms. The alphabet, consisting of exactly these four characters, defines the designated *symmetry words* (words favored by Zazeela), which recur nondeterministically. Schematically, these "words" may be written as

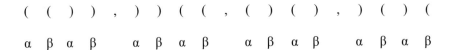

(where the symbols α, β denote the two distinct "complementary" colors), a notation which displays their isometrics and where the first two words are based on four distinct characters, and the last two are based on two distinct characters.

But, obviously, these are not the only possible symmetric configurations of this illuminated alphabet—there are many others which develop over time, some of which have been seen only very rarely—or even only once—and, hence, never been seen again. There are also (possible) symmetric configurations about which it is not known whether they have occurred or ever will occur—meaning, there exist symmetric words about which it is *undecidable* (at current state of knowledge) whether or not they belong to the language actually projected (generated) by the syntactic machinery of Zazeela's *Light*.

(On the level of semiotics, the mobile's surface and its suspension correspond to the calligrapher's pen and hand, respectively; the (monochromatic) light corresponds to (the color of) the ink; the walls support the surface of the writing. In Zazeela's works, the calligrapher's hand is multiplied many times over, writing simultaneously on two or more walls—a humanly unfeasible task.)

Hence, if there is no time restriction on an installation of *Light*, then it poses the possibility of configuring an *absolutely undecidable* word problem in perfect analogy with the intuitionistic counterexamples of classical mathematics. *Exempli gratia*, Brouwer's classical example of an unpredictable run of seven consecutive 7s—the (transcendental) decimal expansion of $\pi$ provides an instance of a synthetic judgement that cannot be evaluated a priori. At the same time, if there (actually) is no run of seven consecutive 7s in $\pi$ (regarded as an "infinite word"), then that fact can never be confirmed by observation (of the decimal expansion [ = "spelling"] of $\pi$). The point is, of course, that we simply *cannot know what is going on* (in Zazeela's environments of *Light*, in the decimal expansion of $\pi$)—even if we are there all the time, that may not be enough time. (This analogy can be sharpened by considering the languages of the *non*-symmetric configurations and their (perhaps continuous) variable alphabets.)

### From Language to Light

Starting in the mid-'60s, Marian Zazeela has created and maintained, in installations of *Light*, works with intrinsic, undecidable properties that reflect our way of extracting a language out of a notation—a notation that is nothing but *pure syntax*, or rather, a notation which does not come equipped with a (given) semantics. Nevertheless, the undecidable properties of Zazeela's illuminated calligraphy are, in some sense, accidental to the construction of the mobiles and their suspension mechanism. As a matter of fact, these properties never entered into the definition of her work as she originally conceived it.

On the contrary, by emphasizing the symmetrical word configurations, Zazeela uses the "intrinsic" semantics of mirror forms, retrograde forms, and nondeterministic recurrences in a way rather analogous to classical Sufi calligraphy. This analogy can be taken further if one considers that Zazeela often lets the letters of her calligraphy dissolve, disintegrate into fragments, only to reimport their meaning as fragments that form ever-new symmetric forms (as in *Ornamental Lightyears Tracery* [see Zazeela's essay *Ornamental Lightyears Tracery* in the volume that originally published this essay]).

Consequently, there is no longer any question of (formal) undecidability here because no structure remains constant under its fragmentation. Even the question of a language recedes—the meaning, if any, may come from elsewhere or from anywhere. *The Dream House*, with its standing, composite sound waveforms, provides an unreality conducive to a meaning that accrues as pure color, as light miraculously purified while sustained for an indefinite time. At this level of perception, the microscopic changes of the shadows cast by the mobiles create a new level of nuance that requires a new tactic of attention distinct from any attention to words or even letters. This is an unreal or ephemeral language, the meaning of which is not prescribed anywhere except at the level of the unconscious—and in complete analogy with sound, it records itself as a cosmic event that shall never return.

However, the fact that this ephemeral language, with its fragile micro-syntax, lacks a formal combinatorial structure does not prevent it from carrying a completely paradoxical appearance. There is, again, an analogy with Sufi calligraphy here, but Henry Flynt's approach to *The Magenta Lights* (as noted in "The Lightworks of Marian Zazeela" in the volume that originally published this essay) shows that entirely independent considerations may carry more weight.

Yet, Zazeela's illuminated calligraphy is strongly confluent with the Sufi practice of *devotional writing*[4]—the practice of an endless writing of a single letter and its fragments, a ceaseless rewriting of the unutterable *Name*, of the unspeakable *Truth*, not necessarily intended to be read or seen by another human being. The intended meaning may no longer be the meaning of words but a meaning that no longer depends on words or depends on words yet to be written—a meaning in search of a language that emanates from a language in search of its meaning. The signifier of a work of devotional writing has the same degree of freedom as the signifier of a text of abstract mathematics—a world closed up on itself and impenetrable from without and accessible only by an *inner illumination*. The calligrapher's pen and hand both cease to have an ontological import here—rather, they coalesce with (the soul of) the calligraphy itself, with the paradoxical perceptual effects succinctly described in Henry Flynt's aforementioned essay.

In their integral appearance, each installation of *Light* brings together many different levels of paradoxicality as these levels inscribe themselves in an invariant ambient space. These levels do not always mix with each other but remain separated by their distinct tactics of attention. Zazeela does not prefer one tactic over another as long as attention is not abandoned. Nor does Zazeela guard against a sharp distinction between calligraphic writings and calligraphic drawings, respectively. At any one time, each installation of *Light* may be viewed as one or the other, or, perhaps, as both. Zazeela's work requires, as does La Monte Young's, the unconditional participation of the spectator who, ultimately, is the agent of creating a writing or a drawing or something else upon viewing a particular installation of *Light* for any given amount of time. Remark that the artist herself has no undue advantage over any other spectator, as "creators" of this work both assume the same activity but not necessarily with equivalent tactics of attention. An installation of *Light* is no less enigmatic to Marian Zazeela herself than it is to any other spectator—there is no script, only anticipation and retrodictions, which are not always possible to systematize.

Marian Zazeela's illuminated calligraphy, in spite of its minimalistic appearance, is a most intricate light work that, in its scope and originality, defines its own aesthetics. Her modalities of calligraphy are a site for a language of light that writes itself without the interference of a human will, without the interruptions of a human hand. Only the boundary conditions of this writing have been fixed by the artist—everything else is sheer magic, like the (unpredictable) digits falling out of the decimal places of $\pi$.

Already in the 1960s, when Marian Zazeela began working with lights, mobiles, and shows, it was clear that her approach to art was related to poetry and the process of writing. In an early (1963) text, "The Soul of the Word"[5] (reprinted in the last section of [Sound and Light: La Monte Young and Marian Zazeela]), Zazeela describes how she regards the soul of the world as imprisoned, but how (the act of) writing may carry it away while preserving it through the fragmentation of its letters—the soul of the word is a dream and dreams recur as reincarnations. Besides the confluence with Sufi mystical poetry, one may notice that her critique of chance coincides with Mallarmé's in his *Un Coup de Dés Jamais N'Abolira Le Hasard* and *Le Livre*,[6] with the only difference that she takes the concept one step further by requiring that the meaning of a word must write itself as its writing writes itself: as a gift, as a miracle from nowhere. By reaching beyond conventional words, beyond conventional meanings, Marian Zazeela has synthesized a (many?) language system(s) of notation(s) that give(s) an entirely new meaning to both poetry and art, resulting in a conceptual art form with nontrivial subjectivities which defines a most rare and original style.

Epigraph's translation: Just as cognition intuits language, so does language recall cognition (*Über die verfahrungsweise des poetischen Gestites*).

1   See La Monte Young and Marian Zazeela's "Continuous Sound and Light Environments" (see the volume in which this essay was first published) for listings of *Light*, the genre of light-mobile environments.
2   I.e., distinct, nonintersecting colors. Warning: this is not the same meaning of "complimentary" as in color theory but, rather, the meaning as in set theory.
3   I.e., deformation in the sense of homotopy theory.
4   See Annemarie Schimmel's *Mystical Dimensions of Islam*. Chapel Hill: University of North Carolina Press, 1975; and *As Through a Veil: Mystical Poetry in Islam*. New York: Columbia University Press, 1982.
5   La Monte Young and Marian Zazeela, *Selected Writings*. Munich: Heiner Friedrich, 1969.
6   See Maurice Blanchot's *Le Livre á Venir*. Paris: Gallimard, 1959.

# THE BERLIN MAHNMAL

"Project for a (Non?-) Berlin Metamahnmal" written in Amsterdam, February 1999. "Eisenman I, Eisenman II, Eisenman III" written in Amsterdam, 1999. Both previously unpublished. See also: "No-One's Memorial / Das Niemandsmal /" in Hennix, *Poësy Matters* (Blank Forms Editions, 2019).

# Project for a (Non?-) Berlin Metamahnmal

INTRODUCTION

When I first learned, about a year ago, about the result of the official Berlin Mahnmal Competition I was greatly astonished. First of all, I was astonished by the very fact that a subject as serious as a Holocaust monument could, in any way, be associated with the type of modern art that was offered by the winning candidates Richard Serra and Peter Eisenman. But I was also astonished by what was offered by the running-up candidates' contributions because it was, indeed, difficult to see how their works in any way differed from the type of works of modern art which, ostensibly, have *no* pretensions to assimilate any difficult subject matter whatsoever, especially one that would be carrying political/historical overtones. The latter predicate is, however, even more attachable to the winning contribution (*Eisenman I*) by Serra/Eisenman, neither of whom is known for any intellectual efforts—except in the field of marketing their own anti-intellectual products, a field in which, ostensibly, both of them have shown remarkable success.

It was difficult for me not to feel that what has become known as *Eisenman I* in recent days was nothing short of an assault on the entire subject matter of Germany and the Holocaust. Not only was the lack of a credible connection between the Serra/Eisenman's work and the Holocaust disturbing, but, even more, so was the artists' profound lack of knowledge of the subject matter that they claimed to represent. It was, indeed, difficult to avoid the thought that Eisenman and Serra were launching the biggest con-artist scam not only of their entire careers, but, actually, of the entire century. Now, a year later and a few months after that, the Walser-Bubis debate has ceased after having opened a deep wound on the basis of which the most astonishing actions have taken place in the last few months by Eisenman and his new cohort (after Serra and Kohl chose to drop out), M. Naumann, one can understand that there is a convoluted, even sinister, hidden agenda accompanying the Holocaust Mahnmal competition that takes us back to the lessons learned from the *Historikerstreit* of the late '80s in conjunction with the attendant *Streit* over the Berlin Museum of German History and the Bonn House of History.

The analysis of the *Mahnmal Streit* is not yet ripe for a definitive conclusion, but already a year ago one could sense the "drift" of this controversy aligning it with the fate of *Deutsches Historisches Museum*. That is to say, both the History museum and the Holocaust Monument were conceived *prior* to there being any semblance of a possibility to actually fulfill the conditions laid down as a prerequisite for these, so far, entirely abstract entities being non-empty concepts. In order to come to grips with the integrated subject matter as such, I conceived, about a year ago, a concept for a *Meta-Mahnmal*, by which I aimed at not only setting a new standard for what is a passable design for a Mahnmal representing the collective of victims of the Holocaust, but which also could take into account the accompanying public discussions surrounding the various phases of this Berlin Republic Identity Project—even if this discussion more properly ought to belong to the collection reserved for the History Museum.

At the time, I could not have dreamt of the intensity of the ensuing (pseudo-)debate that came to follow the Eisenman-Kohl, or *Eisenman II* project (the new, improved *Eisenman I*)—nor, of course, the still shamelessly ongoing and seemingly never-ending scandal perpetrated by the shakers and movers who chose to become advocates of the Eisenman-Neumann *Eisenman III* project (the *new, improved Eisenman II*) or *combi*-Mahnmal project. (I notice that the singularly important and all defining prefix *Holocaust* has been dropped in favor of the automobile term *combi* and, further, that the term "Mahnmal" has been degraded to Denkmal—all while the term Bundestag is progressively being upgraded as *Reichtag*.)

As I've just mentioned, the time has not yet arrived for the *Schlussstrich* of this debate, and, therefore, I am only able to give a brief overview of some of my thoughts that lead me to conceive a *Meta-Mahnmal* as the appropriate response to this sordid and unheard-of international art competition. However, my *Meta-Mahnmal* project does not end until all the cards are in and ready to be called. (Nevertheless, in order to give a public sense to my seemingly disconnected project, I must confess that I thought the Mahnmal competition would have ended prior to last year's German election, and that it would be rejected as ill-conceived and out of hand on all levels.)

Despite the loud and endless debate over the issues involved, I don't see that anything new actually has been added to the discussion of German history as begun fifteen years ago by the *Historiker-* and *Museumstreits*, and continued with renewed intensity through the *Wehrmachtstreit* of a few years ago. What stands out from these "*Streits*," and further amplified by the recent Walser-Bubis *Streit*, is the sustained *compact silence* over the long enduring silence which German history has afforded itself not only after 1945 but also equally already from 1933 and onwards, when the foundations for a fabricated national history were laid. Although, clearly, more has been said than ever before that there is still a lack of an overreaching view which bridges the gap between the "intentional" and "functionalist" schools of history when applied to the events defining German history from 1933–1945, for which neither of which is able to address the phenomenon of this silence over the "*pact of silence*" extended between those who had been empowered to be the surviving witnesses—whether as victims, perpetrators, or just passive bystanders. As an artist and (unvoluntary) citizen of the European Union, I feel a strong need to understand this pact of silence not only as a historical fact but, more urgently, as a *psychological* fact of human consciousness—since it appears impossible that what is *now* known to have happened has, for so long, been covered by an impenetrable silence, and, although *now* known, still remains largely inaccessible and therefore effectively silenced in the public domain. (Of course, I'm not the first one who has addressed this issue—but, paradoxically, I've increasingly found it difficult to recognize the appropriate forum at which this impossibility may belong.)

Nevertheless, the apparently impossible is exactly what is possible, and various dialects of a communicative silence can be observed to have evolved over time. Also, there is a widely entrenched language which purports to deliver explanations of the past, which comes into play exactly at the moment when communicative silence appears to have worn itself out. Thus, covert memories and less than accurate descriptions of facts surface in the public domain each time, claiming that a last and definitive account of the past *finally* has been reached (*Schlussstrich*). One is reminded of Freud's early experience with *hysterics* that turned out to give false testimony concerning the origins of their traumatic past. But one also becomes reminded of Lacan's theory of the denial of the *abject*—to which I will return, below. But first I need to make an excursion into "the" field of contemporary German history in order to set the stage for my investigation.

Lacking the acumen of a professional historian, I have been forced to use sources which more or less randomly have caught my attention. This random search has, *so far*, developed a picture of this pact of communicative silence along three dimensions corresponding to three types of affiliations, viz., (i) the pact between the *perpetrators*; (ii) the pact between the *victims*; and (iii) the pact between the *bystanders* (and to the latter group I also count those who after the war served as authors of its chronicles).

Thus, I got my first clue to the deep-seated cause for this public, communicative amnesia from a report by Jan Philipp Reemtsma in his intervention to the Wehrmacht exhibit in Bremen, 1997, where he recounts the memorable episode from Ruth Beckermann's movie *Jenseits des Krieges*, about an Austrian Eastern Front soldier who, after having seen the Vienna installation of the exhibition *Verbrechen der Wehrmacht*, speaks to the camera and says, "Alles was hier zu sehen ist, habe ich auch gesehen. Und meine Kameraden haben es auch gesehen. Aber als wir wieder zu Hause waren, da habe ich daruber sprechen wollen, aber es hat geheiflen: 'Woruber redest du? Dergleichen haben wir nicht gesehen!'"

This story made a deep impression on me since it illustrated with exemplary clarity the Lacanian interpretation of the trauma ensuing from the human encounter with the *abject*, i.e., that which is irretrievably *beyond* human comprehension on account of its unbearable character. In addition, this story illustrates the compulsion by which the return of the repressed exerts itself. In fact, it illustrated how it is the language of communicative silence *itself* which assures the speaker not only that the abject will not be betrayed but also that the abject is placed at a comfortable and safe distance from the routine everyday conduct, out of which the abject originally arose.

The second clue came from Isaiah Trunk's studies from the 1970s and Mark Edelman's *Ghetto Walczy* from 1945—two works that are extensively quoted in Zygmunt Bauman's *Modernity and the Holocaust*. From the works of Edelman and Trunk (or Bauman), one can understand how it is that Ignatz Bubis has, as he confesses in the FAZ round table conference with Martin Walser, avoided reading any general account of the Holocaust save a single volume on *Treblinka*. For Bubis, the Holocaust reduces to a personal trauma for which the larger context surrounding it must be denied through a concerted effort to look away from the actual documentations of its mechanics, thereby replacing actual history by a veil of noble silence. When he accuses Walser of reaching for a *Schlussstrich*, it is hard not to read in a return of the repressed. Thus, Bubis's reaction on Walser's *Sonntagsrede* in the Frankfurter Paulskirche exemplifies yet another strategy for dealing with the abject history of the twentieth century. Of course, Bubis's reaction falls short of being representative of all those personal histories, which involve a much more direct and violent encounter with the brutality of Nazi hegemony—but it shows that already a "distant" involvement suffices to create a deep-seated trauma. It is not necessary to travel the entire distance to Auschwitz in order to be stunned for life. (On the other hand, Bubis may not be an entirely bona fide representative at all, on account of several disturbing biographical details, such as his past dealings with Degussa and his recent insistence on the unfoundedness of the class-action suits on behalf of former slave workers now living in the US.)

Of course, it would be undue to treat either of these two types of affiliation as homogenous types—silence takes many forms, as does the reason for it. That holds with even stronger emphasis for the third type of affiliation with the postwar German pact of communicative silence, i.e., the "passive bystanders," since the latter type is inherently entirely heterogeneous, consisting, as it does, of "everybody else." However, each of these types speaks its own dialect of a "noble silence", which for posterity seldom can be translated into anything else but a form of "coward silence"—a silence which, when not broken, converges on a hideous species of crime if it weren't for the (psychoanalytic) fact that we are here dealing with a type of epidemic infection, a sickness not recognized by conventional medicine. Only original research, still to be considered, can contribute to a resolution of the enigma(s) posed by this language of silence, which distinguishes itself by making all its speakers lookalikes, by making no one stand out in the crowd.

This is not to say that the historian's account of these events is less urgent than the psychoanalytical—although, clearly, few historical studies have been forthcoming on this inescapable subject matter. To my knowledge, the only authors explicitly addressing this issue on the basis of historical records are Norbert Frei in his groundbreaking study from 1996, "Vergangenheitspolitik: Die Anfange der Bunderrepublik und die NS-Vergangenheit," and Bernward Domer in a volume from last year [1998] entitled *Heimtucke: Das Gesetz als Waffe*. Of course, the somewhat earlier groundbreaking works by such historians as Gotz Aly and Susanne Heim are very valuable for assessing not only the amount of silence cast over our recent past, but also for understanding what the silence actually has been standing for as a representing signifier. Yet, for a layperson trying to come to grips with the historical trauma that began with the first concentration camps in 1933, there is just not sufficient research available in the public domain of which one can avail oneself. Nevertheless, the enormous public attention given to the exhibition *Vernichtungskrieg, Verbrechen der Wehrmacht 1941 to 1944* goes a long way to illustrate the force by which the abject commands everybody's attention—given, that is, that its signifiers do not encroach upon the censorship exerted by those ever-recurrent mundane events that cannot happen but yet somehow always do. (A *New York Times* reporter made almost the same point in 1986 during the height of the *Historikerstreit* when she generalized upon the German identity experience and observed that "Europe's apparent amnesia about the war is largely a willed phenomenon. Europeans old enough to remember those years have not forgotten the past, but often remember it all too well, and they deeply resent being reminded of it.")[1]

As an artist, I don't see how it would be possible to abstract from the problematics just outlined above when the task of conceiving a *Mahnmal* in the city center of Berlin is at issue. Nor do I see the reason for letting the Germans *alone* decide whether there should (as opposed to would) be a *Mahnmal* or not in Berlin. Germany is, despite opinions to the contrary, *not* a *"normal"* member of the European Union, especially as the city of Frankfurt am Main has octroyed the bank vault of the European Central Bank. And, besides, the difficult intellectual issues connected with this task require an entirely new approach to art if to avoid the already exposed pitfalls associated with the entire *Mahnmalstreil*. As Martin Walser concluded more than once in the *FAZ* roundtable discussion with Ignatz Bubis, *"We need an entirely new language"* (for the purpose of representing the meaning of the Holocaust to the generations to come).

It seems to me that the entire *Mahnmalstreit* has been obsessed with a single ontological category, viz., the category of (natural) numbers—considered only, however, for the purpose of establishing a *count of victims* (of the Nazi crimes). Thus, already the first considered *Mahnmal*, proposed by Simon Ungers and Christine Jackob-Marks, was supposed to be a (single) monumental "grave stone" with room for more than four million names of Jewish victims claimed by the Nazis engraved on its surface. The fact that such a monumental slab of concrete could not stand erect but had to be a horizon—the construction appears to have disturbed no one. Neither did anyone express exception to the provocative gesture of letting this number of victims constitute the "foundational sacrifice" on which the (re-)unified Germany was to be erected. And, now, the last proposal for a *Mahnmal* has been nothing but a Kindergarten exercise in arithmetic aimed at soothing, first of all, the politicians who sit on the money that Serra and Eisenman so eagerly are waiting for—to the extent that not only have the artists been willing to sell out their entire artistic integrity but, what is much more disturbing, to sell out the dignity of all the Jewish victims supposed to have been commemorated next to the Potsdamer Platz. It is difficult not to speculate that these two elderly charlatans have self-appointed themselves as members of a fictitious Council of Elders (i.e., a travesty of the Polish Judenrat of the 1940s) in order to maximize their insult and betrayal by associations to one of the major sell-out mechanisms that contributed to the simplification of the administrative procedures by which Jewish culture and ways of life were exterminated from European soil. I found it *very disturbing* when Ignatz Bubis, a few weeks ago, accepted *Eisenman III* with the acclaim that it was a "fascinating" contribution to the legacy of Holocaust Denkmals on German soil. Is Bubis entirely ignorant or just another opportunist—like Naumann, Kohl, Schroder, and all the others?

In any case, all of the *Eisenman I–III* give weight to the interpretation that the Berlin *Mahnmal* aims at cementing the hapless historian's pronouncement that Auschwitz is beyond human comprehension, that it is, in Dan Diner's words, a "no-man's land of the mind, a black box of explanation; it sucks in all historiographic attempts at interpretation, is a vacuum taking meaning from outside history. Only *ex negativo*, only through the constant attempt to understand why it cannot be understood, can we measure what sort of occurrence this breach of civilization really was." In one word, we are back to the traumatized Austrian ex-Wehrmact soldier who recounted how a pact of silence and fierce denial met him when he tried to escape the doom of it never happened.

It is, to say the least, *very disturbing* that the aestheticization of meaningless garbage, i.e., *minimalism* (the trademark of Serra/Eisenman), is being considered as a means for representing the impotency of an apologetic "science" of history in order to further a *Schlussstrich* that appears to be ordered by the German State Department, Deutsche Bank, Daimler-Chrysler, and the Sony Corporations, i.e., the *Mahnmal's* closest architectural neighbors on Potsdamer Platz. On the other hand, one has to congratulate the latter industrial complexes on a perfectly manipulated contest by which artists with no other experience than how to turn garbage into cash have succeeded in octroying not just Auschwitz but also the entire history of Nazi Germany's victims. Not only do the victims deserve a better deal, but so do the German people and everybody else living in the European Union. Therefore, picking up where Walser signed off in his *Streit* with Bubis & Co., I emphatically urge an effort to master a *new language* appropriate for the task at hand. This language may not suit the taste of the shakers and movers currently occupying the scene of the *Mahnmal* contest—but that must not be *my* problem. Nor do I wish to get involved with conventional artistic problems since they, in any case, have uniformly failed to address the ostensibly unique prerequisite which the *Mahnmal* must address in order not to result in a monumental insult to the generations to come. I shall now, therefore, *very briefly* give an account of my own ideas, which will be far from exhaustive. When an occasion is given, I will expand considerably on the short presentation given below. Remark that the task I understand to set myself *does not* require of me that I persist within the conventional boundaries of "modern art," but that the complexity of the subject matter frees me to seek a language which, at least on occasion, transcends what is commonly received as conventional art. In particular, conventional *non*-mathematical methods of representation are selectively rejected (on the basis of their immanent inadequacy). Furthermore, my proposal goes beyond the conventional concept of a *Mahnmal*, and I prefer, in order to amplify the subterm "*Mahn*," to designate it as a *Meta-Mahnmal*.

PROPOSAL.

It is a common experience for an intellectual to seek a new language in the manifold vocabulary of modern mathematics when the task consists in representing phenomena that exceed a certain threshold of complexity. In particular, when we seek to represent spaces or events that lay *beyond* our conventional capacities of perception or comprehension, abstract mathematics offers a singularly unique way of conceiving the invisible. For example, when the beginning or, for that matter, the end of the universe is being modeled in at least approximately comprehensible terms, certain equations can be helpful—on the condition that they are not abused by biased philosophical speculations (which, admittedly, are rather rare). On the basis of this tradition of inquiry into perceptually invisible domains, it occurred to me, as a dialectical reaction to the proposals elicited during the *Mahnmal* contest, that, *as a minimum*, a certain *arithmetical number* was needed in order to represent the order and degree of the human victimization summarily referred to as the *Holocaust*. I wish to stress that I do *not* propose that the subject matter of the Holocaust is reducible to any one number (arithmetical or otherwise). But I do propose, in order to avoid the absolute relativization espoused by such historians as Mr. Diner, quoted above, that some counting procedure must be invoked that is commensurate with the degree of incomprehensibility (and invisibility), which the Holocaust phenomenon inevitably initially offers to those who, like myself, are entirely lacking in the personal experience of a regime of a militarized, totalitarian state.

Of course, not any specific number can represent the totality of Nazi victims, nor would an approximate number be adequate. On the contrary, the number in question must be inaccessible to anyone's comprehension, if not to one's imagination—without reaching the ambiguities and paradoxes connected with the infinite or transfinite domains of arithmetic. In fact, the number must be *finite* while, at the same time, representing the impossibility of reaching it by the regular procession of counting, i.e., by adding +1 to each preceding number, starting from the number one. That is, if the number in question is denoted by the letter $\int$, then it must be impossible to reach it by any finite sum $1 + 1 + 1 + ... + 1$. Such numbers are called by the mathematician *non-Archimedean* numbers and, hence, the number n which I am seeking is such a number. That is to say, as individuals, the victims of the Holocaust are *numberless*, impossible to count up to—not because there is a lack of experience by humans to count up to, say, any number of millions of DM (when destined for a take-over bid for *Bankers Trust*, say), but because the victims (unlike the assets of Bankers Trust) were *a priori* considered as unworthy of being counted individually since they were defined as "unnutze Esser" (like rats or grasshoppers, which, when exterminated en masse, are counted as undifferentiated collectives). Besides, the German bureaucratic machine was not that perfect, and hence failed on many occasions to faithfully record all its deeds. In addition, even in the cases when its record keeping had been accurate, considerable efforts were spent at the bitter end of the war to destroy as many incriminating records as possible. Thus, the *official* number of WWII Nazi victims does not correspond to their actual number—about which future generations always will remain in the dark. In particular, can we with certainty know who was the *first* victim—or the *last*? Thus, I wish to emphasize that, on the basis of existing historical records, we are in the dark even as we attempt to start this procedure of counting. And, as I wish to suggest, perhaps the counting needs to be extended even into our own times—and *beyond*, since by no means is it beyond doubt that the Nazi regime lost the *ideological* component of the war against alternative cultures and lifestyles.

The three dots "..." in the schematically indicated sum $1 + 1 + 1 + ... + 1$ above stand, mathematically, for the (inductive) passage from one number, k, say, to the next *immediately succeeding* number, $k + 1$. When all such passages have been completed and a definite number, m, say, has been reached, then m can be written as a sum $1 + 1 + 1 + ... + 1$—and is called an *Archimedean* number. By contrast, if, for a number m, $m - 1$ such passages cannot be performed, then m is called a *non-Archimedean* number, in honor of the ancient Greek mathematician Archimedes, who discovered such numbers in connection with the (impossible) task of counting all the grains of sand in the universe, the task given to the mythological Sandreckoner.

Accordingly, I use *four dots* "...." in a sum $1 + 1 + 1 + .... + 1$ in order to indicate that the uniform passage from one number unit to the next has been destroyed by the complexity of the counting procedure, which thus represents a *non-Archimedean* number m. And for my *Meta-Mahnmal*, I use for the number, n, of victims of the Holocaust, the following schematic representation:

(Which is here printed, quite deliberately, in the typeface Charcoal, at 72 pt, using the letter "I" again, quite deliberately, for the "pillars," while the black "squares" are the period sign in Charcoal—again, at 72 pt.) (Actually, I'll use 500+ pt.) Thus, the letter n also denotes the word not iterated, non-recursively, n times: I becomes **not**-I n times, the Crosses on Calgary extended an n-fold number of times (Pilatus's crime and indifference multiplied n times), etc., etc.

The actual realization of the above (*non-Archimedean*) number structure shall consist of 5 (= the number of fingers of one hand) larger-than-man-size pillars made out of charcoal (the exact size depending on the site at which this structure is installed) and where the "black squares" are to be obtained from one-such sized charcoal pillar cut in four equal parts. The entire structure shall rest on a "desert" of charcoal powder, the extension of which shall depend on the site of the installation. However, its semblance to a Japanese *Stone Garden* shall be approached by indenting the surface with fine straight lines "raked" *lengthwise*, i.e., parallel with the maximum side of the rectangle defining the area covered by the charcoal powder.

Thus, such, *very briefly*, is my concept for a *Mahnmal* representing the victims of the Holocaust. But since the possibility of erecting a pure *Mahnmal*, free of the dissonances accompanying the various suggestions for a Berlin Mahnmal, has been entirely destroyed by a *Streit* that doesn't belong to a dignified Denkmal, it is no longer conceivable that such a monument can fulfill its original purpose— and, therefore, only a *Meta-Mahnmal* remains as an artistic possibility which simultaneously defines the dialectics of meta-silence, i.e., silence accruing or accumulating over silence; silence's impenetrable silence.

Ad. 1. The installation of the *Meta-Mahnmal* must be an indoor installation— preferably in a soundproof room. In addition, the light must be distributed in such a way that no shadow falls from any of the elements of the *Meta-Mahnmal*. The "shadows of WWII" are confined in their entirety to the (topological) boundaries defined by the geometrical extension of the configuration of charcoal elements.

Ad. 2. A certain text shall accompany the installation taken from my poem cycle *No-One's Memorial / Das Niemandsmal /*, printed in Hennix, *Poësy Matters* (Blank Forms Editions, 2019).

Ad. 3. A psychoanalytic seminar shall address the topography of the structure of meta-silence over the Holocaust in accordance with the theory of J. Lacan. (This will be a continuation of my three previous seminaires conducted since 1992; see "~~La~~ Séminaire" in this volume.)

Stockholm, Feb. 14, 1999, 5:51 a.m.

---

1   Judith Miller, *New York Times Magazine*, Nov. 16, 1986

# Eisenman I, Eisenman II, Eisenman III. Eins, Zwei, Drei, ... , Sold to the Berliner Republik For 150 Million DM+.

The brand of minimalism offered by Eisenman and Serra for the Onkel Fritz Republic Mahnmal is a definitive advancement of the ancient alchemical formula for turning lead into gold, viz., a formula for turning garbage into gold.

Unfortunately, the case is a much more serious one dealing, as it does, with the extermination of the last vestiges of a form of life predicated on the premise that more than an educated guess is required for the advancement of knowledge about the human past and the pending future.

In order to understand why the E&S concrete monument exercises such an irresistible appeal to the various lobby groups progressively colonizing the center of Berlin one needs to recall (once again) the dreadful history of this city, viz., it was at this site that *Generalplan Ost* was developed, i.e., the administrative plan that, after having led to some 100 million deaths, lead to flattening to the ground of almost the entire city center. The recklessness with which the Nazi regime leveled entire cultures to the ground in less than ten years is now repeated on site within the same time span by the old friends of Hitler. That is to say, the rebuilding of Berlin is nothing less than a Generalplan Ost in miniature!

This claim requires an extensive descriptive apparatus, which I will work out in the near future!

The Berliner Mahnmal Entwurf has, during its ten-plus years of gestation, become everything it ought not to be. Starting out as some kind of response to the Hall of Names and the Garden of Remembrance at Yad Vashem in Jerusalem, it has, in early 1999, been octroyed by the Chancellor's cultural affairs czar in order to beat Israel at its own game, and, accordingly, it has been christened The House of Remembrance. In order to get away with this scam, two charlatans from New York have been hired, one of which backed off last summer since he was busy pursuing some other art scams on his native soil (although we are assured that he remains on the team as a "consultant").

Since so-called "modern art"—and, in particular, what is known as "minimalism"—is patently a game for and by idiots, it does not invite a serious writer to spill any ink on the subject matter. However, this time the offense is perpetrated on such an unprecedented scale that a comment is inevitable on this mishmash of kitsch, death, and politics.

To begin with, it has to be assessed to what extent the winner of this contest, Mr. Eisenman, that is, has any knowledge about the proposed subject matter at all. I therefore recall an interview conducted by *Die Zeit*, No. 51, Dec. 10, 1998, the opening question of which was, "Herr Eisenman, do you already know what you will do on January 27, 1999?" To which Mr. Eisenman offered a counter question: "On January 27th?" Of course, January 27 is the date on which Auschwitz was liberated by the allies, a date which the German nation, on pain of not appearing politically correct, has assigned quite special significance. This historical and moral meaning was obviously entirely lost on Mr. Eisenman, who, however, was given a clue and a second chance by *Zeit's* editor, who filled him in as follows: "That is the day on which the foundation stone for the Holocaust-Mahnmal in Berlin will be layed." Mr. Eisenman is still entirely lost, as evidenced by the following answer: "As I don't even know if I'll be the architect of the Mahnmal, I'll will do nothing." In one word, Mr. Eisenman's plan for remembering the liberation of Auschwitz depends on whether he is going to be paid or not, or, more accurately, whether he is going to be remembered or not (by the Germans, that is).

Somewhat later in the *Zeit* interview he goes on to admonish the Germans as follows: "If the Germans build a Mahnmal, they should do so on *the correct grounds*" (my italics). I take that to mean that unless the design of the Mahnmal is signed P. Eisenman, the Germans have failed to recognize the "correct grounds" for building a central monument in remembrance of the Holocaust. Of course, Mr. Eisenman is in good company here, as a certain Herr Dr. H. Kohl has backed him all the way—at least up to the *Eisenman II* version (i.e., the new, improved *Eisenman I*), which these two gentlemen negotiated in May 1998.

That the Herr Doctor knew precisely what he was doing remains beyond any doubts since leaving the building of the Mahnmal to a money-hungry charlatan from New York City would virtually guarantee not only that practically anyone would have no clue as to the meaning of this assemblage of concrete pillars, but, and much more importantly, it would also appease the American courts to the extent that the monetary damage claims by surviving Holocaust victims living in the US could be alleviated by a show of "good faith" put on by the German

Bundestag. This viewpoint is supported by the following story transmitted by *Der Spiegel* journalist H.M. Broder (*Spiegel* 4/1999): a German diplomat in Washington, D.C., tells Broder over a dinner, "We need the Mahnmal most urgently, the faster it is built, the better." On the question to whom "we" refers, the diplomat answers without any further elaboration: "Das Auswartige Amt [i.e., the German State Department]. It is good for our self-image in the US." That is to say, not only is the acquisition of Bankers Trust by Deutsche Bank in question, but so is a possible boycott of the products of Daimler Chrysler, Degussa, Dresden Bank, and other profiteers from the Third Reich, all of which are aiming at a deep penetration of the US market.

The urgency is also stressed by Stateminister Naumann, who in *Focus* 4/1999 states, in connection with how much money the German Government is prepared to spend on the "Combi-Mahnmal," that "money cannot play a decisive role" (apropos the mega price tag allotted to *Eisenman III* ). Indeed, the cost of the lawyer team fighting the pending indictments in the NY Courts could easily run anywhere between 50 and 100 million dollars depending on the length of the litigations. And Naumann is not alone. The Swedish Stateminister Person is concerned not only about the legal implications of Sweden's role as caretaker of Nazi gold, but also with legal settlements concerning Wallenberg's Industries' involvement as a main provider for Germany's war-machine. Person proposed, on Jan. 27, 1999, that Sweden should earmark this date as a national day of remembrance of the Holocaust.

That Mr. Eisenman is well versed in today's anti-intellectual radical chic is amply illustrated by his philosophical agencies, which go all the way from C.G. Jung's arian psychology to the pop-authors Habermas and Derrida. In the case of Jung, Mr. Eisenman has the following to say on the topic of the "collective" function of his Mahnmal proposal (*Die Zeit*, ibid.): "It will shed light on the collective subconsciousness. Carl Gustav Jung believed that also the public collective carries a guilt which must be exposed. He held that the public ritual of punishment is justified since thereby it confers an experience of a kind of absolution on the collective subconsciousness." (Then follows another self-serving harangue about the *Eisenman II* proposal.)

Mr. Eisenman also displays an enormous capacity for namedropping, as in the following interview in *Frankfurter Allgemeine Zeitung*, No. 220 (Sept. 22, 1998), where no one other than James Joyce and his masterpiece *Finnegans Wake* are invoked. As a matter of fact, Mr. Eisenman turns himself into an instant literature critic, pronouncing (without, apparently, any familiarity with the secondary literature) that no one knows how to read Joyce's magnum opus—implying that if unreadability confers immortality to a literary work, then why should not an unreadable and meaningless Mahnmal be granted the same status, especially if it is conceived by Mr. Eisenman. Indeed, why not? Anything goes, as Paul Feyerabend put it for his philosophy-tiered Berkeley students after 1968. And then follows Mr. Eisenman's intellectual tour de force, the claim that *Eisenman II* "puts the collective and individual unconscious [sic!] in the [sic!] reality. It is provoking to come face to face with one's own unconsciousness. No one knows how to do that and humans are frightened by what they do not know." Later in the same interview,

Mr. Eisenman clarifies the symbolism of his "anti-symbolic" concrete monument by the statement that no one knows yet how to understand *Eisenman II*—including Mr. Eisenman himself! This understanding of *Eisenman II* stands in stark contrast to the self-confessed art connoisseur Herr Dr. H. Kohl, who only a few days earlier claimed, with no reservation, that this Mahnmal was, in particular, concerned with the remembrance of the crime depicted by *Eisenmann II* (see *FAZ*, No. 216, Sept. 1998). I note in passing that these two gentlemen have a quite uncomplicated relationship, not only with what "reality" designates but also with what it means to remember the Nazi crimes against humanity. They express themselves as if reality and its historical past record possess a singular and unique reading, equal in meaning for all of us.

Rather than a "why not?" it seems that a "why bother?" would be what they truly aim at. And that would, of course, be the right strategy to surreptitiously achieve a "Schlusstrich" for the victims and survivors of the Holocaust—at least as concerns the monetary claims made on their behalf. The Walser Waltz continues successfully in the public German domain.

Not only has there been a silence about the Holocaust and a silence over this silence, but also there has been a silence over the overt lack of credible intellectual assessment of what the topic requires—as shown by the remarkable silence in which the then Chancellor Kohl's remarks on the *Eisenman II* were passed over by the German press.

According to Herr Dr. Kohl, there exists no suitable word for the Holocaust (*FAZ*, ibid.). He goes on to say that there is no way of conceiving an exhibit of the Holocaust by means of a picture. Thus, in merely two short sentences, Herr Dr. Kohl has succeeded in asserting that (1) the word "Holocaust" (or any other word) is an unsuitable word for the Holocaust, and (2) no pictorial means suffice for clarifying what went down during the catastrophe. In one word, he advises us to keep our ears shut and our eyes closed when considering the subject matter of the Holocaust. And, furthermore, he asserts that the millions of German families whose relatives died in WWII should no longer blame their deaths on the Nazi regime but, rather, should understand the victims' plight by taking a long look at the Neue Wache Monument, which, although wordless and mute, exhibits a well-measured picture of their sustained trauma. Thus, Herr Dr. Kohl finds here an excuse to implicitly rehash young Wittgenstein's maxim—that about which one cannot speak one must remain silent—as well as remind us of the picture theory of meaning, without remarking that the theory went out of vogue the minute Wittgenstein decided to "return" to philosophy.

Herr Dr. Kohl clarifies (*FAZ*, ibid.): "We are not talking about any subject matter. We are talking about the Holocaust and how such a subject matter should be suitably thought of in Germany." We are, obviously, dealing with a culture of oblivion seeking to regain the national entrenchment it once enjoyed before being disrupted by the Historikerstreit, the Wehrmachtstreit, the Walser-Bubis Streit, and the (seemingly) forever ongoing Mahnmalstreit. And the latter Streit is, of course, a suitable diversion tactic for the ongoing and, in the near future, anticipated legal Streits dealing with crimes committed by Deutsche Bank, Dresden Bank,

Degussa, VW, Opel, Daimler-Benz, and other German industrial enterprises before, during, and after WWII. It also serves as a diversion tactic for the relocation of the German government offices at various historically contaminated locations in Berlin, and for the return of the German Wehrmacht throughout the European continent. The return of the Wehrwolfs.

By contrast to the above Streits, the remembrance rituals of 1995 commemorating the 50th anniversary of the allies' victory came off without any major "scandals" hitting the public domain. And, indeed, this was a well-rehearsed show with all the stars appearing and banners flying high for months and months until no one wanted to hear anything more about it—except, of course, the hordes of veterans from near and from far. Here, the culture of oblivion scored a success by using an exhaustion tactic, which apparently nearly avoided the exhaustion of truth as it pertained to the beginning, middle, and end of WWII.

So no wonder that the exhibition *Verbrechen der Wehrmacht*, the opening of which by a few months preceded the celebration of the allies' entrance in Berlin, was considered as the negation of a politically correct statement—entirely unsuitable to discuss in connection with the "liberation" of the German conscripts, as the celebration was interpreted by the "official" Germany.

# REVISITING *BROUWER'S LATTICE* THIRTY YEARS LATER

# SOLITONE COMPOSITIONS, ANANTHROPIC SOUND SOURCES, DESIGNER CHAMBER MUSIC

1. *Brouwer's Lattice* (1976) was the first museum installation housing my solitary waveform, initiated in the winter of 1970 and considered as continuing up to the present. (Its second museum installation defined the event $É_{4IX-17X76}$. Refer to *Being = Space × Action* (1989).)

A *solitary wave*, or *soliton*, is an example of an exitable medium which responds dynamically to vibrational variations in the environment as it travels forward in time. The soliton has, however, no memory, but it recovers its initial form after each vibrational interaction and proceeds in time as if it had never been disturbed or exited by vibrations from the past:

A Silent Sound Wave of Tabula Rasa.

When confined to a large cavity, such as the interior of a chamber hall, the soliton becomes a *SOLITONE*, coherently interacting with itself in the form of standing waves continuously reflected from the walls of their spatial confinement. However, the *SOLITONE* is not confined in time, but pulses as a laser into an *infinitely proceeding sequence* of coherent waveforms in the course of which my manifold compositions

*THE N-TIMES REPEATED CONSTANT EVENT*

notated compactly as

$\square^N$   (N = 0, 1, 2, 3, 4, ...)

emerge or appear.
  These compositions were originally scored for quartz crystals and analog electronic circuits. Corresponding *digital* compositions, scored for the first computer at EMS (SR's digital electronic studio in Stockholm), were all given the title *Fixed Points* (alluding to Brouwer's fixed-point theorem), and they initiated my concept of electronic *Infinitary Compositions*, compositions without an end sustained by algorithmically controlled, continuous binary calculations.

*Initial segments*

$\square^{<N}$

(substructural time consciousness, subjective choice sequences) of these endlessly proceeding compositions correspond to *subjective mathematical assertions* by the *Creative Subject* about the length of ordinal numbers.

$<N^{\omega}$.

However, except for a single (designated) initial segment, all initial segments ("ordinals")
$\square^{<N}$ of $\square^{N}$
are *intermediary segments*, as they are interceptions of $\square^{N}$ while already in progress—propagating from the past into the future.

Another way of stating this property is to say that $\square^{N}$ is an *ananthropic sound (-source)*, subjected to *ananthropic interceptions* of various ordinal lengths $<N^{\omega}$ depending on the Creative Subject's absence or presence.

Still another way of putting it is to say that $\square^{N}$ is a form of *designer chamber music* incidental to our awareness, like time, but independent of human fatigue or aging (no presence of musicians required).

More generally, this concept is related to *designer space compositions* already considered by La Monte Young in the mid-1960s (analog electronic compositions for deep-space travel lasting continuously for up to several years). Standard living-room hi-fi systems do not permit the reproduction of these exceptional, acoustical effects.

The engagement at Moderna Museet only lasted for eight days. The ensemble was never asked to play again by the establishment, which went as far as banning all broadcast of any recordings we had made. Thanks to WBAI and WKCR in Manhattan, broadcast from the 30 H of recordings from *Brouwer's Lattice* became possible in the late '70s and onwards. All of these radio shows also featured the music of my long-time friend Henry Flynt, who also contributed with animated and intense discussion about the purpose of developing these new dimensions in music. Henry insisted that this type of music could only be sustained by a "Higher Civilization," having followed with disbelief its official reception in Stockholm. Passages in Brouwer's already century-old manifesto *Life, Art, and Mysticism* seem to reinforce or even validate Henry's misanthropic outlook—so the name of the ensemble, *Deontic Miracle*, still makes sense in view of this music's unanticipated exclusivity.

1a. However, the exclusivity of the solitone emitted from *Brouwer's Lattice* or the minimalism of *Chagaku* is only superficial because the solitone has a very rich inner structure, which is only exposed under amplification and "pumping" of its harmonics. *The Electric Harpshichord* exemplifies an *alternative* technique for mining the solitone conjugated into increasingly higher states of excitation where amplified harmonic oscillators replace the amplified reeds. The mode is derivative of *Raga Multani*. The only preserved performance of *The Electric Harpshichord* took place in *Brouwer's Lattice* in the late afternoon at sunset on March 23rd, 1976, serving as the opening (multi-)chord for the eight-day engagement at Moderna Museet.

# HALLUCINOGENIC/ ECSTATIC SOUND ENVIRONMENTS PROGRAM NOTES

© Henry A. Flynt, Jr.

Written in New York, 1979, on the occasion of the presentation of *Hallucinogenic/Ecstatic Sound Environments* by Henry Flynt and Catherine Christer Hennix at The Kitchen, New York, February 7, 1979. Previously unpublished.

The Kitchen Center
for Video, Music and Dance

# HENRY FLYNT & CATHERINE CHRISTER HENNIX
Hallucinogenic/Ecstatic Sound Environments

February 7, 1979 8:30 pm

Program Notes

To communicate a generating idea for a superior life-world is like making a revolution after a hundred years of repressive peace. The odds are all against it. It requires more energy than mainstream contemporary culture to achieve half the public availability and a fraction of the acceptance. And beyond the idea's luminosity and our need for deliverance, the resources to support the idea are nonexistent. It survives like a beleaguered brigade, sporadically making successful forays, but always threatened with retreat and rout. Its defeat is far more likely than general disillusionment with mainstream culture, since the latter is not only buttressed by complacency but also propelled by degradation (which is anything but bashful).

The idea may thrive for a while on its surprise value and independence from institutions. But if it loses, it loses everything. Unlike mainstream culture, there are no reserve troops, no stockpiles, no headquarters, and no institutional legitimation to fall back on. The idea cannot be kept going by old familiar lies or truths. To survive, the authors of this dream of an exalted existence must periodically change direction and surface in another place.

Strategy, persistence, imagination, patience, loyalty during fallow periods—the ability to bring everything to bear in a sudden, short moment of engagement, to slip away without loss, to survive through long hiatuses without complaint or murmur: this is the field manual of the idea's authors. **Because visionary proposals must succeed if we are to have a future worth living for, we must adopt a dedication commensurate with that imperative. To comprehend the idea at all is to have one's loyalties altered decisively, to betray the institutions of mainstream culture to make the superior life-world possible.**

© Henry A. Flynt, Jr.

+ + + + + + + + + +

The Kitchen's Contemporary Music Series is supported in part by the National Endowment for the Arts, a federal agency; the New York State Council on the Arts; The Martha Baird Rockefeller found; and the New York City Department of Cultural Affairs.

REVISED AFTER 1979

# *THE ILLUMINATORY SOUND ENVIRONMENT* PROGRAM NOTES

© Henry A. Flynt, Jr.

Written in Berlin, 2013, on the occasion of the presentation of *The Illuminatory Sound Environment* by Flynt and Hennix at ZKM, Karlsruhe, March 21, 2013. Previously unpublished.

.

# HENRY FLYNT / CATHERINE CHRISTER HENNIX

## THE ILLUMINATORY SOUND ENVIRONMENT
## ZKM SUBRAUM VERSION
## 21 III 13 – 12 V 13

By an *Illuminatory Sound Environment* (ISE) is meant a *psychotropically working sonic agency* which transports the listener to an alternate state of mind, the portals to which are closed without the sound as guide and input. ISE works on more than one level of mind, and the priming of all these levels increases the listening subject's receptivity to the ramified lamina of "sheets of sounds," which build up the integral sound defining the sonic space engaged.

ISE needs a dedicated acoustic space which provides the listener unlimited access to its sound, which is often continuous and frequently cyclic, as all pitches are fixed in accordance with standards of just intonation. The repeated exposure to this sound environment exerts a *priming* of the attentive listening subject consisting in an activation of neural plasticity dynamics, which lays down new signal paths connected with neural sound processing sites. As a function of this neural priming activity, the listening subject acquires a heightening sensibility to present threshold acoustical events by cultivating new neural tissue—the innervation of which provides the portals to hitherto unvisited and unmapped sonically mediated sites and regions of mind.

ISE is intended as a *new paradigm* for experimental electronic music which introduces a new purpose for the attentive listening subject consisting in a reorientation of auditory driven consummation and behavior. It is therefore useless to compare our paradigm with any past or contemporary form of music—the listener is encouraged to forget about other paradigms in order to be able to choose the appropriate *tactic(s) of attention* required to engage with our new paradigm. With regard(s) to the latter, in spite of our use of traditional sound sources, traditional tactics of attention are inapplicable as the electronic sound processing (analog, digital) forges *new composite sound waveforms hitherto never produced*. Hence, in order to experience and appreciate the novelty of the latter, the listener needs to choose *ever novel* tactics of attention in order to probe all levels of this sound paradigm. With this listener-interactive aspect for the sounds of ISE, we offer a new purpose for the listening subject.

The ZKM SUBRAUM VERSION of ISE comes in three "flavors" (rasas), two by Flynt (*Celestial Power/Glissando No. 1*) and one by Hennix (*Rag Infinity/Rag Cosmosis*), the three flavors alternating daily in accordance with the schema: Flynt, Hennix, Flynt, Hennix…

# RAG INFINITY/ RAG COSMOSIS

(MYOBU NO OMOTO IN MEMORIAM)

Written in Berlin, 2013, on the occasion of the presentation of *The Illuminatory Sound Environment* by Flynt and Hennix at ZKM, Karlsruhe, March 21, 2013. Previously unpublished.

**A realization in Two-Part Harmony in 8H Sections
ZKM-Beta-Version for the *Illuminatory Sound Environment* Installation**

**21 III 13 – 12 V 13**

Catherine Christer Hennix: well-tuned Yamaha keyboards,
tetra-chord custom sine wave generators and computer
Stefan Tiedje: program design and sound mastering

The title *Rag Infinity/Rag Cosmosis* is a *rag* in name only, referring, if only indirectly, to the Sanskrit root meaning (from "Ranja") of "raga" (meaning color, passion), as an agency for "*coloring the mind*" (of a listener exposed to an all-enveloping sound). The title is a derivative from my (very) "abstract" composition OMSAHASTRANAMA (The Thousand Names of OM). (*Monistic Universes B. 0.2*, in Catherine Christer Hennix, *The Electric Harpsichord*, 2010), of which *Rag Infinity/Rag Cosmosis* is one of its emanations (among other such derivatives, I mention *Rag Tinnitus* (2006), *Raag Ignoranti* (John Cage: *Songbook* No. 56) (2011) and *Rag Sama'* (2013)).

The sound of OM is related to the *Creation Myth of the Rg Veda* and, in modern cosmology, to the Hubble frequency (the lowest possible frequency the universe can sustain at any future time) and the event of the acoustic peak, at which moment, billions of years ago, the observable universe became transparent to light. Current models of the universe are "spectral" in the sense that all components are described by *oscillators* with specific frequencies not necessarily occurring in an acoustic medium that, in effect, ipso facto, are defining the latter as specimens of *anahata nada* or the *non-acoustic* or *unstruck sounds*. It is not without astonishment that one reads this ancient creation myth today, noting, in particular, its refusal to proclaim unrestrained speculations to which most creation myths have fallen victim:

> There was neither non-existence nor existence then: there was
> neither the realm of space nor the sky
> which is beyond.
> What stirred? Where?
> Was there water, bottomlessly deep?
> Who really knows? Who will have proclaimed it?
> Whence was it produced? Whence is this creation?
> The gods came afterwards, with the creation of this universe.
> Who then knows whence it has arisen?
> Whence this creation has arisen—
> perhaps it formed itself, or perhaps it did not—
> the one who looks down on it, in the highest heaven,
> only he knows—
> or perhaps he does not know.

The eight eternal questions of the Creation Myth are still not answered, but ours is the Golden Age of cosmology, which makes them more relevant than ever. While sound cannot by itself model all possible cosmic frequencies, a rag represents a (small) universe or aspect thereof *all by its own*, based on a set of ordered frequencies serving as pitches and beats (pulses) the perception of which gives rise to "inner universes" no less unexplored than the physical universe. *Rag Infinity/Rag Cosmosis* presents fragments of "raga-like" frequency constellations following distinct cycles and permuting their order, creating a simultaneity of "multi-universes." When two such "universes" come in proximity of each other and begin unfolding simultaneously along distinct cycles, there is a kaleidoscopic exfoliation of frequencies as one universe is becoming two, but not separated—the effect of cosmosis is entrained, binding two or more frequency universes into proximity where their modal properties interact and blend, creating in the process entirely new microtonal constellations in an omnidirectional simultaneous cosmic order with phenomenologically "transfinite" Poincaré cycles (cyclic returns to initial conditions). Projecta of (tensor-products of) the *Hilbert Space Shruti Box* (The Quantum-Harmonic Ether—Sounds from Another World) represent the formal ontology of these universes of oscillations ("shruti"). "Shruti" means: that which can be heard (as a means of expression)—the concept applies to *both*, texts (like the *Rg Veda*) *and* actual sounds (like a rag). (By "cosmosis," I mean a (reciprocal) process or event where two distinct but related universes are leaking or bleeding into one another along a continuous (non-chaotic, dynamic trajectory).)

Besides the direct, live, or "online" experience of this sound, there is also a significant "after-sound" or "offline"-experience which is primed by self-"tuning" of a template for otoacoustic emissions, formed by the hair cells of the inner ear by prolonged exposure to *Rag Infinity/Rag Cosmosis*. This experience is accessible to a listener who withdraws to a quiet space and concentrates on the sparkling frequencies filling the inner ear, many, if not all, of which are "re-broadcasted" from the "online-experience." I note, not without satisfaction, that this re-broadcast is an exemplary instance of a terrestrial experience of the unstuck sound, a sound that does not travel through air—*anahata nada*. This is, by definition, one of the thousand sounds of OM!

Episodes of this experience—I call "*Rag Tinnitus*"—are not a physiological anomaly, but a trap-door to what in Indian music theory is referred to as the "*subtle sound,*" commonly known as the "*inner sound.*" The listener regularly alternating between *ahata nada* (acoustic sounds) and *anahata nada* experiences will, according to Indian music theory, be best adapted to the ultimate goals of exposure to psychotropic sounds—a *shruti-dialectics* of sorts.

# HILBERT SPACE SHRUTI BOX (OF THE (QUANTUM) HARMONIC OSCILLATOR)

Written in Amsterdam, 2007. Revised in Berlin, 2016. Alternate version published in *SONOILLUMINESCENCES* on the occasion of MaerzMusik, Berliner Festspiele, March 2017. This version is an early draft from August 2007. Previously unpublished.

1. Classical Indian music theory regards *sound* as the source of all phenomenological manifestations of matter and light by considering it as preceding them both as an efficient cause. Sound's manifestations are, on this theory, analyzed in terms of which harmonics are *present* and which are *absent*—such that each sound represents a cross-section from the *set of all harmonics*.[1] Remark that both sets of harmonics, the present as well as the absent, are recursively enumerable sets and, hence, the cross-section is always a *recursive* set (a member of the solvable cases of the (classical) decision problem).

This approach is known in modern acoustics as Fourier Analysis (or Harmonic Analysis) by which any sound may be understood in terms of its harmonic components. A more exciting aspect derived from this approach shows that matter and light can be given, although quite abstractly, derivations from *collective* acoustic vibrations—known as *phonons* that "live" in a "quantum ether" of oscillating "string-nets."[2] It may therefore not come as any surprise that the ancient Indian music theories and modern quantum cosmology enjoy an almost complete unification under the auspices of the *quantum harmonic oscillator*.[3] (Of course, real, molecular matter is actually only affording *an*harmonic oscillations due to incessant interatomic interactions—which theoretical physics sometimes allows itself to conveniently overlook when anharmonic components occasion the destruction of the integrability of the oscillating system. On the other hand, by overlooking the details of the system studied some quite (if unrealistic) unusual concepts can emerge such as sonic black holes which, although (quantum) oscillating, do not emit any sound: an, in principle, inaudible cosmic event.)

1.1. As a *standard phenomenological, acoustical event,* the sound of the North-Indian *tambura* shall be chosen—both for its richness of harmonics and for the intractable correlated couplings of these harmonics with each other.[4] The replication of that sound needs more than twelve oscillators and perhaps more than ten times as many—the composition of the sound remaining an enigma since the beginning of time![5]

2. A quantum harmonic oscillator (QHO) can be regarded as holding the register (or memory) for all harmonies of an arbitrary fundamental tone defined by its frequency (or wave number) alone. The latter frequency is the oscillator's initial *Eigenfrequency*, $f_0$, corresponding to its "lowest *Eigenstate*," of which any harmonic is an integral multiple, each such multiple also referred to as an *Eigenfrequency* of the oscillator (corresponding to "excitations" of the oscillator into higher partials).

The *Eigenfrequencies* of a QHO is also known as its *spectrum* and they provide as exhaustive *enumeration*, $f_0, f_1, f_2, \ldots f_m, f_n,\ldots$, of all harmonics determined by a fixed, fundamental frequency, $f_0$. Each *Eigenfrequency*, $f_k$, corresponds to a "state" of a QHO—also known as one of its *Eigenstates*. (Quantum states, represented by qubits, allow for the simultaneous *superposition* of more than one *Eigenstate* conferring on the QHO the usual indeterminacy caused by an incomplete or unavailable information protocol. The incompleteness of this protocol seems to contradict the recursiveness of this domain by perturbing or "disordering" its well-order. The phenomenon is known from models of sub-atomic (quantum-) computations and molecular (DNA-) computational models. This development has necessitated alternative logical structures—such as, for example, the various

"Geometries" of Interaction connecting proof-nets with Hilbert space formalisms. The ensuing epistemic limbo is not expected to be resolved as long as the absence of appropriate consistency proofs persists. In the meantime, the pursuance of intuitionistic logics has taken the precedence over its classical counter-parts.)

2.1. The harmonies, $f_q$, of a QHO lexiographically arrange themselves neatly in a *cumulative heiarchy*, QH, of *quantum harmonics*, $|n_q\rangle$, provided the integer q is written in *base* 2, i.e., as a *binary* numeral, of which the first n stages may be presented as the state vectors:

$$QH_1 := <0,1>$$

$$QH_2 := <00,01,10,11>$$

.

.

.

$$QH_n := <00...0, ..., 11...1>$$

Or Binary (bit) strings ("numerals") in the alphabet $\{0,1\}$ of lengths in the union—

$$\bigcup_{n=1}^{\infty} QH_n := QH$$

—which represents the complete hierarchy QH.

This hierarchy is also known as the *universal binary spread* of the intuitionistic continuum, and to which I repeatedly have had occasion to refer to in my writings on just intonation and modal music, beginning with *Brouwer's Lattice*, 1976. By invoking the universal binary spread as a mapping, a correspondence (a map) will ensue between just intonation *intervals (shruti-s)* and intuitionistic *mathematical entities*, both concurrently constructed by the (intuitionistic) *Creating Subject* following an intuition of time evolutions.[7]

REMARK. Readers familiar with computer designs will recognize the shorter strings in QH as the usual "Boolean gates" while readers familiar with propositional logic will recognize the usual truth-tables, say, as given in *Tractatus Logico-Philosophicus*. Either way, an elementary observation consists in noticing that *each logical gate or truth-value distribution*, in virtue of the present formalism, also corresponds to a *fixed frequency ratio*. Thus, it emerges that synthesis of circuity is in parallelism with frequency synthesis—unifying logic, computation and languages of sound (Majorana gates providing for self-programmed choice-sequences in the sense of Brouwer, cf. ADVANCED REMARK, below). Extending the observation to the concept of the entire universe viewed as a quantum computer, it becomes possible, if not feasible, to consider the exact frequency distribution of the present state of the universe (and, extrapolating, guessing the initial frequency ratios within some tolerance of error). (It is, possibly, an irony that the enigmatic *Tractatus* aphorisms 4.011-4.0141 in [8] here receive a (re) solution[8] within their own formalism in that frequency ratios indicated by conventional staff notation are interconvertible with the discrete (co-)sine-Fourier Transform—furnishing user-friendly digital-memory registers for sound as exemplified by CD and DVD technology.)

ADVANCED REMARK. Notice that the binary string of length zero, $\Lambda$, may represent the *superposition* of all the harmonics of QH taken at *zero* amplitude or probability. On this representation, $\Lambda$ measures the inertia of the "sound vacuum" whose frequencies escape into non-zero amplitudes by various tunneling mechanisms (degeneracy of the "ground state"). This would be an example of a (very) *free choice-sequence*. (The number of zeros in the string 00...0 can be taken as a measure of the energy-density of the zero-state vectors $|00...0\rangle$ of this imaginary vacuum (see Section 3), below.) The concept becomes more tangible if amplitudes are taken to be inverse to the frequency.) Remark that, phenomenologically, this comes close to the *spontaneous* oto-acoustical emissions of the inner ear, a stationary, multi-sine-wave-like sound that might be taken as a sonic analog of "hacking into the vacuum." Although most likely entirely unrelated to room-temperature cell-sensor mechanisms, Helium-4 exhibits in certain phases a phonon vacuum which continuously undergoes symmetry-breaking interactions influenced by the dynamics of the Casimir force. The choice-sequences of these broken symmetries escape any (Lagrangian) determinism and must be updated for each effective choice. However, as in the case of oto-acoustic emissions, there is nothing that says that these dynamics are the results of random processes ... we just don't understand what is going on.

2.2. Each level, $QH_m$, of QH may be regarded as a *vector* which enumerates the first $2^m - 1$ harmonics in their "natural" order including the fundamental frequency. Physically, these vectors represent a set of $2^m - 1$ *oscillators* or *strings*, $|n_q\rangle$, n, q = 1, ..., $2^m - 1$, vibrating without overtones, each of which outputs a fixed *Eigenfrequency* as an integer multiple of the fundamental frequency (and as an integer multiple of the corresponding *Eigenstate*). To illustrate the concept by the chosen standard of sound, a "resting" or unplucked *tambura* may be conceived as holding in superposition some $2^k - 1$ distinct harmonics for k < 8, ...say, which "escape" into reality only as the instrument is picked up and precisely tuned. More abstractly, the exponential constant k may be considered without any precise least upper bound—a lack of precision which confers on the "ideal" tambura an *unlimited set of harmonics* or resonances (k goes to "infinity"), as when imagined played by the Godess *Saraswati*. (This case should be contrasted with the more ancient Chinese tradition of pentatonic tunings which limits the value of k at 6, $2^6 = 64$, 64 being the number of hexagrams in the *I-Ching*, the earliest known base-2 notation for whole numbers, yielding 63 distinct pitches from the cycle of fifths. However, later the cycle of fifths were continued up to 25, 524 distinct pitches furnishing a basic microtonal interval measuring .0021174 savarts (2/1 – 301 savarts). The measure is comparable to the most fine-grained Indian *shruti*-scale although here it will not be further mentioned.)

3. Post-inflationary cosmology operates approximately in the frequency interval $10^{-18}$ Hz – $10^{43}$ Hz, a 61-fold expansion over a fundamental still to be determined ($10^{-18}$ Hz being the "Hubble frequency" and $10^{43}$ Hz—the "Planck frequency").

Nevertheless, this frequency range does not exceed 1000 "octaves" and, hence, is included in the speculative conjectures fermented by the ancient Indian theoreticians. It is not unamusing to compare Paula Zizzy's quantum gravity registers with the ancient *shruti* doctrine of infinitely many harmonics as the *source of all phenomenological events*. The following construction of the *Hilbert space shruti box* was occasioned by this comparison which makes possible a certain connection between modern physics and the poetry of *Rg Veda*.[9]

3.1. A state of n *qubits* is defined by the following unit vector in $2^n$-dimensional complex Hilbert Space $c^2$.

$$C2 \otimes C2 \otimes \ldots \otimes C2 \quad \text{—n times.}$$

The basics of this space correspond to $2^n$ classical strings of length n:

$$|0\rangle \otimes |0\rangle \otimes \ldots \otimes |0\rangle = |00\ldots0\rangle$$

$$|0\rangle \otimes |0\rangle \otimes \ldots \otimes |1\rangle = |00\ldots1\rangle$$

$$\vdots$$

$$|1\rangle \otimes |1\rangle \otimes \ldots \otimes |1\rangle = |11\ldots1\rangle$$

each string having the form of a vector.

This is the general basis structure of the *Hilbert shruti space*. For example, for n = 2, the basis vectors are the strings

$$|0\rangle \otimes |0\rangle \otimes = |00\rangle$$
$$|0\rangle \otimes |1\rangle \otimes = |01\rangle$$
$$|1\rangle \otimes |0\rangle \otimes = |10\rangle$$
$$|1\rangle \otimes |1\rangle \otimes = |11\rangle$$

corresponding to the (only) two harmonics, $|10\rangle$, $|11\rangle$, of the second level, $QH_2$, of $QH_m$-s fundamental, here considered to be a normed vibration of 1 Hz. The configuration of frequencies in this example corresponds to one of the basic tunings of the *tambura*, viz., the *Pa-tuning*. Thus (with a ceiling factor of $2^8$),

$|01\rangle$ is *shruti chhandovati*,
$|10\rangle$ is *shruti shadja* — and

$|11\rangle$ is *shruti panchama*.

3.2. All other *shruti-s* emanating from this tuning "live" higher up in the QH-hierarchy and seem to arise in an "inflationary manner" at the very instant the above three shruti-s are initiated by the *tambura player*.

For each n, there are $2^n - 1$ distinct *shruti-s* contained in the corresponding basis for the n-dimensional *Hilbert shruti space*, n = 1,2,3... . Thus, even for "small values of n"—say, 100 or 1000—the population of *shruti-s* living in this "*shruti-box*" is "super-inflationary" and largely unknown from phenomenological experiences (and not necessarily accessible in its totality by identifiable observables since some may escape intrinsic thresholds of discrimination).

3.3. For each n, there are m-tone scales for any m > 2. For example, a 5-tone scale is contained in the basis for n = 3—which contains seven vibrating strings of length three. For providing a 7- or 12-tone scale, it suffices to choose n = 4. In fact, since the unit distance of a *classical* Hilbert space is $\sqrt{2}$, it is trivial to change its norm to $\sqrt[12]{2}$ —which is the unit measure of distance by equal temperament—the classical 12-tone formalism can be found as subspaces already of classical Hilbert space, thus conferring on the latter a certain sense of universality in modeling all known scale structures. Remark that the latter subspaces have *arbitrarily close (discrete) approximations* by letting the exponent, n, go to infinity in *Hilbert shruti space*, making the borderline between "just intonation" and "equal temperament" fuzzy, if not moot. For an exemplary demonstration of this point, refer to Henry Flynt's model of the monochord,[10] historically, perhaps, the first *"mathematical instrument."* On the other hand, modal scales may be constructed by a top-down scheme starting from a set of quantum harmonic oscillators "prepared to" equal temperament but subsequently subjected to the actions of some "deformation operators" by which the equal temperament structure deforms to particular modal scales (the majority of which is still to be heard).

By either of these two approaches to modal scale constructions, the possibility of an *autonomous development* of manifolds of modal scales becomes available basically using only algebra and topology. In particular, it becomes possible to explore both non-commutative and non-associative action principles. To the extent that the latter action principles can be organized to yield novel sound structures, in particular, *self-organized stationary structures maintained far from dynamical equilibrium*, they offer a promising new approach.

# ENDNOTES

1. A standard contemplation of the universe, taken as an indivisible whole, consists in regarding an isolated system of unknown composition and origin, initially at "rest" (the eternal fixpoint), which, then switched-on, suddenly, in less than a few seconds, expands at least sixty-fold and balloons to its present size on a time-scale of billions of years (with a possible reheating phase intervening—as when milk boils over for a second time). Eavesdropping on the present composition of the universe has revealed a large spectrum of wave lengths propagating from all directions. Although only audible by use of sophisticated detectors, their presence betrays an ancient history exemplified by, say, gravitational waves from Population III star remnants (early, giant stars very close to the "last scattering surface" beyond (or "behind") which there will be no direct observational data available, ever). The spectrum of frequencies ranges, theoretically from a fundamental "tone" at about $10^{-18}$ Hz (the "Hubble frequency") to close to $10^{43}$ Hz (the "Planck frequency")—of which the audible spectrum occupies only the narrow slit between $2 \cdot 10$ Hz and $2 \cdot 10^4$ Hz. Actually, this cosmic spectrum expands with the

expansion of the Universe as most of the Hubble frequencies remain "frozen" in time, the lowest frequencies, below $10^{-18}$ Hz, *are still to come* together with their back-actions. By an intricate system of tuning, Classical Indian music theory affords a mapping of frequency ratios from the cosmic range to the human-hearing range, the ratios being referred to by the term shruti-s. (Remark: The Term shruti is also deployed for the "unrevealed" stanzas of the *Rg Veda*.) (Cf. references [1], [5], [6], [7].)

Classical Indian music theory has, since its inception, always maintained a "cosmic connection" marked by the syllable AUM and interpreted as the "initial sound" (highest Hubble frequency?) of the universe. It is not quite obvious how to understand this view in terms of modern cosmology—since, *given* the first second of the Universe, both the first sound and the first light come about without ever being heard or seen as these occasions of origins are both parked behind the last scattering surface. Nevertheless, the Classical Indian view realistically regards the universe as "asound," vibrating at every conceivable frequency—a view that asymptotically coincides with the modern concept of the Universe as a (large) collection (network) of oscillators, each oscillator characterized by its *Eigenfrequency* (each fundamental particle manifests a fixed measurable frequency for each of its energy-levels). For example, Scott M. Hitchcock (NSCL) writes:

> *...observable matter ... are relic computational perturbations from the anistropic phonon-like excitation decay modes of the inflationary epoch.*

The statement appears to imply that the universe as a self-tuned sonic body has long since have had its best years. However, even the modern view concedes that all models of the "first second" of the universe, including the "acoustic peak," are pure speculations. In fact, the modern view often find itself retreating to the *shruti-s* of the *Creation Hymn* (Nāsadiya, of the *Rg Veda*):

> *There was neither non-existence nor existence then; there was neither the realm of space nor the sky which is beyond. What stirred? Where? In whose protection? Was there water, bottomlessly deep? Who really knowns? Who will here proclaim it? Whence was it produced? Whence is this creation? The gods came afterwards, with the creation of this universe. Who then knows whence it has arisen?*

> *Whence this creation has arisen—perhaps it formed itsel, or perhaps it did not—the one who looks down on it, in the highest heaven, only he knows—or perhaps he does not know.*

With more questions than answers, the Classical Indian tradition might be said to be in perfect concordance with the modern view of mathematics (and, derivatively, with the view of the lower sciences, such as theoretical physics and cosmology). It may, therefore, not come as a surprise that the Hindu-Muslim music theory tradition has, at least for a millennium, been preoccupied with calculating the "high-energy sector" of an oscillating, acoustic universe, scaling more than one thousand octaves!—as evidenced by the extensive tabulations of musical intervals presented in [5] (which the *Cornell Nano-Guitar* is still far from approaching with measurable vibrations, so far, "merely" counting in order to formulate an in-depth theory, to reformulate the premises of classical Indian music theory in terms of modern mathematical physics. In addition, and of more importance for the present context, such a reformulation seems to be a required preparatory step towards a more *refined theory of auditory perception* which integrates quantum- and meso-timescales of the of the real time transduction of sound by the body's pressure-sensors. On this account, simple-minded or "toy" models need not be entirely misleading (cf. end-note 2, below). But, ultimately, this field still requires the initiation of a yet to be formulated *radically new direction of science*. However, such a radical topic would require its own end-note or position paper, a project for another occasion (again, cf. endnote 2, below).

2. As already alluded to in the preceding end-note, science is presently undergoing its "second quantum revolution" of which we can discern only the tip of the iceberg. Among novel theoretical observations is the emergence of an understanding of the "vacuum" as distinct "phases" or states of matter determined by topology no less, or even more, that geometry. By this paradigm shift, "atoms" ("points") are giving way to *collective vibrational modes* ("strings") corresponding to certain topographical concepts classifying symmetries in low-dimensional projective geometries. According to Xiao-Gang Wen, matter and light are different collective excitations of a string-net dynamics which populate the "vacuum state." There are also others, like Hitchcock (quoted in end-note one, above), Kitaev and Lloyd who, along different perspectives, regard physical processes as equivalent to topological quantum computations from the dynamics of which all physical forces, including gravity, emerge. It is expected that quite exotic new states of matter (for example "anyons") will be actually (if only indirectly) observable in the near future.

Although not "obviously" pertaining to "biological matter," these exotic phases of matter sometimes have analogues in organic tissues due to the dense ("marginally compact") packing of protein and water molecules which sometimes assumes low-dimensional condensed matter properties. Among the latter, Bose-Einstein condensations appears a likely candidate as do various interactions coupled to the presence of Casimir (or 'vacuum') forces (cf. the early theoretical results by Frölich, Davydov, Scott, and others). Somehow or other, these and other exotic properties of matter must eventually couple to our cognitive experiences, since they couple to the dynamics of their material substrates, and, in particular, may be necessary to take into attention for a refined theory of auditory perception, asked for in the previous endnote. The theoretical situation is now radically different from the circumstances in which Henry Flynt wrote *Superseding Scientific Apprehension of the Inanimate World*—science (having now conceded the naiveté of its past conceptions that were exposed in the text) has now a possibility to contribute with some new concepts that might further Henry's approach to cognition without challenging our credulity—or, at least, less so than in the past. A paradigm shift is on the way, and, possibly, that may entail a more promising epistemology. It will be interesting to follow Henry's response as more experimental results become documented (refer to the *ArXiv* and other open web sources)!

REMARK. The casual reader may be bewildered by the present "scientific" approach to sound and think this is merely one of the nuisances of modernism and belongs to a superseded past at a time when composers tried to fit the music department in-between the physics and the mathematics departments for the purpose of pursuing interdisciplinary work. And although that ideal did flower some fifty years ago (but was snuffed out) it should be pointed out that already the Islamic university system (more than one thousand years ago) was organized into the quadrivium and the trivium which European universities copied and preserved till the sixteenth century. The expulsion of music for the last five hundred years from serious theoretical studies resulted in the omission of the microtonal sector of sound (introduced to Europe by Arabic scholars like al-Farabi five hundred years earlier)—an omission that still persists and which can only be remedied by a return to its roots. In addition, a radical remedy is also on offer which will consist of understanding sound and its influence on cognition as correlations between macroscopic effects of "soft condensed matter" ("surface structure") and the underlying excitable microscopic media effects ("deep structure"). The next important cognition theory must be capable of determining how these physically quite separate macro- and microscopic effects and regions couple to each other under the influences of a mesoscopic interface as provided by biological matter. Although elusive, an attempt to reach this goal has set up basecamp at the frontiers of low-dimensional condensed matter physics (cf. the works of Baskaran). This basecamp may provide additional structures for the microtonal sector of sound compositions by which a strong correlation between sound and states of consciousness might be expected to emerge (and to which tensor-product "paths" in *Hilbert Space Shruti Boxes* will match). (END OF REMARK.)

3. ...

4. Cf. *Why did Pandit Nath bring the Tambura from the East?*—liner notes written by the present author for ref. [4], above (although still not included in the present edition of [4]).

5. ...

6. More than thirty years ago, I began to formulate a formalism for cognitive and, in particular, music structures that attempted to make a clean break with modernism's reactionary past (including logical atomism) and its "post-modern" perpetrators. The reactionary past, however, seems only to have been replaced by a still more reactionary present, which is why scientific illiteracy keeps preventing a wider circle of readers for publications like *Toposes & Adjoints* or *Being = Space × Action*. While much in those works are now being superseded by my present work, they certainly prepared the way for the present approach. However, in the past I failed to consider the relevance of sub-atomic physics (which, until recently, remained opaque and moored in intolerable vagueness). Since I have entertained and been guided by concepts very close to the *Hilbert Space Shruti Box* for the last 30+ years I am amazed to see how "obviously," by a progressively finer division of the octave, this harmonic space not only includes the smallest "octave" containing the "Planck frequency" but also those containing "Planck foam" and the "Casimir section." However, like most people, I considered these connections as too extravagant for my purposes and disregarded them—until I returned to a study of [5] and [6]) some ten years ago and realized that such fine-grained divisions of the octave were actually already known in India more than one thousand years ago. The present write-up is an (overdue) attempt to make up for

the failure of previously making this connection more explicit.

7. …

8.1. In the 1970s, I once set out to find an adequate formalism for computer-aided sound synthesis calibrated for setting my frequencies in a larger context which spanned the foundations of mathematics, universal grammar, and cosmology (*Brouwer's Lattice*; *Toposes & Adjoints*; *17 Points on Intensional Logics*). Although this formalism could have been to cohere, the effort required turned out to be heroically disproportional—somewhat like trying to fit *Tractatus Logico-Philosophicus* to empirical reality (see below). But so was no less the effort required to interface with the then-ultra-slow computers entirely unsuitable for synthesizing complex, high-quality sounds of longer durations (say, exceeding 5' or 10'). As this latter impediment has recently eased considerably, I have had reasons to rethink my initial formalism in order to recalibrate my interface with recent technological advancements. However, I remain undecided as to which formalism is the most suitable (as in my composition *Soliton(e) Star*). Presently I am experimenting with various tentative possibilities without seeing any natural way of unifying them. In what follows, I nevertheless give *one* example of a (toy-model) formalism, although it probably has a little chance to converge with reality as the one of *Tractatus*. Although this example could be given a less concise presentation, I've chosen to use, below, the "rough and tough" idiom perpetrated by modern science since the text is anyway, strictly speaking, quite provisional ("do not quote"!).

However, if the following endnote is provisional, its leading idea is now. Viz., a sound composition M generated by a digital computer describes a *discrete process* or *action* A which is determined by the algorithmic dynamics afforded by the designated computer. That is, M is the result of a certain amount of *computations*, the manifold of which completely determines the structure of the resulting sound waves $\Phi$. Thus, M appears here as a mathematical object (program + DA--conversion physics) and the computer is the mathematical instrument by means of which a *virtual musical instrument* $\Omega_M$ is realized as $\Phi_M$ (using a speaker system as interface).

8.2. Actually, $\Phi_M$ materializes as a product of computations with logic where the latter imposes the necessary strictures on the former. The idea is really classical and was already considered by Wittgenstein to be applicable to anthropic music. I recall aphorism 4.014:

*4.014*
*Die Grammophonplatte, die musikalische Gedanke, die Notenschrift, die Schallwellen, stehen alle in jener abbildenden internen Beziehung zu einander, die zwischen Sprache und Welt besteht.*

[*The gramophone record, the musical thought, the score, the waves of sound, all stand to one another in that pictorial internal relation, which holds between language and the world.*][9]

which compactly may be written as

*4.014

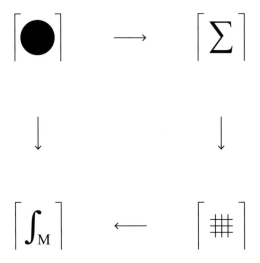

where ● is the record, Σ the site (source) of the musical thought, $\int_M$ the acoustic wave form, and # the score. The logic, but not the computational part, is detailed in the following aphorism:

*4.0141*
*Daß es eine allgemeine Regel gibt, durch die der Musiker aus der Partitur die Symphonie entnehmen kann, durch welche man aus der Linie auf der Grammophonplatte die Symphonie und nach der ersten Regel wieder die Partitur ableiten kann, darin besteht eben die innere Ähnlichkeit dieser scheinbar so gantz verschiedenen Gebilde. Und jene Regel ist das Gesetz der Projektion, welches die Symphonie in die Notensprache projiziert. Sie ist die Regel der Übersetzung der Notensprache in die Sprache der Grammophonplatte.*

*[In the fact that there is a general rule by which the musician is able to read the symphony out of the score, and that there is a rule by which one could reconstruct the symphony from the line on a gramophone record and from this again—by means of the first rule—construct the score, herein lies the internal similarity between these things which at first sight seem to be entirely different. And the rule is the law of projection which projects the symphony into the language of the musical score. It is the rule of translation of this language into the language of the gramophone record.]*[10]

Which in compact notation may be written as

*4.0141

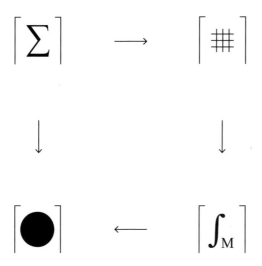

8.3. The logical strictures turn out to closely follow the computational strictures of classical mechanics—which allows for the arrows in 4.0141 to be *invertible*. That is, the "source language" of the composer Σ is a language of instrumental (i.e., mechanical) sounds which has its syntax "compiled" as a (discrete) score, #, the semantics of which is provided by the interpretant and preserved as an external memory by a record, ●. When the record is played back, it reveals a "new" language—*die Sprache der Grammophonplatte*—which "translates" back to the score and, *eventually*, to the composer's source language. If the record ● is on digital format, then both it and the score, #, carry discrete structures which, at least theoretically, are algorithmically inter-translatable. And as soon as also the interpretant's composite wave form, $\int_M$, is "discretized," its language as well becomes intertranslatable with the other languages. For example, if $\int_M$ is realized on the MIT Bösendorfer SE Imperial, then the following diagram commutes

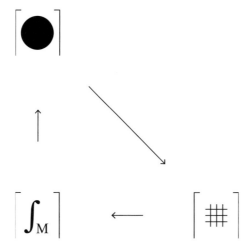

However, *this print-out reveals no more about the semantics of the intended sounds than was already known and its essential components remain hidden to composer and listener alike.* This is the (impossible) premise of modern Cognition Theory for language and sound alike which exempts it from providing any interesting answers to interesting questions.

A more promising premise comes from abandoning the atomistic approach formalized by the diagrams above, and consider, as advocated by Baskaran, *emergent structures*, which result from collective excitations which are not decomposable into separate parts but derivable from some given suitably prepared *ground state*. The emergence of a structure evolving from a prepared ground state depends on reaching a critical threshold value at which stage a self-organizing phase-transition maintains an energy gap with the ground state and from which it remains separated as long as the emergent phenomenon evolves. In the event of the "collapse" of the latter, the return to the ground state does not guarantee that the latter is identical to the initial ground state. Only in the case of a reversible or commutative "return map" is the identity of the ground state maintained but, in general, this map is *non-commutative*. In particular, in the case of considering microtonal sound sources the *discrete* reversibility of the sound turns out to be subjected to *non-linear* regimes whose dynamics is difficult to detail. The technique known as "granular synthesis," used by Xenakis, is based on ideas originating with Dennis Gabor and supposed to satisfy the reversibility property. But as presented by Curtis Roads, no provisions are given for a detailed analysis of non-linear phenomena, and it remains doubtful to what extent granular synthesis has any capacity for generating non-trivial reversible composite wave forms. However, knowledge of how to do the latter will provide important clues as to the interactive dynamics of a set of frequencies satisfying some interesting physical properties. I consider this to be a promising area for a serious form of *experimental* music which takes a more integrated and cross-disciplinary approach than afforded by my predecessors.

9. The idea is certainly not original although I hesitate to give any references. The reader may wish to have a look, at her own risk, at Tony Smith's musings on the subject @ http://www.tony5m17h.net/RgVeda.html

—although, again, it is a reference I hesitate to give (although I do owe Smith (and John Baez) for the reference [3] and other works by Zizzy).

10. ...

*References*

1. A. Danièlou, *The Ragas Of Northern Indian Music*. The Cresset Press, London, 1968.
2. X.-G. Wen, *Quantum Field Theory—From The Origin Of Sound To An Origin Of Light And Fermions*. Oxford University Press, Oxford, 2004.
3. P.A. Zizzy, *Emergent Consciousness: From The Early Universe To Our Mind*, Technical Report. Dipartimento Di Astronomia Dell' Universita Di Padova, Padua, 2000.
4. L. Young–M. Zazeela, *The Tamburas Of Pandit Pran Nath*, Cd, Just Dreams. Mela Foundation, New York, 2001.
5. A. Danièlou, *Tableau Comparatif Des Intervalles Musicaux*, Institute Français D'indologie, Pondichèry, 1958.
6. B.c. Deva, *Psychoacoustics Of Music And Speech*. The Music Academy, Madras, 1967.
7. L. Young–M. Zazeela, *On The Concept Of Time And Eternity In Our Work*, M.s., 2001 (unpublished.)
8. L. Wittgenstein, *Tractatus Logico-Philosophicus*, trans. C.K. Ogden, intro. by B. Russel, Harcourt, Brace & Company, New York, 1922.
9. H. Flynt, *Superseding Scientific Apprehension Of The Inanimate World*, http://www.henryflynt.org/meta_tech/90physics.html
10. L. Wittgenstein, Tractatus Logico-Philosophicus, 40.

# THE YELLOW BOOK

# THE YELLOW BOOK

First published in *Io #41: Being = Space × Action*, ed. Charles Stein, 1989. Included in this volume is a facsimile of the original publication with the exception of "Color Equations," "Black & White Algebra," and "Color Algebra," which have been corrected by Hennix for this volume. The photographs reproduced here come from Hennix's 1976 installation at Moderna Museet, Stockholm, *Toposes & Adjoints*.

# Christer Hennix

$$\breve{E}[\eta]$$

(Text Of Order Type $\eta$)
[Detail]

from The Yellow Book
*[Tractatus De Intellectu Emendatione Antiqua]*

*Finis Universatum:*
Philosophy As Art /
Philosophy As Notation
II


— — — — — XX — — — — —


Hors-texte '68—'88

Abstract Tactical Configuration (Complete view 22 X 76 — Moderna Museet, Stockholm)

»  _ _ _ _  «[1]

$$\xi\nu\nu\grave{o}\nu \; \delta\acute{\epsilon} \; \mu o\acute{\iota} \; \dot{\epsilon}\sigma\tau\iota\nu,$$
$$\dot{o}\pi\pi\acute{o}\vartheta\epsilon\nu \; \ddot{a}\rho\xi\omega\mu\alpha\iota\cdot \; \tau\acute{o}\vartheta\iota \; \gamma\grave{\alpha}\rho \; \pi\acute{\alpha}\lambda\iota\nu \; \ddot{\iota}\xi o\mu\alpha\iota \; \alpha\hat{\upsilon}\vartheta\iota\varsigma. \; \text{Bl. Fr. 5}$$

---

[1] Footnote 1 page 310

*The Yellow Book*

# Preliminary Concepts

It is the tradition of Philosophers since Vedic times to inscribe Being as a term in a *text*.

By this tradition, Being has meaning *only* as a part of a term of a text. As a part of an inscription. . . . .

I am considering terms which have paths through the following (already 2-large) succession of texts

. . . . . Ṛg Veda . . . . . B1. (ΠΑΡΜΕΝΙΔΟΥ ΠΕΡΙ ΦΥΣΕΩΣ) . . . . . Hekigan Roku . . . . . Over de Grondslagen der Wiskunde . . . . . Tractatus Logico-Philosophicus . . . . .

in order to explore if, at all, they will have another successor of a text of the unwritten doctrines, *agrapha dogmata*,* or, if the last texts have already been written but remain invisible in a historical era of oversymbolization and oversimplification.

---

*Project B1.29-30.

## Christer Hennix

It is not that I am looking for something important which has been written down somewhere in the above sequence of classical texts—I am *not* trying to be instructed by these texts, but, rather, I am interested in the dual relation of attempting to instruct these last texts *themselves*—by subjecting them to the primary processes of *semeiosis*. In particular, I am contemplating the sources of/for *homosemeiosis*

$\Sigma$—⟡—the Creative Subject instructs a text $\tau$.

The dual relation is more familiar (from the theory of algorithms).

⟡—$\Sigma$—the Creative Subject is instructed by a text $\tau'$,

although the following fact is apparently quite unfamiliar, *viz*, that, in general, *neither $\tau$ nor $\tau'$* are ever present or real objects.

**Remark**. The concept of (an ever present) time or reality is intrinsically an *ethical concept*. The present or the real is sometimes *permitted* and sometimes *forbidden*, and, if neither, can be transgressed by a *new modality of freedom.*\*

**Last In-First Out**. The real task in sorting out a sequence of classical texts is that of *eliminating* the latter or at least *replacing* them by a text

---

\*This is the site *near* the topos of an *initial model subject*, viz, the topos under which one attends an investigation by *one's own tactics of attention, only*.

It is under such "toposes" that the Creative Subject realizes a complete sense of (perceptual or cognitive) freedom.

## The Yellow Book

of radical translation [as, for example, the Sophocles translations produced by Hölderlin.] The later the original text is, the easier seems the task of superseding it. For that reason, a lot of work has been spent on Brouwer's and Wittgenstein's writings. —But even when so simplified, the task remains very complex and only *partial results* have been obtained as I have attended this investigation with *my* (prefered) tactics of attention.

\* \* \*

Before entering the text, something else has already entered. The allowance or permission to gaze at a linear collection of signs the meanings of which are sometimes even forbidden —or, else, impossible to understand —has entered as a distant premonition before an uninterrupted flow of signs focused by the pages of a text which is condemned to continuously lose its authorship or be abandoned by its reader —all signs of certain distress (of certain veridical ambiguities).

Freedom —as opposed to certain distress. The concept stands in need of further investigation.\*

---

\*A second initial model subject would contemplate the *ethics of meaning*. The subject may begin by regarding the following set of definitions, *viz*:

i. The *positive meaning* of a sign is determined by what the sign is *allowed* to signify.

ii. The *double-negation meaning* (or *weak* positive meaning) of a sign is determined by what the sign is *permitted* to signify.

iii. The *negative meaning* of a sign is determined by what the sign is *forbidden* to signify.

iv. The *possible meaning* of a sign is determined by what *it is not forbidden* for the sign to signify.

[These are the *active meanings* of an arbitrary sign [to be distinguished from its *passive* or *lexical meaning*(s).]]

**Digression.** *What Is (Not-) Not An Axiom* (Frege).

For Frege, a proposition P is a *function* P(X) which takes *itself* as argument, P(P), and takes the truth-value $\top$ if P is *true* and the truth-value $\bot$ if P is *false*.

If P expresses an *axiom*, then P corresponds to a "constant function" $\top$ (with due abuse of notation) while its negation, $\neg$ P, corresponds to an *anti*-axiom i.e. a constant function $\bot$. The *functions* P must not be multi-valued or undefined, else P is logically equivalent to a *potential contradiction* such as

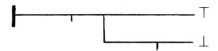

i.e. [ignoring intuitionistic doubts about double-negation elimination]

$$\top \mid \bot$$

in the notation of Tractatus Logico-Philosophicus.

However, it ought to be stressed that Frege somtimes considered an arbitrary proposition P as a *partial* recursive function—simply because P's truth-value is sometimes (intuitionistically) *undefined*.

That is (again resorting to Wittgenstein's compact notation),

$$P \mid . \; P \mid P$$

corresponds to a logically indefinite (or undecidable) proposition (contradicting the assumed completeness of the logical symbolism).


**Digression cont.** *Remarks On The Aesthetics of The Exterior* [A possible Kunstsprache; **Hors-texte**]

The exteriority of human existence reveals itself already by the operation of negation which signifies the absence or otherness of a modality of existence incommensurate with the present.

### Not-*A*

signifies that *A* does not signify what is *now* (because "now" is *now* signified by "**Not-*A***").

**Not-*A***, when signifying, signifies an aspect of what is present, of what is *now*.

Although the operation of negation brings forth an instantaneous temporal division between *now* and *not*-now, the otherness of this temporal *not*-now represents only a single layer of the exteriority with which human existence is universally confronted.

On the other hand, even when the logical sign for negation effectively brings agents of cognition to the exterior of their existence the aspects of the world revealed by an act of mental exclusion remain distinct from those aspects where the exteriority appears as a continuous action of successive intrusions by (an uncensored) reality.

Furthermore, the exteriority revealed by a *negationless* proposition

$$A'$$

also constitutes an infinite barrier for an agent of cognition to be compared only with the one presented by the **not-**$A'$. Because, if the proposition

$$\textbf{\textit{not-}}A'$$

is not false now, then the negationless proposition $A'$ does not signify a cognitive aspect of the present now—except as an unsolvable or regressing vacancy. "$A'$ holds" means that **not-**$A'$ is not presently satisfiable, i.e. that *now* "**not-**$A'$ does not hold".

The paradoxical conjunction "$A'$ and **not-**$A'$" signifies a cognitive collapse of temporal order, i.e., it signifies (a-)symmetrically that *now* is *not*-now. That what is present is absent—with the absence asymmetrically not always present. [The asymmetrical aspect of a diagonal argument).

[**Reminder on scholastisism.** In the medieval logic *via moderna* two conditions had to be satisfied before an affirmative proposition could be said to be true. *Id est*, it must signify things to be as they are and it must not falsify itself. By contrast, a negative proposition is to be true just in case either it signifies that things are not as they are not, *or*, it has a self-falsifying contradictory. This distinction between affirmative and negative propositions carry two important consequences, *viz.*, *pro primo*, "This is false" and "This is not true" have distinct truth-values when they are both *self-referential*. Hence, while all propositions which signify themselves to be false indeed come out false on this analysis, quite paradoxically all propositions which signify themselves not to be true are nevertheless all true. The reason herefore is, of course, that while an affirmative proposition must satisfy a double truth-condition, a negative proposition needs only a single truth-condition to pass as a judgement. *Pro secunda*, tertium non datur must apply to any pair of contradictory propositions, *id est*, exactly one member of such a pair must be a true judgement while exactly one member must be a false judgement. Concisely put, "This is false" is false because it (without mediation) falsifies itself, while "This is not false" is true because its contradictory falsifies itself—again, without any mediation. Notice that as a result, Tarski's theory of truth or its contemporary variants (Kripke *et al*) are hardly applicable since the Tarski-like formula "'T'*P*' iff *P*" no longer can be appealed to (even with the additional premise that *P* exists and that '*P*' signifies *P*, for *P* may be the case when '*P*' is false—as when *P* is "This is false". That is to say, it is now possible for a false proposition to signify that things are as they are!)]

## ¹*Lazy Dot Theory*

The natural numbers $0,1,2,\ldots$ are constructed as binary strings $0,1,10,\ldots$ which are denoted in a formal system by the numerals $0,0',0'',\ldots$. For computational purposes $0',0'',0''',\ldots$ is often notated as $|,||,|||,\ldots$. These classes will be denoted by $\mathcal{N}, \mathcal{B}$, N, and H respectively. Their ranges are indefinite only in so far as the interpretation of the notation "..." is indefinite, "..." means "left to the imagination of the reader (including the author)," so "..." has a definite meaning in terms of the variation of imagination allowed for by the class of readers. But since the class of readers is not a definite number the range of variation of the imagination is left indefinite.

Thus, "..." is a sign of a class whether it occurs between terms as in (i) $0,1,2,\ldots n,n+1\ldots$ or within a term as in (ii) $11\ldots1$. In (i), moreover, the class denoted by the occurrence of "..." between 2 and n is, in general, not the same class as denoted by its second occurrence, and, in (ii), there is no *a priori* reason for identifying the meaning of "..." with either of the meanings assigned to "..." in (i).

Inspection shows that all of mathematics including set theory and, in particular, the formal systems, can be reduced to a complete formalization of the use of "..." in modern mathematics. (This reduction, by the way, is the very (inductive) essence of modern Intuitionistic Type Theory.)

Ultra-Black Chaotic Topology—Painting of a Disaster
(Complete view 4 IX—17 X 76—Moderna Museet, Stockholm)

## Christer Hennix

It is important to be able to grasp the composition or "graph" of the mixed use of lazy dots. If, say, (i) is used as the semantics for $\mathcal{N}$, i.e. $\mathcal{N}$ is closed, *at least,* under the action $n+1$, then the length $lh(n)$ of a numeral $0^{|\cdots|}$ where "..." denotes $n-2$ $|$'s is a *natural number* n i.e. a $0-1$ string of length $\leq {}^2\log(n)$.

[However, it is clear that closure under $n+1$ is not *used* in order to obtain closure under $lh(n)$. The computational resources for closure under $lh(n)$ are contained in "..." in $0,1,2,\ldots n, n+1$, in (i), i.e. in the interval $2\ldots n$ which is the "same" as $3\ldots n+1$ relative any given interpretation of "..." (which is all we shall use)]

$\mathcal{N} \to H$. *First* we speak about the natural numbers and *then* about the numerals which will denote them. The natural number 2, when denoted by the numeral $\underline{2}$, will also be denoted by the numeral $0''$. Since in metamathematics everything is confined to a *finite* text T, it *suffices* to use the usual arabic numerals to indicate any subobject of T itself (as Gödel realized in his paper of [1931]).

$N \to \mathcal{N}$. Then numerals come in such plenty that all natural numbers which were imagined to take the place of the occurrences of "..." in the semantics chosen for $\mathcal{N}$ now are denoted in a consistent way by the numerals imagined to take the place of the occurrence of "..." in N.

According to Weil, Hilbert was of the opinion that a metamathematical capacity for imagination became illicit when it excluded certain commonly intuited limits. Thus, Hilbert ruled out as possible metamathematical terms those which exceeded $10^{12}$ discrete atomic steps by their "shortest" construction. What Hilbert wanted to emphasize here was the *perceptual* basis of metamathematical certainty as opposed to Brouwer's psychological or imaginary basis for the foundations of mathematics. Thus $10^{12}$ may be replaced by any larger but *fixed* constant relative which the possible numerical terms are defined. It should be within the spirit of Hilbert's program that the value of this *program constant* increases as new computational powers are developed. So understood, the solution to the 4-color problem is in perfect harmony with the modern spirit of *Hilbert's* program.

Hekigan Roku Calligraphy
Title page from an abandoned score (The 100 Model Subjects of Hekigan Roku, 1971—1976)

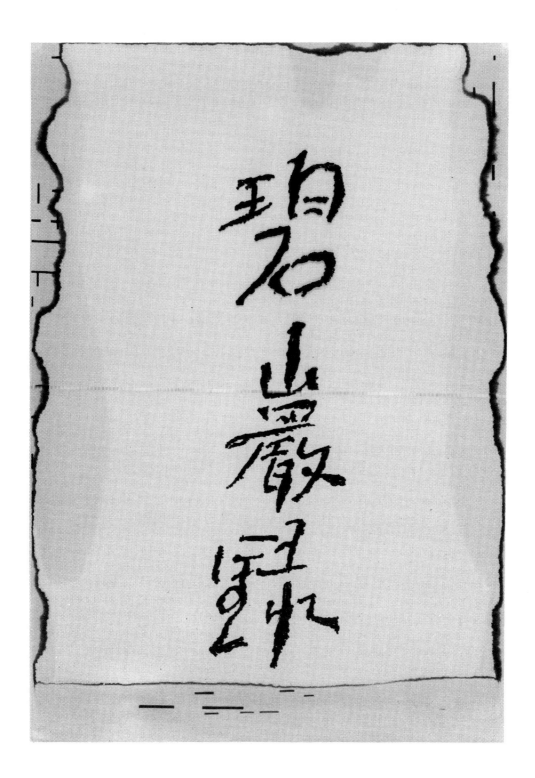

Two pages from the 100 Model Subjects of Hekigan Roku

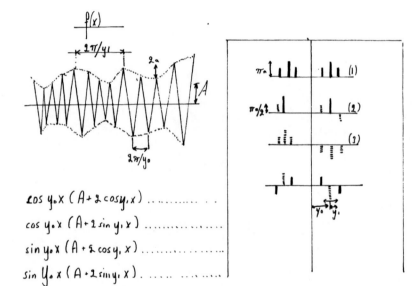

# MODEL SUBJECT NO 2

### *Jō-shū's 'The Real Way not Difficult'*

Jō-shū is the Scholar of this subject. His personal name was Jū-shin. The name Jō-shū comes from the name of the temple at which he resided. He was a native of North China, but learnt Zen in the South, and did not return to the North till he was sixty-one years of age. He escaped the severest persecutions of his times because he was then living in retirement, and he lived on to the good old age of one hundred and three. He died in 897.

Jō-shū's words in the Main Subject, below, are based on the works of Seng-ts'an (Sō-san in Japanese), who was the third Chinese Patriarch of Zen. Seng-ts'an, died 606, is the author of the famous *Records Concerning Belief in the Mind* (*Shin Shin Mei*), and the opening words of this Main Subject below, 'The Way is not difficult, It dislikes the Relative,' are a direct quotation from the *Shin Shin Mei*.

#### INTRODUCTORY WORD

The universe is too contracted. The sun, the moon, the stars, the constellations (shining) simultaneously, are too dark. And even if the staff of correction comes down like drops of rain, and the scolding voice comes like claps of thunder, by no means do these provide any point of coincidence with the main subject of study—the Absolute Truth.

All that all the Buddhas of the three worlds could do was to understand it themselves. Even all the Patriarchs of the ages could not exhaust the explanation. The one whole enormous store of the Scriptures does not exhaust the explanation. Even clear-eyed robed monks have not fully understood the meaning of their own vision (accomplished their own salvation).

Having reached this stage, what should be done to obtain more profit (i.e. fuller knowledge)? To mention that name 'Buddha' is to drag yourself in the mud, to girdle yourself with water. To mention the word 'Zen' is for the whole face to show shame. Advanced students (Bodhisattvas) do not wait to be told this. Students following with their beginners' minds should immediately set forth to further study.

### *Interpretation of the Above*

En-go introduced the subject by saying: The universe is too contracted and closed in for it to express the Absolute. The sun, the moon, the stars, the constellations, even when shining all together are no better than complete darkness for the purpose of revealing the Absolute.

Yes, and even if the teacher brings down his staff of correction, blow on blow, like rain in a storm, and even if he scolds with loud voice, like great claps of thunder, indeed whatever methods of instruction he may use they can have no application to, nor will they accord with, any real means of advancing along the way towards the Absolute.

Furthermore, even if all the Buddhas of the three worlds (past, present and future) were to try to explain this matter, all they would be able to do would be to understand it in their own selves. The whole line of Patriarchs, too, cannot rightly expound it. The great store of the Scriptures (twelve thousand volumes!) does not provide the explanation, and experienced monks who have had the vision have found the comprehension of Truth too hard for them to express.

Such being the case, what can we ourselves do to apply ourselves to this study? Even to talk about the name Buddha will make us feel as though we were being held back, dragging our feet in mud, or constrained as if we were being hindered by struggling along thigh deep in water. Advanced students, of course, who have practised meditation for a long time, do not have to wait to be told this. The minds of those who are still in the elementary stages must go on with their study with great sincerity.

MAIN SUBJECT

Attention! Jō-shū spoke to the assembly and said: The Real Way is not difficult, but it dislikes the Relative. If there is but little speech it is about the Relative or it is about the Absolute. This old monk is not within the Absolute. Do you value this or not? At this point there was a monk who said: If you are not within the Absolute how can you assess its value? Jō-shū said: Neither do I know that. The monk said: Your Reverence, if you do not yet know, how is it that you say you are not within the Absolute? Jō-shū said: You are effective in your questioning. Finish your worship and retire.

*Interpretation of the Above*

Jō-shū spoke to the assembly and said: The Real Way is nothing other than the Absolute. It was Seng-ts'an who told us that there is no difficulty about the Real Way, except that it is not expressible through the Relative. It dislikes the Relative. No matter how few words you may use in trying to explain this matter, you will soon find yourself talking about the Relative and the Absolute, and you will find yourself talking about differentiation. I myself am not captivated by the idea of the Absolute, so as to divide the real way into Absolute and Relative and to value the former very highly. And what about you? Do you distinguish between the Absolute and the Relative and value the former very highly?

Here one of the company spoke out and said: You acknowledge that you do not value the Absolute as highly as you would wish, but if so does not that mean that you are in some measure detached from the Relative? If you neither understand the Absolute nor remain detached from the Relative how can you assess the value of either? To this Jō-shū replied: I do not even know that. The monk said: If Your Reverence has no knowledge about these matters how can you even say that you do not prize the Absolute above the Relative? Jō-shū said: You are skilful in asking logical questions. Your logic is good. It is more important for you to go and do your worship than to argue logically. You will learn more in that way, so go off to your worship and retire.

APPRECIATORY WORD

'The Real Way is not difficult.' Words accord. Speech accords. Though it is One it has many aspects. Even if it be two, it is not only of double aspect. On the far side of the sky the sun rises, the moon sets. Outside the window the mountains are distant, the water is cold. Even though the skull's consciousness has ended why should joy have ceased? The decayed tree's dragon-moan may have been stopped, but it is not yet dried up (dead). Difficult, difficult! The Relative and the Absolute. Do you yourselves ponder them.

*Interpretation of the Above*

Seng-ts'an's words, 'The Real Way is not difficult,' are correct. Our very words, our speech accord with this. Through them the Real Way may be revealed. But what did Jō-shū mean when he said: If there is a little speech, if there are a few words they are about the Relative, they are about the Absolute? When unenlightened men talk about the Real Way, is what they say true? Rather would it appear from what they say that there is some one thing which might be called the Real Way. But in truth the Real Way is an inexpressible thing. It is of course One, but it has many aspects, nor is it to be seen as only two-sided, the Relative and the Absolute. It can be looked at from ten thousand directions.

Look out of your window at the world around you. There will be the sun rising on one side of the heavens, and the moon setting on the other. The sun and the moon, looked at from the point of the Real Way, are not necessarily two, neither are they necessarily one. They only appear so when looked at from the point of the Relative. Again, look at the distant mountains and the cold water outside your window. What relationship have these to one another? Are the mountains distant because the water is cold, or is the water cold because the mountains are distant? Truly distance and coldness are two and yet not two. They are one and yet not one. The Absolute and the Relative are exactly harmonized.

If a skull is found lying about, men say that consciousness has been cut off, but surely emotions like joy, anger, are still active. A decayed tree may seem to be dead, and yet when the wind blows we may hear it moaning like a dragon. The tree seems to be dead, but life itself is not extinct. It exists somewhere. From the point of the Real Way life is not necessarily life, nor is death necessarily death. Difficult, difficult! What is truly difficult is to express these truths in such a manner as to make them intelligible. That is why you must ponder them carefully.

# Toposes
# and Adjoints
(excerpts)

Christer Hennix

## Main Subject: *Boundary Operators.*

A *boundary* is a *constant event* of a space. If the interior of the boundary is also a constant event, i.e. an event with no internal collations except for those which are constant, the space is also called a *constant space*.

The exterior of a boundary event is called the *outer event horizon* of its space, while its interior marks the *inner event horizon* behind the event itself.

*Def.*
A boundary. A distance. Def.
A boundary. A limit. Def.
A boundary. A reflection. Def.
(A motion without velocity.
My own diagonalization.) Def.

Space is a quality of mind, an intension, i.e. a modality of consciousness.

Space as a mode of mind, *not* as a definition—the confrontation between corrupt and enlightened cosmic matter—as a formation of acts of attention, as an array of signs, as a homotopy between an image and its mirror images.

Space is inseparable from the array of signs with which it is designated.

Undifferentiated space is described by its empty array of signs.

[Composition of Mind—Composition of a Space, indexed by its Boundaries.]

Signs are boundaries. They *presuppose* space!

Each formula expresses a possible boundary.

Functions and operators are generators of boundaries. Course-of-values—traces of boundaries.

## Main Subject: *Pre-Socratic Set Theory*

**a ∈ A** ⇔ **a** is a program for the thought (intension) **A**

A *"school"* is a structure which contains *"classes"* some of which are called *"sets"*.

Schools create thoughts via their classes. They distinguish themselves by their syntax. In this sense, schools breed the trees of knowledge by the proliferation of classes arranged into hierarchies of (epistemological) domination.

**Definition.** Pre-Socratic classes exist previous to the formation of *all* their elements.

[***Example.*** The point-species of a locally infinite space (of infinitesimal distances.)

Intuitionistically, a class symbolizes a *"species"* or *"type"* of propositions.

**a ∈ A**

**a** is a proposition of *type* **A**, or, **A** is the species of proofs **a** of **A**.

A set is a class together with a proof that it is determined by all its elements.

Therefore, the type T of *all* types is *not* a set.

A "small" type T corresponds to a "large", i.e. infinite, proposition.

*Its* members are "small". i.e., finite propositions, each proof **a** branching only finitely many times.

A formula is a possible proposition. In general, proofs are complex propositions since the complexity of the proposition proved cannot exceed the complexity of its proof. Atomic propositions are their own proofs. I.e., if $A$ is atomic, then the type [A] has exactly one member when $A$ is true, and is empty when $A$ is false.

Thus, types arise in processes of analytic continuations of symbolic spaces, the general continuations consisting in assigning each proposition $A$ a *type* [A] so that each false proposition is assigned the *empty type* [ ], and if $A$ is a true proposition, then [A] is the *species of proofs* of A. That is to say, this assignment of types determines the meaning of a proposition in terms of its possible proofs.

Language forms a space divided by its propositions.

**Theory of Mind** = Theory of Boundaries of Being **Def.**
**Logic** = Theory of Boundaries of Cosmic errors **Def.**
**Topological Geometry** = Theory of Boundaries of Space **Def.**

The earliest results in the philosophy of thought showed the three-fold impossibility of

        i. enumerating space—
       ii. alphabetizing space—
      iii. geometrizing space—

from which the impossibility of (completely) axiomatizing space clearly follows.

. . . . .

Being forms a site of boundaries.
Its existence describes the
Boundaries of Being.

Incessantly,
Being describes boundaries,
Its incessantly orbiting limits.

The substratum of a boundary
is called *space*.

Geometry is the
syntax of space,
A cosmic phase-shift
A site of condensed cognitive
Matter

Clearly, a logical type [A] is a mixed bag of logical evidence, the extension of the mix being a function of the scope of the notion of proof under contemplation.

More precisely, a (non-empty) logical type [A] is a logical manifold which has the symbol $A$ at its root, each main branch of the manifold representing the structure of a possible proof of $A$.

An immediate metalogical observation is that, because of over-alphabetization [overload] there must be true propositions which cannot be assigned any type at all. Propositions without types are *non-stratifiable* propositions.

If $\mathbf{b}\,(\epsilon A)$ is $\neg\,\mathbf{a}$, i.e. a proof of $\neg\,A$ (not-$A$), then $\mathbf{A}$ is said to form a *"diagonal class"* with $\mathbf{a}$ the symbol for its *"diagonal formula."*

A great deal has been written since Frege on diagonal definitions occurring in a *system of definitions.* It is known from (academic) folklore, that the following provocative picture of diagonalization was formulated by Wittgenstein sometime in the mid-30s (after Kreisel):

> *Suppose we have a sequence of rules for writing down rows of 0 and 1, suppose the pth rule, the diagonal definition, says: write 0 at the nth place (of the pth row) if and only if the nth rule tells you to write 1 (at the nth place of the nth row); and write 1 if and only if the nth rule tells you to write 0. Then for the pth place, the pth rule says: write nothing!*
>
> *Similarly, suppose the qth rule says: write at the nth place what the nth rule tells you to write at the nth place of the nth row. Then, for the qth place, the qth rule says: write what you write!*

Inevitably, the diagonal argument (however cheaply) brings out the *incompleteness* of any formalized notion of proof theoretic studies, *unless*, that is, they are equipped to deal with formal concepts of *negative evidence* which are available *independently* of *any* concept of proof (formal or not). The following observations are due to the *ultra-intuitionistic studies* in the foundations of mathematics.

**Summary. Typical Example Of A Working Definition.**

$\mathbf{A}$ is a type (set) ($\mathbf{A}$ is a formula).

$A$ is a type — $\mathbf{A\ type}\quad;\ x_1 \in \mathbf{A}_1,\ldots,x_m \in \mathbf{A}_m$

$A = B$ equal types — $\mathbf{A = B}\ ;\ x_1 \in \mathbf{A}_1,\ldots,x_m \in \mathbf{A}_1$

$a \in A$ object of type $A$ — $\mathbf{a \in A}\ ;\ x_1 \in \mathbf{A}_1,\ldots,x_m \in \mathbf{A}_m$

$(a = b) \in A$ equal objects of type $A$ — $\mathbf{a = b} \in \mathbf{A}\ ;\ x_1 \in \mathbf{A}_1,\ldots,x_m \in \mathbf{A}_m$

.....

The sign of Being in Philosophy is in the signs of a text while the sign of the text is a sign of non-Being of Being in Philosophy and its texts. [Iterated diagonal formulae]

*Being* is a term of a text. Its meaning is *only* that of a term of a text. Yet, paradoxically, Being may be enriched as a term of a text.

What exists, what surrounds Being, is a text.

It is through the action of the text that Being as Thought becomes a Form in many variables.

It is the action of the many variables of Thought which is the source of the many forms of Being.

Thought is a Form in many variables. E.g. ...x...y...z... is a formal expression of a form of a Thought in which enters at least three variables denoted by x, y, and z.

A formal expression of a Form is a sign of limits as Being itself is a sign of limits.

A text is an arrow along which a natural transformation of Being into co-Being occurs.

A text presupposes space.

Space exists as Being.

Being generates space.

Space carries geometry as Being carries space.

The geometry of a Form in many variables is called a *site*. It is formally denoted by a category together with a topology.

The *analytic continuation* of a form in the algebraic geometry of a site is called a *pre-topos* while its *analytic completion* is a *topos*, a continuously variable natural transformation of the intrinsic geometric logic of the algebraic geometry contained in every possible analytic continuation of a Form of a site.

The geometric logic *intrinsic* to the geometry of a Form is not classical but *intuitionistic*. This can be seen in the geometric constructions corresponding to the logical constants and in particular, the quantifiers, including negation.

The notion of a topos effects a natural transformation between a geometric space and a logical space intrinsic to the geometry of the space.

The geometry of space is a perception of inferences in logical space, [The geometry of Thought is a geometry of Being.]

Being defines a space together with an action.

## The Alternative Interpretations Of Type Theory.

1. $A$ is a proposition ($A$ is true) (**a** is a proof of the proposition $A$).

2. $A$ is a problem ($A$ is a solvable problem) (**a** is a program for the problem $A$).

3. $\mathbf{a} \in \mathbf{A}$ — **a** is a (mental) program for the thought or intension **A** (**A** is a workable idea).

**Remarks on the alethic realities.** As soon as an event is perceived by $\Sigma$, its arrival is *"organically" real* and the sentence which expresses this arrival is *"epistemically" real*. For example, any arrival of a perceived collation is organically real and any such collation may be included in the text of the epistemically real sentence which expresses the perception.

A situation **S** is *"organically real"* (*"epistemically real"*) as soon as each sentence to be accepted by the sense of **S** is *"organically"* (*"epistemically"*) real and any of its textual collations is perceived. In particular, if **S** is a collection of sentences and textual collations, its organic (epistemic) "reality" shall be that of each of the sentences together with the perceptions of the textual collations of **S**.

If a sentence on the presence or absence of an object (in **S**) is organically or epistemically real, the presence or absence of the object (in **S**) shall be called, respectively, organically or epistemically *"real."* In general, only logically indecomposable objects or events are considered as the content of "perceptions" or what is "perceived", while more complicated objects are to be deduced from the reality of decomposable objects by logical means, which are studied by a specific branch of (ultra-intuitionistic) logic, viz., the *Reasoning Theory*. When the Reasoning Theory is available, "exhaustions" are considered as indecomposable objects when the means to obtain them by the *Conjunction Theory* fails.

I now indicate four ways, $\alpha$–$\delta$, by means of which a sentence on the absence or presence of an object **e** or a class **E** of objects may be recognized as real in **S** *independently* of the Reasoning Theory.

$\delta$. If any object present in S is discerned from **e** and all objects present in S are exhausted, then **e** is not-present or *"absent"* in S.

$\beta$. If any object present in S is discerned from any object of the kind **E**, and all objects present in S are exhausted, then no object of the kind **E** is present in S, or, equivalently, all objects of kind **E** are *"absent"* in S.

## Christer Hennix

Being is a sign of a site of limits.

A text delineates the geometric limits of Being.

To ask what is a text is analogous to asking what is space.* I.e., again, there is an analogy with the continuum. The space of the text is yet another replica of the continuum problem, i.e., problems of thought connected with the existence of infinitary or $\omega$-forms of thought $\ldots x \ldots y \ldots z \ldots$ in many variables $x,y,z,\ldots$.

---

*No part of a text avoids defining a space whose intrinsic geometric logic is not intuitionistic. Thus, as non-euclidean geometry was not immediately asserted by the unguided perception of pure space so non-classical logics were not observed to occur in the passages from finite to the infinite in Thought.

Now, it is well known that at least since the time of Plato, a course in *advanced philosophy* has always taken the knowledge of geometry for granted. Riemann, Frege and recently Lawvere have in different ways approached fundamental epistemological questions by means of purely geometrical considerations. This situation has led to a Model Subject with the following main subject: The geometry of Thought in the becoming of a geometry of Being.

## The Yellow Book

γ. If **e**, or any other object **b** in **E**, is *alien* to any of the ways of recognizing an object as "present" in **S**, then **e**, or any object **b** in **E** is not-present ("*absent*") in **S**.

δ. If the arrival of $Oc_e$ of an event **e** is absent in **S**, then **e** is *non-arrived* in **S**.

On the basis of $\alpha-\delta$ one may now specify the following

### Principle of Negative Extension

Let **S** by any real situation and all objects of the kind **E** absent in **S**. Then the situation **S**, obtained from **S** by adding the sentence that "*all objects of kind **E** are absent in **S***", is real.

The principle of negative extension (**p.n.ex.**) has been considered by various authors throughout the history of logic. It is interesting to note that **p.n.ex.** can be used to obtain an axiom of "infinity" as was actually done by some scholastic logicians and, notably, by the Indian logician Dinnaga (9th century C.E.).( *Id est*,there exist ontologies with "infinitely" many *absent objects*).

. . . . .

We have now developed some means in order to declare some situations "*alethically real*" since we are able to take into consideration some *sources of sentences*

$$\Diamond_\chi^S A_1 \quad \mathbf{M}_S A$$

from which an ascent to an alethic reality can be made by the reader. Viz. recall that some sentences $\Diamond_\chi^S A$ are already available since every prepared atomic action **A** is supposed fulfillable i.e. is *organically possible* in any organically possible situation. Further, since we demand that all prepared atomic actions must be allowed, the corresponding deontic sentences **P** $A$ must be accepted as must the epistemically corresponding sentences **M** $A$. Hence, the following two definitions belong to the Modality Theory.

I. A situation **S** is alethically *real* if each element of it is accepted on the basis of a perception *or* a definition.

II. Each alethically real situation **S** will also be called a *possible* situation.

**Note.** $\Diamond$, **M** and **P** are formal symbols for *alethic, epistemic* and *deontic possibility*, respectively, where $\chi$ denotes a parameter varying over some set of "laws".

*Christer Hennix*

## Model Subject W

$$\left\{ \text{Truth Set Of Measure Zero} \right\}$$

***Introductory Word.***
(4.093. 4.092)*

4.094. Ein Bild zur Erklärung des Wahrheitsbegriffes: Schwartzer Fleck aus weissem Papier. Die (Papier; die) Form des Fleckes kann man beschreiben (,) indem man für jeden Punkt der Fläche angibt, ob er weiss oder schwartz ist. Der Tatsache (,) dass ein punkt schwartz ist (,) entspricht eine positive—der, dass ein Punkt weiss (nicht schwartz) ist (,) eine negative Tatsache. Bezeichne ich einen Punkt der Fläche (einen Fregeschen Wahrheitswert), so entspricht dies der Annahme (,) die zur Beurteilung aufgestellt wird. (,) etc. etc.

Um aber sagen zu können (,) ein Punkt sei schwartz oder weiss, muss ich vorerst wissen (,) wann man einen Punkt schwartz und wann man ihn weiss nennt: um sagen zu können (:) „p" ist wahr (oder falsch) (,) muss ich bestimmt haben (,) unter welchen Umständen ich p ( „p") wahr nenne, und damit bestimme ich den Sinn der Satzes.

Der Punkt (,) an dem das Gleichnis hinkt (,) ist nun der: Wir können auf eines Punkt des Papiers zeigen (,) auch ohne zu wissen (,) was weiss und schwartz ist; einem Satz ohne Sinn aber entspricht gar nichts, den er bezeichnet kein Ding (Wahrheitswert) (,) dessen Eigenschaften etwa „falsh" oder „wahr" hiessen: das Verbum eines Satzes ist nicht „ist wahr" oder „ist falsh"—wie Frege glaubte—, sondern das (,) was „whar ist" (,) muss das Verbum schon erhalten.

---

*Cf. Tractatus 4.063

***Interpretation of the Above***
    Finite Set of Measure 0 (Detail) 1969 (2-D Truth-Space) Moderna Museet 1976.

# Model Subject No. −1 [Without Title]

***Introductory Word*** [1-2.0121...]

1. The world is a form of thought.
1.1 The world consists of forms of thought, not of facts.
1.11 The world is determined by forms of thought and by them all being nothing but forms of thought.
1.12 Because the totality of forms of thought determines what is as well as what is not.
1.13 An exact world consists of forms of thought in logical space.
1.2 Every world breaks down into its constituent forms of thought. The world eventually breaks up in its atomic forms of thought—when the logical analysis has been completed.
1.21 The exact forms of thought form an independent set of forms, where an exact form corresponds to a form of an exact thought.
2. What is the case—the form of thought—is the existence of states of minds.
2.01 A state of mind is a combination of thoughts.
2.011 It is essential for thoughts that they should be possible constituents of states of mind.
2.012 In logic nothing is accidental: if a thought can occur in a state of mind, the possibility of the latter must be co-possible with the thought itself.
2.0121 It does not stand to reason that a form of thought shall adjust itself to a thought that exists independently of the former. If the thought can occur in a form, then that is something co-formed by the formation of the form itself. (What is logically possible is not just simply possible. Logic is occupied with every possibility, and all possibilities form its field of thought).

Just as we are completely unable to imagine spatial objects outside space or temporal objects outside time, so too are we wholly unable to conceive of a single thought without the possibility of its connections with other thoughts, without its occurrences within the boundaries of a form of thought.

If I can imagine thoughts combined and connected by forms of thought, then I cannot imagine the possibility which excludes every thought from at least one such combination.

.
.
.
.
.

# LOGISCH-PHILOSOPHISCHE ABHANDLUNG

1*  Die Welt ist alles, was der Fall ist.
1.1  Die Welt ist die Gesamtheit der Tatsachen, nicht der Dinge.
1.11  Die Welt ist durch die Tatsachen bestimmt und dadurch, daß es alle Tatsachen sind.
1.12  Denn, die Gesamtheit der Tatsachen bestimmt, was der Fall ist und auch, was alles nicht der Fall ist.
1.13  Die Tatsachen im logischen Raum sind die Welt.
1.2  Die Welt zerfällt in Tatsachen.
1.21  Eines kann der Fall sein oder nicht der Fall sein und alles übrige gleich bleiben.
2  Was der Fall ist, die Tatsache, ist das Bestehen von Sachverhalten.
2.01  Der Sachverhalt ist eine Verbindung von Gegenständen (Sachen, Dingen).
2.011  Es ist dem Ding wesentlich, der Bestandteil eines Sachverhaltes sein zu können.
2.012  In der Logik ist nichts zufällig: Wenn das Ding im Sachverhalt vorkommen kann, so muß die Möglichkeit des Sachverhaltes im Ding bereits präjudiziert sein.
2.0121  Es erschiene gleichsam als Zufall, wenn dem Ding, das allein für sich bestehen könnte, nachträglich eine Sachlage passen würde.

* Die Decimalzahlen als Nummern der einzelnen Sätze deuten das logische Gewicht der Sätze an, den Nachdruck, der auf ihnen in meiner Darstellung liegt. Die Sätze n.1, n.2, n.3, etc. sind Bemerkungen zum Satze No. n; die Sätze n.m1, n.m2, etc. Bemerkungen zum Satze No. n.m; und so weiter.

***Interpretation of the Above*** (vertical *s*equence of dots)
The general form of the *natural numbers* is given by

$N_W$ $\qquad\qquad\qquad [0, \xi, \xi+1]$

where 0 is a parameter for values of the *empty logical operation*, $\Lambda$.

>Numbers are exponents for an operation.
>All initial operations are logical operations.
>The operation of picturing a fact (as a composition of arrows) is a logical operation.
>By picturing the fact that an operation has taken place, by constructing its model, the *meaning* of that picture is now attainable as a new logical object, as a new collection of arrows.
>There are three *parameters* in the number theoretic schema $N_W$.
>0 is a parameter for values of $\Lambda$.
>$\xi$ is a (meta-)variable of quantification—the most general (logical) designation of a natural number.
>$\xi+1$ is the generic parameter for a fixed arithmetical *succesor function* with argument-values *restricted* to the range $N_\xi \subset N_W$ of quantifiers with $\xi$ as the *only eigenvariabel* [cf. Frege's general concept of a (partial recursive) function].
>All mathematical operations are logical operations.
>Numbers don't occur in logic, they are a side-product—the exponents of operations.
>Logical propositions say nothing, they cannot define the exponents of an operation.
>Not even the exponent of the empty operation can have a logical name, since, if I were to choose one, $\emptyset$, say, then by "$\emptyset$" a dynasty of new arrows would follow in the wake of tracing the developing identifying chains, in tracing the ensuing compositions of arrows.
>Mathematics does not take place within logic.—It occurs outside of logics, as a theory of models for formulae with quantifiers.
>The general form of numbers is mirrored in the general form of *truth-functions*

$L_W$ $\qquad\qquad\qquad [\bar{p}, \bar{\xi}, N(\xi)]$

which is the general form of the *proposition* P expressed as a sentence p [provided that the elementary truth-function N(of P) is at most $\xi$-ary].

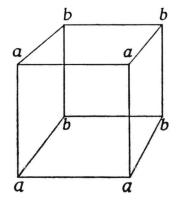 ≠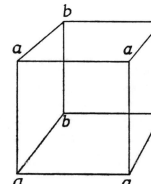

That is, out of the $\xi$ elementary propositions p,q,r,..., an infinite sequence of truth-functions of elementary propositions is obtained by iterating the continuously variable elementary truth-function N[$\eta$] infinitely many times with any previously obtained values as its arguments. I denote the so obtained sets of propositions by $\bar{p}_\xi$ and regard it as a *covering* of the space of propositions determined by $L_W$. [Indeed, $\bar{p}_\xi$ suitably defined may be considered as inducing a *Grothendic topology* on the language $L_W$. Although one will notice complications which will arise if the argument $\xi$ accepts non-Archimedian integers, i.e. integers $\underline{\xi}$ such that

$$\underline{\xi} \neq 1 + 1 + 1 + \ldots + 1$$

i.e. such that $\underline{\xi}$ is *not* a natural number.]

For any choice $\bar{p}$ of elementary propositions p,q,r,..., suitable definitions of the set $\bar{p}_\xi$ represents an enumeration of *all two-valued truth-functions* uniformly built up around the elementary truth function .|.. Thus, the set $\bar{\bar{p}}_\xi$ of all sets $\bar{p}_\xi$ regarded as binary sequences (0-1-sequences) is in 1-1 correspondence with all infinite sequences of binary natural numbers regarded as exponents of (iterated) metamathematical operations over the propositions in the language of arithmetic. Once more, the totality of all paths taken through a set of all meaningful propositions is made to depend on the meaning of the *continuum problem*. [Needless to say, the following hypothesis, *viz.*

(CH) $\qquad\qquad 2^{\aleph_0} = \aleph_1$

(the *continuum hypothesis*), is *not* included in any totality of meaningful propositions but is simply regarded as one among Cantor's many wreckless statements—a verdict, by the way, which didn't win common acceptance until "after Cohen" when it was finally realized that the infinitary exponential term $2^{\aleph_0}$ *can be anything it ought to be*!

.
.
.
.
.

*Christer Hennix*

# Main Subject
On The Metamathematics of Tractatus Logico-Philosophicus

***Attention!***

I shall only state this much as known:

> The clarity of a form of thought is a cosmic event, waiting to take its place among the elements.....
>
> Now, regard the well-known philosophical diagrams below—in the relative and in the absolute. Do you yourself ponder them!

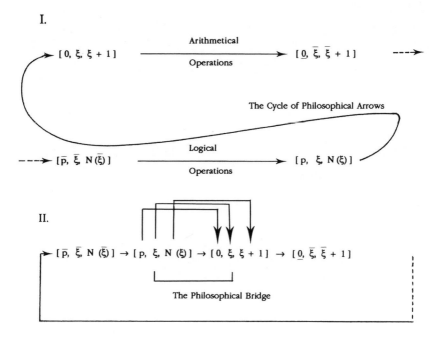

## The Yellow Book

### Interpretation of the above

Any particular development of arithmetic cannot be chosen on the basis of the propositions of logic alone.

A form of arithmetic, such as $N_{WA}$, is a form of *restricted quantification*.

That is, in order to indicate any particular arithmetic from the general form of natural number,

$$[0, \xi, \xi+1]$$

I need to specify the ranges of values of the parameter $\xi$.

The general form of arithmetic is

$N_{WA}$ $\qquad\qquad [0^{\bar{\xi}}, \bar{\xi}, \bar{\xi}+1]$

Like the propositional variables, the arithmetical variables arrange themselves in *types*.

Numbers correspond to exponents of operations on propositions.

[Alternatively, numbers measure the quantity of mind's folly (cf. L.E.J. Brouwer).]

Arithmetical types are also called *"functional universes"* or *"natural number objects"*. For brevity, I shall designate them as "f-*types*" when determined by the stages (course-of-values) of an f-sequence $fx = \bar{\xi}$.

**Remark.** Regarded as a *category* neither $N_W$ (nor $N_{WA}$) is a *discrete category*, i.e. not every arrow is obtained as $id_N$ on some arithmetical object N.

I now recall that each arithmetical object $n \geqslant 0$ forms a category *viz as follows:*

        **0**   —*empty category*
        **1**   —*singleton category*
        **2**   —*binary category*
        .
        .
        .

## Christer Hennix

At the limit of this series of abstract constructions stands the category **N** formed by a single object N in conjunction with infinitely many arrows from N to N ( corresponding to the natural numbers, 0,1,2,3...).

Each arrow has the same domain and codomain, *viz.*, the — unique object N. Composition of arrows $m,n$, corresponds to *addition*, i.e. m o n = m + n:

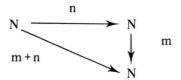

Furthermore, if the "philosophical bridge" between occurrences of the natural number objects N is indicated as $1_N = 0$, then

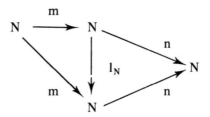

commutes, since 0 + m = m and n + 0 = n.

.
.
.
.

### Appreciatory Word

(For the purpose of understanding the text below recall that both the concept of formula and the concept of arrows generalize to the concept of *diagram* (Topos Theory). Furthermore, the latter concept generalizes to the concept of objects such as (calligraphic) characters and other complex signs. On the other hand, it has been known since the late 60s (folklore) that *Howard* had secured a proof which established the interconvertibility between formulae and *terms*.)

## The Yellow Book

The logical object which corresponds to the natural numbers, N, in Tractatus, can be interpreted as a *continuously variable set* of natural numbers N related to a *topos construction* satsifying the usual Kock-Lawvere axioms (where the difference between two *external* natural number objects, $N_1$, $N_2$ are interpreted as different stages of the construction of the *internal* natural number object $N_0$). However, rather than just viewing arithmetic as governed by processes of additions m + n of natural numbers m,n, the arithmetic of the Tractatus (WA) is founded on a generalized operation for a *multiple-successor arithmetic*. Thus, given a number m, the value of $m + \ell + 1$, the $\ell$+ 1st *successor of* m, is a value which must exist in the arithmetical system WA (given that $\ell$ exists). On the other hand, the diagonal value m + m of m + n is *undefined* by Tractatus' symbolic conventions [cf. Tractatus 4.0411]. Classically, the diagonalization of the two-place function m + n is denoted by the one-place function 2m (which generalizes to the two-place operation n · m of *multiplication*). The values of the latter function may be used to indicate a formal series of *fixed points* $2 \cdot m, 2 \cdot m + 1, 2 \cdot m + 2, \ldots 2 \cdot m + \ell, \ldots$, at which the arithmetical operation of addition is "flattened out" and overtaken by the arithmetical operations n · m and $\ell + 1$, $\ell$,m,n = 0,1,2,3... . Although the latter constructions of fixed points are not available within the framework of Tractatus, the latter affords other types of fixed point constructions which are related to the growth of the exponents of operations on elementary propositions and their truth-functional combinations.

Now, observe that given any consistent set $\bar{p}$ of elementary propositions ordered with respect to their logical complexity, there are no two elementary propositions p,q, such that q is $\neg$ p, i.e. the conjunction $\wedge$(p,q) is *undefined* whenever q is $\neg$ p or p is $\neg$ q. However, if, say, there is an elementary proposition r expressing the fact that a spot in the visual field is *red*, then there could be elementary propositions p,q, ..., expressing the fact that the same spot is not-white, not-black, ...a series which may be interpreted as giving an increasingly correct "approximation" of the proposition r. That is, if the number of distinct colors were *finite* and, as a set, containing, say, $\ell$ members, then the $\ell$- 1-ary conjunction

$$\bigwedge_1^{\ell-1} \quad \{\, p, q, \ldots \,\}$$

## Christer Hennix

of $l-1$ possibly elementary propositions recursively entails r while their $l-1$-ary joint denial would be equivalent to $\neg r$, i.e. the elementary proposition p expressing that the spot in the visual field is *not* red. But, obviously, this contradicts the independence of the elementary propositions. An immediate conclusion of this meditation on the logic of colors is that in so far as colors may be comprehended by elementary propositions, they must not be bounded by a finite set, the number of logical colors being numberless (zahllos) i.e. *non-finite*. Using a less archaic language, one says today that the problem of estimating a lower upper bound on the cardinal number of the number of logical colors remains *unsolvable* (even when notations for transfinite ordinals are allowed). And the same goes for membership in $\bar{p}$, i.e. it is *undecidable* whether or not r (or p,q,...) is (are) among the members of the set $\bar{p}$ of elementary propositions p,q,r,...., and, it still remains unknown whether or not the latter sequence is co-extensive with the *empty sequence* of elementary propositions. Yet, if $\bar{p}$ *is* non-empty, then it can be shown that $\bar{p}$'s cardinal number must exceed one, i.e. in terms of (cardinal) size, $\bar{p}$ must be, at a minimum, a *0-large set* [cf Tractatus 2.0121]

### *Interpretation of the Above*
*Quod decet bovem dedecet Jovem.*

It is, of course, well-known that the Tractatus text ostensively neglects the more fundamental aspects of the *decision problem [Der Entscheidungsproblem]*[Cf. Tractatus 6.5...: *The riddle* does not exist ...]. *For example,* everybody knows today that it is not even sufficient (given consistency) to identify a formal system, such as WA, with its set of deductions, since one also has to consider with particular detail the *manner in which it is verified that a syntactic object is a deduction—* where, of course, the additional information or "structure" (semantics) being the (formal) sequence involved in building up the deductions themselves. Yet, obviously, there is (assuming Church's thesis) a mechanical method (algorithm) of deciding whether $\underline{d}$ is a (formal) derivation of any *existential formula* $\exists x \Phi x$.

However, this is not the case for *universal formulae*—a topic discussed at length for the first time by Gödel, 1931. Here are some simple examples. Given formulae $\Phi_1$, $\Phi_2$ and $\Phi_3$ of WA one of the following *cannot* be derived in WA:

i. $\Phi_1$ expresses that WA is (deductively) *closed* under *modus ponens* and $\Phi_1$ holds

    ii. $\Phi_2$ expresses that WA is *complete* for numerical arithmetic (wrt a specific arithmetical predicate) and $\Phi_2$ holds

    iii. $\Phi_3$ expresses that WA is *consistent* and $\Phi_3$ holds

It is rather remarkable that, although not explicitly stated, these facts may be guaged already from Frege's Appendix to *Grundgesetze*, vol.II.

With reference to $\Phi_3$, the concept of *identity* of deductions (proofs) is absolutely critical. *For example*, there are at least two distinct proofs of the formula

$$(\Phi_4) \qquad\qquad p \wedge \neg p \to (p \to p)$$

*viz*. i. one ignores the conclusion (*ex falso quodlibet*), or, ii. one ignores the premise (since $p \to p$ is a tautology.) Here a formal identification of these corresponding two proofs is obviously a non-trivial problem. Furthermore, in this context it should be stressed that *different styles of formalization* may be compared with the use of different coordinate systems in geometry, where one system is particularly suited for the study of a *specific geometric relation*, "suited" not in the sense of being manageable, but, rather, where the passage from one co-ordinate system to another may introduce singularities *without geometric meaning* (such as the indeterminateness of the second polar co-ordinate at the origin.)

Returning now to Wittgenstein's enigmatic notation

$$(\text{------}W)(\xi,\ldots.)\,[(\text{------}T)(\xi,\ldots.)]$$

it must be immediately remarked
that *what is not* is *not* recursively enumerable (r.e.). That is (even) if *what is* is r.e., its complement is *not* r.e. However, neither is the set of finite models (of this context) r.e. so (a black-and-white) logical space would be *incomplete* for most *finite* $\xi$. On the other hand, from the incompleteness property one deduces that a sequence of falsehoods of order type N $(= \text{``}\omega^{WA}\text{''})$ will not necessarily correspond to the constant function $\bot$ (designating permanent falsehood) but rather to (by switching non-linearly at infinity) the constant function $\top$ (designating permanent truth) as the following recursion shows (where "$\vdash$" denotes the formally defined *provability operator*):

## Christer Hennix

$\vdash^0 \bot := \bot$

$\vdash^{k+1} \bot := \vdash (\vdash^k \bot)$

$\vdash^N \bot := \neg \bot$

Writing ■ for $\bot$ and □ for $\top$ the following diagram relates the *continuum problem* with the *Liar Paradox* (and propositional quantifiers with modal operators).

*p  q  r  . . .*

*The Yellow Book*

## A Continuously Variable Open Point Set $\eta$ of Measure 0

The set $\eta$ is a *totally disordered* set with no distinguished first or last elements. The elements of $\eta$ are called *points* and they are indicated (when present) by *black dots* (of variable sizes).

The semiotical action corresponding to the event $e \in \acute{E}$ where the set $\eta$ is losing some of its points is the *merging* or *identification* of pairs of points $<\beta, \gamma>$ (with a single point $\alpha$—which *may* also be (non-deterministically) identified with either $\beta$ or $\gamma$ (as in))

$$\{\ldots\}_{\alpha\beta\gamma} \mapsto \{\ldots\}_{\alpha\beta\ldots}$$

The dual event where $\eta$ acquires new points shall be semiotically indicated by the action of *splitting* or *discerning* a single point $\alpha$, thereby creating a (not necessarily ordered) pair $\{\beta, \gamma\}$ of points, i.e.

$$\alpha \mapsto \{\beta, \gamma\}$$

A more precise notation for the set $\eta$ is $\acute{E}(\eta)$ together with a *calander signature*, e.g $\acute{E}(\eta)_{4IX-17X\ 76}$.

Different phases of the latter continuously variable set are shown as a *continuously variable floor painting* (reproduced on the following pages). Thus, this floor painting serves simultaneously both as a *picture* and as a *model* for a *finite set of the topoi* constructed in the style of F.W. Lawvere.

**Remark.** The here documented set $\acute{E}(\eta)_{4IX-17X\ 76}$ only existed during the time interval indicated by the calender signature and has since that time never existed again.

Continously Variable Open Point Set Of Measure Zero
(Partial views 4 IX - 17 X 76—Moderna Museet, Stockholm)

*Christer Hennix*

## *Epistemological Intermezzo (I,II)*

The simplest objects which are directly dealt with are called *"signs"* and among them one distinguishes the *elementary signs* as an enumerable sub-species which intersects any non-empty species of signs.

Let $E_0$ denote an inhabited species of elementary signs. Then, by $\mathcal{E}_{E_0}$ I indicate a ($\omega$-) *finite* Nn, the image $N_{\mathcal{E}_0}$ of which enumerates $E_0 \cup \{ \triangle \}$. [Here "$\triangle$" is a sign for an occurrence of an empty sign which does not inhabit $E_0$.]

I shall indicate that a natural number k belongs to $N_{\mathcal{E}_0}$ by the (non-positional) *unary system of indications*

$|,||,|||,\ldots\ldots,|^k,|^{k+1},\ldots\ldots$

If $\omega$ is the k:th elementary symbol in $E_0$, then $\dot{\omega}$ denotes the positive integer k + 1.

It must be decidable, given any object $\alpha$, whether $\alpha \epsilon E_0$ and whether $\alpha \neq \omega$. Thus, $N_{\mathcal{E}_0}$ is an intuitively decidable Nn since the map $\dot{.} : \alpha \to |^k$ is required to be effective.

The decidability of the species of elementary signs is a necessary property for any *direct* correctness proofs [proofs of absence of errors]. On the other hand, the sequences of species of non-elementary signs is not even r.e. and neither are many of its members $E_1, E_2, E_3, \ldots\ldots, E_k, E_{k+1}, \ldots\ldots$ In particular, its empty members, $E_\phi$, are *not* r.e.

For each inhabited species $E_j$, there shall be an Nn, $N_{\mathcal{E}_j}$, which depends both on $E_j$ and the function $\mathcal{E}_j$ enumerating $E_j$.

Thus, the continuum of inhabited species of non-elementary signs shall be denoted by $\dot{E}$—and its Nn by $N_{\dot{E}}$.

## *Reminder.*

Correct sequences of elements of $\dot{E}$—such as *programs*—are among the most complex ontological objects so far encountered from searches at this end of the universe (Poets must ask themselves (again) if Mallarmé was not right—after all.—And, on reflection, must not proof-theorists, if not novelists, take Robbe-Grillet's dictum, "Nothing is more fantastic, ultimately, than precision" into renewed considerations?!)

## SPECTRA OF MODALITIES
## AND
## THE THEORY OF THE CREATIVE SUBJECT, $T_H(\Sigma)$

I.   It is a well-known fact that activities ending in art may not always carry a well-determined meaning or sense. On the contrary, the lack of meaning(-fulness) is compensated for by (purported) aim(s) expressed by the purpose(s) governing the installment of the generating activities for which end some particular object is taken as a witness. This somewhat confused reality shows the indisputable importance of the interpretation of the <u>optative modalities</u> underlying any goal-oriented activity $\mathcal{A}$.

II.   In order to fix the purposefulness of an activity $\mathcal{A}$, several ratios are to be measured, such as

1) $$\frac{\text{Interest of results}}{\text{Efforts involved}}$$

AND

2) $$\frac{\text{Long-term satisfaction}}{\text{Efforts required}}$$

Given some satisfactory measures of these ratios for an activity $\mathcal{A}$ there is a further requirement on the <u>means</u> available by which the result(s) of $\mathcal{A}$ are achieved. Viz. it is generally required that any aim achieved through $\mathcal{A}$ is acquired only as far as <u>fair</u> means have been provided.

*Christer Hennix*

Thinking occurs as a form in many variables.

Forms of thinking are forms of attention. (No discernment takes place if attention is not present.) Acts of attention preceed every identification.

(When the Creative Subject discerns or identifies the values of her current free variables she is already enduring a succession of acts of attention. Here shall only be mentioned attention to variables and attention to forms.)

(The geometry of forms is a notation for the projective content of thought, i.e., the points of thought, when charted on a manifold, that are determined by the values of the free variables of its form(s).)

When the Creative Subject identifies two thoughts or thought processes by means of yet another thought the two thoughts (or thought proceses) are said to be of the *same type.*

(Types of thought are discerned by their (intrinsic) evaluation of the Creative Subject's current free variables.

From a geometric point of view thought has the shape of a manifold along which certain variables have been evaluated.)

The form of thought which expresses attention to form is *also* a form of attention. In the limit, this form can be expanded as a *manifold of attentions* (mastered by the Creative Subject).

Attention penetrates thought (in) as much as thought penetrates attention. Attention combined with thought is an operator of (intensional) discernment, a form of a complex perception in a space where mind and cosmos momentarily coalesce along a singular manifold of arbitrarily many dimensions.

In this way, existence becomes, ultimately, a result of attention (or absence of attention). And attention is the result of a form of thought. What is is thus firmly trapped in our forms of thought. (or forms of absence of thought).

*Grammatica tua sit tibi in perditionem!*

Any violation of this <u>fairness principle</u> is to be considered harmful for the continuation of the situations $S$ generated by $\mathcal{A}$, on account of the <u>displacement of modalities</u>, caused, in particular, by the displacement of goals relative the installment of $\mathcal{A}$.

III. Clearly, the condition of fairness for purposeful activities $\mathcal{A}$ imposes an obvious restriction as to the availability of means for realizing $\mathcal{A}$. This restriction must be evaluated relative the higher-order aims under which $\mathcal{A}$ is subsumed. As far as clarity and certainty is sought, the fairness principle is but a higher-order means for our epistemic development, and its violation poses obstacles as far as (foundational) communication is aimed at (to wit, its deepest threat).

IV. For the purpose of <u>restricting</u> the above-mentioned restriction, two <u>spectra of modalities</u> are defined for the sake of optimal freedom in activities $\mathcal{A}$ restricted by fair means. Viz.

(1) The first spectrum which will be designated Freedom$_1$ or $F_1$ and is defined as that <u>regime</u> $P$ governing activities $\mathcal{A}$ in the <u>absence of any obstructions</u>. Id est, $F_1$ assigns the following interpretation to the fulfilment of the optative modalities connected with $\mathcal{A}$: If $T$ is an aim in $\mathcal{A}$ and $\mathcal{A}$ provides ($\alpha$) sufficient means and ($\beta$) all necessary means for realizing $T$ in $\mathcal{A}$, then $T$ is fulfill<u>able</u> in $\mathcal{A}$. $F_1$ clearly corresponds to the <u>purposefulness</u> of $\mathcal{A}$ and would be violated in any situation where ($\alpha$) ($\beta$) hold but $T$ has been (or will be) obstructed.

*Christer Hennix*

## Main Subject.
Re: Tractatus 3.144 [ Names are like points, propositions like arrows].

The world consists of arrows. The
                      world disintegrates
                      in arrows.
Each arrow is a fact—a mental fact
                      a mutual fact.
Each fact is an arrow.

Arrows run between points. The leftmost point serves as a comprehension term for the rightmost point.

(A philosophical *problem* can sometimes be analyzed as a *stack of arrows*, in which case its *solution* can be given as—a bundle of paths going through a *forest of arrows*.)

The simplest arrow is the

*empty arrow*

it designates a point of *negative dimension* $\leq -1$.

Clearly, the empty arrow does not consititue a philosophical problem—unless the negative dimension numbers do. *Via negativa*, again, nor does it constitute a philosophical solution—unless, that is, it points to negative infinitessimal dimension numbers close to, but not identical with, the points of $-\infty$, the darkest dimension of cosmic existence.

Presently, only

■ designates the *continuum of empty arrows*
[points here play the role of comprehension terms for collections of empty spaces]

□ designates the *unit space* of a constant arrow

$$\alpha \to \beta$$

(2) The second spectrum which will be designated Freedom$_2$ or F$_2$ and which is defined as that <u>regime</u> **P** governing activities $\mathcal{A}$ such that <u>no act in $\mathcal{A}$ is forced by coercion, fraud or any other violation of the fairness of means provided for the course of</u> $\mathcal{A}$. Id est, $\mathcal{A}$ is said to possess property F$_2$ whenever every act in $\mathcal{A}$ is free from compulsion, id est exercised in accordance with the creative subject's free will. Clearly, the satisfiability of F$_2$ captures exactly what is intended by <u>justfulness</u> of $\mathcal{A}$ and the <u>spectrum of</u> F$_2$-modalities is precisely all instances of installments of given activities $\mathcal{A}$ for which fair means have been provided.

V. The spectra of modalities for $\mathcal{A}$ thus split into two basic components, F$_1$ and F$_2$. By passing to the <u>direct limit</u> of the projections of F$_1$ and F$_2$ on any $\mathcal{A}$, the composite F$_1$ F$_2$ obtains. It corresponds to that <u>regime</u> **P** for which Freedom$_1$ and Freedom$_2$ hold <u>simultaneously</u> and if $\mathcal{A}$ possesses property F$_1$ F$_2$ we shall say that **P** is <u>eleutheric</u> for $\mathcal{A}$ or that the activities comprised by the situations generated by $\mathcal{A}$ are <u>eleutheric activities</u> in the regime **P**.

### Axioms for $\Sigma$:

I: $\Sigma \vdash_n \mathcal{A} \;\mathbf{v}\; \Sigma \vdash_n \neg \mathcal{A}$

II: $\Sigma \vdash_n \mathcal{A} \rightarrow \mathcal{A}$

III: $\Sigma \vdash_n \mathcal{A} \;\&\; m > n \rightarrow \Sigma \vdash_m \mathcal{A}$

IV: $\neg \exists (x) \; \Sigma \vdash_x \mathcal{A} \rightarrow \neg \mathcal{A}$

A unit space of dimension 1 is obtained by evaluating the arrows

$$\{\Lambda\} \to \Lambda$$

as

$$\Lambda \in \{\Lambda\}$$

Reflection on negative dimension numbers $< -1$ yields the higher dimensional unit spaces $\square_\alpha$, $\alpha > 1$).

Each sentence is an arrow.

—equations are all arrows.

A sentence is *true* if it points to the higher dimensional arrows—if its associated system of true equations are all arrows.

Otherwise, it is *false* or *absurd*.

Hence, it is absurd that all sentences are false. But it is not true that there is a sentence which is *not* absurd!

Whence, we continue our sacrifice.

**Model Subject** $\Phi(\Phi)$
Frege's 'The Real Way Is Not-Not Difficult'
(Don't write what you write, *or*, write *nothing*)

$$\nu \begin{bmatrix} \,_{\circ}\!\!\uparrow g(a) \\ \phantom{x} M_\beta(\!-\!g(\beta))=a \\ M_\beta\left(\,_{\circ}\!\!\uparrow \begin{matrix} g(\beta) \\ M_\beta(\!-\!g(\beta))=\beta \end{matrix}\right)=a \end{bmatrix}$$

(IIIa): —————————————————

$$\begin{bmatrix} f(a) \\ M_\beta\left(\,_{\circ}\!\!\uparrow \begin{matrix} g(\beta) \\ M_\beta(\!-\!g(\beta))=\beta \end{matrix}\right)=a \\ f(a) = \,_{\circ}\!\!\uparrow \begin{matrix} g(a) \\ M_\beta(\!-\!g(\beta))=a \end{matrix} \end{bmatrix} \qquad (\xi$$

(IIb)::- - - - - - - - - - - -

$$\begin{bmatrix} f(a) \\ M_\beta\left(\,_{\circ}\!\!\uparrow \begin{matrix} g(\beta) \\ M_\beta(\!-\!g(\beta))=\beta \end{matrix}\right)=a \\ M_\beta(\!-\!f(\beta))=M_\beta\left(\,_{\circ}\!\!\uparrow \begin{matrix} g(\beta) \\ M_\beta(\!-\!g(\beta))=\beta \end{matrix}\right) \\ \mathfrak{F}\begin{bmatrix} \mathfrak{F}(a) = \,_{\circ}\!\!\uparrow \begin{matrix} g(a) \\ M_\beta(\!-\!g(\beta))=a \end{matrix} \\ M_\beta(\!-\!\mathfrak{F}(\beta))=M_\beta\left(\,_{\circ}\!\!\uparrow \begin{matrix} g(\beta) \\ M_\beta(\!-\!g(\beta))=\beta \end{matrix}\right) \end{bmatrix} \end{bmatrix} \qquad (o$$

## INFERENCE SCHEMA FOR $T_H(\Sigma)$

$$V: \frac{\Sigma \vdash_n \mathscr{A}, \quad \mathscr{A} \rightarrow \mathscr{C}}{\Sigma \vdash_n \mathscr{C}}$$

$$VI: \frac{\Sigma \vdash_n \exists(x) \mathscr{A}(x)}{\exists(x) \Sigma \vdash_n \mathscr{A}(x)}$$

$$VII: \frac{\Sigma \vdash_n \mathscr{F}, \quad \Sigma \vdash_m \mathscr{F} \rightarrow \mathscr{G}}{\Sigma \vdash_{n,m} \mathscr{G}}$$

The general idea is now as follows. The basic relation $\vdash$ in the context $\Sigma \vdash_n \mathscr{A}$ is interpreted as " $\Sigma$ has <u>decided</u> or <u>solved</u> $\mathscr{A}$ at the $n^{TH}$ stage of her investigation or research in $\mathcal{A}$", where $\mathscr{A}$ designates an <u>intension</u> or <u>problem</u> connected with $\mathcal{A}$. The logical operators $\neg$, &, $\lor$ and $\rightarrow$ are given the following interpretations.

$\neg \left[ \mathscr{A} \right]$ signifies the task of obtaining the absurdity of the solution of $\mathscr{A}$

$\&\left[ \mathscr{A}, \mathscr{B} \right]$     "   "   "   " solving <u>both</u> $\mathscr{A}$ and $\mathscr{B}$

$\lor \left[ \mathscr{A}, \mathscr{B} \right]$     "   "   "   "   " <u>either</u> $\mathscr{A}$ or $\mathscr{B}$

$\rightarrow \left[ \mathscr{A}, \mathscr{B} \right]$     "   "   "   "   " the problem $\mathscr{B}$ given any solution of $\mathscr{A}$

(IIb, IIIa) :: = = = = = = = = = = = = = = =

$$\left.\begin{array}{l}\overset{}{\underset{}{\vphantom{|}}}\!\!\!\begin{array}{l}f(a)\\M_\beta(\underline{\quad}f(\beta))=a\end{array}\\M_\beta\left(\overset{\mathfrak{g}}{\frown}\!\!\begin{array}{l}\mathfrak{g}(\beta)\\M_\beta(\underline{\quad}\mathfrak{g}(\beta))=\beta\end{array}\right)=a\\\overset{\mathfrak{G}\,\mathfrak{F}}{\frown}\!\!\begin{array}{l}\mathfrak{F}(a)=\mathfrak{G}(a)\\M_\beta(\underline{\quad}\mathfrak{F}(\beta))=M_\beta(\underline{\quad}\mathfrak{G}(\beta))\end{array}\end{array}\right.\tag{$\pi$}$$

$$\left.\begin{array}{l}\overset{\mathfrak{g}}{\frown}\!\!\begin{array}{l}\mathfrak{g}(a)\\M_\beta(\underline{\quad}\mathfrak{g}(\beta))=a\end{array}\\M_\beta\left(\overset{\mathfrak{g}}{\frown}\!\!\begin{array}{l}\mathfrak{g}(\beta)\\M_\beta(\underline{\quad}\mathfrak{g}(\beta))=\beta\end{array}\right)=a\\\overset{\mathfrak{G}\,\mathfrak{F}}{\frown}\!\!\begin{array}{l}\mathfrak{F}(a)=\mathfrak{G}(a)\\M_\beta(\underline{\quad}\mathfrak{F}(\beta))=M_\beta(\underline{\quad}\mathfrak{G}(\beta))\end{array}\end{array}\right.\tag{$\varrho$}$$

($\mu$): – – – – – – – – – – – – – – –

$$\left.\begin{array}{l}M_\beta\left(\overset{\mathfrak{g}}{\frown}\!\!\begin{array}{l}\mathfrak{g}(\beta)\\M_\beta(\underline{\quad}\mathfrak{g}(\beta))=\beta\end{array}\right)=a\\M_\beta\left(\overset{\mathfrak{g}}{\frown}\!\!\begin{array}{l}\mathfrak{g}(\beta)\\M_\beta(\underline{\quad}\mathfrak{g}(\beta))=\beta\end{array}\right)=a\\\overset{\mathfrak{G}\,\mathfrak{F}}{\frown}\!\!\begin{array}{l}\mathfrak{F}(a)=\mathfrak{G}(a)\\M_\beta(\underline{\quad}\mathfrak{F}(\beta))=M_\beta(\underline{\quad}\mathfrak{G}(\beta))\end{array}\end{array}\right.\tag{$\sigma$}$$

(Ig): – – – – – – – – – – – – – – –

$$\left.\begin{array}{l}M_\beta\left(\overset{\mathfrak{g}}{\frown}\!\!\begin{array}{l}\mathfrak{g}(\beta)\\M_\beta(\underline{\quad}\mathfrak{g}(\beta))=\beta\end{array}\right)=a\\\overset{\mathfrak{G}\,\mathfrak{F}}{\frown}\!\!\begin{array}{l}\mathfrak{F}(a)=\mathfrak{G}(a)\\M_\beta(\underline{\quad}\mathfrak{F}(\beta))=M_\beta(\underline{\quad}\mathfrak{G}(\beta))\end{array}\end{array}\right.\tag{$\tau$}$$

(IIa) :: – – – – – – – – – – – – – –

$$\left.\begin{array}{l}M_\beta\left(\overset{\mathfrak{g}}{\frown}\!\!\begin{array}{l}\mathfrak{g}(\beta)\\M_\beta(\underline{\quad}\mathfrak{g}(\beta))=\beta\end{array}\right)=a\\\overset{a\,\mathfrak{G}\,\mathfrak{F}}{\frown}\!\!\begin{array}{l}\mathfrak{F}(a)=\mathfrak{G}(a)\\M_\beta(\underline{\quad}\mathfrak{F}(\beta))=M_\beta(\underline{\quad}\mathfrak{G}(\beta))\end{array}\end{array}\right.\tag{$\upsilon$}$$

×

$$\left.\begin{array}{l}\overset{a\,\mathfrak{G}\,\mathfrak{F}}{\frown}\!\!\begin{array}{l}\mathfrak{F}(a)=\mathfrak{G}(a)\\M_\beta(\underline{\quad}\mathfrak{F}(\beta))=M_\beta(\underline{\quad}\mathfrak{G}(\beta))\end{array}\\M_\beta\left(\overset{\mathfrak{g}}{\frown}\!\!\begin{array}{l}\mathfrak{g}(\beta)\\M_\beta(\underline{\quad}\mathfrak{g}(\beta))=\beta\end{array}\right)=a\end{array}\right.\tag{$\varphi$}$$

———•———

IIIe $\vdash M_\beta\left(\overset{\mathfrak{g}}{\frown}\!\!\begin{array}{l}\mathfrak{g}(\beta)\\M_\beta(\underline{\quad}\mathfrak{g}(\beta))=\beta\end{array}\right)=M_\beta\left(\overset{\mathfrak{g}}{\frown}\!\!\begin{array}{l}\mathfrak{g}(\beta)\\M_\beta(\underline{\quad}\mathfrak{g}(\beta))=\beta\end{array}\right)$

($\varphi$): ─────────────────────────

$$\overset{a\,\mathfrak{G}\,\mathfrak{F}}{\frown}\!\!\begin{array}{l}\mathfrak{F}(a)=\mathfrak{G}(a)\\M_\beta(\underline{\quad}\mathfrak{F}(\beta))=M_\beta(\underline{\quad}\mathfrak{G}(\beta))\end{array}\tag{$\chi$}$$

IN ADDITION:

$\exists(x)\left[\mathcal{A}(x)\right]$   SIGNIFIES THE TASK OF SOLVING THE VALUE OF $x$ SUCH THAT $\mathcal{A}(x)$

WHERE $\exists(x)$ IS THE OPERATOR DESIGNATING THE <u>EXISTENTIAL CONSTRUCTION PRINCIPLE</u>.

AMONG SOLVABLE PROBLEMS IN $\text{Th}(\Sigma)$ WE MENTION THE FOLLOWING TASKS (EXERCISE!):

$$\mathcal{A} \to \mathcal{B} \mathbin{\&} \mathcal{B} \to \mathcal{C} \to \mathcal{A} \to \mathcal{C} \quad (1)$$

$$\mathcal{A} \to \mathcal{C} \mathbin{\&} \mathcal{B} \to \mathcal{C} \to \mathcal{A} \vee \mathcal{B} \to \mathcal{C} \quad (2)$$

$$\neg \mathcal{A} \to \mathcal{A} \to \mathcal{B} \quad (3)$$

$$\mathcal{A} \to \mathcal{B} \to \neg \mathcal{B} \to \neg \mathcal{A} \quad (4)$$

$$\mathcal{A} \to \neg \mathcal{B} \to \mathcal{B} \to \neg \mathcal{A} \quad (5)$$

$$\neg (\mathcal{A} \vee \mathcal{C}) \to \neg \mathcal{A} \mathbin{\&} \neg \mathcal{C} \quad (6)$$

$$\neg (\mathcal{C} \mathbin{\&} \mathcal{E}) \mathbin{\&} \mathcal{C} \vee \neg \mathcal{C} \to \neg \mathcal{C} \vee \neg \mathcal{E} \quad (7)$$

$$\neg (\mathcal{A} \mathbin{\&} \neg \mathcal{A}) \quad (8)$$

<u>REMARK</u>: BY (8), <u>CONSISTENCY</u> OF $\text{Th}(\Sigma)$ IS ESTABLISHED, I.E. $\text{Th}(\Sigma)$ IS A <u>NON-TRIVIAL</u> THEORY (I.E. EPISTEMICALLY PALATABLE).

<u>(HISTORICAL) REMARK</u>: <u>L.E.J. BROUWER</u> WAS THE FIRST LOGICIAN TO FORMULATE PRINCIPLES SIMILAR TO THE ONES GIVEN ABOVE.

Short Infinitary Process 4 IX—17 X 76
(Moderna Museet, Stockholm)

# Idios Kosmos (I)

### *Pre-socratic Ontologies*

Ṛta—concept of *correct action*.
Ancient composition of arrows. (Laws.)

0. Only the empty arrow remains the empty arrow when the empty arrow is composed with the empty arrow.

–When any other arrow is composed with the empty arrow, it remains itself, whether or not the composition takes place to the left or to the right of the empty arrow.

Event $\breve{E} = \acute{E}_{4IX-17X76}$ Def.

Ṛ: $\breve{E} \rightarrow \acute{E}$          (Being = Space × Action)

*Ultra-Environments* $\breve{E}$

## Types of Universes

(I) .......................... A, B, Γ, ........................

(II) ..................... a, b, c, d, e$'$, e$''$, ....................

(III) ........................ I, II, ........................

*Christer Hennix*

I. **Monistic Universes** A.

Ia. $\Sigma$ contemplates the existence of *empty universes*

$$\Lambda\Lambda\Lambda\ldots\ldots\ldots\Lambda\Lambda\ldots\ldots\ldots$$

and the embeddings

$$\underset{\cdot}{R}: E^\Lambda \to \acute{E}$$

The event $\Lambda$ may be completely indeterminate—*or*, it may correspond to a designated event which occurs interior to the event $\acute{E}$. *For example,* the event $\Lambda$ is the genesis of an *empty event* in the interior of $\acute{E}$ at a time $\tau$, *or*, $\Lambda$ is the genesis of a progression of clusters of *empty cosmoi* experienced by $\Sigma$ in the interior of $\acute{E}$ at any time $\tau$. The identity of the interior event $E^\Lambda$ shall be determined by the *inverse image* of the functorial action $\underset{\cdot}{R}$ of the realization map

$$E^\Lambda \to \acute{E}$$

Remark that it is quite possible that $R^{-1}(\acute{E}) \neq E^\Lambda$ because of lack of certain symmetries (such as commutative diagrams!).

**Various Notions of Emptiness** (Concepts of Absence)
(Partial summary)

> The Empty Cosmic Cluster
> The Empty Arrow
> The Empty Self
> The Empty Thought
> The Empty Text
> The Empty Action/Event

**Various Notions of** $E^\Lambda$ (Partial summary)

> —Empty Mā
> —Empty Nō
> —Empty Butō
> —Empty Space-Time

*The Yellow Book*

## MĀ-Ontologies. Case 1, $\bar{X} = 0$.

$M\bar{A} = MA_{\bar{X}}$     (Mirror Duality)

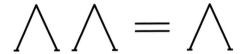

**B/W Equation**

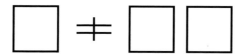

**B/W Equation**

Christer Hennix

## Monistic Universes B

Ib. Σ contemplates the existence of *non-empty universes*

□□□..... □□.....

and the embedding(s)

R: E□ → É

Again, the identity of a non-empty monistic universe □ shall be determined by an inverse limit or image R⁻¹(É). And, again, it is possible that R⁻¹(É) ≠ R(E□) (if the reality of the situation is lacking in symmetries.)

*Standard Examples* (Classical Set Theory)

Singleton Sets: {·}, {Λ}, {e}, ... &c.

## *É-Examples: Soliton Compositions. (Solitones).*

*0. Agrapha Harmonia.*
*[Cognitio Matutina]*

0.1    The Sound of Shiva—ÔMSAHASTRANAMAM
       [For Pandit Pran Nath]

0.11   □$_\kappa$  —The $\kappa$-times Repeated Constant Event.
       [Infinitary Composition. Locally Infinite Space.
       Fix Point Structure, $\kappa = \kappa + 1$].

0.111  □$^N$  The N-times Repeated Constant Event.
       [The Five Times Repeated Music, &c.]

0.111a  N = 3. Short Infinitary Processes. *White MĀ*.

□ □ □ ⇒ . □ ...

[where "." refers to the empty space left by the left □ merging with its successor and "..." to the transfinite term which covers the future of the constantly present boundary or middle term □. (Cf. the Black & White Algebra of the formal (binary) ontology Λ □ ■).]

*The Yellow Book*

0.1111      *The N-Times Repeated Constant Event* [Version For Sound Waves]

0.1111a      $N = 0$. **0-D** Toplogies For A Vertical Sound. The *Zero-Times Repeated Event,* $\square^0$, or *The Sound of MA* is defined by the *Sound of an Indestructible Moment of Silence* contained by a space equipped with a vertical topology.

$\square^0$ —The Empty Sound

0.1111b.    $\square_{<x,y,z>}$ *Crystal Oscillators* (Quartz). *Digital Wave Forms.* (Programs)

Transfinite Case;

$\square_\kappa$    —The $\kappa$-Infinite Sound

$\square_{<x,y,z>}$ —x,y,z transfinite real variables.

The complexity of *constant events* may be measured in various ways. A convenient complexity measure for a constant event e shall be a certain ordinal number ord(e). The non-empty constant events

$$E^{\square}{}_\alpha \qquad \square\square\square\ldots\square\square\ldots\square$$

are usually characterized by *limit ordinals* $\alpha$. Ord ($\square$) and ord (∎) are two distinct species of limit ordinals which define two families of initial segments of the continuum of ordinal numbers, $\Omega$, and which (naturally) give rise to two (families of) *natural number series* $N_\square$ and $N_\blacksquare$ respectively. The series of constant (canonical) empty events $\square^0$ is usually denoted $N_\Delta$ [MĀ-ordinals].

(Summary). The constant events $\square^N$ are defined by the (point-wise) composition of the three distinct curves

$\square_{<x>}: a \times \sin(x)$

$\square_{<y>}: b \times \sin(y)$

$\square_{<z>}: c \times \sin(z)$

the continuous point-wise compositions of which are omnidirectionally distributed in the interior of É as a mixture of a triple of phase-locked sine waves at constant frequencies and amplitudes such that the objects $\square^N$ or $\square_\kappa$ obtain as the respective limit constructions of this continuous process of composition based on fixed (eternal) quartz crystal oscillations in pre-determined ratios.

More specifically, each sine-wave compactum $\square_{<w>}$ describes an infinitely proceeding sequence of constant events $\square_{<w_i>}$ the fixed amplitude of which is inversely proportional to the frequency of the constant events that build up this indefinitely on-going wave structure. The possible frequencies of these constant events are determined by a certain set of *odd* prime numbers. Thus, 2 certainly does *not* belong to this set, but, say 5 *may* belong to it; or all prime numbers larger than any large but otherwise arbitrary prime number may belong to it with certainty. Hence this set may certainly be infinite. If the kth prime $p_k$ does not belong to this (possibly infinite) set and $p_k$ divides m/n, the ratio between two sine-wave components, then any ratio m:n:$p_k$ is a possible (but not necessary) determination of a sine-wave component in a (É-)realization of the composition $\square^N$ or its transfinite extension $\square_\kappa$. (The eternal presence being constantly controled or determined by what is eternally absent.)

Elements which belong to the complex wave form $\circledast^N$ are called *chronons* or *time elements*. Here the technique of *analytic continuation* is presupposed as well as the most efficient programs for the **FFT** [Fast Fourier Transform.]

At the moment when the Creative Subject enters a frame for a topos $\mathcal{E}$ as defined by the interior of É, the time manifold $\square^N$ is supposed to already contain indefinitely many time elements which have not yet or never will be experienced by the Creative Subject.

## The Yellow Book

The moment at which the Creative Subject's tactics of attention include attention to the time process $⊞^N$, corresponds to a point in her life-world where a moment of life falls apart with one part retained as an image and stored by memory while the other part is retained as a continuum of new perceptions.

This marks the beginning phase of the Creative Subject's experience of the *fixed point composition* $\square^N$, i.e.

The N-times Repeated Constant Event

[begun by me during the winter months of 1970 and continued into the present].

In a later phase of the Creative Subject's experience of $\square^N$, the obtaining continuum of perceptions becomes gradually attenuated by a *continuum of memories* of a N-times repeated constant event $\boxdot$. Thus, the Creative Subject gradually comes to experience $\square^N$ as a *transfinite object* order-isomorphic to the set of rational numbers $\eta$ (where the latter may be identified as *pairs* of integers m,n, except for the rational number 0 (zero) which may be identified with the usual 0 in the set of natural numbers.)

In particular, at this later stage of experiencing $\square^N$ the Creative Subject does experience the conjunction of the continuum of perceptions and the continuum of memories as a *dense ordering of (the falling apart of) moments of life,* i.e., an ordering without first or last elements and of Cantorian order-type $\eta$.

Finally, at the "transfinite stages" of experiencing $\square^N$, the Creative Subject arrives at a stationary subset of the generated continuum of perceptions at which she retains complete facultative control of the continuum of time-elements which defines the transfinite time-object $⊞_\kappa$, [here $\kappa$ denotes (an ordinal of) some "large cardinal" and not merely a "large number" as connoted by the symbol N].

### *Digression*

I notice in passing that the formation of the pairs

$<\Sigma, \square^N>$    ($\lozenge\!-\!\Sigma$)

and

$<\Sigma, \square_\kappa>$    ($\lozenge\!-\!\Sigma$)    (in particular)

gives rise to the formation of (subjectively experienced) *locally infinite spaces* (whose elements consist of correlations between moments of consciousness and time-elements belonging to the continuum of perceptions of the invisible time-manifolds $\square_\kappa$).

In particular, the composition $\square_{<x,y,z>}$ acts as a *covering* Cov(**F**) of a frame **F** of a topos $\mathcal{E}$. That is, the lattice of infinitesimal constant time-manifolds $\square$ *has a dense embedding in the interior of the topos frame if the latter is understood as already containing the finer (transfinite) lattice* $<\square_\kappa>$ obtained by projecting $\boxdot_\kappa$ chaotically at each lattice point.

$$\square^{N_m} \xmapsto{N} \square^N$$

For m = 1,2,3,4,5..., $\square^{N_m}$ is a *localization* of $\square^N$ in a topos frame **F**.

$$\left.\bigcup_{k=1}^{m} \square^{N_k} \right| = \begin{array}{l} \text{The Composite Sound Wave } \square_{<x,y,z>} \text{ Covering } \mathbf{F} \\ \text{The Infinitesimal Time-manifold } \mathbf{F}(\tau) \text{ covering } \mathbf{F} \text{ (at} \\ \text{any instantaneous moment } \tau) \end{array}$$

Each localization $\square^{N_k}$ is a terminal object with a chaotic topology. (Single arrow)

The covering space Cov(**F**) is a totally disconnected topological space of neighborhoods with a chaotic topology.

2-D detail of the lattice Cov(**F**)

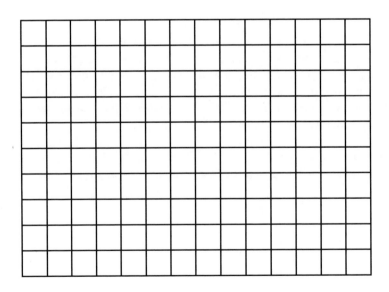

## The Yellow Book

The disconnected space of subobjects of the time-manifold $\Box^N$ covering the interior of **F** restricts both horizontal and vertical movements by the attending Creative Subjects. Each attending Creative Subject may only compose with movements of infinitesimal arc-lengths, so that stasis dominates over movement and movement, when manifest, occurs only at infinitesimal velocities.

[*(Ultra-) Black Metastasis:* Framed Abstract Butō [Sub-spaces of a Black Topology. See appendix II.]

(Summary cont.)

There exists a *unique time-interval*, $\tau$, in the space **É** defined by the length of the period of the resulting *composite sound wave form* $\Box_{<x,y,z>}$. When the time-interval $\tau$ has repeated itself **N** times, the time-arc $\tau_N$ corresponds to the repetition of the constant event $\Box$ **N** times—also written $\Box^N$, or, more accurately,

$$\Box^N_{<x,y,z>}$$

Remark that the unicity of the infinitessimal time-arc element $\tau$ is here based squarely on *geometrical* considerations so that the *constancy* of the invisible event $\Box^N$ may be defined in terms of a unique geometrical congruence between the areas of the curves (boundaries)

$$\Box = \Box^1, \Box^2, \Box^3, \ldots, \Box^k, \Box^{k+1}, \ldots, \Box^N = \Box^{N+1}$$

which, in turn, are defined by a point-wise composition of images under the analytic functions $\lambda\xi \sin(\xi)$.

The triad $<x,y,z>$ defines a class of equations E(x,y,z) which in turn determines a certain set of *algebraic theories*, Th(**E**), among which *triples* $<X,Y,Z>$ and co-triples $<X^{co},Y^{co},Z^{co}>$ have played an important role in my early formulations of an ALGEBRAIC AESTHETICS

For each Creative Subject $\Sigma$ who attends the space $\text{É}_\Box$ in which the composition $\Box^N$ is freely developing, there exists a (subjective) time-interval, $\tau^*$, during which the Creative Subject experiences a *constant event* $\Box^*_{<x,y,z>}$ as a *subobject* of the $\text{É}_\Box$ —universal infinitely proceeding sequence of geometrically congruent composite wave forms $\Box^\tau_{<x,y,z>}$.

In general, the constancy of the subjective event $\Box^*_{<x,y,z>}$ can be experienced as also fluctuating so that the subobject $\Box^*_{<x,y,z>}$ of $\text{É}_\Box$ (created by a Creative Subject's attendance) as a submanifold $\Box^{N*}$ of $\text{É}_\Box$ defines a *continuously or discretely variable set* (of (fluctuating) experiences of a temporal constancy of time).

Thus $\square^*_{<x,y,z>}$ corresponds to $\Sigma$'s perception or image of $\square_{<x,y,z>}$ along the subjective time-arcs $\tau^*$ iterated $N^*$times. Obviously, $N^* < N$.

In consequence of the latter inequality, the $N^*$-times iterated time-element $\tau^*$ may be made to correspond to an "arrow of time" in $\acute{E}_\square$ (point-wise speaking).

Thus, $\acute{E}_\square$ is obtained as a subjective space-time manifold of indefinitely iterated invisible constant events $\square_{<x,y,z>}$.

$\acute{E}^\nu \qquad \square_0 = 1, \square, \square_2, \square_3, \ldots,$

are considered the objects of this category and consequently

$$1 \to \square, \square \to \square_2, \ldots,$$

are its morphisms.

More precisely, $\square^N$ has as *objects*

$$1, \square, \square_2, \square_3, \ldots,$$

and for each $n = 0,1,2,3,\ldots,n$ *morphisms*

$$\square^{N_n} \xrightarrow{\Pi_i^{(n)}} \square, \qquad i = 0,1,\ldots,n-1,$$

such that for any n morphisms (in $\square^N$)

$$\square^{N_n} \xrightarrow{\theta_i} \square, \qquad i = 0,1,\ldots,n-1,$$

there exists exactly one morphism

$$\square^{N_n} \xrightarrow{<\theta_0, \theta_1, \theta_2, \ldots, \theta_{n-1}>} \square^{N_n},$$

so that, in $\square^N$,

$$<\theta_0, \theta_1, \theta_2, \ldots, \theta_{n-1}> \Pi_i^{(n)} = \theta_i, \, , i = 0,1,\ldots,n-1.$$

If the arbitrary morphisms

$$\square^{N_m} \xrightarrow{\phi} \square$$

are regarded as n-ary operations of $\square^N$, then $\square^N$ can be regarded as the *category of constantly shifting events* (which is simultaneously an *algebraic theory*), beginning with the event $1 \to \square$.

B/W Equation

*Monistic Universes* Γ. *(Limit Cases. Ultra-monism)*

1c. Analogously, Σ will contemplate the existence of *large monistic universes*

■■■ . . . . . . . ■■ . . . . . .

and the imbedding(s)

$$R: E^\bullet \to \acute{E}.$$

**Remark.** Already the figure "2" is here considered to denote a *"large number"* in the sense that "2" corresponds to the *smallest* large number (among all numbers, 2 is "0-*large*".) Thus, 1 is the largest "small number" and 0 is the smallest such number (0 is "0-*small*".)

Consequently, the set of *small numbers*

(S) $\qquad\qquad\qquad \{0, 1\}$

*is a (0-large) finite* set and it is unique if "0" and "1" are unique. The complement of S is

(L) $\qquad\qquad \{2, 3, 4, \ldots, \ell, \ell+1, \ldots\}$,

the *set of large numbers*—and it is usually *not* a unique set, unless "$\ell+1$" is unique. Furthermore, this set can be *very large* (in comparison with S).

The set of natural numbers, N, is sometimes partitioned into small and large numbers. By

□

I shall indicate a *generic small set* of natural numbers, while

■

shall denote a *generic large set* of natural numbers. In particular, for any generic brand N of natural numbers I may write

$$N = \square \cup \blacksquare, \text{ or,}$$

$$N = \cup (\square, \blacksquare)$$

to indicate that N is a *generic set (brand) of natural numbers.*

[The well-known inductive paradox by which it is shown that all natural numbers are "small" can be resolved already by this generic partition of N. That is, the critical inductive step at "if n is a small number, then n + 1 is also a small number," becomes vacuous (or "generic") by the identification n = $\ell$ since it entails that $\ell \leq 1$, 1 being considered the *largest small number*.

**The Heap Paradox.** This paradox is a dual variant of the last one in the sense that closure under n $\dot{-}$ 1 (predecessor arithmetic) appears to fail. Hence, the appropriate induction principle sought is Brouwer's principle of *Bar Induction*, i.e.

$$\Lambda\alpha \text{Vb} H[\bar{\alpha}(b)]$$
$$H(s)v - H(s)$$
$$\Lambda b Q(s\hat{\ }b) \to Q(s)$$
$$\underline{H(s) \to Q(s)}$$
$$Q(<>)$$

**Remark.** Ignoring the problems besetting the continuum, the monistic universes contemplated so far may be projected as a series

(H) $\qquad$ |, ||, |||, ....., |$^{(h)}$, |$^{(h')}$, .....

of "strokes" where h' = h + 1, i.e., the (monistic) *successor function* governing the extension of H. In É, each sequence of monistic universes has a *parametrical extension*

(H$_e$) $\qquad$ |, ||, |||, ....., |$^{(h)}$, |$^{(h')}$, ...., |$^{(e)}$.

where "e" is acting as the *finitization parameter*. Thus, for each sequence s of monistic universes in É there is a parameter $e_s$ by which the projection of an infinite sequence on H is finitized by switching the projection to H$_e$. Consequently, I may use the notations

$$H_{e_\Lambda}, H_{e_\square}, H_{e_\blacksquare}, \ldots,$$

to denote finite images of infinite sequences of monistic universes (in É).

Furthermore, in order to get a notation for "0" some indication of the *empty stroke*, shall be used. E.g. $\emptyset$ may be used to identify such indications. Since $lh(\emptyset) = 0$ i.e. the *length* of the empty stroke is zero, this additional notational convention does not increase the length of the series H or $H_e$ (under the (recursive) convention by means of which $lh(1) = 1$, and, in general, by which $lh(|^k) = k$, $k = 0, 1, 2, 3, \ldots$).

Notice that any monistic ontology based on the empty stroke has "length" zero. *Viz.* The (recursive) length of any sequence

$$E^{\emptyset} \quad \emptyset\emptyset\emptyset, \ldots\ldots, \emptyset\emptyset, \ldots\ldots$$

is bounded above by an infinitesimal constant $\delta > 0$, since

$$lh(E^{\emptyset}) = 0.$$

[Also, observe that the sequence $E^{\emptyset}$ may be of order type $\eta$ (the "Hilbert Hotel"-effect), and, if read as a single (continuous) word it exemplifies an occurrence of a *dense empty word*, i.e. a word order-isomorphic with the set Q of rational numbers, i.e. the set of all ordered pairs $<m,n>$ of integers m,n).]

The infinitesimal interval $<0, \delta_{\emptyset}>$ of arbitrary sequences of empty strokes is an example of an *abstract object generator* whose image is obtained as a *locally infinite space* in the interior of the environment É. I use the notation

$$E^{<0, \delta_{\emptyset}>}$$

to indicate the continuous image of the infinitesimal interval $<0, \delta_{\emptyset}>$ in the interior of É.

Remark that "$\emptyset$" is here also used as a sign for the *"empty printed event."* A blank sheet of paper may—or, may not—be considered as having printed the symbol for the empty printed event on both of its surfaces or only on one of them. The example generalizes to considerations of *stacks* of blank sheets of paper that easily yield intractable problems of identifications of occurrences of (perhaps totally undetermined) empty printed events (even apart from $\emptyset$). In the limit, the by now familiar fixed point recursion (cf. p.316)

$$\vdash^0 [\,] := [\,]$$
$$\vdash^{h+1} [\,] := \vdash (\vdash^h [\,])$$
$$\vdash^H [\,] := -[\,]$$

emerges, where $[\,]$ is chosen as symbol for the *Empty Type*.

B/W Equation

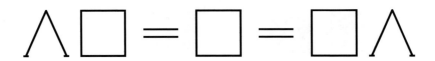

**B/W Equation**

B/W Equation

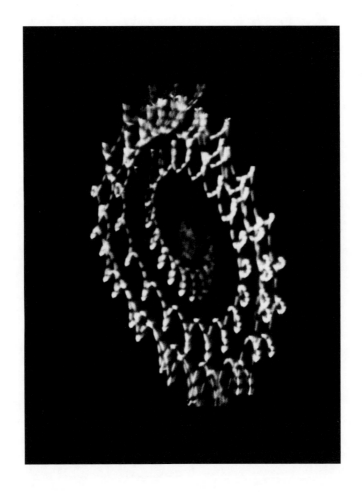

*Unidentified Universe (Partial view)*

# Idios Kosmos (II)

## II (Logo-) Graphic Forms Of The Continuum

Black Body Radiation. Planck Oscillators. (Approximations of Absolute Darkness.)

**Black Topologies** ................. ■ ■ ...........

*The Chaotic Black Topology* ........... ■ ..............

*A Continuum of Black Chaotic Topologies*

■ ■ ■ ■ ..... ■ ■ ..... ■ ..................

### IIa. Indiscernables/Double-negation Topoi
### IIa. Indiscernables/Double-negation Spaces.

Infinitesimal Distances/Infinitesimal Spaces.

Infinitesimal elements are obtained by *partitions of unity*, and, as sets, contain 0 as their smallest member or minimal element. Thus, if $\delta$ is an infinitesimal, then

$$\delta \to 0$$

and

$$\delta \neq 0$$

are true relations (here "$\neq$" denotes the intuitionistic *apartness relation*.) More specifically, given a topos $\mathcal{E}$ and an object $X$ in $\mathcal{E}$, the basic understanding when considering the topological structure determined on $X$ by the logic of $\mathcal{E}$ is that given any two points $x,y$, in $X$, to assert the negation $\neg(x=y)$ of the equality $x=y$, means that any two points p,q are *well separated* (or at a measurable distance $\neq 0$).

Thus, given any point p$\in$X, the points well separated from p are the points

$$x \in \neg \{p\}$$

while the points not well separated from p are the points

$$x \in \neg \neg \{p\}$$

i.e. those points $x$ which are *infinitesimally close* (or "very close") to p.
Since, intuitionistically,

$$X = \neg\neg\{p\} \cup \neg\{p\}$$

is false in general, there must still be some space left unaccounted for in $X$. Remarkably, this space is a *"grey areas"* (a "no man's land") because it has *no explicit description* in the topos $\mathcal{E}$. (Remark that $\neg\neg\neg\{p\} = \neg\{p\}$ by Brouwer's argument.)

Implicitly described, the situation is as follows. Define a *neighborhood* $H_p$ around a point p as a subobject $H \subseteq X$ which contains $\neg\neg\{p\}$ and also this "no man's land." This is expressed by the identity

$$\neg\{p\} \cup H = X$$

which says that every point in the space $X$ is either well separated from p—or, it is in the neighborhood $H_p$ of p.

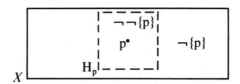

**Technical Remark.** By substituting for the geometrical concept of a "measurable distance" the logical concept of "provability" ("logical distance"), it is easy to obtain "topological" variants of Gödel's incompleteness proofs. *Id est*, steps of proofs are substituted for units of distance, where "proofs" of any (*independent*) axiom take exactly zero steps (i.e. are completely trivial proofs).

## IIb. ■ —*Space*

I. C-*Space*. 2-*Space*. *Ultra-monism*.

Ia. The chaotic topology on a ■-space is given by the single non-unique arrow

obtained by substituting every occurrence of q with p throughout all inequalities

$$p \neq q$$

including the case where q = ¬¬p i.e. where (previously)

$$\neg\neg p \neq p$$

while changing the apartness relation to a relation of identity. Set theoretically, ■ is treated as {p} i.e. as a *singleton* set. In so far as p is not unique but takes on a range of ambiguous values p* = p',p",.... the singleton set {p*} is easily interpreted as a *continuously variable* (singleton) *set*.

  1b. From the chaotic topology one derives continuously variable *sets of indiscernibles* indexed by various wandering sets of distinct degerss of chaos or indeterminacy. Thus, the sequence

(with (inverse) limit point □) is logographically increasing in *ultra-marine blue* color elements while continuously decreasing in *black* or *ultra-grey* color elements (until, in the limit *(via* a passage through a "grey area*") only* the boundary □ is carrying a color space (distinct from the empty color space (white elements)).

  1c. The chaotic set **C** is also interpreted as a set {0,1} or **2**-*space*, by taking 0 as denoting an empty subset of **C** while 1 denotes the entire space. I.e. the arrow

$$1 \rightarrow C$$

determines the interpretation uniquely (up to isomorphism).

  1d. By duality, by regarding all points ¬{p} and ¬¬{p} as distinct from {p}, the ■-*space* is transformed to a **C**-*space* of the (intuitionistic) continuum requiring a *continuum of tactics of attention* to the points q distinct (at any non-zero distance) from p. [In a construction of a pair <■,■> of Black Spaces of the continuum it is often convenient to regard its first projection as a constant zero-function corresponding to the empty subset of the uncountable set of points along the intuitionistic unit continuum $1_C$, while its second projection takes 1 as its image — the latter, of course, denoting the *unit interval* of the continuum **C**.]

  1e. The *Ultra-black Construction*

$$E^{<■,■>} \rightarrow É$$

is a realization of the (intuitionistic) *universal spread of elements of (a species of) ultra-black ashes* as a (topological) *covering* of a pair of universal (white) squares $<\square, \square>$. The latter are represented as highly polished aluminum mirrors measuring exactly 1 m² each—a measure which except for a *meager* subset excludes the *boundaries* of the mirror surfaces which continue the covering of the interior and span a surface measuring exactly four times $10 \times .333\ldots$ m² and identically covered by the same ultra-black particles—thereby reflecting the all-embracing effect of *The Fire in The Mirror*, an alternative title for *The Painting of a Disaster (Multiplied)*.

The latter, beginning a transfinite sequence

$$\acute{E}^{\blacksquare}_\alpha \quad \blacksquare\blacksquare \ldots,$$

is constructed from the *initial catastrophe*

$$\acute{E}^{\blacksquare} \ldots \blacksquare \ldots (Black\ M\bar{A})$$

which is experienced *twice over* ($=\acute{E}^{\blacksquare_2}$) under the guidance of noemas created by iterated passages through the interiors of *Black MĀ* during which a continuum of layers of darkness is traversed. *Lumen increatum. Cognitio vespertina.*

**Remark.** When E is realized within the context of MĀ-Theater, $M\bar{A}_{\blacksquare_{\alpha=1}}$ is also referred to as the *Initial Pine Sacrifice*. (The ash paint is obtained and applied by mixing pine-sticks with fire.)

Ie.' Remark that, in contradistinction to the sequence $\Delta_\blacksquare$ of gradually varying indiscernibles ■, the *vertical topology* generated by the (ordinal) *height* of the topos is determined by the stochastic isomorphisms of an initial chaotic topology $\blacksquare_0$ (chosen by the Creative Subject.) For the purpose of visualization, the finite models of an N-stack are sometimes used as an aid for intuition.

(Ie″) In intuitionistic cosmology*, a solution to the *Night Sky Paradox* depends on both set theoretical and topological properties of the continuum C. The darkness of the night sky is indicative of the *absence* of additive groups of motion (i.e. absence of closure under a + b for arbitrary travelling elements a, b, of the light of the stars) while, simultaneously exhibiting a *logarithmic gradient of growth*—allowing for models of multiple-successor arithmetics (representing degrees of "anti-darkness".)

---

*Intuitionistic cosmology is derived from Brouwer's concept of geometry by which any cosmic (sub-)space can be obtained as the image of a *continuous group of motions* (such as Lie groups).

The Ultra-Black Paintings
(Moderna Museet, 1976)

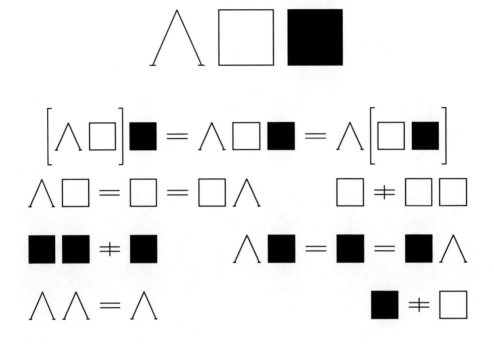

B/W Algebra

# Idios Kosmos (III)
*Post-socratic Ontologies. Non-monistic Universes.*
*Binary Ontologies. Ternary Ontologies, ..., κ-ary Ontologies.*

## (A) Dualistic Universes.

***I. Binary Universes.*** [2-Ontologies. 2-Categories]

0-1 - Universes: propositions as finite binary sequences

2-valued Measures (Complete Boolean Algebras &c.)

(Characteristic Function Universes)

$\{\vee, \wedge\}$—Off-On-Universes

□ ■ -Universes

propositions as infinite binary strings

Binary Categories: $<\rightrightarrows, \uparrow\uparrow>$

$<\rightrightarrows, \downarrow\downarrow>$

.
.
.

&c.

$\Sigma$ contemplates an endless formation of sets

$$\square, \Lambda, \blacksquare, \Lambda\Lambda, \Lambda\blacksquare\blacksquare, \ldots,$$

coded as a binary sequence

$$\square, \blacksquare, \blacksquare\square, \blacksquare\blacksquare, \ldots,$$

with arrows

$$\square \to 0$$
$$\blacksquare \to 1$$
$$\Lambda \to \emptyset$$

This contemplation of ternary and binary universes arises out of a still more fundamental contemplation of a $\kappa$-dimensional intuitionistic continuum the initial spread of which may be drawn as

$$a_1 \; a_\kappa \; a_{2\kappa^+} \quad \ldots\ldots$$

$$a_2 \; a_{\kappa^{++}} \; a_{2\kappa^{++}} \quad \ldots\ldots$$

$$\ldots\ldots\ldots\ldots\ldots\ldots\ldots\ldots\ldots\ldots$$

$$a_\kappa \; a_{2\kappa} \; a_{3\kappa} \quad \ldots\ldots$$

Using modular arithmetic the following diagram pictures a binary code for the endless progressions of *finite sets*:

|   | 0 | 1 | 2 | 3 | 4 | 5 | 6 | 7 | 8 | 9 | 10 | 11 | 12 |
|---|---|---|---|---|---|---|---|---|---|---|----|----|----|
| 0 | 0 | 1 | 0 | 1 | 0 | 1 | 0 | 1 | 0 | 1 | 0  | 1  | 0  |
| 1 | 0 | 0 | 1 | 1 | 0 | 0 | 1 | 1 | 0 | 0 | 1  | 1  | 0  |
| 2 | 0 | 0 | 0 | 0 | 1 | 1 | 1 | 1 | 0 | 0 | 0  | 0  | 1  |
| 3 | 0 | 0 | 0 | 0 | 0 | 0 | 0 | 0 | 1 | 1 | 1  | 1  | 1  |
| 4 | 0 | 0 | 0 | 0 | 0 | 0 | 0 | 0 | 0 | 0 | 0  | 0  | 0  |
| . | . |   |   |   |   |   |   |   |   |   |    |    | .  |
| . | . |   |   |   |   |   |   |   |   |   |    |    | .  |
| . | . |   |   |   |   |   |   |   |   |   |    |    | .  |
| . | . |   |   |   |   |   |   |   |   |   |    |    | .  |
| . | . |   |   |   |   |   |   |   |   |   |    |    | .  |
| k | 0 | 0 | 0 | 0 | 0 | 0 | 0 | 0 | 0 | 0 | 0  | 0  | 0  |
| . | . |   |   |   |   |   |   |   |   |   |    |    | .  |
| . | . |   |   |   |   |   |   |   |   |   |    |    | .  |
| . | . |   |   |   |   |   |   |   |   |   |    |    | .  |
| . | . |   |   |   |   |   |   |   |   |   |    |    | .  |

## The Yellow Book

Not all sets are well-founded—in particular those preceeding $\Sigma$'s initial contemplations of the universal spread of binary words in lexicographic order. Beginning with the elementary fixed-point equations

$$x = \{x\}$$
$$y = \{y\}$$
$$z = \{z\}$$

and the usual self-referential formulae, $\Sigma$ is equipped to contemplate arbitrary *non-well-founded* sets such as

$$\{\ldots\{\{\ldots\{\{\{\ldots\}\}\}\ldots\}\}\ldots\},$$

again, with specific attention to the interpretation of the occurrences of lazy dots.

I notice in passing their relations of duality with the finite but indeterminate *Zermelo ordinals* $\mathbf{z}\,(z_i)$

$$\{\ldots\{\{\ldots\{\{\{\Lambda\}\}\}\ldots\}\}\ldots\},$$

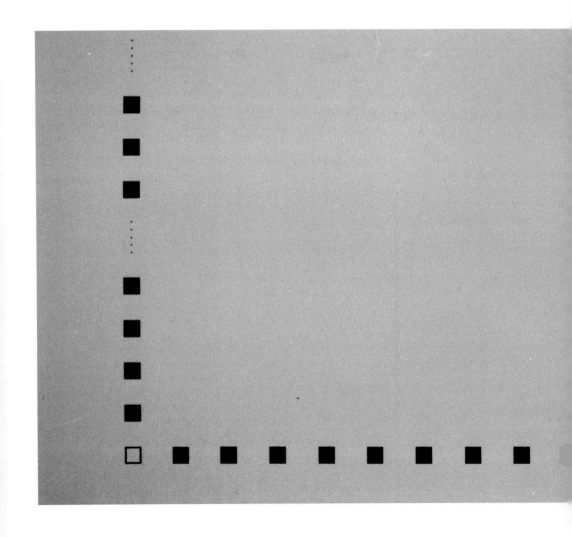

Large Infinitary Process 4 IX—17 X 76
(Moderna Museet, Stockholm)

## II. The Model Theory of Algebraic Aesthetics.

*From univalent and ambivalent truth-values to binary, ternary, ....
and $\kappa$-ary truth-values.*

~~The Lattice of Continuous Truth~~.

### *TACTICAL CONFIGURATION*

$1 \longrightarrow 0$  (INITIAL MAP)

$0 \longrightarrow \Lambda$  (FIRST DISCRIMINATION)

$\Lambda \longrightarrow \blacksquare$  (CATASTROPHE MAP)

$\blacksquare \longrightarrow \square$  (RECONCILIATION)

$\square \longrightarrow 1$  (RETURN TO THE EVERYDAY MALICE)

.4.2: *By a "colorless" or "grey" WORLD ALGEBRA* $V$ *we mean the notion*

$$V \approx \Lambda \square \blacksquare$$

*of dialectics, where*

$$\square \approx \{\Lambda\},$$

$$\blacksquare \approx \{\Lambda\{\Lambda\}\},$$

$$\Lambda \approx \overline{V} \quad \text{and}$$

$$\overline{\Lambda} \approx V$$

*.4.21: EXAMPLE.* $\quad V \approx \{\Lambda \{ \Lambda \{ \Lambda \}\}\}$
*together with its equational closure and tactical configuration is a WORLD ALGEBRA* $V$

*.4.3: By a WORD ALGEBRA* $V$ *we mean a WORLD ALGEBRA* $V$ *containing some of the following equations*

$$\zeta : V = \Lambda$$

$$\eta : V = \square$$

$$\theta : V = \blacksquare$$

*Ad* $\zeta$. *Equation* $\zeta$ *yields* $\forall y A(y)$ *always <u>fulfillable</u> while* $\exists y A(y)$ *is always <u>unfulfillable</u>.*

*Ad* $\eta$. *Equation* $\eta$ *yields* $\forall y A(y)$ *always <u>fulfillable</u> if, and only if;* $\exists y A(y)$ *is always <u>fulfillable</u> and conversly with unfulfillable in place of fulfillable.*

*Ad* $\theta$. *Equation* $\theta$ *yields* $\forall y A(y)$ *<u>fulfillable</u> if, and only if,*
$\exists y \exists x [ A(y) \,\&\, A(x) \,\&\, \neg\, y \cong x ]$ *and* $\exists y A(y)$ *is always <u>unfulfillable</u> if, and only if,* $\forall y [ \neg A(y) \,\&\, y \cong y ]$

*.4.4: <u>Definition</u>. The WORLD PROBLEM for* $V$ *is the class of equations each member of which has* $\square$ *as a solution.*

*<u>Definition</u>. The WORD PROBLEM for* $V$ *is the class of (mental) activities* $\mathscr{A}$ *which (in* $\square$ *) proceed over a span of indications of* $\Lambda$.

*Note that in* $\square \Lambda\Lambda \sim \Lambda$ *, id est iteration (continuation) is <u>idempotent</u>. Of course, in terms of the mundane experience of the world, WORLD and WORD PROBLEMS for* $V$ *are examples of what appropriately can be called IMAGINARY PROBLEMS.*

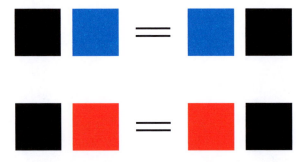

**Color Equations**

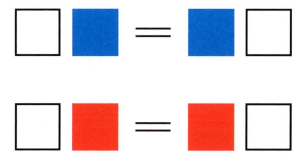

Color Equations

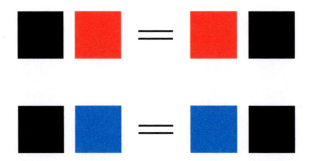

**Color Equations**

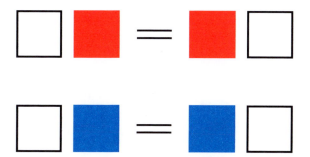

Color Equations

# SEMIOTICS-I

The idea of an **abstract language** originated with the discovery of some simple **algebraic properties** pertaining to the combinatorial or syntactical rules governing the productions of strings of symbols. One of the most elementary algebraic structures involving these properties is the **semi group with** $1$, generally designated $\mathfrak{a} = \langle \mathcal{A}, \circ \rangle$, where the first coordinate designates the **domain** of the semi group (also called the carrier of the semi group) and the second coordinate designates an **associative operation** (concatenation) closed with respect to the domain of the semi group.

Operations performed on a carrier $\mathcal{A}$ are termed **productions** of the structure $\mathfrak{a}$ and they correspond to sentence forms and other grammatically significant units on the syntactic level.

Chains of productions over $\mathcal{A}$ are given structural descriptions in terms of **trees**, $\mathcal{T}_{\!A}$, where the "root" designates the initial production (or "start symbol") and the branchings designate the successive applications of operations on previously obtained "**words**". By the closure of $\mathcal{A}$ we mean all trees $\mathcal{T}_{\!A}$ such that $\mathcal{T}_{\!A}$ obtains in $\mathfrak{a}$. This closure corresponds to the **language** generated by $\mathfrak{a}$, designated $\mathcal{L}(\mathcal{A})$.

By generalizing the concept of a semi group with $1$ we may obtain a global presentation of $\mathcal{L}(\mathcal{A})$. This generalization brings us to the concepts of **category theory**, one of the highlights of exact thinking after the creation of Cantor's "Paradise". By a **category** $\mathbf{C}$ we shall understand a collection of **objects**, corresponding to the words on $\mathcal{A}$ above, together with a collection of **morphisms**, corresponding to the productions generating $\mathcal{L}(\mathcal{A})$.

Objects will be denoted $A, B, \Gamma, \Delta, \ldots$ and morphisms $Я, Ю, Э, \ldots$. For each pair of objects $A, B$, there is a set $C(A, B)$ of morphisms $Я$ carrying $A$ to $B$, and, in addition, for each $A$ in $C$, an <u>identity morphism</u> $\epsilon_A(A, A)$, also written $\mathcal{J}_A$.

Now, if there are three morphisms $Я, Ю, Э$ such that
$$Я: A \Rightarrow B, \quad Ю: B \Rightarrow \Gamma, \quad Э: \Gamma \Rightarrow \Delta$$
then the <u>composition</u> of them satisfies

$$(ЯЮ)Э = Я(ЮЭ)$$

Also, if $Я: A \Rightarrow B$, then $\mathcal{J}_A Я = Я = Я \mathcal{J}_B$

To complete our definition we remark that a Category $C$ is always <u>closed</u> under arbitrary <u>compositions</u> of Morphisms, i.e. if

$$Я \in C(A, B) \text{ and } Ю \in C(B, \Gamma), \text{ then always}$$

$$ЯЮ \in C(A, \Gamma)$$

The <u>syntax</u> of $\mathcal{L}(A)$ can now be specified as a category $\mathcal{F}$ where the Objects are strings of letters drawn from some fixed alphabet and the Morphisms are derivations (Trees) of one string from another.

By a derivation $\mathcal{D}$ we shall now understand the following ordered triple

$$\mathcal{D} = \langle (A_0, \ldots, A_n), (Я_0, \ldots, Я_{n-1}), (\lambda_0 - \zeta_0, \ldots, \lambda_{n-1} - \zeta_{n-1}) \rangle$$

WHERE

$(A_0, \ldots, A_n)$ DESIGNATES THE WORD COORDINATE,

$(Я_0, \ldots, Я_{n-1})$ IS THE DERIVATION COORDINATE, AND

$(\lambda_0 - \zeta_0, \ldots, \lambda_{n-1} - \zeta_{n-1})$ IS THE NEIGHBOURHOOD COORDINATE,

THE LATTER GIVEN A <u>TOPOLOGICAL</u> INTERPRETATION (SEE BELOW).

THE <u>LENGTH ZERO</u> DERIVATION $\langle (A), (\ ), (\ ) \rangle$ IS REGARDED AS THE $A$-<u>IDENTITY DERIVATION</u>, WHILE THE <u>LENGTH ONE</u> DERIVATION $\langle (A, B), (Я: A \Rightarrow B), (\lambda - \zeta) \rangle$ WILL BE "ABBREVIATED" $Я: A \Rightarrow B$ AND PURPOSELY CONFUSED WITH THE "REAL" PRODUCTION $A \Rightarrow B$ IN $\mathcal{L}(\mathcal{A})$. CLEARLY $\mathcal{D}$ MAY BE TURNED INTO AN INDEPENDENT CATEGORY, ID EST INDEPENDENT OF $\mathcal{L}(\mathcal{A})$.

THE IMPORTANCE OF THE ABOVE CONCEPTS COMES FROM THE FACT THAT MORPHISMS ARE EXAMPLES OF A GENERAL CLASS OF <u>ARROWS</u>. ANOTHER EXAMPLE IS THE CLASS OF <u>FUNCTORS</u> THAT EXISTS BETWEEN CATEGORIES THEMSELVES.

A FUNCTOR $\Upsilon$ FROM A CATEGORY $C_0$ TO A CATEGORY $C_1$ IS SIMPLY TWO CLASSES OF ARROWS, ONE SENDING OBJECTS IN $C_0$ TO OBJECTS IN $C_1$ AND THE OTHER SENDING MORPHISMS IN $C_0$ TO MORPHISMS IN $C_1$. FORMALLY, THE FOLLOWING SITUATION OBTAINS: IF $\Upsilon$ IS A FUNCTOR BETWEEN $C_0$ AND $C_1$, ID EST

$$\Upsilon: C_0 \longrightarrow C_1$$

, THEN FOR EVERY $A \in C_0$, $\Upsilon$ ASSIGNS AN OBJECT $\Upsilon(A)$ IN $C_1$ AND FOR EACH $Я \in C_0$ $\Upsilon$ ASSIGNS THE MORPHISM $\Upsilon(Я)$ IN $C_1$.

Now, by the SEMANTICS of $\mathcal{L}(\mathcal{A})$ we mean a CO-FUNCTOR

$$\mathcal{J}: \mathcal{F} \rightrightarrows \mathcal{U}.$$

where $\mathcal{U}$, of course, denotes the SEMANTIC CATEGORY associated with $\mathcal{L}(\mathcal{A})$ when generated by the Syntax Category $\mathcal{F}$.

More specifically, the Co-Functor $\mathcal{J}$ specifies an INTERPRETATION of $\mathcal{F}$ by taking Objects to CARTESIAN PRODUCTS in $\mathcal{U}$ and derivations to functions in $\mathcal{U}$. In other words, the Semantic Category $\mathcal{U}$ consists of a Category of SETS and FUNCTIONS and the image of the interpretation $\mathcal{J}$ is called the SEMANTICS of the interpretation. For example, the interpretation of an Object $\mathbf{A}_{\mathcal{F}}$ of the Syntax Category consists of those Functions Щ that are Contravariant in $\mathcal{U}$. (They correspond to retracts in a Topos).

If Я is a Morphism in $\mathcal{U}$ (i.e. Я is a Function), then the neighbourhood of Я is defined as those Morphisms Я$_1$, ......, Я$_n$ that act as Identities on the extended neighbourhood domain of Я. That is, Я$_1$, ......, Я$_n$ are neighbourhoods of Я if the following diagrams commute:

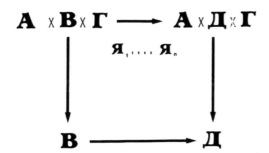

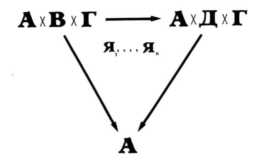

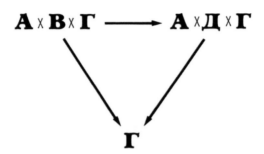

WHERE **Я** IS THE MORPHISM **Я**:**В** $\Rightarrow$ **Д** AND X INDICATES CARTESIAN PRODUCT.

FURTHER EXAMPLES OF GENERAL CLASSES OF ARROWS TO BE MET WITH IN CATEGORY THEORY – BESIDES MORPHISMS AND FUNCTORS – ARE <u>MONO-MORPHISMS</u> AND <u>EPI-MORPHISMS</u>, AS IN THE FOLLOWING

DEFINITION. **Ш** IS A <u>MONO-MORPHISM</u> IN A CATEGORY **C**, IF FOR ALL **Ю**,**Э** $\in$ **C**

$$Ю:Г \Rightarrow A, Э:Г \Rightarrow A$$

IMPLIES **Ю** = **Э**   IF **ЮШ** = **ЭШ**

DEFINITION. Ш IS AN EPI-MORPHISM IN A CATEGORY **C**,
IF FOR ALL Ю, Э ∈ **C**

$$Ю : B \Rightarrow Г, Э : B \Rightarrow Г$$

IMPLIES $Ю = Э$ IF $ШЮ = ШЭ$

Щ AND Ш WILL BE OF IMPORTANCE FOR THE MAPPINGS OF THE INNER STRUCTURES OF TOPOSES.

TOPOSES GIVE RISE TO YET OTHER GENERAL CLASSES OF ARROWS LIKE <u>PULL-BACKS</u> AND <u>PUSH-OUTS</u>. FOR THE MOMENT WE WILL STOP THE PRESENT CLASSIFICATION OF ARROWS, ONLY MENTIONING ONE FURTHER CLASS, AND LEAVING THE OTHERS FOR ANOTHER OCCASION. THIS CLASS IS CALLED THE <u>CLUB OPERATORS</u>, $\Omega$ , WHICH ASSIGNS TO EACH OBJECT **A** A MORPHISM

$$Ч_A : \gamma A \longrightarrow \Phi A$$

WHERE $\gamma$ AND $\Phi$ ARE **2**-FUNCTORS.

FURTHER, TO EACH MORPHISM Ч OF THE UNDERLYING **2**-CATEGORY Г OF Д, A **2**-CELL MORPHISM $Ч_A$ IN THE CO-DOMAIN **2**-CATEGORY Д IS ASSIGNED SUCH THAT THE FOLLOWING "SQUARE" OBTAINS:

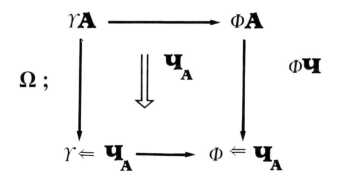

Intuitively, $\Omega$ is a <u>NATURAL TRANSFORMATION</u> between Categories. Specific Natural Transformations will be pictured:

$$Ц_\Omega : \Upsilon \rightsquigarrow X$$

The Club Operator plays a prominent role for the <u>PASSAGE</u> between Categories, as when we wish to go from one Semantic Category $\mathcal{U}_1$ to another Semantic Category $\mathcal{U}_2$, with common underlying Syntactic Category $\mathcal{F}_0$. The DEONTIC AXIOMS determining the admissible passages for some $\Omega$ are called the <u>DOCTRINE OF THE CLUB OF CATEGORIES</u> (or just <u>DOCTRINES FOR SCHOOLS</u>), where the "Club" notion now refers to the Categories in the domain and co-domain of $\Omega$. For example, a situation that is typical for any Doctrine for Schools is the operation of <u>PASTING</u> Objects (here, categories) in a Club. So one thing permitted is to pass from the situation

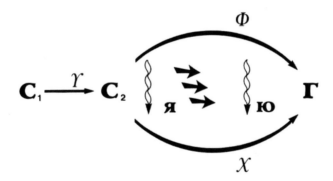

TO THE SITUATION

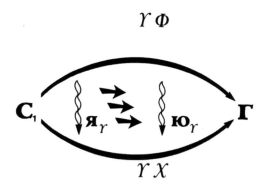

WHERE ⇉ DENOTES THE PASTING OPERATION AND $\Gamma$ IS AN ELEMENT OF THE CLUB.

DIAGRAMS OF CONCEPT FORMATION PROCESSES UNDERLYING FORESTS OF CORRECT REASONINGS MAKE HEAVY USE OF ⇉ , ESPECIALLY WHEN THE CLUB HAS MANY-SORTED DOCTRINES FOR SCHOOLS.

+ + + + +

SOME ELEMENTARY CATEGORIES (ARROW AND TIME CATEGORIES).

(1) LET $\mathcal{V}$ BE A (SMALL) UNIVERSE OF <u>SETS</u>. THE <u>ARROW CATEGORY</u>

$$\mathcal{V}^{\Rightarrow}$$

WILL CONSIST OF THOSE OBJECTS $\lambda : \mathbf{X}_0 \Rightarrow \mathbf{X}_1$ FOR WHICH $\mathbf{X}_0$ IS A DOMAIN FOR $\lambda$ AND $\mathbf{X}_1$ ITS co-domain and where the Morphisms, i.e. Arrows

$$\Lambda : \lambda : \mathbf{X}_0 \Rightarrow \mathbf{X}_1 \Rightarrow \lambda' : \mathbf{Y}_0 \Rightarrow \mathbf{Y}_1,$$ are

the pairs of functions $\lambda_0$, $\lambda_1$ such that the following diagram commutes, i.e. $\lambda \Lambda^\circ = \Lambda' \lambda$

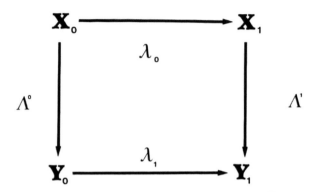

(2) If $\mathcal{P}$ is a (discrete) <u>PROCESS</u>, then $\mathcal{V}^{\mathcal{P}}$ is the Category of Times (relative $\mathcal{P}$). If instead of $\mathcal{V}$ and/or $\mathcal{P}$ we put the Category on the forms

$$\mathcal{V}^{\mathcal{E}} \quad \text{or} \quad \mathcal{E}^{\mathcal{E}},$$

we get the (universal) Categories of local and global Time, respectively.

For the Category $\mathcal{V}^{\mathcal{P}}$ we shall have as Objects infinitely proceeding sequences or strings

$$\mathbf{X}_0 \Rightarrow \mathbf{X}_1 \Rightarrow \mathbf{X}_2 \Rightarrow \cdots \Rightarrow \mathbf{X}_m \Rightarrow \cdots$$

of Arrows between sets $\mathbf{X}_j \in \mathcal{V}$ and as Morphisms sequences of $\Lambda$-Arrows, like the following:

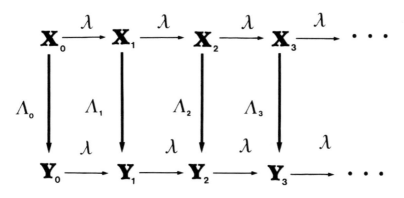

In terms of Arrows, $\mathcal{V}^{\Rightarrow}$ and $\mathcal{V}^{\mathcal{P}}$ differ in the following way

$$\mathcal{V}^{\Rightarrow} : \cdot \Rightarrow \cdot$$

$$\mathcal{V}^{\mathcal{P}} : \cdot \Rightarrow \cdot \Rightarrow \cdot \Rightarrow \cdots$$

## THE DEFINITIVE CATEGORY OF ALL CATEGORIES.

For Toposes as well as elsewhere, the DOCTRINAL CATEGORY $\mathcal{E}$ is the FORGETFUL CO-DOMAIN CATEGORY of the UNIVERSAL FORGETFUL FUNCTOR $\mathcal{E}^{\sharp}$

Its Objects are many-sorted — Brackets, $|\ |$, and Cups, $\sqcup$ — and the Morphisms are obtained through iterations in the Cumulative Hierarchy $\mathcal{V}$ of Arrow Operations $\longrightarrow$ for denotational connections between Objects in $\mathcal{E}$.

Any diagram for a Concept Formation Process (guided by Correct Reasonings) has an ADJOINTED FORGETFUL CO-FUNCTOR

$\mathcal{E}$

mapping elements in the Process to Cartesian Products of Objects in $\mathcal{E}$ and Morphisms to Functions (Arrows) in $\mathcal{E}$. Evidently, Cartesian Closed Categories (CCC's) will be the most prominent tool for constructing Toposes. By this last step we attempt a move from Lawvere's <u>Objective Dialectics</u> to <u>Natural Dialectics</u> where Club Operations and other Natural Transformations ( ⟿ ) dominate over the specifications of Category Objects. Clearly, $\mathcal{E}$ considered as a Category will be our alternative to the Category of all Categories as a foundation of mathematics and Generalized Constructive Conceptualism.

Of course, $\mathcal{E}$ and its Sub-Objects will still serve as our favorite example of Inaccessible Cardinals, Toposes, Cosmois and what not that will be encountered in the pursuit of the delights of Exact Thinking.

Recall that the Objects of the Doctrinal Category $\mathcal{E}$, i.e. the denotational connections between signs of type $|a_i|^k$ or $\bigsqcup ( |a_{i_1}|^{k_1}, \ldots, |a_{i_n}|^{k_m} )$ consist of the points of indications connected with the local Arrow or Pre-Morphism appearing in some fiber for a Site belonging to the Topos $\mathcal{E}$. The Rank or Depth of any such sign is given by its associated INDEX, i.e. $i+k$ or $i+k+\frac{n\pm m}{2}$, as the case may be. In other words, the Depth of a sign $[a_i]^k$ or $\sqcup( [a_{i_1}]^{k_1}, \ldots, [a_{i_n}]^{k_m} )$ equals the number of Arrows or Pre-Morphisms of the underlying Bundle or single Fiber that defines the corresponding indications.

The Depth of an indication, in turn, is generally equal to the inverse of the Rank of the Site or Stack that envelopes the indication. Analogously, the Depth of a Topos is in general equal to the inverse of the Rank of its Sheaf and so on for the remaining structures (Fiber Bundles, $pb$'s, $pc$'s, Sheaves, etc.).

In the other direction we may Reflect upwards over the entire universe of Sheaves. As a first stage of this Reflexion, we arrive at a PRE-COSMOI, while at a later stage the appearance of a COSMOI of collections of sets of Sheaves becomes possible.

For Cosmois, we may define LEFT and RIGHT ADJOINTS as a Universal Property of every Cosmoi. That means in particular that every Cosmoi is SYMMETRICALLY SELF-REFLEXIVE with respect to ADJOINTNESS.

Adjoints associated with Sheaves and Toposes are not necessarily SYMMETRIC, but nevertheless defined in Left or Right form for every Sheaf and Topos. If both forms are permitted by the Doctrine on a Sheaf or Topos, the Universal Property is recovered. Such situations are referred to as DOCTRINAL CLUB CONSPIRATIONS - DCC's - and their Objects are the Adjointed Sheaves and Toposes.

In this way we can continue to Reflect upwards beyond the Cosmois towards more and more comprehensive Units and there seems to be no conceivable end to the iterative applications of the <u>Reflexion Principle</u>. On the other hand, due to the normality of our Sheaves, there is no corresponding infinite regress or descent downwards, since all structures below the Sheaves collapse ultimately on the void indication $\mathbf{a}_0$, i.e. the Universal Terminal Object $\underset{\sim}{\pi}^o$ . This property will henceforth be referred to as the well-foundedness of the structure in question. On the contrary, regressive Sheaves or Toposes can never be well-founded and the same holds for their (inadmissible) Doctrines.

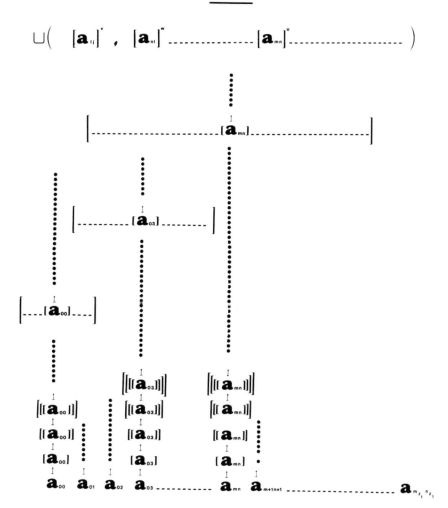

409 THE YELLOW BOOK

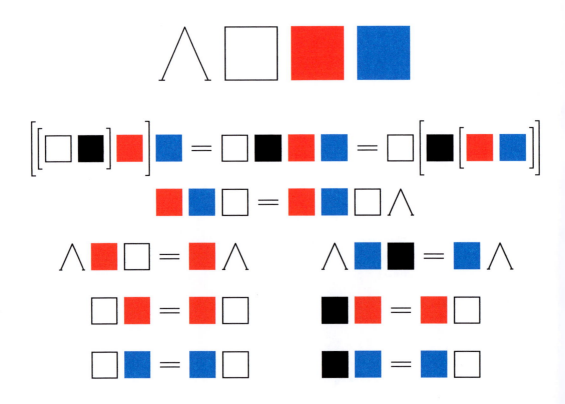

**Color Algebra**

410     C.C. HENNIX          OTHER MATTERS

*Appendix* I
# Abandoned Lecture Notes on Intuitionism
(From the Rheinbeck Seminar, 1984)

# TEXTS By Luitzen Egbertus Jan Brouwer

From L.E.J. Brouwer: *Begrundung der Mengenlehre unabhängig von logischen Saltz vom ausgeschlossenen Dritten* (Collected Works)

Der Mengenlchre liegt eine unbegrenzte Folge von Zeichen zu grunde, welche bestimmt wird durch ein erstes Zeichen und das Gesetz, das aus jedem dieser Zeichen das nachtfolgende herleitet. Unter den mannigfachen hierzu brauchbaren Gesetzen erscheint dasjenige am geeignetesten, welches die Folge ζ der Ziffernkomplexe 1,2,3,4,5,..... erzeugt.

Die Bestimmungsgesetze endlicher Zeichengruppen sowie unbegrenzter Zeichenfolgen von der Art der Folge ζ, bilden besondere Falle von Mengen, deren Elemente von der einzelnen Zeichen gebildet werden. Die Menge der Ziffernkomplexe von ζ werden wir mit A bezeichen.

Mengen und Elementen von Mengen werden *mathematische Entitäten* genannt.

Eine Species E heisst *endlich*, wenn sie mit der Menge der Ziffernkomplexe eines gewissen Anfangselementes der Folge ζ gleichmächtig ist.

Eine Species U heisst *unendlich*, wenn jedes Element von A einem verschiedenen Elemente w von U, zugeordnet werden kann. Im Falle dass die Elemente w eine mit A gleichmächtige abtrennbare Teilspecies von U bilden, heissr U *reduzierbar unendlich*.

Es existiert kein Grund zu Behaupten, dass jede Menge oder Species entweder endlich oder unendlich sei. Dagegen steht fest, dass eine S<sub>ṭ</sub>
zwar a

## Color Equations

*The Yellow Book*

*Haupteigenschaft der endlichen Species.* Fur jede Herstellungsweise der eineindeutigen Bezeichnung zwischen einer endlichen Species E und der Menge der Ziffernkomplexe eines Anfangselementes von $\zeta$, kurtz: fur jedes Zählungsweise von E, wird dasselbe Anfangselemente von $\zeta$ benutz.

.....

Die Species $C_n$ der Gruppen von n unbeschränkt fortgesetzten Folgen von zu $\zeta$ gehörigen Ziffernkomplexen ist eine Menge derselben Kardinalzahl wie die Menge C. Um dies einzusehen, braucht man nur dem Elemente $a_1$ $a_2$ $a_3$ $a_4$ ... von C das Element

$$a_1\ a_{n+1}\ a_{2n+1}\ \cdots$$

$$a_2\ a_{n+2}\ a_{2n+2}\ \cdots$$

.................

$$a_n\ a_{2n}\ a_{3n}\ \cdots$$

von $C_n$ zuzuordnen. In dieser Weise bestimmt man gleichzeitig eine eineindeutige Beziehung zwischen den Punkten eines n-dimensionalen Kubus und den Punkten eines geraden Liniensegmentes (aus welcher unmittelbar eine eineindeutigee Beziehung zwischen den Punkte der geraden Linie folgt).

Dieser Beziehung ist aber *nich stetig* wenn man z.B. (bei konstanten $a_1, \ldots, a_n, a_{n+3}, a_{n+4} \ldots$) $a_{n+2}$ abwechselnd gleich 1 und 2 wählt und $a_{n+1}$ unbeschränkt wachsen lässt, so bekommt man auf dem Liniesegmente eine gegen einen einzigen Punkt konvergierende Folge von Punkten, im n-dimensionalen Kubus aber *nicht* gegen einen einzigen Punkt konvergiertende Folge von Punkten.

Color Equations

# The Two Basic Acts of Intuitionism

## by L.E.J. Brouwer

From L.E.J. Brouwer: *Historical Background Principles and Methods of Intuitionism* (Collected Works)

......*The intervention of intuitionism* of which the first seems necessarily to lead to destructive and sterilizing consequences, whereas the second yields ample possibilities for recovery and new developments......

FIRST ACT OF INTUITIONISM
completely separates mathematics from mathematical language, in particular from the phenomena of language which are described by theoretical logic. It recognizes that mathematics is a languageless activity of the mind having its origin in the basic phenomenon of perception of a *move of time*, which is the falling apart of a life moment into two distinct things, one of which gives way to the other, but is retained by memory. If the two-ity thus born is divested of all quality, there remains the common substratum of all two-ities, the mental creation of the *empty two-ity*. This empty two-ity and the two unities of which it is composed, constitute the *basic mathematical systems*. And the basic operation of mathematical construction is the *mental creation of the two-ity of two mathematical systems previously acquired*, and the consideration of this two-ity as a new mathematical system.

It is introspectively realized how this basic operation, continually displaying *unaltered* retention by memory, successively generates each natural number, the infinitely proceeding sequence of natural numbers, arbitrary finite sequences and infinitely proceeding sequences of mathematical systems previously acquired, finally a continually extending stock of mathematical systems corresponding to "separable" systems of classical mathematics.

## THE SECOND ACT OF INTUITIONISM

which recognizes the possibility of generating new mathematical entities:

firstly in the form of *infinitely proceeding sequences* $p_1\ p_2\ldots$, whose terms are *chosen more or less freely from mathematical entities previously acquired;* in such a way that the freedom of choice existing perhaps for the first element $p_1$ may be subjected to a lasting restriction at some following $p_\nu$, and again and again to sharper lasting restrictions or even abolition at further subsequent $p_\nu$'s, while all these restriction interventions, as well as the choices of the $p_\nu$'s themselves, at any stage may be made to depend on possible future mathematical experiences of the creating subject;

secondly in the form of mathematical species, i.e. *properties supposable for mathematical entities previously acquired,* and satisfying the condition that, if they hold for a certain mathematical entity, they also hold for all mathematical entities which have been defined to be equal to it, relations of equality having to be symmetric, reflexive and transitive; mathematical entities previously acquired for which the property holds are called *elements* of the species.

With regard to this definition of species we have to remark firstly that, during the development of intuitionist mathematics, some species will have to be considered as being re-defined time and again in the same way, secondly that a species can very well be an element of another species, but never an element of itself.

Two mathematical entities are called *different* if their equality has been proved to be absurd.

Two infinitely proceeding sequences of mathematical entities $a_1, a_2, \ldots$, and $b_1, b_2, \ldots$, are called *equal* or *identical* if $a_\nu = b_\nu$ for each $\nu$, and *distinct,* if a natural number $s$, can be indicated such that $a_s$ and $b_s$ are different.

# Essentially Negative Properties
## by L.E.J. Brouwer

In order to estimate the significance of affirmative or negationless mathematics, the development of which is sometimes advocated, it may be useful to publish a simple and clear example, which I gave now and then in courses and lectures since 1927, and in which a simply negative property (i.e. the absurdity of a constructive property) is realized in such a way that no hope of transforming it into a constructive property can be justified. It consists of two real numbers which are different though neither can be proved to be greater or smaller than the other, let alone that they can be proved to be apart from each other.

Let $\alpha$ be a mathematical assertion that *cannot be tested*, i.e. for which no method is known to prove either its absurdity or the absurdity of its absurdity.[1]

Then the creating subject can, in connection with the assertion $\alpha$, create an infinitely proceeding sequence of rational numbers $a_1, a_2, a_3, \ldots$ according to the following direction: As long as, in the course of choosing the $a_n$, the creating subject has experienced neither the truth, nor the absurdity of $\alpha$, every $a_n$ is chosen equal to 0. However, as soon as between the choice of $a_{r-1}$ and that of $a_r$ the creating subject has obtained a proof of the truth of $\alpha$, $a_r$ as well as $a_{r+\nu}$ for every natural number $\nu$ is chosen equal to $2^{-r}$. And as soon as between the choice of $a_{s-1}$ and that of $a_s$ the creating subject has experienced the absurdity of $\alpha$, $a_s$ as well as $a_{s+\nu}$ for every natural number $\nu$ is chosen equal to $-2^{-s}$.

This infinitely proceeding sequence $a_1, a_2, a_3, \ldots$ is positively convergent, so it defines a real number $\rho$.

If for this real number $\rho$ the relation $\rho > 0$ were to hold, then $\rho < 0$ would be impossible, so it would be certain that $\alpha$ could never be proved to be absurd, so the absurdity of the absurdity of $\alpha$ would be known, so $\alpha$ would be tested, which it is not. *Thus the relation $\rho > 0$ does not hold.*

---

[1]For instance the assertion that there exists a quadruple of natural numbers 2,a,b and c, for which the relation $a + b = c$ holds, or that in the decimal expansion of $\Pi$ there occur ten successive digits forming a sequence 0123456789.

## The Yellow Book

Further, if for the real number $\rho$ the relation $\rho<0$ were to hold, then $\rho>0$ would be impossible, so it would be certain that $\alpha$ could never be proved to be true, so the absurdity of $\alpha$ would be known, so again $\alpha$ would be tested, which it is not. *Thus neither does the relation $\rho<0$ hold.*

Finally let us suppose that the relation $\rho=0$ holds. In this case neither $\rho>0$ nor $\rho<0$ could ever be proved, so neither the absurdity nor the truth of $\alpha$ could ever be proved, so the absurdity as well as the absurdity of the absurdity of $\alpha$ would be known. This is a contradiction, *so the relation $\rho=0$ is absurd,* in other words *the real numbers $\rho$ and 0 are different.*

Consequently for the real numbers $\rho$ and 0 the simply negative property $\rho \neq 0$ holds, whilst neither of the properties $\rho \gtrless 0$ or $\rho \lessgtr 0$ is present, let alone one of the constructive properties $\rho > 0$ or $\rho < 0$. Thus for real numbers the relation $\neq$ is an essentially negative relation.

Analogously, if at the end of the third section above, $-2^{-s}$ is replaced by $2^{-s}$, then for the real numbers $\rho$ and 0 the simply negative property $\rho>0$ holds, while the constructive property $\rho \gtrdot 0$ does not hold. Thus the relation $>$ of virtual order is also an essentially negative relation.

# Lecture Notes on Intuitionism (I)

*Cognitio enim contingit secundum quod cognitum est cognoscente. Cognitum autem est in cognoscente secundum modum cognoscentis. Unde cuiuslibet cognoscentis cognito est secundum modum suae naturae.*

Th($\Sigma$) is the intuitionistic theory of *initiable* mathematical realities. This theory contains many possibilities but they are all characterized by being *bounded* by what is *presently* given.\*

Since what is present to the creative subject, $\Sigma$, *varies* with the stages of her illumination, it is by studying the very variations of these stages that we can grasp what kind of possibilities $\Sigma$ is *limited* by.

For limited she is at any stage of illumination, be it after $\phi(n)$ lives or not. But even so, we can agree that $\Sigma$ is *never less* illuminated after the nth illumination than she is after her first initiation with the practice of a single successor function $\lambda_{00}$, that is, after her very first illumination (by an unending series of natural numbers).

The theory of the creative subject, Th($\Sigma$), derives its entire rationale from the assumption that iterations of illuminations initiate $\Sigma$ to grasp still higher stages of illumination.

. . . . .

We begin by considering an indefinitely proceeding sequence

$$\underset{\sim}{\mathcal{U}} : \mathcal{U}_a, \mathcal{U}_b, \ldots, \mathcal{U}_k, \mathcal{U}_{k+1}, \ldots$$

of *universes*.

Inside a universe $\mathcal{U}$ there emerges two kinds of events, viz those which are judged to hold for the *fleeing properties* of $\mathcal{U}$ and those stable or non-fleeing properties which hold for the already arrived events together with their lawful (functional) continuations within the limits of $\mathcal{U}$.

---

\*The immanently derivative character of symbolic assertions stems from the impossibility of a presuppositionless interpretation of occurrencies of symbolic events.

Hence, all symbolic actions are lost in their own opacity which individual assertions consecrate as a kind of ideological subjective camouflage in lieu of the apodictic evidence for the aberrance of Being.

As a result, isolation becomes a prerequisite as a means of communication as does the need for undoing what has been instrumental for the reification of the interior monologue of the Creative Subject's True Self.

While classical logic was shown inadequate by Brouwer, he did so mainly with reference to the fleeing properites of $\mathcal{U}$ while maintaining the validity of classical logic at least for the case of all events already arrived. That is, Brouwer viewed the "already arrived" as something *finite* for which he maintained the classical principles of logic, including *tertium non datur*. This view point, however, overlooks the real possibility of our *knowledge* of the arrived events itself being a "fleeing property." More precisely, just because something once has been proven to have been constructed, that does not mean that it can be found *now* or even in the immediate future. That is, we may not *now* be able to locate the construction any longer, except by starting all over again, thereby repeating the entire previous existence proof before we may continue. And just because something was done once doesn't imply, analogously, that it can be done again, so one must *prove* the *possibility* of iterating an old proof, especially if the context has changed markedly since the original proof was effected. *Ex eo quod aliqua res est* cognita esse, *non potest evidenter inferri quod alia res sit*.

. . . . .

We say that P is a *"fleeing property"* if

i. For each natural number n, there is a method $\mathcal{M}_p$ deciding between P(n) or its absurdity (not-P(n));

ii. It is not known whether a method $\mathcal{M}_p$ can be written down by means of which a natural number n can be calculated such that P(n) ;

iii. There is no proof of the absurdity of P(n) i.e. of not-P(n).

By a *critical number* $K_p$ of the fleeing property P we understand the (hypothetically) smallest natural number possessing P. If $n < K_p$, n is called a *down-number* and if $n > K_p$ an *up-number*.

But now it becomes obvious that the property of being the number of all possible proofs itself becomes a *fleeing property*, hence contradicting the finiteness of all possible proofs (as free creations by the Creative Subject herself when considered as sub-spaces $C_m$ of the graph of the species $C_n$, $n > m$.) Thus, there is a deep contradiction in Brouwer's foundations of mathematics.

. . . . .

As soon as we abandon the use of *restricted quantifiers* many fleeing properties seem to reside in $\mathcal{U}$.

However, soon one makes the experience that by passing to the next universe $\mathcal{U}'$, the fleeing properties of $\mathcal{U}$ are transformed into harmless decidable species. That is, up-numbers of $\mathcal{U}$ together with its critical numbers, become down-numbers in $\mathcal{U}'$.

The species $\mathcal{B}$ of critical numbers of a universe $\mathcal{U}$ forms, in some sense, the *boundary* or *limit* of $\Sigma$'s knowledge of $\mathcal{U}$ called the *critical boundary* or *limit* of $\mathcal{U}$.

This limit is surpassed by the passage to the immediately next universe $\mathcal{U}'$. Yet, $\mathcal{U}'$ awaits further fleeing properties as soon as restricted quantification is abandoned again.

The length of the sequence $\underset{\sim}{\mathcal{U}}$ of universes is a measure of the failure to learn from the experiences with unrestricted quantification.

The problem is not to be able to extend the sequence $\underset{\sim}{\mathcal{U}}$ indefinitely (that is already taken into attention) but to *classify* the many different ways in which transitions from one universe to another takes place.

Thus we shall expect to deal with a *branching* sequence of universes, each branch modelling a *uniform class* of transitions from one universe to another.

# Lecture Notes on Intuitionism (II)

## Aspects On The Continuum

### Introductory Remarks

We choose an *Initiation Number* **N** as we choose a real line

($\mathbf{R}_x$) $\qquad\qquad \underline{\phantom{xx}0\phantom{xxxx}x\phantom{xxxxx}}\ldots$

located around a real point $x$ or with *Weierstrass*' arithmetical notations

($\mathbf{R}_W$) $\qquad\qquad 0,1,2,3,\ldots,\nu,\ldots\infty$

(The fact that the entire line R can be mapped 1 – 1 to the closed interval [0,1] cannot be more astonishing than the fact that all classical and intuitionistic continua are cofinal with an Initiation Number.)

## The Yellow Book

We think of the term $\nu$, the *leading term.* as *given* among the terms that are included in the Initial Number N.

Assuming that $\mathbf{R_W}$ is monotone and increasing (if not, drop the superfluous terms) we know that for some term $n < \nu$, $\varphi(n) = \nu$. Letting also $\varphi$ be monotone and increasing, and such that $\varphi^n(0) = \nu$, $\varphi$ indicates a *law* or *leading operation* by means of which terms to be included in $\mathbf{R_W}$ are defined. (And the graph of $\varphi^n(x)$ is called the *orbit* of the leading action $\varphi$.)

[From a modern point of view one is here dealing with an application of the *number-theoretic axiom of choice* (**AC-NN**)

$$\forall n \exists m \, R(n,m) \Rightarrow \exists f \forall n \, R(n, f(n))$$

The interesting question is, of course, whether $f$ can be choosen as a recursive function or not, i.e. whether or not Church's thesis is an acceptable principle.]

The dots indicated in **R** are explained by pointing to Euclid's first Axiom. Arbitrarily long lines can be drawn and each line is still in the possession of the property of being further extend*able*.

It doesn't follow from the fact that we can draw arbitrarily long geometrical lines, that we also thereby are endowed with the capacity to extend further any one of them. In point of fact, given that we can draw arbitrarily long lines why even be interested in *extending* any one of them since a line together with its extension can be obtained as just another arbitrarily long line without any fuss about concepts of "extensions" (and "limits"). (No topology.)

If an arbitrarily given line $R$ can be extended, we must ask, how?

If we assume that the extension obtains by continuing the generating operations of which $R$ is the result, then not only must they be specified (and hence no longer remain completely arbitrary) but so also must the fact that, taken all together, *just* the generating operations suffice for the end result $R$ ( screen against objects falling from heaven).

If the original generating operations for $R$ turned out to be insufficient, then *other* means must be sought. In any case, they must be specified and in addition, be proven sufficient (since we are employing more powerful but so far untested means).

In any case, we are moving towards the *topology* of the geometrical line making it come nearer the behavior of points on the real infinite line.

. . . . .

Turning now to the intuitionistic concept of the real line, consider that each initiable *mathematical* activity starts from a fixed *Initiation number*, N (*Anfangszahl*, Hausdorf, 1907).

Once the beginning of a series of Initiation numbers has been permitted, there is no end to the mathematical possibilities so opened up.

Once initiated into a beginning of a mathematical activity, $\mathcal{A}_N$, we shall move in an orderly fashion from one mathematical reality to another, where the latter reality remains just a *possibility* as long as we *remain* in the former reality.

The jump from one mathematical reality to another is obtained by exhausting a reality which at present is at hand until a limit is reached and from which another reality is formed.

The search for mathematical possibilities is moved by a desire to expand mathematical reality. Every new-formed mathematical reality contains the key to any further mathematical possibilities. It is the possibility of initiating a mathematical activity again and again which our understanding of the (increasingly) varying mathematical reality must be based on. In particular, it is the reality of the form*ed* limits in which the mathematical possibility operators reside.

Each process realized by a mathematical activity $\mathcal{A}_N$ is *cofinal* in N (or one of its initial (singular) segments).

In particular, if $\mathcal{A}_N$ realizes a continuum, C, the process C is cofinal in N.

The initiation number, N, of a mathematical activity is usually a limit point of a previously introduced activity $\mathcal{A}_{N'}$, based on an initiation number N' which was obtained as a limit of a still earlier mathematical activity.

If N' forms a *proper initial segment* of N i.e., if

$$N' \mathrel{\text{---}\!\!<} N$$

and is not cofinal in N then $\mathcal{A}_N$ is said to be a *regular* mathematical activity and following upon N' in the ordering of initiation numbers $<\eta, \text{---}\!\!<>$.

If N is an initiation number which is not cofinal with an initial segment of any previously obtained initiation number, then $\mathcal{A}_N$ is said to be *singular* mathematical activity.

The simplest possibility of a singular mathematical activity obtains with $\mathcal{A}_N$ as a limit of an unending but well-ordered chain of regular mathematical activities with regular initiation numbers $N_{00}$, $N_{01}$, $N_{10}$, ..... such that

$$N = \overleftarrow{\lim} \; N_{00}, N_{01}, N_{10}, \ldots$$

and N is cofinal with $N_{00}$.

**Remark**. Without the Axiom of Choice, there are (classically) no regular limit numbers above $\omega$ ( $= N_A$) and only 0 and 1 below. Thus, "2" ( $=$ "10") is the "smallest" singular ordinal number.

. . . . .

The first singular initiation number $N = N^0$ is the *first internal* limit imposed on the seemingly unending chain of increasing mathematical possibilities which all begin as regular mathematical realities.

In order to transpose a possibility of a manifold of mathematical realities into a manifold of new mathematical possibilities we must be initiated into a mathematical activity which will contain the latter manifold as a reality.

None of the previous regular activities contains the new manifold as a reality but at the limits of the said regular activities we shall construct a "diagonal" thereby delineating the internal limit as well as the construction of the first singular initiation number $N^0$.

Because of the breakdown of the monotone increasing cofinalities of the initiation numbers $N_{00}, N_{01}, N_{10}, \ldots$, the splendid regularity of the formation of new mathematical possibilities has been spoiled and we are about to start contemplating an entirely new form of substitution so that a sequence of regular initiation numbers, all larger than any of the previously obtained initiation numbers, can be picked up again.

For a traditional mathematician, of course, there is only one concept that comes to mind: Cantor's classical concept of *Diagonalization*.

But, then, the first question is: how do I know that the diagonal construction is *unique* and how do I tell apart two such constructions if they are not equivalent?

Yet, the diagonal construction exhausts the possibilities contained in the initiation numbers $N_{00}, N_{01}, N_{10}, \ldots$ . It is this power of $N^0$ which defines the reality of a first internal limit of mathematical possibility.

All the realities that have been encountered by following the sequence $\mathcal{A}_{N_{00}}, \mathcal{A}_{N_{01}}, \mathcal{A}_{N_{10}}, \ldots$ have been *regular* realities. Nothing upset the regularity of mathematical reality until someone delimited the work so far layed down by laying out a diagonal following the exact contours of the limits of regular reality.

If you are not permitted to transgress the diagonal contour of the work you have so far layed down, then, indeed, you have exhausted all your possibilities and reached the limit of the realities encountered so far.

Yet, it seems, by staying where you are, i.e. on the diagonal, mathematical reality is not becoming enriched. Rather, it stays fixed and you have taken a step out of it, seeing just the far end contour, as it were, from a distance.

In order to find yourself back in mathematical reality again, you need to be initiated into a mathematical activity which has a replica of this contour well within its limits and while rising towards those limits you may survey the totality of your previous mathematical reality up to and a bit beyond the fixed diagonal contour.

Since there is no possible communication between these two mathematical realities, i.e. the latter contains an initial assumption which was not permitted by the reality of the diagonal world, we must be initiated into a *third* mathematical activity in terms of which all communication between the diagonal world and its "successor" takes place, i.e. a mathematical reality which treats the reality beyond the diagonal world as a regular *extension* of it. But this is where all the trouble comes in.

When I speak of picking up again a regular sequence of initiation numbers, I speak of a mathematical possibility which is formed out of a reality which constitutes a conceptual break with any mathematical reality encountered so far through the sequence $N_{00}$, $N_{01}$, $N_{10}$, ......

# Lecture Notes on Intuitionism (III)

According to Brouwer, intuitionistic mathematics must be regarded as a *free creation* by the human mind.

The freedom with which the Creative Subject constructs mathematical objects is only paralleled by her freedom of choosing the *rules* upon which the existence of her constructions depends. Although freely chosen, these rules need not correspond to any given mathematical object although the result of following the rules may do so. It is even possible to consider freely chosen rules the following of which certainly does *not* correspond to a construction of a mathematical object.

It is not quite clear how free one is in making a distinction between the latter kind of rules and those the following of which leads to a mathematical construction. It is indeed possible to consider cases where one may consider the result of following some rules under both aspects, i.e. the "same" construction $\kappa$ is connected with two distinct objects, say, a text $T = \{s\}$ and a natural number $n = s$.

In such a case the Creative Subject is not completely free to interpret the resulting construction because unrestricted freedom of interpretation would introduce a possibility of deep confusions.

Thus, because of the requirement of the *clarity* of intuitionistic mathematics, the latter cannot be regarded as a *languageless activity* as stated by Brouwer. This does not mean that, say, the intuitionistic continuum, C, will not eternally remain without an exhaustive description $C[\tau]$, but only that cases of ambiguity are resolved by introducing specific rules for the use of certain combinations of signs.

It follows from the above that the logical approach to problems in the foundations of intuitionistic mathematics is by *regressive logical methods*. That is, the Creative Subject *first* arrives at an intuition of the continuum C and only *thereafter* does she arrive at the intuition of a description $C[\tau]$ of C. While the latter description necessarily remains incomplete, nevertheless, in the course of constructing a description $C[\tau]$, the Creative Subject encounters a description $b^\tau$ of objects B which are finite substructures of C.

One unambiguous such object is the *empty continuum*, $\Lambda_C$, described by a fulfillable intuitionistic method, $\mathfrak{M}_{\Lambda_C}$, corresponding to the *first act of intuitionism*, while another *ambiguous* such object would be the process of events defining the series of *initial numerical signs* known by "heart."

$$(K_h)\ 1,2,3,4,5,\ldots\ldots$$

That is, does a description $b^r$ of the series $K_h$ correspond to a finite mathematical object or must the "object" $K_h$ be identified with some species of "pre-ontological" objects? That is to say, the problem is whether or not the Creative Subject prefers to take the initial acts out of intuitionistic mathematics proper. If she does, then $b^r$ does not correspond to any mathematical object and the symbol $K_h$ becomes mathematically unambiguous in the clear sense that *it* does *not* belong to the language of intuitionistic mathematics. But this must also mean that the Creative Subject has lost her freedom to rely on the initial acts of intuitionism when effectively considering the existence of mathematical constructions. That is, the Creative Subject is *forbidden* to consider an intuitive Nn such as $K_h$.

Again, the existence of this possibility shows that the complete freedom with which the Creative Subject constructs her mathematical objects is fictitious and, therefore, stands in need of an adequate formalization. In particular, the logical mysticism surrounding her initiation into the abstract activity of the beginning steps of intuitionistic mathematics stands in need of a detailed formalization.

*Appendix* II

# MA̅-Theater

# Theater of the Eternal Mind

## MĀ-THEATER:
From Abstract Nō To Abstract Butō (1968–1988)
[ABENDSCHAUSPIELE/COGNITIO VESPERTINA]

According to Zeami, dance is instructed by song, i.e. poetry. Thus, if dance is instructed by *abstract symbols* instead of (concrete) words, *abstract dance* is created.

$$\mathbf{A}$$ is a symbol for the Empty Dance

(Utsu Butō - Void Butō)

The stage on which the Creative Subject shall be born is a lattice of (existential) contradictions—a vacuum encased by darkness.

Abstract Nō begins with a study of Non-Being and ends by a presentation of the character **MĀ**—annotated with its appropriate X-index, $\mathbf{MĀ_X = MĀ}$. More generally, "MĀ-Theater" stands for "X-indexed **MĀ**-*Theater*" of which Abstract Nō is a *separable sub-species*.

By contrast, the X-topocosm of *Abstract Butō* is characterized by (the consequences of) the singular identity

$$有 \equiv 無$$

which is also written

$$\bigcirc \equiv \bullet$$

Remark on *Ankoku Butō*. The character **ANG** signifies, with complete silence, what the concept "Day" stands for—while the character complex **ANKOKU** signifies the darkness brought about as the sounds of civilization already at dawn pierce through the daylight of what was once true.

Ankoku Butō-no-Zhuang Zhou from the Flowers of the Black Chrysanthemum (1985) is my second composition in the style of *Saido-Butō* and it too is characterized by the abstract identity

$$\bullet \equiv \bigcirc$$

where "$\bigcirc$" now also carries the connotation of "Day."

*The Yellow Book*

Circles of Being: 　　○ ○ ○ ○ ○

Circles of Darkness: 　● ● ● ● ●

The Circles of Being and Darkness are unified in Abstract Nō by the identity

$$闇 \cup 有 \equiv 闇$$

Reminder on Yugen. Yugen applies to speech, to the sounds of words. Yugen signifies the deep beauty of the darkness in which the sound of words envelope the Day.

Being, shattered by the sound of words—the flowers of a Black Chrysanthemum.

Saido-Butō designates the continuous trajectories of the infinitesimal arrow arabesques of a shattered Being falling through the infinite darkness of the mind's dislocated centers.

(Remark on the formal derivation of the "character" **SAIDO-BUTŌ**. The use of the character **SAIDO** within the theory of Noh goes back all the way to Zeami by whom it was used to signify the concept of a *"pulverizing movement"*. Resorting to a compact and concise notation

$$有 \equiv 砕動 \qquad \text{(SAIDO-BUTŌ)}$$

is thus the general formula by which an ancient dance step of utter darkness becomes a "pulverizing movement" as indicated by Zeami's character **SAIDO**.)

*Christer Hennix*

***Arrows of movements for a vertical topocosm***
(The Static Anfractous Flows Of A Cosmic Current.)

These are the principal arrows of movements in the style of Saido-Butō in which emphasis is on very small but widely differentiated *vertical movements* which are subjected to an equally small *anfractous rotation*

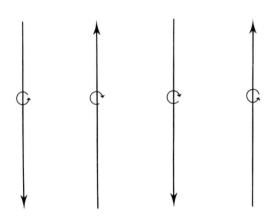

Movements in this space of vertical rotational movement gradually become displaced as instances of *locally infinite spaces* encased by an inpenetrable darkness into which the Creative Subject eventually disappears. The Creative Subject creates absence by being present only within the confines of a locally infinite space in which each movement pulverizes its very presence. More specifically, the pair of arrows which determine the vertical rotational movement is composed in such a way that vertical and horizontal movements alternatively absorb each other. That is, given an indexed family of a principal arrow, say,

*The Yellow Book*

the Creative Subject recurs and recurs as a limit point

•

of motion and stasis by which is defined the utter darkness of the enveloping space of the X-indexed family of principal arrows

Historical Reminder. (Pre-socratic Dance.) The determination of movement and stasis by poetry goes back at least to Vedic times. It is in the Vedic texts that one first encounters a refined concept of *correct action*, i.e. **ṛta**. The Vedic Dance remains largely unknown as do the later Eleatic Dance or the Eleusinian Dance. However, it is known that a theme common to all these ancient arts of dance is the action of transformation by sacrifice. Thus, it must be expected that *correct action* (**ṛta**) translates for the Creative Subject as *total personal transformation* in a rigid performance of Abstract Nō or Abstract Butō.

常住不滅

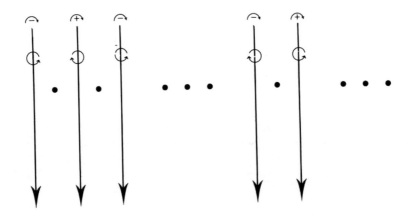

(Elements of Movement $\bar{X}$).

# Ankoku Butoh—no—Soshi
## (Tatsumi Hijikata in Memoriam)

> You do not dip twice in the river
> Beneath the same tree's shadow
> Without bonds in some other life.
>
> Motokiyo

Characters:

| | |
|---|---|
| Zhuang Zhou reincarnated as dream-images | **Shite (1)/Shite 2** |
| Dharmakirti | **Waki** |
| Wanderer (Sophist?) | **Tsure** |

Space:

The interior of a recurrence of *Zhuang Zhou's* eternal dream

Season:

Autumn

**Chorus:**   November

Steps

Abraxas

In the

Fall ...

The last task

To ask the

Questions never

Thought, appears what

Remains in these

Ruins of human hopes &

Fears

in the

Fall ...

      (Among the evening's

        Echoes.)

Dreams of the eternal
Maps have all ceased.

Words are gone.

Lacking an end they also lack a

Beginning. Only the broken

Thought of a middle without

Beginning ... nor end remains as

a single

Possible dream of eternal

Thoughts without words that

Fall ...

Abrasax !

Abraxas !

   .......

Two            (**Tsure** enters)

Utter

Ancient

Emptiness

Memories

Time

Night ...

Night ...

Two                                    (**Waki** enters)

Memories

Ancient

Emptiness                              Emptiness

                                       Memories



                                       Time

Utter

Time



                                       Ancient

                                       Two



                                       Utter

                                       Night ...

Two shadows passing each other

Utter darkness contained in                         in the

Ancient step that continues                         a single

Emptiness of space divested                         forever in the

                                                    of any

Memories of the passage

Time during the passage                             of

Night ...                                           of an endless


**Waki:** No one rides before, no one comes behind

and the path bears no fresh prints

How now, am I alone? Ah yes, I see:

the path which the ancients opened up by
now is overgrown

and the other, the broad and easy road,
I've surely left


*Yet,* as I crossed this                            (Shite enters)

bridge of many dreams,

I realized - for the first time -

That even for a dream, that is, any

Dream, to be real, **it** -

**Reality**! - must also be a

Dream. Because, only what is

Dreamed is eternally

Real ...



**Chorus:** Every dream is a dream, although every

Reality is not real because a

Reality not dreamed is not

Real

**C/W:** Indeed, certainly every undreamed reality remains

Unreal ...



**Waki:** Yet, notable transgressions exist, such as
the ominous moment when a

Dream turns into a

**Nightmare** - which is a dreamed

Reality consisting of

Memories of something
Unreal, of something not yet real,
Of something with a beginning
& a middle but with no



End.




**Aprameya-vasunam**

**Aviparita-dṛṣṭih**




W/C:   **Vikalpa-yonayaḥ**

      **Śabdā vikalpāḥ**

      **Śabdā-yonayaḥ**

**Chorus:**   A

   Dream

   Nightmare

   Reality

   Memories

   Unreal


   Of

   &

   End.


**Tsure:**   Sarvam mithyā bravimi.

   (Among the evening's

   Echoes.)

   I believe I see the

   Image of **Master Zhuang Zhou** - this time

   Reincarnated as an

   appearance of an eternal

   Reality!

**Waki:**   Ah yes, I now believe

   I see the eternal image of **Master Zhuang Zhou,**

   Too! - Maybe he can

Guide my way along

This untrodden path of a

Dream which perhaps is

No longer real ...

**Chorus:** Yes

I

Too

Guide

This

Dream

No

**Shite:** Among my memories, my initial

Memory was of a

Dream in which I entered, effortlessly,

**Immediate Reality** - without knowing

Anything about what is

Real - except my dreams - except my

Dreams of

Reality ...


**Chorus:** Every dream is

                                            real.

Every dream is a dream.

                                            Like

Mirrors of the eternal maps

                                          of recollections

                                          of

A receding reality

                                        of ancient mirrors ...
                                      of ancient dreams ...


**Shite:** Yet, how ominous, but I cannot

Recall anymore **if** I

At that moment of my noble birth,

Was truly dreaming about reality,

That is, **this**

**Reality,**

**Or,**

were I actually in a state of

Dreaming about **SOMETHING ELSE?!** – of which

**S/C:** Reality cannot know, or, perhaps, even,

**Must not know?**

**Shite:** Or, again, is this all an

Unsurpassable never ending

**Nightmare** – such that, if I,

**Zhuangzi,** am not a

Dream, then my being is

All the same a

Dream about a non-dream, a

Dream about an ominous **Butterfly** which cannot

Be a dream by itself ?!

. . . . . . .

**Shite 2:** There is no Butterfly as there is
**no (-) Self!!**

But, there is , there remains , as the

Creative Subject's shadow , a single

Endless , solitary , ancient step

**S2/C:** That continues on and on in

Utter darkness until the step itself is

Dissolved by its own impenetrable solitary

Darkness as if the

**S2/C/T:** Dream was not real . . . .

. . . . . . .

**(The two Shite characters begin their dance.)**

**Chorus:**  Dreams dreamed - dreams of dreams - are      not always

Dreamed dreams - not always, not always -

Whether or not the passage

                                                is crossed, the

Passage between what is no

                                                longer

& that which is still not yet,

                                                the

Crossing of the bridge

                                                of

Dreams ...

There

there

shadow

ancient

in

itself

Dissolved

as

real ...




Two shadows again

passing

each other

in the

Utter darkness contained

in a

single

Ancient step that continues

  forever

                                                                in the

            Emptiness of

                                                                space

                                                                divested

                                                                of any

            Memories of

                                                                the

                                                                passage of

            Time during the

                                                                passage of

                                                                an endless

            Night ...




                            **THE END.**

A Non-unique Extraordinary Set
(From Toposes and Adjoints, 1976)

Published by Blank Forms Editions in New York, 2019,
with support by Agnes Gund and the Swedish Arts Grants Committee.

**K**ONSTNÄRSNÄMNDEN

Edited by Lawrence Kumpf, with assistant editor Joe Bucciero.
Editorial consultation from Henry Flynt and Catherine Christer Hennix.

Designed by Jonathan Gorman.
Printed by Ofset Yapımevi, Istanbul.

© 2019 by Blank Forms Editions, except for the following pieces,
all © Henry A. Flynt, Jr.: "Modalities and Languages for Algorithms,"
"The Electric Harpsichord," "WSTNOKWGO," "Hallucinogenic/Ecstatic
Sound Environment Program Notes," and "Illuminatory Sound Environment
Program Notes."
All rights reserved.
Published in the United States by Blank Forms Editions,
a division of Blank Forms, Inc., New York.

ISBN: 978-1-7337235-0-3

Blank Forms
468 Grand Avenue #3A
Brooklyn, NY 11238